THE GREAT YORKSHIRE ELECTION OF 1807

Mass Politics in England before the Age of Reform

The Great Yorkshire Election of 1807

BY
ELLEN GIBSON WILSON

EDITED BY
EDWARD ROYLE AND JAMES WALVIN

The publication of this book has been assisted by grants from
The Marc Fitch Fund and the following local organisations:
the Leeds Philosophical and Literary Society, the Sheldon
Memorial Trust, the Yorkshire Archaeological Society,
the Yorkshire Architectural and York Archaeological Society,
and the Yorkshire Philosophical Society.

First published in Great Britain in 2015
by Carnegie Publishing Ltd
Carnegie House,
Chatsworth Road
Lancaster, LA1 4SL

Copyright © Ellen Gibson Wilson, 2008

The right of Ellen Gibson Wilson to be identified as the author
of this work has been asserted by her in accordance with the
Copyright, Designs and Patents Act 1988.

All rights reserved. No part of this publication may be
reproduced, stored in a retrieval system, or transmitted, in any
form or by any means, electronic, mechanical, photocopying,
recording or otherwise, without the prior permission of the
copyright owner.

A CIP catalogue record for this book
is available from the British Library.

ISBN 978-1-85936-223-5

Designed and typeset in Monotype Baskerville
by Carnegie Book Production
Printed and bound in Great Britain by Jellyfish Solutions

Contents

List of Illustrations	vii
List of Maps	viii
Acknowledgements	ix
Preface	xi
Maps	xiv–xv
Introduction	1

PART I   BACKGROUND

1	The Prize of Yorkshire	12
2	Land, Wool, and Iron	20
3	The Political Past: Reform and Reaction	33
	Reform (1770–1784)	33
	Reaction (1784–1802)	49
4	The Election of 1806: A Rehearsal	61
5	A Note on Contests and Factions	81

PART II   THE CONFRONTATION OF 1807

6	The Dissolution	88
7	The Adversaries	97
	The Hon. Henry Lascelles	99
	Charles William Wentworth Fitzwilliam, Viscount Milton	106
	William Wilberforce	111
8	The Canvass, 27 April–13 May	119
	Wilberforce Goes to the County	124

	The Return of Lascelles	129
	Milton, the 'Infant Candidate'	140
9	Nomination Day in York	155
10	Preparing to Poll	166
11	The Public Argument	185
	Abolition	185
	Popery	191
	Coalition?	201
	The view from Etridge's and Wentworth Woodhouse	202
	The View from York Tavern	206

PART III THE POLL

12	The First Ten Days, 20–30 May	212
13	The Final Stretch, 1–5 June	239
14	Afterwards	259

Appendix General Summary of the Whole Poll	287
Bibliography	288
Index	301

List of Illustrations

The plates appear between pages 144 and 145

1. 'A Sheffield Cutler'
2. 'The Cloth Makers'
3. Gillray, 'A Kick at the Broad Bottoms'
4. The Hon. Henry Lascelles
5. Lord Viscount Milton
6. William Wilberforce
7. The White Cloth Hall, Leeds
8. A plan of York Castle
9. The arrangement of voting booths in Castle Yard
10. Gillray, 'Orange Jumper'
11. A Milton plumper jug
12. Title page from the County of York 1807 Poll Book

List of Maps

The maps appear on pages xiv and xv

1 Yorkshire, showing the three Ridings and major towns
2 The North Riding, showing wapentakes
3 The West Riding, showing wapentakes
4 The East Riding, showing wapentakes

Acknowledgements

Acknowledgement is made to the following libraries, galleries, museums and societies for permission to reproduce the illustrations in this volume. Figs 1 and 2 are from George Walker, *The Costume of Yorkshire* (1885), photography © University of York. Figs 3, 5, 6 and 10 were supplied by the British Museum Free Image Service and are © Trustees of the British Museum. Fig. 4 is © National Portrait Gallery, London. Fig. 7 is from a drawing by Percy Robinson and is © The Thoresby Society, the Leeds Historical Society. Fig. 8 is from T.P. Cooper, *The History of the Castle of York* (1911), photography © University of York. Fig. 9 reproduces the sketch in Jonathan Gray, *An Account of the Manner of Proceeding at the Contested Election for Yorkshire, in 1807* (1818). Fig. 11 is © Hull Museums and is reproduced by permission. Fig. 12 is a reproduction of the title page of *County of York. The Poll, for Knights of the Shire, Begun on Wednesday, May 20th, and finally closed on Friday, June 5th, 1807* (York, 1807). Map 1 is taken with minor modifications from the Yorkshire Ridings Society's web site at http://www.yorkshireridings.org/news/yorkshire-map.html; and Maps 2, 3 and 4 are taken from http://en.wikipedia.org/wiki/List_of_wapentakes_in_Yorkshire [accessed 20 September 2013] and are here used under the Creative Commons Attribution-ShareAlike License.

We are also grateful to the following libraries and archives for their assistance during the original research and the subsequent preparation of the manuscript for publication, and for any necessary permissions to use and quote from documents in their possession: Bodleian Libraries, University of Oxford; Borthwick Institute, University of York; The British Library Board; Brotherton Library, University of Leeds; The Syndics of Cambridge University Library; City of York Council Archives; Dr Williams's Library, London; Doncaster Archives; Hull Museums, Wilberforce House; Mr John Goodchild and the John Goodchild Collection, Wakefield; Leeds City Libraries; The Library Committee of the Religious Society of Friends in Britain; The National Archives, Kew; Northamptonshire County Record Office; North Yorkshire County Record Office, Northallerton; St John's College Library, Cambridge;

Sheffield City Archives; Shropshire Records and Research Centre, Shrewsbury; Wakefield Library and Museum; West Yorkshire Archive Service, Kirklees; West Yorkshire Archive Service, Leeds.

The Wentworth Woodhouse Papers have been accepted in lieu of Inheritance Tax by HM Government and allocated to Sheffield City Council; extracts are reproduced with permission from The Milton (Peterborough) Estates Company and the Director of Culture, Sheffield City Council. Extracts from the Fitzwilliam (Milton) Papers are reproduced by kind permission of the Milton Estate, copyright reserved.

Preface

ELLEN GIBSON WILSON died in 2008. Among her papers was this full-length study of the Great Yorkshire Election of 1807. For some reason it was never published, although she was basing lectures on the completed manuscript during the last twenty years or so of her life. Her interest in the subject arose out of her earlier researches which had resulted in three important studies published between 1976 and 1989. The first, *The Loyal Blacks* (1976) told the remarkable story of freed slaves who sided with the British during and after the American War of Independence. Then her *John Clarkson and the African Adventure* (1980) provided another innovative book, rooted in exhaustive research and narrating in her compelling style the story of Clarkson's expedition to take some of those freed slaves 'back to Africa'. Thirdly came her biography of *Thomas Clarkson* (1989) which was not fully and publicly appreciated until 2007, when the bicentenary of abolition in 1807 generated widespread attention to the British abolition of the slave trade. It may have been that the initially less enthusiastic reception of this third volume dissuaded Ellen from seeking a publisher for her work on the Great Yorkshire Election. Instead as she entered her late seventies she turned her attention to local Yorkshire history of a different kind, editing for the Yorkshire Archaeological Society *The parish register of Bulmer, 1571–1837* (Leeds, 1995).

By training and trade Ellen Wilson was a journalist and a student of practical politics, both of which gave her insights and skills which contributed to the qualities of this manuscript. She graduated from the University of Wisconsin in 1941 in History and Journalism. Beginning on a small local newspaper she moved to the *Milwaukee Journal*'s State desk in 1943, the first woman to do so. She specialized in welfare reporting and in 1950 was the first woman to be awarded a Reid fellowship to enable her to study the new welfare state, and the emerging new towns in Britain. This interest led to her appointment as a public relations officer for the new John Kennedy administration in Washington in the early 1960s. It was there that she met

Harry Wilson, an English historian of Africa. Following their marriage, she moved with him first to Aberystwyth and then to York.

Following Ellen's death Harry Wilson passed this manuscript study of the Great Yorkshire Election to James Walvin, to see what use could be made of this important study of the only fully contested parliamentary election fought by William Wilberforce, almost immediately following Wilberforce's great political triumph with the abolition of the British slave trade in 1807. Walvin, in turn, passed the text to Edward Royle whose interests lay more generally in Yorkshire history. We were both agreeably impressed by the quality of the work, in terms of the depth of the research and its narrative style. Accordingly we decided to seek a publisher for the work. We recognized that in places the text would need factual amendment in the light of subsequent research, and that it would need setting in the context of more recent scholarly emphases and interests, but we felt that the body of the narrative had stood the test of time remarkably well and so should be preserved with almost no alteration for the reader to enjoy and appreciate. In its clarity it possessed the qualities of good, readable journalism, and we did not wish to detract from the reader's appreciation of Ellen's invigorating style. At the same time, we have preserved the lengthy references to indicate the depth of scholarship underlying the study, correcting them only where archival reference numbers and locations are no longer current.

In three respects we failed. When she originally undertook the research for this volume, Ellen Wilson had access to the private papers of the late Mr C.E. Wrangham of Caterick, a descendant of Wilberforce. These papers were acquired by the Bodleian Library, Oxford, in 1988, but the item referred to as 'Robert Grimston's account of the election' is not listed there and has not been traced elsewhere. She also quoted from 'To the Memory of the Spinning Wheel' by B. Hebblethwaite, a copy of which she had located in the Piece Hall Museum, Halifax. This museum is currently in storage at the Piece Hall, and the attempt by Dee Weaver of Halifax to unearth this work for us has not been successful. We are grateful to her for her efforts. Finally, she consulted the Harewood Papers when they were held in the Leeds City Archives, later part of the West Yorkshire Archives Service. These papers were assigned new call numbers by the West Yorkshire Archives Service (Leeds) and we have been unable to identify the location of 6/92, Lord Harewood's Accounts, to which there is one reference. The Harewood House archive is currently closed.

This publication has been made possible through the kind offices of Alistair Hodge of Carnegie Publishing, and the staff of the many libraries and archives listed on the Acknowledgements page who originally helped Ellen and have since helped us. Grateful acknowledgement is also made to The Marc Fitch Fund, the Leeds Philosophical and Literary Society, the Sheldon Memorial Trust, the Yorkshire Archaeological Society, the Yorkshire Architectural and

PREFACE

York Archaeological Society, the Yorkshire Philosophical Society, and the University of York Department of History, without whose support this book would not have been published. But chiefly we are grateful to Harry Wilson for rescuing his late wife's work and for making it available to us, and to Ellen herself for writing it. We dedicate this work to her memory and close this Preface with some words of her own in which she set out, like the good journalist and historian that she was, her own political prejudices on the subject in question. She wrote with characteristic wit at the end of her original Introduction:

> My own village of Heslington on the outskirts of York in 1807 contained 21 electors (in a population of nearly five hundred) who divided 12 for Wilberforce and Lascelles, 6 for Wilberforce alone, 2 for Milton only, and a solitary plumper for Lascelles.[1] Had I lived then, I should have tried to persuade my husband to choose Wilberforce and Milton, but I am afraid that he would have plumped for the young lord.

Edward Royle
James Walvin

---

[1] All figures on the 1807 vote are taken from *County of York. The Poll, for Knights of the Shire, Begun on Wednesday, May 20th, and finally closed on Friday, June 5th, 1807* ... (T. Wilson & R. Spence: York, 1807).

Map 1 Yorkshire, showing the three Ridings and major towns. (*Source*: Based upon a map on the Yorkshire Ridings Society's website at http://www.yorkshireridings.org/news/yorkshire-map.html [accessed 20 September 2013])

Key:
1. Gilling West
2. Hang West
3. Gilling East
4. Hang East
5. Allertonshire
6. Halikeld
7. Langbaurgh West
8. Birdforth
9. Bulmer
10. Ryedale
11. Langbaurgh East
12. Whitby Strand
13. Pickering Lythe

Map 2 The North Riding, showing wapentakes. (*Source*: Based upon http://en.wikipedia.org/wiki/List_of_wapentakes_in_Yorkshire [accessed 20 September 2013])

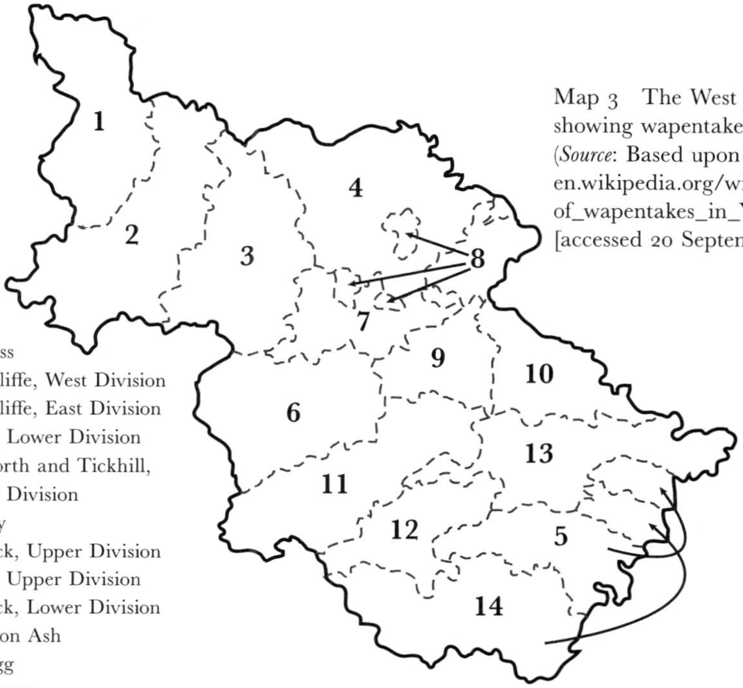

Map 3 The West Riding, showing wapentakes. (*Source*: Based upon http://en.wikipedia.org/wiki/List_of_wapentakes_in_Yorkshire [accessed 20 September 2013])

Key:
1 Ewcross
2 Staincliffe, West Division
3 Staincliffe, East Division
4 Claro, Lower Division
5 Strafforth and Tickhill, Lower Division
6 Morley
7 Skyrack, Upper Division
8 Claro, Upper Division
9 Skyrack, Lower Division
10 Barkston Ash
11 Agbrigg
12 Staincross
13 Osgoldcross
14 Strafforth and Tickhill, Upper Division

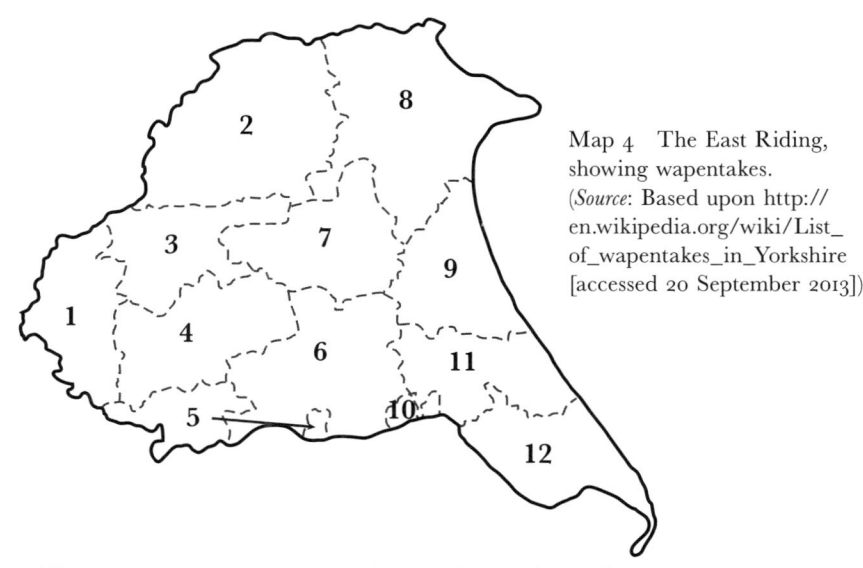

Map 4 The East Riding, showing wapentakes. (*Source*: Based upon http://en.wikipedia.org/wiki/List_of_wapentakes_in_Yorkshire [accessed 20 September 2013])

Key:
1 Ouse and Derwent
2 Buckrose
3 Harthill, Wilton Beacon Division
4 Harthill, Holme Beacon Division
5 Howdenshire
6 Harthill, Hunsley Beacon Division
7 Harthill, Bainton Beacon Division
8 Dickering
9 Holderness, North Division
10 Kingston upon Hull (county corporate
11 Holderness, Middle Division
12 Holderness, South Division

xv

Introduction

THE outcome of the great Yorkshire election of 1807 was settled in the spring of 1806 at a stormy encounter in the lobby of the House of Commons when a nettled Henry Lascelles, MP for Yorkshire, intemperately assured John Grant and Robert Cookson, trustees of the White Cloth Hall in Leeds: 'You may hoot me, and scout me, and do what you please – I don't care a damn for you all!'[1] The targets of his outburst claimed to represent 19,000 clothiers and the incident was related the length and breadth of the populous wool-working West Riding.

The Yorkshiremen were in London to oppose attempts to repeal a clutch of Elizabethan statutes which sheltered their 'domestic system' of manufacture from the creeping growth of large-scale factory production. At this time most of the clothiers in Yorkshire still scrubbed, carded, spun and wove wool from their rural cottages, employing their wives, children and sometimes a journeyman or two. A few acres, a garden and a cow added to their comforts. Anyone who wished to become a cloth maker had first to serve a seven-year apprenticeship. The clothier carried his lengths (or 'pieces') to the cloth halls in Leeds or Bradford, Wakefield, Huddersfield or Halifax, and sold them to merchants who undertook the finishing and marketing.[2] For several years the more enterprising merchants and some large master clothiers had glimpsed the riches that might accrue if they organized all stages of production under one roof, making full use of the machines that were already transforming the cotton industry over the Pennines in Lancashire.

When the introduction of gig mills in the woollen centres of Wiltshire, Gloucestershire and Somersetshire in 1802 led to riots and machine-breaking, all severely quelled, the cloth workers of England re-discovered the archaic

---

[1] *Leeds Mercury*, 28 October 1806 and 9 May 1807.
[2] See *The Diaries of Cornelius Ashworth, 1782–1816*, ed. R. Davies, A. Petford and J. Senior (Hebden Bridge Local History Society: Hebden Bridge, 2011). For an idealised view of a clothier see Plate 2.

regulations by which their trade had been regulated in Tudor times, and demanded that they be enforced. The merchants responded in 1803 by seeking repeal of these 'obsolete' constraints. Repeal was not enacted but Parliament agreed to suspend the laws for a year to prevent further prosecutions. An investigation was promised. The suspension was renewed in 1804 and 1805 to the mounting distress and anger of the cloth makers. In 1806, therefore, the Yorkshire and West of England clothiers petitioned for relief. At last a Select Committee of the House of Commons was appointed. It sat from 18 March to 10 June, taking some evidence from working men but even more from burgeoning capitalists. Both Lascelles and William Wilberforce, the other MP for Yorkshire, were on the committee and Wilberforce composed the report which went to the House on 4 July 1806. The committee recommended (with some compassion, thanks to Wilberforce, for the domestic tradition) the abolition of virtually all the protective laws which, in the committee's view, prevented the woollen industry from modernizing and expanding as befitted one of a great trading nation's principal industries.[3]

The Hon. Henry Lascelles, a conscientious MP and second son of the first Earl of Harewood, whose country home was only eight miles from Leeds, the nation's leading wool town, saw the future as the merchants did, with an industry flourishing on large-scale capital investment and mass production. Like them, and his fellow committeemen, he was disturbed by symptoms of unity and class consciousness shown among the cloth workers as was demonstrated by their well-organized and well-funded lobbying. Certainly, Wilberforce and Lascelles agreed that if restrictions on production were to be abandoned elsewhere they must not be allowed to survive in Yorkshire. The committee had hardly behaved impartially, however, and the clothiers who testified were subjected to unforgettably hostile questioning.

Doubts were thrown on their evidence and veracity. Had 19,000 Yorkshire clothiers indeed signed a petition to protect their livelihoods? They 'would sign any Thing for a Tankard of Ale', retorted Lascelles, 'with one of his usual contemptuous smiles'. When the Yorkshire workers faced the Select Committee, 'To puzzle them with intricate Questions, and, by cross Examination, to take advantage of their simple and undesigning evidence, appeared to be [Lascelles's] constant aim', their spokesmen complained, 'and a significant shrug, a doubting look, and an unbelieving sneer, he had

---

[3] *Parliamentary Debates, House of Commons*, vol. 6, cols 347–9 (4 March 1806), cols 424–5 (12 March 1806), cols 432–3 (14 March 1806); vol. 7, cols 1010–14 (9 July 1806); Report and Minutes of Evidence, on the State of the Woollen Manufacture of England, *Parliamentary Papers*, Reports from Committees (268, 268a), 1806, vol. 3, pp. 567, 595; R.G. Wilson, *Gentlemen Merchants: The Merchant Community in Leeds, 1700–1830* (Manchester University Press: Manchester, 1971).

ever ready at command when a clothier was under examination; but when a Factory Owner, or a Man of large Property or Influence appeared, he was all Candour, Complacency, and Civility'.⁴

Yorkshire's 1807 election was the first contest for both county seats in 73 years and the last before 1830.⁵ Many national themes were played upon in the election. Loyalties to old political dynasties were invoked and the dormant cause of parliamentary reform affected many votes. The cry of 'No Popery' was raised against Viscount Milton, the lanky, red-headed, barely 21-year-old heir of the Earl Fitzwilliam. The voters were constantly reminded both of Wilberforce's leadership of the recently successful anti-slave trade campaign and of the Lascelles family's connection with slavery and the West Indies from which they derived about a third of their considerable annual income.⁶ But the insulted clothiers remembered above all Lascelles's cool disdain for their doomed struggle to defend the domestic system of manufacture. They brushed aside his protests of concern for the long-term welfare of the nation as it entered an economic and social upheaval not yet labelled the industrial revolution, as they streamed into York on foot, on horseback, on wheels and in boats to plump for the young Lord Milton.

In Wakefield two preemer lads (apprentices who cleaned the teasels of bits of wool and acted as general dogsbodies) from different croppers' shops met in the street during the election struggle. One had Lord Milton's orange card stuck in his hatband. The other wore no tag. 'If I wortee,' said the former to the latter, 'I'd put a Lord Milton paper e my hat, thau may goa to t' printer and taul get one.' 'Nay, dang it,' sighed his friend, 'I dar'nt if I did a'r maister od kick my a—.' 'Why, then,' the first replied, 'I'd get a Lashille color or summot.' 'Nay, nay, if I did tat, a'ar men od murder me.'⁷

Relatively few clothiers gave their second votes to Wilberforce, who had critics among them but no real enemies and who was almost universally respected in Yorkshire for his moral character and twenty years' devotion to the abolition of the slave trade. Wilberforce, like Lascelles, had voted in

---

⁴ *York Herald*, 1 August 1807; E.P. Thompson, *Making of the English Working Class* (Gollancz: 1963; 2nd edn, Pelican Books: Harmondsworth, 1968), pp. 576–8.

⁵ For the 1830 election, aborted after one day when the fifth candidate withdrew, see N. Gash, 'Brougham and the Yorkshire Election of 1830' in *Pillars of Government and other essays on State and Society, c.1770–c.1880* (Arnold: 1986), pp. 77–92.

⁶ S.D. Smith, *Slavery, Family and Gentry Capitalism in the British Atlantic. The World of the Lascelles, 1648–1834* (Cambridge University Press: Cambridge, 2006; 2010 edn), pp. 89–90 and p. 250, Table 8.7.

⁷ *Wakefield Star*, 29 May 1807. On the significance of electoral symbols, see K. Navickas, '"That sash will hang you": Political Clothing and Adornment in England, 1780–1840', *Journal of British Studies*, 49:3 (July 2010), pp. 540–65.

committee against their perceived interests, but he had done it sympathetically. They were confident he would win on the votes of other freeholders, in any case, and they abhorred his friendly leanings towards Lascelles. Wilberforce, less optimistic, had unwillingly to fight the only contested election of his 45 years in Parliament. Significantly, the clothiers were joined by other artisans and craftsmen in their political protest.

The 1807 Yorkshire election was possibly the most flamboyant and certainly the most expensive in British parliamentary history. Approaching a quarter of a million pounds (some said double that) was spent, equal to several millions in our day. The only modern parallel might be found in the United States, where comparable sums can sometimes be spent by candidates seeking election to Congress.[8]

In the following chapters the events of 1807 are set first in the longer-term context of the Yorkshire economy and county politics. The earlier electoral history of the county is outlined, especially the campaign in 1806 which prepared the way for the 1807 election and illustrates the sometimes narrow distinction to be made between a contested election that did not lead to a poll and one which, untypically, finally did so. The three candidates are then introduced and the steps they took to organize their supporters in readiness for the poll are set out in some detail. The aim in the central chapters of the book is to give some sense of the military-style organization necessary to mobilize the largest electorate in the largest parliamentary constituency in Britain, in what everyone knew would be a tight and expensive contest. Despite interpretations of pre-Reform politics which concentrate on personalities and so-called corrupt influences – both of which were prominent in this as in other elections – it was really issues which dominated the campaign in 1807, though the ways in which both anti-slavery and anti-Catholicism were used could be both unprincipled and, in the rival outpourings of political propaganda, entertaining. In the final section of the book the drama of the actual fifteen days of the poll is described as, hour by hour, the fortunes of each candidate ebbed and flowed until the result was declared, with Lascelles the loser by the narrowest of margins. The narrative concludes with a review of the poll book such as the candidates themselves conducted to see where support had been won and lost.

Even before the poll was over, Henry Lascelles was heard to mutter that he would rather have the money than the seat. And Lord Harewood for years

---

[8] The most expensive winning campaign in the 2012 election to the House of Representatives cost the candidate the equivalent of about £13 million and the average winner about £1 million; election to the Senate could cost an average of about £7 million with the most expensive winner spending over £30 million: see http://www.opensecrets.org/bigpicture/elec_stats.php?cycle=2012 [accessed 25 October 2013].

carried in his pocket a little card with the ominous figure '£100,000' written on it which he produced as his 'unanswerable argument' whenever anyone ventured to hint in his presence at another election contest.[9]

Although electoral politics in the unreformed era have attracted scholarly attention, much of this has focused either on elections in general or on specific borough elections.[10] The most comprehensive survey, which draws evidence from Yorkshire as part of its national overview, is by Frank O'Gorman.[11] Studies of the elections for Middlesex in the era of Wilkes are included in works by Ian Christie and others, but few British county elections of this time have been examined in depth.[12] The 1784 Yorkshire election, which was aborted on the eve of the poll, is the subject of an article by Alexander Loch, and the principal published work on the Yorkshire extravaganza of 1807 is E.A. Smith's article in *Northern History* (1967) and then more briefly in his subsequent political biography of the Earl Fitzwilliam. Robert Worthington Smith's study of Yorkshire elections in the *American Historical Review* (1969) covers the event and it is also described in the numerous biographies of William Wilberforce.[13] There are also succinct accounts of the constituency

---

[9] [Lord Granville Leveson Gower], *Private Correspondence 1781 to 1821*, ed. Countess Castalia Granville, 2 vols (J. Murray: 1916), vol. 2, p. 251; A.M.W. Stirling, *Letter-Bag of Lady Elizabeth Spencer-Stanhope*, 2 vols (John Lane: 1913), vol. 1, p. 143; Henry Clarkson, *Memories of Merry Wakefield* (Wakefield, 1887), p. 186.

[10] See for example, M. Hinton, 'The General Elections of 1806 and 1807', unpublished Ph.D. thesis (University of Reading, 1959) and J.A. Phillips, *Electoral Behaviour in Unreformed England. Plumpers, Splitters, and Straights* (Princeton University Press: Princeton, 1982) and *The Great Reform Bill in the Boroughs. English Electoral Behaviour, 1818–1841* (Clarendon Press: Oxford, 1992).

[11] F. O'Gorman, *Voters, Patrons and Parties. The Unreformed Electorate of Hanoverian England, 1734–1832* (Clarendon Press: Oxford, 1989).

[12] I.R. Christie, *Wilkes, Wyvill and Reform. The parliamentary reform movement in British politics, 1760–1785* (Macmillan: 1962) and P. Thomas, *John Wilkes. A Friend to Liberty* (Clarendon Press: Oxford, 1996). Other studies of county elections include E.G. Forrester, *Northamptonshire County Elections and Electioneering, 1695–1832* (Oxford University Press: 1941); R.J. Robson, *Oxfordshire Election of 1754* (Oxford University Press: 1949); B. Bonsall, *Sir James Lowther and Cumberland and Westmorland Elections, 1754–1775* (Manchester University Press: Manchester, 1960); and L.P. Curtis, *Chichester Towers* (Yale University Press: New Haven, 1966) (on a Sussex by-election in 1741).

[13] A. Loch, 'The Electoral Management of the Yorkshire Election of 1784', *Northern History*, 47:2 (2010), pp. 271–96; E.A. Smith, 'Yorkshire Elections of 1806 and 1807: a study in electoral management', *Northern History*, 2 (1967), pp. 262–90; E.A. Smith, *Whig Principles and Party Politics: Earl Fitzwilliam and the Whig Party, 1748–1831* (Manchester University Press: Manchester, 1975); R.W. Smith, 'Political Organization and Canvassing: Yorkshire Elections Before the Reform Bill', *American Historical Review*, 74 (1969), pp. 1538–60;

and the candidates in the relevant volume of the *History of Parliament*.[14] The only recent contribution to the published literature on the 1807 Yorkshire election itself is by Kirsten McKenzie, who looks at the use of anti-slavery rhetoric by the clothiers to assert their freedom, independence and common humanity.[15]

The events of 1807 as narrated in the following chapters can be interpreted on two levels. On the one they exemplify the narrow political world of unreformed élite politics in which events were dictated by money and powerful male aristocratic interests, though Yorkshire was unusual on account of its size and the fact that one of the candidates – Wilberforce – had neither the money nor the pedigree expected of the usual aspirants to a county seat in Parliament. On the other level they demonstrate the extent to which popular participation by both men and women formed an essential part of such elections. The political world was never as narrow as it at first seems. As recent studies have emphasized the street theatre attendant upon electoral contests meant that electoral participation involved far more than casting ballots. Contests were popular in the sense both that they involved the people and they were desired by the people.

The rituals of political campaigning that surrounded all elections in the pre-Reform era were important because they were the means by which politics were embraced by the whole community, incorporating voters and non-voters, men and women alike.[16] The parading of candidates, the unhorsing of carriages so that supporters could draw their champion into town, the political meetings, the canvassing, the rituals of nomination day and the hustings with their spectacle, speeches, heckling, and opportunity for popular acclaim (or the reverse), were essential features of an election and not ones to be denied to the people.

Similarly, the campaign literature and language, the partisan symbols and colours all followed a set and expected pattern, and aligned elections with

---

R. Furneaux, *William Wilberforce* (Hamilton: 1974); J. Pollock, *Wilberforce* (Constable: 1977); S. Tomkins, *William Wilberforce: a biography* (Lion: Oxford, 2007); and W. Hague, *William Wilberforce. The life of the great anti-Slave Trade campaigner* (Harper Perennial: 2008).

[14] R.G. Thorne (ed.), *History of Parliament. The House of Commons, 1790–1820*, 5 vols (published for the History of Parliament Trust by Secker & Warburg, 1986).

[15] K. McKenzie, '"My voice is sold, & I must be a Slave": Abolition Rhetoric, British Liberty and the Yorkshire Elections of 1806 and 1807', *History Workshop Journal*, 64:1 (2007), pp. 48–73. There is also an unpublished thesis by H. Donaldson, 'The Yorkshire election of 1807' (MA thesis, University of York, 2006).

[16] At Nomination Day in York in 1807 it was alleged that over three-quarters of those present were non-electors: *Yorkshire Election. A Collection of the Speeches, Addresses, and Squibs, Produced ... During the Late Contested Election* (Edward Baines: Leeds, 1807), p. 66.

other popular ceremonies and occasions, not least horse racing which provided a vividly colourful opportunity for tribal celebration bringing together the highest and lowest in society in a common passion. At an election, all men were equal, as candidates and electors alike asserted their 'independence', and even lords and their ladies deferred to humble freeholders who possessed a highly prized vote. Finally, at the close of the poll, the successful candidates were chaired for a victory parade. All this ritual was a necessary contribution to the carnival atmosphere in which victory was celebrated. In 1807, Wilberforce was too ill to take part but Milton exulted in his new role, girding on his sword as a knight of the shire and being paraded around the city of York like a warrior returning from some great victory. The modern cheering at the declaration of the poll in some dingy municipal hall pales into insignificance in comparison, though the open-top bus parade which greets a successful sporting team perhaps captures a little of the public spectacle of an election in the era before reform sanitized the event.[17]

The political meetings, the heckling, the scurrilous broadsides and ballads that made up the rough-and-tumble of a vigorous campaign afforded little protection to the gentleman or aristocrat who sought the votes of that minority of the population who actually had the right to vote. This was true of many seats, both county and borough, but was especially true of a county such as Yorkshire where the lower end of the electorate merged into the body of non-electors in a shared interest. Lascelles discovered this to his cost when confronted by workers in the woollen and worsted industries of the West Riding after 1806. And, as McKenzie has argued, this interest extended beyond economics. Lascelles, the apparent supporter of both West Indies black chattel slavery and of what Richard Oastler was later to call the 'Yorkshire Slavery' of the new textile mills, failed to recognize the sense of moral outrage that underpinned popular opinion among some of the electorate and the wider public alike. He was not helped by his own personality, diffident and appearing dismissive. Though Wilberforce could also be introverted, and hated the turmoil surrounding elections, he warmed to the popular mood

---

[17] F. O'Gorman, 'Campaign Rituals and Ceremonies: the social meaning of elections in England, 1780–1860', *Past & Present* 135 (May 1992), pp. 79–115; D. Eastwood, 'Contesting the Politics of Deference: the rural electorate, 1820–60', in J. Lawrence and M. Taylor (eds), *Party, State and Society: Electoral Behaviour in Britain since 1820* (Scolar Press: Aldershot, 1997), pp. 27–49; A. Clark, 'Class, Gender and British Elections, 1794–1818', in M.T. Davis and P.A. Pickering (eds), *Unrespectable Radicals? Popular Politics in the Age of Reform* (Ashgate: Aldershot, 2008), pp. 107–24; Navickas, 'That sash will hang you'. The contemporary meaning of 'independence' and its association with classical notions of citizenship are explored in M. McCormack, *The Independent Man: citizenship and gender politics in Georgian England* (Manchester University Press: Manchester, 2005).

and was a good speaker, exuding moral concern. Milton, the new-comer to elections, surprised all with his warmth and natural gift for communication. These things mattered.[18]

Elections were popular also because, although they might disrupt business, they were also great generators of business. The coins dispensed by the candidates with apparently limitless generosity went into thousands of pockets, not only those of voters who were also, naturally, consumers, but also of printers and their assistants, innkeepers, victuallers, owners of coaches and carts and, not least, glaziers and others who followed in the wake of any electoral demonstration or celebration. Elections were carnival and ritual; they were employment and profit. The candidates and their supporters were as much victims as masters of the situation, exploited by as well as exploiting the system by which élite politics were maintained.

A detailed local study of Yorkshire politics in the pre-Reform era is not without precedent, with the four hundred pages of Herbert Butterfield's study of a few months in 1779–80 being one of several works devoted to the closing decades of the pre-Reform era.[19] An in-depth study of the 1807 Yorkshire election can be rewarding because it provides both a way into the inner workings of the electoral politics of the period and a gripping story that captures the imagination now as much as it did at the time. Building on the work of the many scholars listed in the bibliography, and drawing upon new sources in scattered archives and the Yorkshire press, this detailed study adds tones of light and shade to the picture sketched more briefly and partially by E.A. Smith over half a century ago and furthers work done since by scholars on other constituencies. As John Markham observed in his study of the 1820 election in the Yorkshire borough of Hedon, it takes a parliamentary election to make one see the frequently ludicrous relationship between great affairs and the trivialities of everyday life.[20] If further justification were needed for a study of what one Yorkshire MP has rightly called 'one of the most hard-fought and expensive elections for a single constituency in the whole course of British history', it is to be found in the observation of Robert and Samuel Wilberforce in their *Life* of their father, that the 1807 Yorkshire election 'was even then unique; and since, from the changes of 1833 [*sic*], it can never be

---

[18] McKenzie, 'My voice is sold, & I must be a Slave'; for Oastler and slavery, see J.A. Hargreaves and E.A.H. Haigh, *Slavery in Yorkshire. Richard Oastler and the campaign against child labour in the Industrial Revolution* (University of Huddersfield Press: Huddersfield, 2012).

[19] H. Butterfield, *George III, Lord North and the People* (Bell: 1949), N.C. Phillips, *Yorkshire and English National Politics, 1783–1784* (University of Canterbury Publications: Christchurch, 1961); Christie, *Wilkes, Wyvill and Reform*.

[20] John Markham, *The 1820 Parliamentary Election at Hedon: a study of electioneering in a Yorkshire borough before the passing of the Reform Act* (J. Markham: Beverley, 1971).

repeated', it must remain so. Consequently, they concluded in 1838, 'a more minute account of its events may possess much interest for the future student of English manners in the beginning of the nineteenth century'. What follows is offered in this hope.[21]

---

[21] Hague, *Wilberforce*, p. 362; R.I. Wilberforce and S. Wilberforce, *Life of William Wilberforce*, 5 vols (J. Murray: 1838; 2nd edn, 1839), vol. 3, p. 316.

PART I

BACKGROUND

CHAPTER ONE

The Prize of Yorkshire

THE county of Yorkshire, which exists no more since the administrative map was redrawn in 1974 with bureaucratic indifference to ancient pride and traditional geographical distinctions, was in 1807 'first in the kingdom, in territory, population, and opulence'.[1] It stretched like a giant moth in beautiful variety of mountain, moorland and vale across the north of England from Lancashire and the Pennine dales on the west to the cliffs of what was then called the German Ocean on the east and dropped 90 miles from County Durham on the north to the Humber River, Nottinghamshire and Derbyshire on the south. Its 'circuit' totalled 460 miles and enclosed more than three and a half million acres. With a snobbery once shown by its cricket selectors, Yorkshire elected to Parliament only men born in the county or long and substantially associated with it.[2] In the House of Commons Yorkshire members shared with those from London the privilege of designated seats – next to the privy councillors. Every other MP 'sitteth as he cometh'.[3]

But in the unreformed Parliament, there were only two representatives for this vast principality, as for the smallest rotten borough, say, Dunwich, where two patrons chose two members long after most of the place had slid under the sea; or Old Sarum, an uninhabited hill to which a handful of voters were given title deeds shortly before an election (returnable afterwards); or Midhurst, of which nothing survived but a few stones in a wall.

Yorkshire's population in 1801 was 858,892 (almost a tenth of the inhabitants of England and Wales) of whom two-thirds (563,953) dwelt in the West Riding,

---

[1] T.H.B. Oldfield, *Complete History, Political and Personal, of the Boroughs of Great Britain*, 3 vols (B. Crosby & Co.: 1792; new edn, 1805), vol. 2, p. 265.
[2] John Bigland, *Beauties of England and Wales, XVI, Yorkshire* (Vernor & Hood: 1812), pp. 60–1.
[3] Smith, 'Yorkshire Elections', p. 62; Edward Porritt, *Unreformed House of Commons: Parliamentary Representation Before 1832*, 2 vols (Cambridge University Press: Cambridge, 1903, reprinted Kelley: New York, 1963), vol. 1, p. 426.

one of the three Saxon trithings into which the county then divided. Ten years later, when the county had grown to 973,113, most of the gain – 89,362 – was in the West Riding with its flourishing manufacturing towns. The predominantly agricultural North Riding actually declined in numbers during the decade, from 155,506 to 152,445, while the East Riding, where fishing, whaling and the Baltic trade supplemented farming on the billowing chalky wolds, grew from 139,433 to 167,353. No other county held such a mingling of the old and the rising elements in English society.[4] A total of 23,007 male freeholders voted in 1807 and numerous qualified electors were still unpolled when the clock struck three on the fifteenth day and a cannon signalled the end of the contest in the Castle Yard at York. Informed conjecture put the full number of eligible voters (there were no registers) at between 28,600 and 40,000.[5] The 'political nation' at this time was judged to be no more than 400,000 men, of whom the veritable backbone – the landed – probably amounted to 125,000. With the Yorkshire electorate thus between seven and ten per cent of the whole, and constituting as well a microcosm of Britain in its blend of landed and town folk, a Yorkshire election reflected the sense of the people to a degree only matched by the London constituency of Middlesex. 'Yorkshire and Middlesex between them,' observed Charles James Fox, 'make all England.' Yorkshire MPs, it followed, were heard with respect. In the context of the pre-Reform era, they were proudly independent, for they owed their seats to labourers as well as lords, pig jobbers and parsons, brewers and barristers, nailers and knights.[6] Elections in Yorkshire, Lord Milton declared to freeholders gathered in the Piece Hall at Halifax during his 1807 canvass, 'teach the rich not to despise the poor, and they shew the poor that they are not altogether dependent on their more opulent neighbours. They express the collective wisdom of the country.'[7]

Where the three ridings touched stood the walled city of York which, with its own county (or Ainsty) also returned two members of Parliament with a

---

[4] Thomas Allen, *New and Complete History of the County of York*, 6 vols (J.T. Hinton: 1828–1831), vol. 1, p. 220; Smith, 'Yorkshire Elections', p. 63.

[5] In a list of estimated electorates in 1790, Yorkshire is given as 20,000. The next largest English counties were Kent and Somerset, each with 9,000; 7 Irish counties each had more than 9,000 voters, the largest being Tyrone with an estimated 10,000–20,000: *History of Parliament. The House of Commons, 1790–1820*, vol. 1, pp. 358, 366. For a plan of York Castle Yard see Plate 8.

[6] *York Courant*, 25 May 1807; G.S. Veitch, *Genesis of Parliamentary Reform* (Constable: 1913, reprinted 1965), p. x; Asa Briggs, *Age of Improvement, 1783–1867* (Longman: 1959), p. 113; G.E. Mingay, *English Landed Society in the Eighteenth Century* (Routledge & Kegan Paul: 1963), p. 26; N.C. Phillips, *Yorkshire and English National Politics*, p. 19.

[7] *Halifax Journal*, 16 May 1807.

standing nearly equal to that of the knights of the shire.[8] To enjoy the ripe flavour of unreformed Yorkshire politics requires a dip into the complex and at times corrupt world of the parliamentary borough. Of Yorkshire's 59 market towns, 13 were designated by royal charter to send two members each to Parliament for reasons which had vanished with time. Together with York, the boroughs returned 28 MPs on a total electorate of about 7,000. Leeds, Sheffield, Bradford, Halifax and the other prospering industrial centres had no voice save through the county members. Yorkshire had, in all, 30 seats but in terms of the proportion of window tax paid per capita, it should have had 46 and distributed quite differently.[9]

The franchise in the boroughs was vastly more elitist than for the county as a whole. Few Yorkshire boroughs fell into the delightfully named 'scot and lot' or 'pot-walloper' categories, which by enfranchising individual households could be called the most representative. In a pot-walloper constituency, all householders who could claim a separate doorway and a hearth could vote so long as they had not ever, and were not now, receiving poor relief. Only Pontefract in Yorkshire had the makings of such an electorate but it was a hotly debated point there whether households or burgage tenures, chiefly the property of Lord Galway, carried the vote. The only scot and lot boroughs were tiny Aldborough where in theory all males resident for six months who paid church (scot) and poor (lot) taxes could vote but where in practice the Duke of Newcastle, who owned nearly all the houses, chose the MPs, and Malton, where the chief proprietor, Earl Fitzwilliam, virtually always succeeded in persuading, by judicious cash gifts, his largely working-class householders to accept the candidates he designated.[10]

In the larger boroughs such as York, the franchise lay with the freemen, residents who obtained their freedoms by inheritance, apprenticeship, purchase (£25 in eighteenth-century York) or, occasionally, gift. Freedoms were licences to practise a trade or set up a business. York, with around 2,500 freemen, was the least susceptible to one-man domination, although the Marquess of Rockingham was for many years a determining influence and York's earlier

---

[8] Lewis Namier and John Brooke, *History of Parliament. The House of Commons, 1754–1790*, 3 vols (Oxford University Press: 1964); I.C. Collyer, 'Politics in 18th-century York', York Georgian Society *Annual Report* (1955–56), p. 13.

[9] Oldfield, *History*, vol. 2, p. 265.

[10] On the boroughs, Namier and Brooke, *History*, vol. 1, pp. 10–34; Veitch, *Genesis*, 5–7; Oldfield, *History*, vol. 2, pp. 267–88; Smith, 'Earl Fitzwilliam and Malton: a Proprietory Borough in the Early Nineteenth Century', *English Historical Review*, 80 (1965), 53; F.M.L. Thompson, *English Landed Society in the Nineteenth Century* (Routledge & Kegan Paul: 1963), p. 205; R.A. Butlin (ed.), *Historical Atlas of North Yorkshire* (Westbury Publishing: Otley, 2003), pp. 120–1.

reputation under the first two Georges was one of a city open to the highest bidder. Five guineas a vote was what some freemen expected.[11] In Kingston upon Hull, also a county and a town in itself, the poorer order of the 1,400 freemen (or burgesses) 'charged' two guineas a vote (four, if a single vote or plumper was pledged). His first election at Hull in 1780 cost 21-year-old William Wilberforce between £8,000 and £9,000.[12] Beverley's thousand freemen tended to follow the wishes of the Pelhams and some would not say no to a guinea since freemen came in many guises, from labourers to merchant princes. It was generally considered bad form for the richer freemen to accept 'the guineas'.

Not so, however, in little Hedon in the watery plain of Holderness with its 200 freemen in a population of 592. Situated on a haven off the Humber, secure from pirates, Hedon was a wealthy seaport when it was granted parliamentary representation, but it continued to return two members even though by the sixteenth century it had lost all of its importance to nearby Hull and was simply a quiet market town. Not only were the electors greedy – they had been known to ask up to £100 for a vote although the nominal price was £20 – but they also were mostly absentees. In the 1807 general election, of the 206 voters, only 82 actually lived there. The selling of freedoms was a lucrative line for the Corporation and the candidates were not only obliged to purchase their freedoms – the going rate at the start of the nineteenth century was 200 guineas – but also to give generously to some local good work such as new church chimes or cottages for the aged. These adopted sons were milked at election time when they came down from London to cast their votes for candidates who, in the early nineteenth century, were approved by the borough patron, William Iveson, and then spoke for the East India Company. 'The families of several burgesses have almost lived by their exactions,' asserted a parliamentary reformer.[13]

In the remainder of the Yorkshire boroughs, burgage-holds or tenures carried the privilege of voting and the occupants largely did the bidding of the lords of the manor. Boroughbridge, the village twin of Aldborough, was another pocket borough of the Duke of Newcastle who controlled, in all, seven parliamentary seats. The duke of the day returned members for the two small Yorkshire boroughs for 130 years. At Thirsk, 49 of the 50 tenures belonged to Sir Thomas Frankland. The Peirse and Lascelles families shared the seats for Northallerton where some of the burgage houses had become stables or fallen

---

[11] Collyer, 'Politics in York', pp. 14, 15.
[12] Furneaux, *Wilberforce*, p. 15.
[13] Markham, *1820 Election at Hedon*, pp. 7–22; M.T. Craven, *New and Complete History of the Borough of Hedon* (Ridings Publications: Driffield, 1972), pp. 20–2, 70, 159–61; Oldfield, *History*, vol. 2, p. 277.

into ruins but retained the chimneys that denoted their status. Any structure which carried a vote was worth an extra £100 on the market.[14] At Ripon, it was the Aislabie family, at Knaresborough the Duke of Devonshire, and Richmond followed where Sir Thomas (later Lord) Dundas led.

Scarborough was Yorkshire's only example of a borough where the franchise was vested in the self-perpetuating Corporation, in this case made up of 40 to 50 men generally loyal to the interests of the Duke of Rutland and Lord Mulgrave.

In contrast to that in most boroughs, the electorate in counties throughout Britain was composed of freeholders possessing property worth a rental of 40 shillings or more a year and assessed for the land tax. Over the years, since its introduction in 1430, the 40 shilling qualification came to include lifetime leases, ecclesiastical benefices and other evidences of solid citizenship. In 1430, of course, 40 shillings-worth of property clearly described the middling and upper classes. By 1807 the unaltered qualification had brought the vote to tradesmen and artisans and smallholders who could boast property with an equivalent capital value of only £60. It was not necessary to live on the property to vote in the county where it lay. In the 1807 election, 3.6 per cent of the voters lived outside Yorkshire. On the whole, county elections were less vulnerable to manipulation, provided the best insights into the public mind and were the least predictable.

This accounted for the prestige of county MPs, who sat on select committees, were listened to on local issues such as turnpike, canal and enclosure bills, and who affected the appointments of tax collectors and other servants of the Crown. The possibility of honours and the certainty of patronage lured many to seek these seats. These members (knights of their shires) alone could wear spurs in the House. They deferred less to the court or the government of the day, which made certain that its leaders sat for safe – if rotten – boroughs. In 1807, the *Leeds Mercury* took savage pleasure in pointing out that the ten chief ministers newly installed by the king represented a total of just 1,214 people: not one sat for a county or a city. Centuries-old laws and customs shored up such privilege. One hundred and eighty-two individuals selected 326 of the 658 MPs; seventy others were 'placemen' of the court or government of the day, and forty were chosen through some compromise of contending interests. This left 222 MPs whose chances were affected by any body of citizens.[15]

---

[14] The deeds by which in 1754 and 1779 the Lascelles and Peirse families agreed to elect one MP from each house (when Henry Peirse was a minor the Lascelles occupied both seats, 1754–74) are in the Harewood Archives (WYAS(L)) at WYL250/6/3/28. B.A. English, 'Harewood MSS.', *Bulletin of the National Register of Archives*, 12 (1963), 9–14.

[15] Arthur Male, *Treatise on the Law and Practice of Elections* (J. Butterworth: 1818; 2nd edn, 1820), pp. 250–7; Namier and Brooke, *History*, vol. 1, p. 2; Forrester, *Northamptonshire County*

Yet the system suited a complacent and still largely rural society. In this day of the universal franchise at 18 and the secret ballot, the old way may look intolerable but it persisted because it did represent with surprising accuracy the landed interests, trades and professions of a stable, hierarchical society. Interests, rather than individuals, were what mattered and, as a closer examination will reveal, the system was open to manipulation by lowly as well as landed interests. Trevelyan, himself from a patrician political family, portrayed a disarming but simplistic scene when he wrote that the 'British working man, then called the "honest yeoman" or the "jolly 'prentice", was quite happy drinking himself drunk to the health of the "quality" at election time. And even if he had no vote, he could stand cheering or hooting in front of the hustings, while the candidate, possibly a Peer's son, bowed low with his hand on his heart and a rotten egg in his hair, addressing the mob as "gentlemen" and asking for their support.'[16]

Undeniably, unreformed Parliaments contained more talent than the system implied. Pitt came in effortlessly, aged 21, from a rotten borough in a 1780 by-election. 'I have seen Sir James Lowther,' he wrote to his mother. 'Appleby is the place I am to represent, and the election will be made (probably in a week or ten days) without my having any trouble, or even visiting my constituents.' Pitt's father, afterwards Earl of Chatham, began his parliamentary career in 1754 from Aldborough, and Boroughbridge's former MPs included General Sir Henry Clinton, commander-in-chief of the British army in the American Revolution; William Murray, who became the first Lord (Chief Justice) Mansfield, and Sir Richard Steele, author of *The Tatler*.[17]

Sir Francis Burdett's father-in-law, the London banker, Thomas Coutts, fixed him up with the Boroughbridge seat in 1796. As Burdett recalled: 'I was told, one day, that I was returned for Boroughbridge. ... The matter was arranged, as such matters usually are, by other parties, a sum of money was received on the part of the noble Duke of Newcastle and paid on mine. ... I am bound to say that the sum which procured me the seat was not by any

---

Elections, p. 2: Porritt, *Unreformed House*, p. 25; Elie Halévy, *History of the English People in 1815* (1912; reprinted, Penguin Books: 1937), pp. 167–8; *Leeds Mercury*, 25 April 1807; Walter Fawkes, *Speech ... on the Subject of Parliamentary Reform, Delivered at the Anniversary Celebration of the Election of Sir Francis Burdett* (Ridgway: 1813).

[16] G.M. Trevelyan, *History of England* (Longmans: 1926; 3rd edn, repr. 1948), p. 514.

[17] Quoted in Henry Jephson, *The Platform: Its Rise and Progress*, 2 vols (Macmillan: 1892), vol. 1, p. 34; John Ehrman, *The Younger Pitt: The Years of Acclaim* (Constable: 1969), pp. 25–6; W.W. Bean, *Parliamentary Representation of the Six Northern Counties of England, 1603–1886* (C.H. Barnwell for the author: Hull, 1890); H.S. Smith, *Parliamentary Representation of Yorkshire* (J.R. Smith: 1854).

means unusually large ... it amounted to £4,000 and for that I was guaranteed for six years.'[18]

The Marquess of Rockingham, and later the Earl Fitzwilliam, gave Malton to Edmund Burke from 1780 until his retirement in 1794, unharried the whole time by constituency affairs. And a seat for the notional Midhurst was purchased by Lord Holland in 1768 for his adored son, Charles James Fox, while the latter, barely 19, was in Italy. Fox entered the Commons still 18 months under the legal age, was an instant success and achieved office at 21.[19]

Members of Parliament were drawn almost exclusively from the upper classes. The income of a county member had to be at least £600 a year from land; £300 was the lower limit for borough members. A few, like Fox and Pitt, were younger sons of peers who having completed their educations and the grand tour were presented with seats in the nation's legislature. Absolutely barred from sitting in the Commons for 'the supposed want of discretion, or imbecility' were infants (that is, all under 21, a frequently flouted disqualification), women, deaf mutes, idiots, madmen, aliens, felons and Roman Catholics. Parliament was so nearly a nest of interconnected families that an MP might spot fifty relatives on the green benches.[20]

To the majority of the British people, politics and elections were entirely spectator sports. The unenfranchised included the propertyless, paupers, idiots, lunatics and all Catholics who were unable in conscience to swear the oaths of allegiance and supremacy. Dissenting ministers, who were moved about at the will of their congregations, and Methodists with their itinerant preachers, were apt to be disqualified while Anglican clergy, removable from their livings only for exceptional reasons, could qualify through the church property they occupied.

Women could not vote but as property holders they could sometimes in effect control the votes of others as Mrs Jane Osbaldeston of Hutton Buscel demonstrated at the 1807 election; and other women were borough patrons, such as Elizabeth Allanson of Ripon. In medieval York tradeswomen were admitted as freemen of the city, and in 1807 Simon Appleton of South Cliff promised a plumper to Lord Milton's canvasser 'in the right of his wife'. But some confusion surrounded women's rights, or lack of them, as Milton's Wetherby agent revealed when he asked the committee at York to 'have

---

[18] Quoted in Fred Singleton, *Industrial Revolution in Yorkshire* (Dalesman: Clapham, 1970), p. 97; M.W. Patterson, *Sir Francis Burdett and His Times (1770–1844)*, 2 vols (Macmillan: 1931), vol. 1, pp. 36–9.
[19] Christopher Hobhouse, *Fox* (Constable: 1947), p. 10; J.W. Derry, *Charles James Fox* (Batsford: 1972), p. 18.
[20] A.D. Harvey, *Britain in the Early Nineteenth Century* (Batsford: 1978), pp. 28–9; Mingay, *English Landed Society*, p. 114; Male, *Treatise*, p. 34.

the goodness to say whether or no a Female can vote as I have several of that distinction held waiting for my acceptance'. So experienced a politician as Walter Spencer Stanhope reported that the county's gentlemen agreed beforehand that 'the ladies who were entitled to vote should not exercise this privilege unless it should be found essential'. No women's names appear in the 1807 poll book.[21]

---

[21] Male, *Treatise*, p. 242; R.Y. Hawkin, *History of the Freemen of the City of York* (City of York Guild of Freemen: York, 1955), p. 8, 12, 13; SCC:LAI: WWM E51, Harthill canvass book; E160/1, Royston to Milton committee, 6 May; Stirling, *Letter-Bag*, vol. 1, p. 142.

CHAPTER TWO

Land, Wool, and Iron

THE economic underpinnings of Britain's early nineteenth-century world power were all to be found in Yorkshire, and the county's diversity fostered the Yorkshire electorate's vaunted independence, often contrasted with the truckling of voters in more feudal counties. No single grandee could 'deliver' Yorkshire.

From at least the mid-eighteenth century, the West Riding had been the key to political success. By 1811, 53 per cent of all Yorkshire families lived by manufacturing, handicrafts or trade and most of them were in the West Riding.[1] This decisive influence can be identified in the two eighteenth-century contests which preceded the election of 1807. In the bitter struggle of 1734, the Whigs, then the ministerial party with great strength among the landed aristocracy of the North and East Ridings and in the Established Church, were opposed by a 'Country Interest' determined to assert its independence from the Crown and its dislike for Walpole's government. The Whigs were led by the Earl of Carlisle and Sir William Strickland, then Secretary at War and MP for Scarborough. The Country Interest drew upon the small freeholders in the cloth-making districts and the old Tory landed families of the West Riding with the Earl of Strafford in their van. After a seven-day election in May 1734, the Country Interest candidate, Sir Myles Stapylton, topped the poll and although the Whigs kept the other seat with Cholmondeley Turner, their favourite, Sir Rowland Winn, came third.[2] Seven years later, in a poll lasting eight days to fill one seat, Turner was re-elected not only because of the Whigs' superior resources and his own good standing, which brought him three-quarters of the landed vote, but because the opposition was split over issues of wool supply and cloth quality control with the Leeds and Wakefield

---

[1] Smith, 'Yorkshire Elections', p. 63, note 7.
[2] C. Collyer, 'Yorkshire Election of 1734', *Leeds Philosophical and Literary Society Proceedings*, 7:1 (1952), pp. 53–82; H.E. Chetwynd Stapylton, *Stapletons of Yorkshire* (Longmans: 1897), pp. 300–2.

merchants pitted against an alliance of smallholders, gentlemen owners of fulling mills and ordinary clothiers.[3]

It is so tempting to think of the West Riding as the 'workshop of the world' it became in the later nineteenth century that the importance of its landed proprietors and the agricultural interest can be overlooked. In 1807 it held an 'astonishing number' of small freeholders farming 20 to 60 acres and 330 country seats – more than half the total in the county. Their owners already were profiting from a fortuitous location above vast coal fields and iron ore deposits. Easily the most splendid seat was Wentworth Woodhouse, a country palace near Rotherham which the fourth Earl Fitzwilliam inherited in 1782 from his uncle, the second Marquess of Rockingham. But close to it in grandeur was Harewood House, seat of the Lascelles, north of Leeds. These were the strongholds from which the 1807 election was fought.

As much as one family could, the Rockingham interest dominated Yorkshire politics in the latter half of the eighteenth century. The connection began with the election of Thomas Watson Wentworth (afterwards Lord Malton and the first marquess) for the family borough of Malton in 1714. He was to be an unwitting founder of a Whig dynasty – his elder daughter married the first Earl Fitzwilliam – but his own lifetime preoccupation was the rebuilding of Wentworth House on a magnificent scale. The second Marquess of Rockingham, who succeeded to the title and an annual rent roll of £24,000 in 1750, made the house the political and social centre it long remained.[4]

From his lavish coming-of-age party in 1751 until his elaborate burial in York Minster in 1782, Rockingham was a potent force. The election of Sir George ('Independent') Savile for the county in 1758 secured the Rockingham ascendancy, for Savile was immensely popular and nowhere more so than in the West Riding. A Rockingham Club was founded in 1753 and for more than 30 years it brought together at the George Inn in Coney Street, York, freemen, clergymen and gentry.[5]

---

[3] C. Collyer, 'Yorkshire Election of 1741', *Leeds Philosophical and Literary Society Proceedings*, 7:2 (1953), pp. 137–52.

[4] *Ibid.*; Smith, *Whig Principles*, pp. 3, 29–30.

[5] C. Collyer, 'The Rockinghams and Yorkshire Politics, 1742–1761', *Thoresby Miscellany* (Thoresby Society: Leeds, 1954), p. 361; T. Whellan & Co., *History and Topography of the City of York; and the North Riding of Yorkshire*, 2 vols (Beverley, 1857), vol. 1, p. 272; Allen, *History of York*, vol. 1, p. 121; WYAS(K): Ramsden Family Papers, Records, WYL109/20/1/104; 'Extract from Mr Hunter's letter' [undated but perhaps July 1782] – an account of Lord Rockingham's death; E.C. Black, *The Association: British Extra-parliamentary Political Organization, 1769–1793* (Harvard University Press: Cambridge, Mass., 1963), p. 7; D.E. Ginter (ed.), *Whig Organization in the General Election of 1790: Selections from the Blair Adam Papers* (University of California Press: Berkeley, 1967), p. xlvi; Collyer, 'Politics in York', p. 16.

Rockingham is often dismissed on the national stage as something of a tongue-tied mediocrity – although he headed two administrations – but he understood well the need to create alliances. His rule was to 'follow, not to lead, the sense of the county'. His eloquent protégé, Edmund Burke, in an epitaph asserted that Rockingham 'far exceeded all other statesmen in the art of drawing together ... the concurrence and co-operation of various dispositions and abilities of men ... for it was his aim through life to convert party connexion and personal friendship ... into a lasting depository of his principles; that ... the British constitution might be preserved according to its true genius'. The Rockinghamites, largest of the factions produced by the Whigs, saw themselves as the natural guardians of the 1689 settlement which followed the Glorious Revolution. Rockingham's Yorkshire influence ran long after his death. In 1808 a new weekly paper bearing his name was introduced in Hull to defend Whig principles and the 'purity of the constitution'.[6]

In the House of Lords Rockingham sided with the woollen interest. Yorkshire knew him as an agricultural improver and decent landlord, one of the county's greatest patrons of racing and a conciliatory and effective lord lieutenant and chief magistrate. By the opening of George III's reign, he carried unique weight among the landed and commercial interests of the county and with the freemen of the city of York. He cemented his bonds with the Leeds and other West Riding merchants when in 1761 he backed Edwin Lascelles for the second county seat on the death of Lord Downe. But opposition to this imposing influence was never lacking in the county and there were many families of rank who objected on principle to the interference of peers or to alliances with commerce, and developments in the economy were to create new political divisions between a Tory-commercial partnership and a combination of gentry and clothiers under aristocratic Whig leadership.[7]

At the onset of the industrial revolution, the West Riding contained a wool cloth production area in the constellation of towns and villages near Leeds and a southern metal-working region around Sheffield. Issues relating to the import, manufacture or sale of wool busied Parliament for centuries but far less controversy burdened the newer, less tradition-laden trades of Sheffield and its

---

[6] Namier and Brooke, *History*, vol. 1, p. 42; Burke's epitaph, J.B. Morrell, *Biography of the Common Man of the City of York As Recorded in His Epitaph* (Batsford: 1947), pp. 59–61; Smith, *Whig Principles*, p. xii; *Rockingham*, 2 January 1808; for critical views of Rockingham, R.J. White, *Age of George III* (Heinemann: 1968), pp. 94–9; John Brooke, *King George III* (Constable: 1974), p. 209.

[7] Collyer, 'The Rockinghams', pp. 369–76; C. Collyer, 'The Rockingham Connection and Country Opinion in the Early Years of George III', *Leeds Philosophical and Literary Society Proceedings*, 7:4 (1955), pp. 251–2, 253, 263; Smith, *Whig Principles*, p. x.

vicinity. Smoke from 1,700 forges stained Sheffield's handsome new houses (and even its inhabitants) without complaint. A royal visitor, the Duke of Clarence, viewed with 'uncommon curiosity and delight' the manufactories turning out hand tools, nails, screws, scissors, razors and silver plate in 1806, followed from one workshop to the next by a large but seemly crowd. The plentiful coal in the neighbourhood supplied more family-sized shops in the scattered villages of the wooded valleys roundabout and the hillsides were decorated with the pretty villas of the newly rich 'Cyclops'.

Sheffield, now nearing 40,000 in population, was a nursery of inventions and ideas, and it supported in addition to its churches, seven dissenting chapels. 'They are a social people,' William Hutton noticed in 1803, 'attend more to business than to quarrelling; and, I hope, are acquiring fortunes, as a recompense for subsisting upon smoke.' The artisan class was dominant and large employers rare. A manufactory (vulgarly known as a factory) consisted of the master and his journeymen and apprentices who had every reason to expect to go into trade on their own eventually. Rotherham, six miles north-east, was a small and sooty sister to Sheffield, thriving on its trade in coal and cattle and on the Walkers' cast iron works over the bridge at Masborough.[8]

Like the wool towns, these communities were not represented in Parliament. The aspirations of its people made Sheffield a centre of radicalism. The Sheffield Constitutional Society, founded in 1780 and revived a decade later as a Society for Constitutional Information, drew thousands to meetings which called for a fairer voice in Parliament. Unlike the Yorkshire Association for Parliamentary Reform of the same vintage, the Sheffield activists were as concerned with wages, pensions and welfare benefits for needy mothers and children as with manhood suffrage, and they were of course condemned by the rich as dangerous extremists. In the 1790s the Sheffield society was the largest in the North and the first with entirely working-class origins – 'four or five persons, Mechanics', men of good character and sense, whose peaceable object was to educate workers to the need for reform so that they would be willing to join 'persons of consequence' in pursuit of more adequate representation. Although the society alarmed many observers by its interest in

---

[8] Bigland, *Beauties XVI Yorkshire*, pp. 611–12, 818–27; Smith 'Yorkshire Elections', 63; *Doncaster Gazette*, 7 November 1806; Allen, *History of York*, vol. 3, pp. 2–3, 31–9; [Louis Simond], *Journal of a Tour and Residence in Great Britain, During ... 1810 and 1811, By a French Traveller*, 2 vols (Constable: Edinburgh, 1815), vol. 1, p. 78; W. Hutton, *A Tour to Scarborough in 1803; including a Survey of the City of York* (Nichols, Son & Bentley: 1804; 2nd edn, 1817), pp. 8, 9, 10.; D. Hey, *Yorkshire from AD 1000* (Longman: Harlow, 1986), pp. 221, 225–9. For a cutler's workshop, see plate 1.

Thomas Paine's republican notions, others considered it a wholesome advance on the disorderly gatherings which had troubled the area shortly before.⁹

Meanwhile, Sheffield turned to the county members, and the proposed pig-iron tax was the most recent local issue at the 1807 election. All the wartime taxes were unwelcome, but Sheffield toolmakers felt especially threatened by Lord Henry Petty's 1806 bill to levy an import duty on the Swedish bar iron they used. They believed it would undermine their trade and reduce their ability to export profitably. Farming spokesmen chimed in to complain that it would double the cost of horseshoes. Henry Lascelles declared that iron wares like Sheffield's were already made and sold more cheaply in Germany and that the tax would make it even easier for foreigners to undercut the Yorkshire manufacturers. Wilberforce, 'having made myself master of the subject', in a long and able speech on 9 May 1806 fought for his constituents whom he hailed as 'men of athletic make, and great bodily vigour' in contrast with those in unnamed occupations which produced a 'feeble and degenerate race ... without spirit or ability to defend their rights'. Never had he felt more pleasure than when returning to Sheffield, a once barren spot now 'covered with the fruits of human industry'. In only nine years, iron manufacture had soared from 100,000 tons a year to 250,000. Pitt had proposed such a tax 10 years ago but when that great man perceived his error he had abandoned it. In vain did the Foxites argue that all this talk proved that the flourishing iron trade was now 'ripe enough to produce a revenue'. By a majority of ten the House recommitted the bill and Lord Henry dropped it. But he had no better luck with a substitute measure to tax home-brewed beer.¹⁰

As small shops dominated the iron and steel industry, so was woollen cloth production, in the main, on a family scale. Living in his stone house with its long mullion windows, surrounded by up to fifteen acres of land with pigs, poultry, a cow and a horse (often that small and sturdy breed known as the galloway), the Yorkshire clothier was as much agriculturalist as artisan, and the combination of pursuits gave the industrious weaver a comfortable living. He needed little capital to buy his materials and he owned his tools. Each member of the household had a task and the larger clothmakers had

---

⁹ Donald Read, *English Provinces, c.1760–1960: a study in influence* (Arnold: 1964), pp. 35, 46–7; S. Maccoby, *English Radicalism, 1786–1832* (Allen & Unwin: 1955), pp. 51–2, 66–7; Rev. Christopher Wyvill, *Political Papers, chiefly respecting the attempt of the County of York and other ... districts commenced in 1779 ... to effect a reformation of the Parliament of Great Britain*, 6 vols (W. Blanchard: York, 1794–1802), vol. 5, pp. 43, 46–50; Harvey, *Britain*, p. 51; Black, *Association*, pp. 223, 224; F. O'Gorman, *Whig Party and the French Revolution* (Macmillan: 1967), p. 82.

¹⁰ *Parliamentary Debates, House of Commons*, vol. 6, cols 948–50 (28 April 1806); vol. 7, cols 74–92 (9 May 1806); col. 255 (19 May 1806); Wilberforce, *Life*, vol. 3, pp. 263–4; BI: TAY/1/109, Wilberforce election broadside.

their journeymen and apprentices or sent work out to neighbours who wove part-time. From the clothier's looms came between two and ten 'pieces' a week, which were carried on the galloway for weekly exhibition and sale at the cloth hall. By 1800 the West Riding was turning out three-fifths of Britain's woollens – the nation's largest export – and some clothiers dealt directly with colonial markets. Yorkshire-made blankets covered sleeping slaves in the American South and Yorkshire woollen was tailored into the greatcoats worn by the British soldiers, and, war notwithstanding, the troops of Bonaparte and Russia as well.[11]

In the last two decades of the eighteenth century, the domestic clothiers absorbed the new flying shuttle, scribbling, slubbing and carding machines and the spinning jenny from the Lancashire cotton industry, expanding in some cases their numbers of workers and looms. The division between producers and sellers (the merchants also finished or dressed the cloth) was maintained, however. The appearance of factories, combining all stages of production, was slow in Yorkshire and the clothiers' worst fears of being displaced entirely or forced to toil for wages in mills were not realized until after 1815.[12]

Cornelius Ashworth of Waltroyd farm in the Wheatley valley near Halifax was typical of many smallholders who wove on the side. He cultivated eight fields of corn, oats and hay, and worked at his handloom for a near-by clothier in afternoons and on rainy days. When a piece (about 30 yards) was completed, he carried it to the master clothier, or perhaps to the Piece Hall itself. On average, working part-time at his loom, Ashworth could produce a piece of cloth in about two weeks, probably earning him around 35 shillings.[13]

The doughty independence of weavers like Ashworth was sometimes criticized on the grounds that it encouraged sloppy work, sloth, even dishonesty.

---

[11] Herbert Heaton, 'Leeds White Cloth Hall', *Thoresby Society Miscellanea*, 22 (1915), pp. 132–3; *Baines's Account of the Woollen Manufacture of England*, ed. K.G. Ponting (David & Charles: Newton Abbot, 1970), pp. 33–4; Wilson, *Gentlemen Merchants*, pp. 4–7; Frank Peel, *Risings of the Luddites, Chartists and Plug-Drawers* (Senior & Co.: Heckmondwike, 1888; 4th edn, Cass: 1968), p. ix; Frank Peel, *Spen Valley: Past and Present* (Senior & Co.: Heckmondwike, 1893), pp. 18, 221, 222, 229; Briggs, *Age of Improvement*, pp. 162–3; [John Ryley], *Leeds Guide* (J. Ryley: Leeds, 1806), p. 101.

[12] Wilson, *Gentlemen Merchants*, pp. 91, 33, 56–9; W.B. Crump (ed.), *Leeds Woollen Industry 1780–1820* (Thoresby Society: Leeds, 1931), pp. 17–36. J.L. Hammond and B. Hammond, *Skilled Labourer, 1760–1832* (1919; second edn, Longmans: 1920), pp. 139, 149–50, 164, 177–87; Hey, *Yorkshire*, pp. 230–9.

[13] T. Hanson, 'Diary of a Grandfather: Cornelius Ashworth, of Waltroyd Wheatley', *Halifax Antiquarian Society Papers* (1916), pp. 233–48. Hanson speculated that a piece would have earned about 5 shillings, but for the revised estimate see *The Diaries of Cornelius Ashworth*, ed. Davies, Petford and Senior, pp. 59, 67.

Henry Lascelles allegedly once cited, and appeared to believe, an accusation from a supposedly respectable source in Leeds that many petitioning clothiers were 'idle Vagabonds, who wish to have their Work in their own Houses, to embezzle their Masters' property'. On Mondays and Tuesdays their looms worked to the slow chant of 'Plen-ty of time. Plenty of time' and on Thursdays or Fridays clacked swiftly to 'A day t' lat. 'A day t' lat [A day too late]', or so it used to be said. But to others these pre-factory days were idyllic:

> When Spinning Wheels were us'd in every Cot,
> Contentment dwelt each happy with their Lot; ...
> How happy were the Days, when each good Wife,
> Could spin and sing and keep her tongue from strife,
> Her Husband happy, and their Children dear,
> Where taught the Laws t'obey, their God to fear,
> How chang'd the Scene, now to the Mills they go,
> Where Immoralities in Torrents flow ...[14]

Partly because of wartime uncertainties, by 1800 scarcely twenty manufactories had been established in the West Riding but the concentration of marketing in the cloth halls and the rise of merchant capitalists would lead inevitably to investment on a grander scale. Best known among the pioneers of factory production was the young merchant Benjamin Gott who (as Messrs Wormald, Gott & Wormald) built at Bean Ing on the river Aire in 1792 the first real factory in the Leeds district, and followed it in the next few years with establishments at Armley and Burley. The Bean Ing plant cost £17,000, was enclosed by a high wall and used a water wheel and a 40 horsepower steam engine to run its machines.[15]

In one shed, Gott employed 80 croppers or shearmen, the aristocrats of the clothworkers, who raised the nap with teasels then trimmed it with iron shears that weighed some 30 pounds. If these jobs were done by gig mills and shearing frames, which allowed several pairs of shears to operate simultaneously and were not banned by law, a man and two boys could replace eighteen men and six boys. Whenever Yorkshire employers attempted to introduce these innovations, the croppers resisted. But the machines made their inexorable inroads. It was the protesting shearmen who had reacted violently to such changes in Wiltshire in 1802 and shortly afterwards Yorkshire croppers walked

---

[14] *York Herald*, 1 August 1807; Hanson, 'Diary of a Grandfather', p. 234; B. Hebblethwaite, 'To the Memory of the Spinning Wheel', copy seen at former Piece Hall Museum, Halifax.
[15] Crump, *Leeds Woollen Industry*, pp. 4–26; Wilson, *Gentlemen Merchants*, pp. 90–1, 96–7, 60, 243–4; *Baines's Account*; Singleton, *Industrial Revolution*, pp. 30–1; BRO: MS 193, Benjamin Gott Business Papers; [Ryley], *Leeds Guide*, p. 103.

out in a body when Gott, in defiance of the widely disregarded statutes, hired two lads too old to serve out their apprenticeships before the age of 21. The merchants of Leeds met, passed resolutions declaring that the strikers would be blacklisted and then discovered that they faced a solid front of some 900 workmen with support from other trades. The men had a fund which could pay a striker 18 shillings a week and no cropper could be found as far off as Somerset to take their places. Pitt's Combination Acts had made trade unions illegal, but the croppers' 'institution', representing some 5,000 men, provided a worrying alternative. Members carried 'tickets' – their passports to work – and during the parliamentary inquiry, Henry Lascelles called attention to this body which he alleged was acting in unholy alliance with the 'rioters and criminals' of the West Country. It was true that Yorkshire and the South West were in regular contact. Lascelles threatened to freeze their funds (they were said to have raised £2,000 to finance the petition and their other needs such as sick benefits or, it was darkly hinted, jacobinical activities). The committee report showed deep concern over the clothworkers' 'systematic, and organized Plan, at once so efficient and so dangerous' that it warranted a parliamentary investigation. The croppers could earn five shillings a day, but toiled from 4 a.m. to 8 p.m. for it. They had a reputation for being troublesome because they worked in groups where the 'contaminating influence of vice spreads with fatal rapidity'. This rather prevalent belief contributed to the resistance among some merchants to embark on factory production.

The croppers' steadiness in the face of the united merchants in the Leeds strike was alarming. 'God only knows where it is to end,' John Beckett wrote despairingly to Earl Fitzwilliam after attending the meeting of merchants where he saw the hundreds of croppers gathered in the yard of the White Cloth Hall to await the outcome. When the merchants were called upon to prove their charges of a workers' combination, there was 'perfect silence'. To a croppers' delegation, the merchants declared that they would have nothing to do with them until they went back to work, whereupon the croppers 'made us a very contemptuous bow' and left.

A committee from each side finally reached an agreement which the strikers saw as a victory. The merchants feared that if they prosecuted under the Combination Acts, and an appeal followed conviction, their shops would be idle for three months. If they had held out only a fortnight longer, the croppers would have run out of money but these hard men had 'learnt the trick of acting in a body so well' that the merchants 'caved in', Beckett declared, and this 'pusillanimity' was a thoroughly bad example for society in general. The Combination Acts had been invoked in the Wiltshire protests but in Yorkshire were considered 'quite inefficacious'. 'I don't know that they ... ought to exist at all,' Fitzwilliam commented, much as he disliked any interference with trade. The croppers he branded the 'Tyrants of the Country, their power and influence has grown out of their high wages, which enable them to make deposits, that puts them beyond all fear of inconvenience from misconduct', as he reported to the Home Office. The croppers kept gig mills and shearing frames out of Gott's factory for twenty years.[16]

The towns of the wool district had each its own character. Leeds, the emporium of the trade with 60,000 inhabitants in its parish bounds, had a high church and Tory local government but also a substantial body of reform-minded Nonconformists, as well as the potentially unruly working class. About twenty families, connected by wool, dominated the Corporation, and having no parliamentary representation, this oligarchy was exceptionally interested in the county elections. Built on the north bank of the Aire, Leeds was divided into halves by broad Briggate where the open market was held. At the upper end, a row of crumbling buildings, the Shambles, in the centre of the street left only narrow passages on either side. The Coloured (or Mixed) Cloth Hall and the White Cloth Hall were vast quadrangular salesrooms which, when open for business for an hour on Tuesdays and Saturdays, astounded visitors. One defined a cloth hall as the 'joint property and warehouse of 2,000 private manufacturers, half-farmers', each of whom attended at his 2½ foot-wide stand with his cloth stacked behind him and samples in his hand while merchants strolled the galleries looking over the goods and buying. Much business was transacted with very few words 'although many of the stands are occupied by women', one tourist remarked. The Leeds cloth halls, as those elsewhere, were the venues for public meetings, electioneering, balls and assemblies, or such spectacles as Mr Lunardi's balloon ascent. Leeds had grown rapidly with the century and was full of modern buildings and well-planted squares, with neat labourers' cottages filling the spaces between workshops. It gave a prosperous impression to travellers who admired all that was new and dismissed York, 25 miles away, as 'an old town, and of course very ugly'.[17]

---

[16] Hammond, *Skilled Labourer*, pp. 135, 136; Cecil Driver, *Tory Radical: The Life of Richard Oastler* (Oxford University Press: New York, 1946), p. 17; Wilson, *Gentlemen Merchants*, pp. 99–100; Singleton, *Industrial Revolution*, pp. 146–7, 164; [George] Walker, *Costume of Yorkshire* (Longman: 1814), Plate V; [Ryley], *Leeds Guide*, p. 10; Harvey, *Britain*, pp. 58–9; *Report on the State of the Woollen Manufacture*, pp. 17, 19, 35, 49, 75; *York Herald*, 1 August 1807; SCC:LAI: WWM F45/117, Beckett to Fitzwilliam, 28 January 1803; Crump, *Leeds Woollen Industry*, p. 40; NRO: F(M), X515/6/3, Fitzwilliam to Laurence, 25 September [1802?].

[17] W.G. Rimmer, *Marshalls of Leeds, Flax-Spinners, 1788–1886* (Cambridge University Press: Cambridge, 1960), pp. 17–19; A.S. Turberville and F. Beckwith, 'Leeds and Parliamentary Reform, 1820–1832', *Thoresby Society Miscellany*, vol. 12 (Thoresby Society: Leeds, 1954), p. 18; Bigland, *Beauties XVI Yorkshire*, pp. 775–96; Allen, *History of York*, vol. 2, pp. 469–532; [Simond], *Journal*, vol. 2, pp. 76–7, 67; W.G. Rimmer, 'Leeds and Its

Bradford, ten miles west of Leeds, was the centre of worsted making, a newer and smaller section of the trade which used long wool requiring less processing. Large employers were more common. Pleasantly sited at the meeting of three valleys, Bradford was becoming, thanks to the coal and iron in its vicinity, a manufacturing town where the 'rattling of looms and … the smoke of steam engines' impressed travellers. More than 7,700 people inhabited the stone-built town where an elegant Methodist meeting house was one of the attractions. Cloth was sold at a fine piece hall.[18]

At Dewsbury south of Leeds, the 5,000 residents clustered on the hillside overlooking the river Calder, with as many more in the parish roundabout. The greater part of them made blankets and coarse broadcloths. Because its birth rate was twice its mortality, Dewsbury was held up as proof that manufacturing was not bad for the health.[19] Halifax, eight miles south-west of Bradford, looked hurriedly built – part traditional stone and part fashionable new brick – long and narrow and surrounded by hills; it had indeed grown rapidly to almost 9,000. Through public subscriptions the residents had provided a theatre, a circulating library, a news room and a dispensary. At the heart of the town was the splendid Piece Hall built around a square against the backdrop of Beacon Hill. With 315 small display rooms on three galleried levels, the hall was open from ten until noon each Saturday. Today it provides the only chance in Yorkshire to see how the woollen trade functioned at the height of the domestic system.[20]

Huddersfield, equidistant from Halifax and Dewsbury on the south-western edge of the constellation of wool towns, was a community of 7,000 with double that in its parish. Again the focal point was the Cloth Hall, here a circular brick building with a central courtyard. The last of the West Riding wool towns and by some considered the handsomest was Wakefield, nine miles south of Leeds, second to Bradford in worsted manufacture. It also had an important corn market. On the fine stone bridge over the Calder stood a redundant Gothic chapel which had been converted into a news room for gentlemen. The manufacture of fancy cloth had enriched Wakefield. Most of

---

Industrial Growth', *Leeds Journal*, 24:11 (1953), p. 391; Herbert Heaton, *Yorkshire Woollen and Worsted Industries* (Clarendon Press: Oxford, 1920; 2nd edn, 1965), p. 378; D. Fraser (ed.), *A History of Modern Leeds* (Manchester University Press: Manchester, 1980). For the White Cloth Hall, see Plate 7.

[18] Heaton, *Yorkshire Woollen Industries*, pp. 273–4, 297; Bigland, *Beauties XVI Yorkshire*, pp. 771–2; D. James, *Bradford* (Ryburn: Halifax, 1990), pp. 11–46.

[19] Bigland, *Beauties XVI Yorkshire*, pp. 767–70.

[20] *Ibid*; pp. 742–7; A.M. Teale, 'Methodism in Halifax and District, 1780 to 1850', unpublished M.Sc. thesis (University of Bradford, 1976); J.A. Hargreaves, *Halifax* (Edinburgh University Press and Carnegie Publishing: Lancaster, 1999), pp. 25–115.

it was marketed at Leeds or Huddersfield but the cloth hall here (called the Tammy Hall) was tasteful if small.[21]

Extraordinary exertion would be needed to canvass so large and varied a region as the West Riding with its combination of commerce and agriculture. But in the North and East Ridings, the landed influence faced little competition, Hull apart. The East Riding landowner dynasties of Constables, Grimstons, St Quintins, Vavasours, Saltmarshes and Hildyards were being joined by and integrated with mercantile families such as the Sykes, Broadleys and Denisons who handled their share of the obligations of the rich, serving as justices of the peace, deputy lieutenants or militia officers. There were more than ninety country seats. Land was power and as soon as his purse – perhaps after a fortunate marriage – allowed, the lawyer or merchant established himself in the country where, with servants, labourers, tenants and the clergyman to whom he presented the living, he built the 'interest' which could be thrown in the way of one or another political kingmaker. This interest he expanded by 'constant entertaining, by giving favours ... and by getting jobs for importunate individuals'. The landowners were basically conservative but liberty loving and jealous of their independence. Most of them kept a foot in both town and country, maintaining a London house for the season. Thus, 'nobody is provincial in this country', a foreigner observed, 'nobody above poverty who has not visited London once in his life; and most of those who can, visit it twice a-year. ... In France, the people of the provinces used to make their will before they undertook such an expedition.'[22]

Yorkshiremen still sounded like Yorkshiremen, however, for public school accents had not yet suffocated regional speech among the well-to-do, but times were changing: rude and rough Sir Tatton ('Tatters') Sykes, the passionate horseman who created an agricultural empire on 34,000 East Riding acres, used to be tucked out of sight in his London mansion when his wife gave smart parties.[23]

---

[21] Bigland, *Beauties XVI Yorkshire*, pp. 767, 804–6, 931; W.B. Crump and G. Ghorbal, *History of the Huddersfield Woollen Industry* (Tolson Memorial Museum: Huddersfield, 1935), p. 74; Philip Ahier, *Legends and Traditions of Huddersfield and Its District*, 2 vols (Advertiser Press: Huddersfield, 1940–45), vol. 1, part 4, pp. 205–8; Heaton, *Yorkshire Woollen Industries*, pp. 271–2; E.A.H. Haigh (ed.), *Huddersfield. A most handsome town* (Kirklees Cultural Services: Huddersfield, 1992).

[22] J.T. Ward, *East Yorkshire Landed Estates in the Nineteenth Century* (East Yorkshire Local History Society: York, 1967), p. 6; Mark Girouard, *Life in the English Country House* (Yale University Press: New Haven, 1978), p. 184; Mingay, *English Landed Society*, p. 116; Thompson, *English Landed Society*, pp. 25–6; [Simond], *Journal*, vol. 1, p. 185.

[23] Ward, *East Yorkshire Estates*, p. 6; Christopher Sykes, *Four Studies in Loyalty* (Collins: 1946), pp. 12–15.

Notable along with the vast estates in the North and East Ridings were the numbers of small holdings owned and occupied by yeoman farmers. The North Riding township of Pickering alone had 300 in the late eighteenth century and no one man owned a £300 a year estate there. In the early nineteenth century, it was estimated that a third of the property in the Riding was in small farms valued at up to £200 a year, while the rest was in estates worth £700 to £20,000. Most of the larger owners lived at their country seats the year around. Among tenant farmers annual leases which could be terminated on six months' notice were common. Their votes, it could be assumed, would be at the landlord's disposal, but the ultimate penalty of dispossession was rarely invoked. Long-standing tenants (often freeholders of other property) as well as enfranchised employees or local tradesmen gave votes or pledges more often from loyalty and a sense of kindred interest with the landed gentry than from duress. It was the large landowners, after all, who maintained the roads, dug canals, set up village schools, dispensed charity and, in many cases, kept rents within bounds – such things as we now expect from our governments. The electors frequently believed they were acting independently in pleasing themselves even while at the same time pleasing the lord of the manor.[24]

The North Riding reached from the Pennine fells to the bold sea coast and descended through fertile uplands into the flat rich Vale of York. The stony tracks that connected the scattered market towns had wild and lonely stretches where travellers met only a few small and 'miserable looking' sheep. But the new turnpikes were excellent and mercifully free from tolls, thanks to the subscriptions of landlords and the 'statute labour' of the people. Facing the sea were Whitby, a lively fishing port with some trade links to northern Europe, and Scarborough whose fisheries and trade were more extensive. Apart from seafaring occupations and some cottage linen weaving, agriculture was the whole livelihood of the Riding's inhabitants.[25]

The East Riding, Yorkshire's south-east corner, was gentler and smaller, although each of the Ridings could easily have formed an English county on its own. Here the coastline dropped from the fishing village of Filey and the outcrop of Flamborough Head to the treeless plain of Holderness which ended in the narrow hook of Spurn Point where the Humber emptied into the sea. Like Scarborough to the north, Bridlington was becoming a popular summer resort. But Hull, with a population of 30,000, was the regional capital, a port

---

[24] [William] Marshall, *Rural Economy of Yorkshire*, 2 vols (T. Cadell: 1788), vol. 1, p. 20; Bigland, *Beauties XVI Yorkshire*, pp. 65–8, 93–105; [John] Tuke, *General View of the Agriculture of the North Riding of Yorkshire* (W. Bulmer & Co.: 1794); Phillips, *Yorkshire and National Politics*, p. 21; Smith, 'Yorkshire Elections', pp. 62–3; Smith, 'Earl Fitzwilliam and Malton', pp. 51–2; Namier and Brooke, *History*, vol. 1, p. 2–3.
[25] *Historical Atlas of North Yorkshire*.

on the Humber with the largest coasting trade outside of London, important links to the Baltic and a major whale fishery. Dorothy Wordsworth dismissed Hull as a 'frightful, dirty, brick-housey, tradesmanlike, rich, vulgar place' but even she found the river beautiful with its drifting sails and changing lights. Docks, wharves and warehouses were connected by narrow streets lined with the new houses and offices of merchants who often also had country residences at nearby Cottingham, Kirk Ella or West Ella. The house in the High Street where William Wilberforce was born in 1759 tells us much of Hull's one-time opulence. From this dignified seventeenth-century mansion, with its oak panelled rooms and mullion windows, Wilberforce's father and grandfather ran their lucrative Russia trade. Inland from the coast the swelling wolds were the scene of an agricultural revolution as pastures were turned into cornfields and the Riding became an important exporter of bacon, butter and potatoes as well as horses and sheep. The jewel among the inland market towns was Beverley, nine miles from Hull, where a majestic minster and almost equally regal parish church bathed worshippers in grandeur and gave landmarks to travellers.[26]

---

[26] *Journals of Dorothy Wordsworth*, ed. E. de Selincourt, 2 vols (Macmillan: 1959), vol. 1, p. 172; Bigland, *Beauties XVI Yorkshire*, pp. 387, 529–30, 582–3; Isaac Leatham, *General View of the Agriculture of the East Riding of Yorkshire* (W. Bulmer & Co.: 1794); A Harris, *The Rural Landscape of the East Riding of Yorkshire, 1700–1850* (Oxford University Press: 1961).

CHAPTER THREE

The Political Past: Reform and Reaction

Reform (1770–1784)

As the American Revolution drew France, Spain and Holland into conflict with Britain, woollen exports sank and unemployment or low wages, bankruptcies and street riots were the gloomy consequences in the manufacturing parts of Yorkshire. Apart from the physical distress, there was intellectual unease over a conflict inspired in part by taxation of an unrepresented people and the colonists' determination to curb the power of the Crown, a Whiggish objective. The waste and incompetence of government exposed by the stubborn prosecution of the unpopular war, added to the burdens of taxation and the drain on manpower, fed the first flickers of the parliamentary reform movement.[1]

It was easy in the provinces now to follow national and international events. In Leeds in the late eighteenth century the weekly *Mercury* and *Intelligencer* were well-established rivals while York had its *Chronicle* and *Courant*, and by 1807 there were a dozen Yorkshire weeklies. Their four dense pages were heavily devoted to parliamentary reports, court news, London gossip and foreign dispatches, all lifted from the London papers delivered to Yorkshire by the new mail coaches in around 30 hours. With the London papers, a pot of paste and a pair of scissors, the provincial printer was in business. The papers were expensive at sixpence a copy (which included a 3½d. stamp duty) but were readily available to non-subscribers at coffee houses, some workshops, inns and news rooms. A column or so of local news was put together by the printer, largely from contributed paragraphs. A space for tasteful verse on

---

[1] Wilson, *Gentlemen Merchants*, pp. 47–50; R.K. Webb, *Modern England from the Eighteenth Century to the Present* (Allen & Unwin: 1971), pp. 91–2.

page 4, variously known as the 'Muses' Bower' or simply 'Poetry Corner', was sacrosanct except in extremities of war or electioneering. The London papers were rarely independent, deriving their bread and butter income from government or, later, a political faction. The Yorkshire press likewise had its patrons, and it was read in London and other parts thanks to a network of booksellers, printers' agents and coffee houses where the latest copies could be found.[2]

One message which came out of Yorkshire in the late 1770s was aversion to the American war. The Rockingham Whigs consistently opposed the government's colonial policies and in 1765 the first Rockingham administration repealed the extension of the Stamp Tax which had infuriated the American settlers. The Yorkshire trading towns presented addresses of thanks to the marquess during race week in York in 1766. Later, when it became clear to everyone but George III that the war could not be won, questions about the balance of power between Crown and Parliament were heard once more.[3]

Yorkshire also was embroiled in the lengthy controversy over the seating of John Wilkes, repeatedly elected for Middlesex and as often denied his parliamentary place, and Rockingham took the popular side. Leeds, Bradford, Wakefield and other towns seethed with indignation and Wilkes's release from prison in 1770 was celebrated with bells, fireworks and 'Wilkes and Liberty' placards displayed everywhere.[4]

In 1779, at the end of a disheartening year in the American war, an important step towards popular government was taken by Yorkshire gentry and merchants, led by the Rev. Christopher Wyvill who through marriage had acquired the North Riding estate of Constable Burton with annual rents

---

[2] Edward Baines, *Life of Edward Baines, Late M.P. for the Borough of Leeds* (Longmans: 1851), p. 42; Donald Read, *Press and People, 1790–1850: Opinion in Three English Cities* (Arnold: 1961), pp. 61–7; Donald Read, 'North of England Newspapers (*c.*1700–*c.*1900) and their Value to Historians', *Leeds Philosophical and Literary Society Proceedings*, vol. 7:3 (1957), pp. 202, 212; Alexander Paterson, 'Yorkshire Journalism in the Eighteenth Century', in *Old Yorkshire*, ed. William Smith, new series 2 (Longmans: 1890), pp. 183, 184, 191–5; H. Barker, *Newspapers, Politics and Public Opinion in Late Eighteenth Century England* (Clarendon Press: Oxford, 1998), pp. 135–78.

[3] Webb, *Modern England*, p. 77; Brooke, *King George III*, pp. 209–20; Collyer, 'Rockingham Connection', p. 272.

[4] Smith, *Whig Principles*, p. 17; Collyer, 'Rockingham Connection', p. 265; J. Brewer, *Party Ideology and Popular Politics at the Accession of George III* (Cambridge University Press: Cambridge, 1976), pp. 178–9; Edward Parsons, *Civil, Ecclesiastical, Literary, Commercial and Miscellaneous History of Leeds, Bradford, Wakefield, Dewsbury, Otley, and the District Within Ten Miles of Leeds*, 2 vols (F. Hobson: Leeds, 1834), vol. 1, pp. 65–6; Read, *English Provinces*, pp. 6–7; *Victoria History of the County of York*, 3 vols (1913), vol. 3, p. 432.

of £4,000 a year which enabled him to quit his Essex rectory and devote the rest of his life to the reform of parliament. The time was right because men of property were thoroughly alarmed by the 'ruinous' expense of the 'cursed American war' and careless accounting by ministers.

'Never was there a time when old England was so precariously situated,' Henry Maister of Hull complained. 'It is too late to quarrel with those who have brought us into this scrape ... but let us cordially join to extricate ourselves, & then I hope they may be punished who deserve it.'[5]

Around Wyvill and the Rev. Canon William Mason, a Hull native, prebendary of York Minster and a poet of some distinction, a committee formed to initiate a county meeting on 30 December 1779 at York's Assembly Rooms to consider the 'present critical state of public affairs'. They set up headquarters at the York Tavern in nearby St Helen's Square and dispatched hundreds of invitations. It was unheard of for a self-appointed body to call a county meeting, but the high sheriff, who had the power to respond to requests for such portentous gatherings, had just died. Wyvill's oddly matched precedents were the public rally for Wilkes in 1769 and a 1745 meeting at which Yorkshire had voiced its fervour for the king against the Scottish Jacobites.[6]

There was a hearty response from nobility, clergy and lesser freeholders eager to deplore the sinking ship of state, their intolerable grievances, the 'torrent of unbounded ministerial interference' and the government's total lack of accountability for the sacrifices wrung out of the inhabitants of this 'once very happy & envied Island'. The more cautious replies assumed that measures to 'promote Public Oeconomy' or 'destroy abuse & promote regularity' were the sole objectives. In Sir Robert Hildyard's words, the result should be a petition to the Commons for a 'strict Enquiry' into the public expenditure and an attack upon 'Useless Places, Sinecures, & the Enormous Perquisites of Others ... to save Annually a large Sum of Misapplied Money & to cut of [sic] at the same time the source of Parliamentary corruption'.

Of this mind was Rockingham, who responded, 'I cannot sufficiently express the Satisfaction I feel at the steps ... taken ... as a Yorkshireman, feel a Pride, that the County of York will stand foremost, in shewing anxious Sollicitude for the welfare, Freedom, & Happiness of their Country.'

Few refused Wyvill's request to use their names in advertising the meeting but he was clearly casting a wider than usual net. In the search for fresh

---

[5] Webb, *Modern England*, pp. 79–81, 92; I.R. Christie, *Wilkes, Wyvill and Reform*, pp. 70–4; W. Belsham, *History of Great Britain from the Revolution to the Commencement of the Year 1799* (R. Marchbank: Dublin, 2nd edn, 1825), p. 6; ERALS: DDGR/42/29, R. to J. Grimston, 23 December 1779; Maister to Grimston, 24 June 1779.

[6] NYCRO: ZFW 7/2/2, Minute Books of the Yorkshire Committee 1779–81, largely printed in Wyvill, *Political Papers*, vol. 1.

political allies, invitations went to men with no freeholds in Yorkshire or to persons who modestly declined because of their obscurity. Some pointed out that it was notoriously easy to get signatures and that a small, highly respectable list would be preferable to avoid ridicule. William Walker of Leeds urged that only names of the 'first consequence in the County as to Fortune or Profession' be published. One invitation reached a minor who was only visiting the county and another man replied in a fury that 'Whosoever you are' had dared think him a 'Promoter of Sedition'.[7]

Nevertheless, nearly everyone of importance wanted to come and 600 men, including six peers, squires, clergy, MPs and other substantial persons, together representing property worth £800,000 a year, crowded into Lord Burlington's Egyptian hall. When Savile presented the ensuing petition bearing nearly 9,000 signatures and calling for an investigation into 'gross abuses' in public spending, he declared with relish that the initiators at the 30 December meeting were worth more than the whole House of Commons. The king, however, remained unimpressed by 'Mr. Wyvile's Congress'.[8]

With a method rarely if ever seen before a county committee of 100 was established with a smaller York-based sub-committee sitting regularly at the York Tavern, and the Yorkshire Association for Parliamentary Reform came into being in March 1780.[9] William Gray, a pious, hard-working young York solicitor, became its paid executive secretary and proved to be a gifted organizer. He circulated petitions, filled the sympathetic *York Chronicle* and *Leeds Mercury* with letters and paragraphs and created a network of agents in every wapentake. The committee entered into correspondence with bodies that sprang up in several counties on the Yorkshire model.

'Economical [we would say administrative] reform', along with opposition to the American war, was unanimously blessed by the December 1779 meeting.

---

[7] YA: M25, Letters, 1779–1786, fols 171, 143, 31, 155, 168; ERALS: DDGR/42/29, Hildyard to Grimston, 2 December 1779.

[8] Belsham, *History*, p. 7; Sir John Fortescue (ed.), *Correspondence of King George the Third from 1760 to December 1783*, 6 vols (Macmillan: 1927–28), vol. 5, p. 209.

[9] In addition to NYCRO: ZFW 7/2/2 and YA: M25 cited above, the following section draws upon Smith, *Whig Principles*, pp. 57, 58–9; Collyer, 'Rockingham Connection', p. 266; I.R. Christie, *Myth and Reality in Late Eighteenth-Century British Politics* (Macmillan: 1970), pp. 261, 264–6, 269–70, 277–83; Wilson, *Gentlemen Merchants*, p. 168; A. Gooder, *Parliamentary Representation of the County of York, 1258–1832*, Yorkshire Archaeological Society Record Series, vol. 96 (1938), pp. 146–8; Herbert Butterfield, 'Yorkshire Association and the Crisis of 1779–80', *Transactions of the Royal Historical Society*, 4th series, 29 (1947), p. 79; J.R.M. Butler, *Passing of the Great Reform Bill* (Longmans: 1914), p. 6; Read, *English Provinces*, pp. 12, 13; *Appeal to the Nation by the Union for Parliamentary Reform* (J. Willan: Halifax, 1812), pp. 99–100.

But the formation of the Association with more radical intentions of altering the electoral system was to split the Rockingham Whigs. Rockingham would go along with triennial parliaments but many of his friends would not. To them the King was the real source of potential evil, his right to give or withhold honours and offices and through patronage to make Parliament a rubber stamp the one clear target. Tampering with the franchise would strike at the roots of aristocratic power.

Yet the Yorkshire Association's proposals were relatively moderate for the time. They sought 100 more county members (to be found by the abolition of pocket boroughs); a three-year limit on the life of a parliament (instead of the present seven), household suffrage, the abolition of sinecure places and undeserved pensions, and frugality in public expenditure. Annual parliaments, universal male suffrage and representation for the new industrial towns were on the agendas of others.

The rippling effects of the Yorkshire Association and its counterparts are well treated elsewhere. Here it can simply be recognized as a nearly mass movement which trained a generation of Yorkshiremen politically. The Association was an unlikely medley of aristocrats, gentry, clergy, new industrialists, tradesmen and artisans. Hundreds actively solicited subscriptions or canvassed for signatures. Of the thousands who signed, it was notable that fewer than two per cent had to make their mark. Tenants were unafraid to put down their names even when landlords disapproved. In Leeds, the Association won over 'every dissenting merchant in the town'. The Earl of Effingham, a great landowner with a seat at Thundercliffe Grange near Rotherham, was unswerving in support, persuaded that 'by the Long Duration of Parliaments, the unequal Representation, & the encreased Influence of the Crown, the People at Large have ... had very little, if any, more share in the Legislature of Great Britain than in that of China'.

The new politics was put to the test in the 1780, 1783 and 1784 elections. Parliament was dissolved during the Association's first year on 1 September 1780 and of the two old county members, Savile was secure but Edwin Lascelles had broken with the Rockingham Whigs to support the American war and North's ministry. (The Lascelles family stake in West Indian sugar may have assisted his conversion.) He also was hostile to every reform measure. Lascelles was the son and heir of an earlier Henry Lascelles, born in 1713 in Barbados when his father was Collector of Customs there. Later this Henry founded a successful sugar factor firm in London. Edwin involved himself in the family's Caribbean interests and thenceforth the family exercised a more direct management over their numerous slave properties. He spent some of the fortune which the West Indies interests brought on building Harewood House in the sumptuous new Palladian style in 1759. He was thought to be socially ambitious, perhaps angling for a peerage, but was a generous local benefactor.

He had not, however, paid much heed to recent events in Yorkshire. 'He has allways appeared too Illustrious & too Great for his Office' was the verdict of Stephen Croft of York, an active reformer.[10]

The Association now commanded nearly 6,000 members and found an impeccable candidate to replace Lascelles in its own committee: Henry Duncombe of Copgrove near Knaresborough, a son of Thomas Duncombe of Duncombe Park, Helmsley, and grandson of Sir Thomas Slingsby of Scriven. The Rockinghamites approved, and using Gray's efficient machine the county was canvassed and a £14,000 subscription pledged to finance – or, so it was hoped, scare off – a contest. Lascelles met his friends (as gentlemen then spoke of their supporters) ten days before the election, but when they did not fasten eagerly on his broad hint that they should raise an equivalent war chest for him, he bowed out, accepting the family seat at Northallerton then warmed by his brother Daniel. Lord Loughborough for one thought Lascelles too timid; there was no cause for his retreat in either the canvass or the subscription. The *Leeds Intelligencer* sympathetically recorded that Lascelles had declined 'upon mature deliberation ... on account of his advanced age [he was 67], and the mischief a contest might make in this large county'. But Canon Mason boasted that the reformers had 'plucked away every peacock's feather out of the tail of that strutting carrion crow L[ascelles], and has ... frightened the Lord Paramount of the West India Islands out of the contest'.[11]

Savile claimed that the outcome was a triumph for the people. 'Hitherto,' he was quoted, 'I have been elected in Lord Rockingham's dining room. Now I am returned by my Constituents.' Savile and Duncombe did not need to spend a shilling of their own for the Association paid all expenses and hoped that this would set a precedent for independent elections in other parts of the kingdom.[12]

In Hull that year, the Rockinghamite member, David Hartley, one of whose 'eccentricities' had been in 1775 to introduce the first motion against

---

[10] Black, *Association*, pp. 68–70; Gooder, *Parliamentary Representation*, p. 149; Namier and Brooke, *History*, vol. 3, pp. 22–3; vol. 1, p. 84; Smith, *Slavery*, pp. 184–9; *Leeds Mercury*, 27 May 1780; *Leeds Intelligencer*, 22 September 1767 and 5 January 1779.

[11] Black, *Association*, pp. 69–70; Wyvill, *Political Papers*, vol. 3, p. 201 and vol. 1, p. 5; Namier and Brooke, *History*, vol. 2, pp. 352–3 and vol. 3, pp. 22–3; Royal Commission on Historical Manuscripts [C.8551], *Fifteenth Report, Appendix Part VI, Manuscripts of the Earl of Carlisle* (1897), pp. 444–5, Loughborough to Carlisle, 18 September 1780; *Leeds Intelligencer*, 19 September 1780; *Horace Walpole's Correspondence with William Mason*, ed. W.S. Lewis, 2 vols (New York, 1955), vol. 2, p. 79, Mason to Walpole, 20 September 1780.

[12] Wilberforce, *Life of Wilberforce*, vol. 1, p. 57; YA, M25/325, Yorkshire Association Letters, John Hatfield to William Gray, 2 October 1780; M32/6, Yorkshire Association Papers, Resolutions of County Meeting, 14 September 1780.

slavery to be heard in the Commons, was routed by a newcomer, William Wilberforce, whose mercantile connections, 'charm and purse', added to warm memories of the roast ox and good ale provided for the 'lower order of freemen' on his 21st birthday on 24 August, carried him in with Lord Robert Manners, the sitting MP, almost unanimously.[13]

The Rockingham-reform alliance continued briefly and uneasily. Although public petitions were cast into some disrepute by the 'No Popery' Gordon Riots in London in June 1780, the Yorkshire reformers intensified their demands and at a York meeting in November 1782 the Association called for additional electoral changes including the vote for 40 shilling copyholders (tenures subject to the will of the lord of the manor) as well as freeholders.[14] The Associators were not appeased by the reforming steps taken by Rockingham Whigs during the preceding two years. Twice, in 1780 and 1781, Burke had introduced unsuccessful bills which would have cut national spending and curbed court influence, and when the North ministry fell in March 1782, Rockingham was called upon to form the new government. He was not the King's first choice (Shelburne was) because he made his acceptance conditional on the King's recognizing American independence and accepting the measures that would reduce Crown influence. But when it was clear that Shelburne could not proceed without Rockingham's support, the King gave in to a coalition.[15]

Now Burke's economical reforms were carried. Patronage jobs were to be abolished aiming to save almost £73,000 a year. Thousands of revenue officers were to be disfranchised and government contractors were barred from seats in the Commons. Burke as Paymaster General cut the huge rewards of his own office, making it merely a salaried post, and even the expenditure of the royal household came under mild regulation.[16] The resolutions of the House

---

[13] *Cobbett's Parliamentary History*, vol. 18, cols 1049–50, 1056 (7 December 1775); Furneaux, *Wilberforce*, pp. 14–15; Hague, *Wilberforce*, pp. 35–6. Wilberforce, *Life of Wilberforce*, vol. I, p. 15.

[14] I.R. Christie, *Wilkes, Wyvill and Reform. The Parliamentary Reform Movement in British Politics, 1760–1785* (1962), p. 115; *Annual Register, 1781* (1782), History of Europe, pp. 137–8; Wyvill, *Political Papers*, vol. 2, pp. 17–22.

[15] *Cobbett's Parliamentary History*, vol. 21, cols 1–73 (Commons, 11 February 1780) and cols 73–4 (Commons, 14 February 1780); copy of Burke's Establishment Bill, vol. 21, cols 111–35 (Commons, 23 February 1780); col. 150 (Commons, 2 March 1780), cols 171–217 (Commons, 8 March 1780); *Cobbett's Parliamentary History*, vol. 21, cols 1223–92 (Commons, 15 February 1781); Black, *Association*, p. 80.

[16] Civil List (22 Geo. III cap. 82): *Cobbett's Parliamentary History*, vol. 22, cols 1269–73 (Commons, 15 April 1782), cols 1412–16 (Commons, 6 May 1782), cols 1273–5 (Lords, 15 April 1782); vol. 23, cols 121–7 (Commons, 13–20 June 1782); cols 139–47 (Lords, 3 July 1782); Contractors (22 Geo. III, cap. 45): *Cobbett's Parliamentary History*, vol. 22, cols 1333–6

concerning John Wilkes were expunged from the record. William Pitt, a Cambridge contemporary and now a close friend of Wilberforce, made his brilliant maiden speech in 1781 in support of Burke's proposals for reform and in 1782 proposed an inquiry into the reform of parliamentary representation, a motion which was lost by only 20 votes. What the reform movement remembered most clearly about the Rockingham administration was Pitt's interest in their cause.[17]

Rockingham's government was cut short by his death from influenza on 1 July 1782. His heir, the Earl Fitzwilliam, wrote sorrowfully to Burke, 'I can never emulate his character; I will imitate, as I ought to do, at an awful distance.'[18] His uncle's estates, added to Fitzwilliam's own, gave him huge tracts of Yorkshire, Northamptonshire and Ireland, but political influence was more difficult to bequeath. In a sense, he had been his uncle's loyal apprentice; he shared the same principles but he lacked experience in forging interests. Not until 1798 was he appointed lord lieutenant of the West Riding with its control over the military and civil establishment.[19]

Two crises faced Fitzwilliam in Yorkshire in the autumn of 1783, both portents of the price the Rockingham Whigs were to pay for failure to unite behind the reform movement. First came a defeat in York. That October Sir Charles Turner, the Rockingham member since 1768, died. Fitzwilliam, without adequately consulting old allies in the Corporation, the Minster and the Rockingham Club, almost casually agreed to support Charles Duncombe, Henry's brother, in Turner's place, even though 'some think him a little too blue'. A hostile crowd speedily discouraged Duncombe, and Fitzwilliam then proposed his brother, George, but the Yorkshire Association knew George Fitzwilliam as an MP who had voted against Pitt's motion. The Associators chose Lord Galway, whose carriage was dragged through the streets by cheering admirers to the Guildhall where he was elected by acclamation.[20]

(Commons, 12–19 April 1782); cols 1356–82 (Lords, 1, 6 May 1782); vol. 23, cols 74–5 (both Houses, 22–30 May 1782); Revenue Officers (22 Geo. III, cap. 41): *Cobbett's Parliamentary History*, vol. 22, cols 1336–44 (Commons, 16–25 April 1782); vol. 23, cols 95–101 (Lords, 3 June 1782); Paymaster General (22 Geo. III cap. 81): *Cobbett's Parliamentary History*, vol. 23, cols 134–5 (Commons, 26, 28 June, 2 July 1782). *Annual Register, 1784–1785* (1787), *History of Europe*, p. 143; D.L. Keir, 'Economical Reform, 1779–1787', *Law Quarterly Review*, 50 (1934), pp. 368–85.

[17] *Cobbett's Parliamentary History*, vol. 22, cols 1407–11 (3 May 1782); *Cobbett's Parliamentary History*, vol. 21, cols 1261–6 (Commons, 26 February 1781); vol. 22, cols 1416–38 (Commons, 7 May 1782); Wyvill, *Political Papers*, vol. 4, pp. 56–62.

[18] *Correspondence of Edmund Burke*, vol. 5, pp. 7–8, Fitzwilliam to Burke [3 July 1782].

[19] Smith, *Fitzwilliam*, pp. 29–38, 56–7.

[20] Smith, *Fitzwilliam*, pp. 65–8.

The second blow was Sir George Savile's sudden decision in November 1783 to retire after 25 years as a county MP and a man who, in Wyvill's words, was the 'key-stone ... by which the Nobles and the People, as parts of the same political arch, were united and kept together'. In an uncontested by-election, and in almost their last act of co-operation, the Fitzwilliam party and the Association agreed upon Savile's nephew, Francis Ferrand Foljambe, to replace him. This seemed to be Savile's wish, although Fitzwilliam was warned that Foljambe was acting entirely for the Association – 'our worst enemies'. The Association was determined, certainly, to return 'friends to reform' but Wyvill insisted it must not be seen to interfere actively. Nevertheless the Association's methods on this occasion, which included the calling of a caucus of members the day before the county meeting, aroused some criticism. 'Leave it to the real & unbiassed Choice of the Landed Interest,' the Earl of Fauconberg protested.[21]

Following peace with the United States and its allies in 1783, Lord Shelburne, who had succeeded Rockingham, resigned and the King with utmost reluctance (he even threatened to remove to Hanover) accepted an 'infamous' coalition of Lord North and Charles James Fox, erstwhile bitter enemies, under the titular leadership of the Duke of Portland. The King and Fox shared one passion – a mutual hatred. To George III Fox was the political personification of his own dissolute heir. Within a year he found an excuse to get rid of Fox in the India bills, devised by Burke to curb the freebooters of the East India Company who were building an empire quite free of government control. The bills proposed seven government-appointed commissioners – four supporters of Fox and three of North – with nine assistants named by the Company to run the commercial side. Fox's closest friend, Fitzwilliam, was to head the board. A Company director, admittedly elderly, died of shock on reading the bills. Opponents were loud in their denunciations of 'jobbery'.[22]

The bills easily passed the Commons and the Lords voiced little objection until the King made it known that any peer who voted for them would henceforth be his enemy. Within hours of their defeat in the upper chamber on 17 December, the King rudely dismissed the coalition and brought in William Pitt as prime minister at the age of 24. It seemed a flimsy convention that the King governed with the consent of Parliament.[23]

---

[21] Wyvill, *Political Papers*, vol. 4, p. 165 and vol. 2, pp. 285–6; Black, *Association*, pp. 106–7; Smith, *Fitzwilliam*, pp. 68–9; Wyvill, *Political Papers*, vol. 2, pp. 277–8, Fauconberg to Stephen Croft, 9 December 1783; Smith, *Fitzwilliam*, pp. 71–6. A. Loch, 'The Electoral Management of the Yorkshire Election of 1784', *Northern History*, 47:2 (2010), pp. 271–96.
[22] John Cannon, *Fox–North Coalition* (Cambridge University Press: Cambridge, 1969), pp. 65–81; Smith, *Fitzwilliam*, pp. 100–1 and pp. 44–5, 47.
[23] Cannon, *Fox–North Coalition*, pp. 106–44.

His action was not unpopular, however. In parts of Yorkshire it was the 'received Notion amongst the Inferiors ... that Mr. Fox was attempting to dethrone the King and make himself an Oliver Cromwell'. Some of Fox's natural allies were not so angry as they should have been for they were offended that he had taken office with North in the first place. Walter Spencer Stanhope, the Yorkshire squire and MP who deserted Fitzwilliam for Pitt, likened the coalition to 'a chimney-sweeper and a miller embracing each other, by which was formed a *black* and *white*, a *pye-balled Administration*'.[24]

Pitt's administration was swiftly branded a mince pie, not expected to last beyond Christmas. Fox still dominated the Commons and Pitt had trouble finding ministers. He soldiered on with the King's trust and not inconsiderable aid in rewarding politically powerful anti-Foxites with peerages. The King was genuinely loved in the country and Fox had as unsavoury a public image as the Prince of Wales. Loyal subjects were warned that opposition to Pitt would pull down the King and install the Prince. Addresses thanking his majesty for sacking the coalition were instigated all over the kingdom and 230 poured in as a preliminary to an early general election. 'I wish we had a good paragraph put into the York & Leeds papers ... to state the dispute betwixt the K[ing] and parliament properly,' John Carr, the York architect and alderman, wrote to Lord Fitzwilliam, 'for it is amazing to think how ignorant people are on the subject.'[25]

No loyal address was more urgently desired than one from Yorkshire. Wyvill led the 100 freeholders who called for a county meeting in York's Castle Yard on 25 March 1784. Carr scoffed at most of the names on the requisition as 'never before heard of'; they were chiefly from the West Riding towns or Hull. Pitt relied upon Wilberforce to swing Yorkshire and the Hull MP left London on 21 March and arrived at York the next day. He lodged with Mason, almost his sole acquaintance in the city, and they with Wyvill and Lord Fauconberg composed the address which would be put to the public meeting, a gathering which would catapult the unknown Wilberforce into an extraordinary career.

The hopes of Wyvill and other Associators were pinned on Pitt. Fox was discredited in their eyes because of his promise to North that the coalition would not take up the reform question. Commercial interests supported Pitt because of a supposed threat to property implicit in Fox's India bills and out of anger at a sales tax introduced by Lord John Cavendish, member for York

---

[24] R. Parker to Fitzwilliam, 26 April 1784, quoted in Smith, *Fitzwilliam*, p. 81; Wyvill, *Political Papers*, vol. 2, p. 339.

[25] Wilberforce's Diary, 22 December 1783, quoted in Wilberforce, *Life*, vol. 1, p. 48; Cannon, *Fox–North Coalition*, p. 155–62, 185–9; SCC:LAI: WWM, F/34/59, John Carr to Fitzwilliam, 8 March 1784.

and the coalition's Chancellor. The new alliance of Associators and Pittites was indeed a 'strange monster'; even Wyvill saw it as a 'very extraordinary junction'.[26]

Other motives than simple devotion to Pitt sent Wilberforce so eagerly to York. In later years, he shrank from party combat, but the religious conversion which was to transform his life was still to come. In this cold spring, he was merely a clever new member and a sparkling addition to London clubland. A glimpse of Wilberforce with Pitt and a tableful of friends drinking, 'singing and laughing a gorge deployée' as he left the House one night caused George Selwyn to wish he were 20 again. Wilberforce sang the best, he informed the Earl of Carlisle, first explaining who Wilberforce was.[27]

It was now Wilberforce's ambition to sit for the county, such a mad scheme, considering that he was the grandson of a Hull merchant adventurer, young and almost totally unacquainted with the aristocracy of Yorkshire, that he confided in no one, not even Pitt. He did not own a country seat – almost a disqualification in itself. Although he loved breathtaking scenery, and later spent months on end in the Lake District, Yorkshire's beauties did not seem to evoke any special attachment, although he knew them well enough to advise tourists. He had inherited land at Markington, Coniston and Holderness. His curious – and in its day, inexplicable – disinterest in property was captured in his hilarious reaction to a passing call paid at Markington: 'Went on to look at my land; my land just like anyone else's land.' Men of property never understood why Wilberforce squandered his life in a 'quixotic crusade against public wrongs and remote injustice' but neglected the more imperative (and steadying) duties of supervising his estates.

Yet in March of 1784, he prepared as carefully as any actor for his entrance on the Yorkshire stage. Had the opportunity arisen a year or two later, when he had become 'serious', he never would have sought to 'carve for myself so freely', or to ingratiate himself with the odd alliance which was his only hope for success.[28]

Warned that any attempt to prevent a county meeting and a loyal address would do more harm than good, Fitzwilliam decided he must at least make sure that the Whig case was heard, although canvassers were reporting that he could not rally a tenth of the crowd he would need to carry the show of

---

[26] Pollock, *Wilberforce*, p. 26; Wilberforce, *Life*, vol. 1, p. 52; Smith, *Whig Principles*, pp. 7, 1–4; YA: M25, fol. 517.
[27] *The Manuscripts of the Earl of Carlisle, preserved at Castle Howard*, ed. R.E.G. Kirk (Eyre & Spottiswoode: 1897), p. 602.
[28] Wilberforce, *Correspondence*, vol. 1, pp. 270–3; Wilberforce, *Life*, vol. 1, pp. 310, 383–4, 56–7; *Quarterly Review*, 62 (June 1838), pp. 225–6; J.S. Harford, *Recollections of William Wilberforce* (1864), p. 203; Furneaux, *Wilberforce*, pp. 28–9.

hands. Even George Osbaldeston, an Associator but stout friend, feared to lose his Scarborough seat if he showed his face at the meeting: 'The story of my being pinned on your Ldps & Mr. Fox's sleeve I have stopped; but an appearance at York would produce a revival.' However, he promised that no one under his influence would sign the address.[29]

March 25th dawned bitterly cold, with lashing winds and bursts of hail. It had been a harsh winter, the river Ouse frozen solid enough to walk upon for eight straight weeks. Coal sloops could not reach the staithes and fuel carried overland was scarce and dear. Although Fitzwilliam had contributed generously to those in want – a third of the city's population needed the bread and coal purchased by fund raising – he was not politically astute enough to patronize the local shops and tradesmen extensively or call forth now the loyalties of the Rockingham Club.

Heedless of the weather, 7,000 Yorkshiremen swarmed through Castlegate postern into the open-air arena. The great men drew up in their coaches, the freeholders arrived on horseback or on foot. Speaker after speaker climbed upon a table beneath a makeshift canopy to harangue. The case for an address was put by Fauconberg, Henry Duncombe, Sir Christopher Sykes, and Walter Spencer Stanhope among others. Lords Surrey (later Duke of Norfolk), Carlisle and Cavendish orated against it. Fitzwilliam, personally abused for agreeing to head the proposed East India board, defended himself and Fox unreservedly, observing that since government had loaned the Company vast sums it had a rightful interest in the Company's management. He admitted that he was no parliamentary reformer for he had not yet seen a practical plan for it, but he did not believe Pitt was serious on that issue. He invoked Rockingham, averring 'every principle in this breast comes from him'. People and peers must stand together: 'If your Liberties are destroyed, the Peerage must perish in the Ruins; we should, as in all arbitrary Governments, have it in our Power to oppress our Inferiors, and be oppressed ourselves; but this I will say, that were the Friends of Liberty to be oppressed by the Court, I should have the darkest Dungeon.'[30]

After nearly six hours, Wilberforce mounted the table, facing a chilled, tired, wet and somewhat noisy crowd. As if by magic, he caught its ear and for an hour heaped eloquent scorn on the coalition. Standing in the audience

---

[29] Smith, *Whig Principles*, 75–6; SCC:LAI: WWM, F34/75, Osbaldeston to Fitzwilliam, 14 March 1784.

[30] Phillips, *Yorkshire and English National Politics*, pp. 38–46; Allen, *History of York*, vol. 1, p. 122; Smith, *Whig Principles*, p. 74; *Proceedings of the General Meeting of the Freeholders of the County of York ... March 25, 1784* (A. Ward: [1784]), pp. 18–19; Wilberforce, *Life*, vol. 1, pp. 52–6; A.M.W. Stirling, *Annals of a Yorkshire House from the Papers of a Macaroni and His Kindred* (John Lane: 1911), pp. 184–8; Wyvill, *Political Papers*, vol. 2, pp. 325–7, 345–6.

was James Boswell on his way to Edinburgh with Dr Johnson. Later in a letter to Henry Dundas he described how he had seen 'a little fellow on a table speaking – a perfect shrimp. But presently the shrimp swelled into a whale.'

As if on cue, a King's messenger pushed through the throng and handed Wilberforce a letter from Pitt written at noon the day before. With complete aplomb Wilberforce instantly digested its contents and announced to brilliant effect that Parliament was dissolved and the sense of the people would be taken at a general election. He begged the Yorkshire voters to demonstrate at the poll their support for Pitt. 'Take care to keep all our friends together,' Pitt's letter had also said, 'and to tear the enemy to pieces.' Pitt advised that Sir Robert D'Arcy Hildyard might be a good choice to displace Foljambe who was tainted by his Fitzwilliam backing. This was no part of Wilberforce's plan. He was pleased at his own debut before the county: 'I have scarcely ever spoken better.' The motion on the address was called for and the high sheriff signed Yorkshire's loyal tribute.[31]

Pittites and reformers celebrated at the York Tavern while the vanquished Whigs collected at Bluitt's to dine and talk of candidates. The county election would be on 7 April. It joined the long list of 'uncontested' Yorkshire elections but it was a classical battle of bluff waged from command posts at the two inns.

As the bottles went round at the York Tavern, it was Wilberforce who mollified the ill-suited wings of the new coalition, reminding them of their common bond in opposition to Fox. They were in cheerful concord that Henry Duncombe should be re-elected. For the second seat, Harry Pierse of Bedale proposed the day's best orator and to cries of 'Wilberforce for ever!' the merrymakers dispersed. By morning, thoughts of the cost of a contest had cooled some passions, although young Richard Slater Milnes of the Wakefield merchant family declared they had £10,000 towards it in that room alone. The waverers swung behind the brave when a message arrived from Francis Hawksworth, speaking for the gentlemen at Bluitt's, who had agreed to nominate Foljambe again and asked concurrence on this in return for their support of one York Tavern nominee. The whiff of compromise rallied the new coalition (luckily for Wilberforce) and it adopted Duncombe and Wilberforce, 'a wonderful young man', enthused Robert Athorpe to the Duke of Leeds.[32]

The answer sent to Bluitt's, however, was that the York Taverners felt incompetent to decide the election so privately and had requisitioned the high

---

[31] Pollock, *Wilberforce*, pp. 26–8, 313 n. 31; Furneaux, *Wilberforce*, pp. 29–30; Harford, *Recollections*, p. 204; Gooder, *Parliamentary Representation*, pp. 151–2; *York Chronicle*, 26 March and 9 April 1784.

[32] Wilberforce, *Life*, vol. 1, pp. 58–9; Pollock, *Wilberforce*, 28–9; YA: M90, Election Papers, 46, Hawkesworth to Gentlemen of the York Tavern; BL: Add Ms 28,060, fols 121–2, Athorp to Leeds, 10 April 1784.

sheriff to call a county nomination meeting. Whereupon the Whigs at Bluitt's endorsed their own slate of Foljambe and William Weddell of Newby Hall, MP for Malton, one of the county's wealthiest landowners and brother-in-law of the widowed Countess of Rockingham.

Duncombe could be sure of his county seat. Wilberforce could not, so he rushed to Hull to secure his place there. David Hartley, a Fox supporter, had been returned once more after Lord Manners' death in 1782. Wilberforce canvassed with his Pittite cousin, Samuel Thornton, spent £8,807 and came in top of the poll with Thornton second. As he was chaired, Wilberforce was pelted with snowballs – some electors obviously felt disgruntled by his plain intention to resign if he also won a county seat. But an engaging speech from the window of his old nursery in the family home so charmed the crowd that Wilberforce later could name his successor for Hull, Spencer Stanhope.[33]

A furious county canvass by each side filled the following week. Thanks to William Gray's superb organization, land tax assessment lists, agents and clerks were readily available to the coalition. Horses, chaises and public houses were speedily engaged to convey and accommodate voters for a poll at York. The combined reformers and Pittites were strong in the North and East Ridings (in the Pickering Lythe wapentake, for example, their canvassers reported 530 promises for Duncombe and Wilberforce to 20 for Foljambe and Weddell) and rich in pledges from the West Riding. 'In the trading part of the county,' gloated a partisan, 'our enemies can do nothing, & the Clothiers thank the Gentlemen that come to canvass for standing up for the King & Mr. Pitt.'

The King and Mr Pitt were not timid about reinforcing the people's enthusiastic patriotism with the resources of the Treasury and the City, and the rusty Rockingham party could not match this political powerhouse. Sir Thomas Gascoigne served as chairman for the Whig committee with Fitzwilliam as his deputy. Some forty followers who were members of the Association's committee resigned from it in the vain hope that the movement might now be 'totally knock'd up'. They were not keen for a contest but would not be bullied into an alliance with Pitt.[34]

Plans to erect the hustings and polling booths in the Castle Yard were agreed at a joint conference on 2 April. Colour bearers and chair men were hired and poll watchers appointed. Subscriptions were tallied. The two York

---

[33] YA: M90, Election Papers, 45, successful requisition for a County Meeting; WYAS(K): RA, WYL109/vol.III/42(1): Mr Weddell to Mrs Weddell from York 26 and 27 Mar., 1784; Black, *Association*, pp. 72, 112; Wilberforce, *Life*, vol. 1, p. 60.

[34] R.W. Smith, 'Political Organization', p. 1545; YA: M32, Yorkshire Association Papers, 12; BL: Add Ms 28,060, fols 123–4, Tooker to Leeds, 1 April 1784; Smith, *Whig. Principles*, says 23 resigned from the committee.

Tavern candidates pledged £2,000 each but their committee rejected their tenders, preferring to stand the cost from the more than £22,000 available. In the end, the Yorkshire Association brought in Wilberforce and Duncombe for only £4,000.

On election eve, the Association and its friends made known that they had 10,812 promises for and 2,758 against their men, neutral or undecided. The Whigs calculated 6,000 for, 1,600 against and 3,000 doubtful. Their campaign coffer held a promised £15,000.[35] Later that night, Weddell and Foljambe withdrew. Wilberforce drily chronicled the next day's triumph: 'Up early – breakfasted tavern – rode frisky horse to castle – elected – chaired – dined York Tavern.' That his election was an affirmation of independent principles he did not doubt. To Pitt this was a glorious result and with similar successes in 200 other constituencies he vindicated his election gamble.

The Fitzwilliam party endured another debacle in York city. Determined to take both seats again, the earl put up Sir William Milner with Lord John Cavendish. The Association and Pitt men backed Lord Galway with Richard Milnes and won after a six-day poll. 'By the late glorious election, the ... power and patriotism of the trading interest [is] exemplified and confirmed,' boasted a contributor to the *Leeds Mercury*. But R. Hay Drummond of Doncaster assured Fitzwilliam, 'the republican spirit of the Dissenters and the arbitrary notions of the High Tories ... can never hold long together'. Weddell spoke of the 'senseless noise of Pitt & Fox & King & I know not what' which had such telling effect on the 'lower people' with too little time to 'set them right, & so ye County has got its representatives made without ye strength of Landed property'. 'We were certainly not deserted by the better part,' agreed Fitzwilliam, 'but beat by the ragamuffins.' Stephen Croft had another post mortem verdict. A member of both the Association and the Rockingham Club, he helped to settle accounts after the election and concluded that the Whigs had been 'too delicate of our cash'.[36]

It was a useful practice run for 1807. Both sides, having brought the county to the brink of a contest, drew lessons from the experience. Thomas Plummer, a York attorney, volunteered to Fitzwilliam to reduce to one sheet a regular system to prevent the 'Inconveniences of any unexpected vacancy', while

---

[35] YA: M90, Election Papers, 47, subscription lists; 48, minutes of meeting to decide on the conduct of the election; 53; Smith, *Whig Principles*, pp. 79, 84 notes 48 and 51; R.W. Smith, 'Political Organization', pp. 1546–8; Furneaux, *Wilberforce*, p. 30. The figures differ somewhat in each source.

[36] Wilberforce, *Life*, vol. 1, pp. 63–4; Smith, *Whig Principles*, pp. 80, 74, 91; Wilson, *Gentlemen Merchants*, p. 168; WYAS(K): RA, WYL109/vol.III/50: Mr Weddell to Mrs Weddell from Newby, 9 April 1784; NRO: F(M), 37, Croft to Fitzwilliam, 24 April 1784.

William Gray added to his Association files a six-page 'Hints for Conducting the Business of a Contested Election'.[37]

The Yorkshire Association, however, did not survive its own success, although its principles continued to guide a substantial number among the county electorate. Article 4 of the Plan of Association bound members until reasonable reforms had been achieved to support no candidate who did not join the Association or otherwise signify that he would support its aims. Wyvill for one never yielded on this point. The leadership was splintered over the juncture with Pitt and the committee met no more. Pitt was to abandon the cause of parliamentary reform; he owed no special debt to the reformers and neither the King nor his ministers favoured it. Wyvill clung to the hope that Pitt would act and after an interview with him in December 1784 was convinced, and so told the Yorkshire press, that a reform bill would appear. Wilberforce and Wyvill did help Pitt to draw up a bill to buy out 36 rotten boroughs and re-distribute the seats but it failed. In 1785 and 1786, the Earl of Stanhope, Pitt's brother-in-law, offered a county voters registration bill which would permit balloting at numerous places on a single day instead of voters being taken, usually at the expense of a candidate, to the 'tumult and debauch of the election saturnalia at the county-town'. Wilberforce was asked to introduce it in the Commons. With scant support from Pitt, it was defeated by the King's friends and Whig aristocrats. The idea of polling close to home was not popular in Yorkshire and the county MPs with Wyvill worked on a compromise that would simply register electors by parishes. In 1788 Stanhope was able to get through the Lords a registry bill dividing the country into polling districts and it passed the Commons but the Yorkshire MPs opposed it, despite Wyvill's warnings that if some such measure were not adopted they could not be re-elected with such 'eclat' as they had been in 1784. The act was suspended the following year and soon even the most modest parliamentary reform excited the opposition of all opponents of the French Revolution.[38]

---

[37] NRO: F(M), 37, Plummer to Fitzwilliam, 12 April 1784; YA: M90, Election Papers, 52, Memorandum or Hints for conducting the business of a Contested Election in the County of York.

[38] Wyvill, *Political Papers*, vol. 1, pp. 139–47; YA: M25, Letters, fol. 517; Maccoby, *English Radicalism*, pp. 15–16; Pollock, *Wilberforce*, pp. 35, 42–3, 100–1; Smith, *Whig Principles*, pp. 76, 77–9, 92–3; Gooder, *Parliamentary Representation*, pp. 151–2; J.R. Dinwiddy, *Christopher Wyvill and Reform, 1790–1820*, Borthwick Papers no. 39 (St Anthony's Press: York, 1971).

Reaction (1784–1802)

Fitzwilliam's formidable duty was to repair his political bequest. In the country he was deputy leader of the Whigs (under the Duke of Portland) and a liberal party financier. But however important in Whig councils, he preferred his county role. The Fitzwilliam seat was at Milton in Northamptonshire, but the family now spent its summers at Rockingham's Wentworth Woodhouse. The birth of his son on 4 May 1786 completed his acceptance as Rockingham's heir.

Even in the rancorous aftermath of the 1784 defeats, the Rockingham Club in York continued to celebrate the marquess's birthday and most of the respectable tradesmen turned up. The earl attended in great style the York races and other events which brought out leading families. A Yorkshire dining club was founded in London, and Portland and Fitzwilliam financed a Whig Club there. William Adam, the lawyer and political intimate of Fox, became the Whigs' effective fund raiser and whip. In 1785 Fitzwilliam strengthened his influence with the York Corporation when Sir William Milner was elected an alderman and distributed £400 (Fitzwilliam's) to the poor at Christmas. Charles Bowns, then clerk to the agent at Wentworth, was assigned to build a skeleton organization for future county elections.[39]

In Yorkshire as in London the Whigs took a new interest in the press. When in 1788 both the *York Courant* and the *Chronicle* refused to print a letter signed 'A Whig' because of Dr Burgh's influence, Fitzwilliam helped Thomas Wilson to establish the *York Herald*, directing advertisements to it and paying for copies that went into public houses.[40] Much hard work was undone in the regency crisis of 1788–89 which pitted Fox against Burke. The King fell ill – he is now thought to have succumbed to porphyria which produced symptoms resembling madness – and because Fox was a particular friend of the heir to the throne, the prospect of a regency tantalized his followers. Yorkshire opinion with much of the country disliked this unseemly eagerness. The King's temporary recovery in the spring of 1789 left a taint upon the Whigs.

Fitzwilliam invited the Prince and his brother, the Duke of Clarence, to York races that August hoping to win back some of the public favour, and at Micklegate Bar a crowd unharnessed the horses and drew Fitzwilliam's carriage with its royal occupants to the Deanery where they stayed the night. An address in a gold box was presented by the Corporation and a dinner party held at the Mansion House. The Prince left behind 200 guineas for the debtors

---

[39] Smith, *Whig Principles*, pp. xi, 87, 113, 90–1, 95, 111–12; O'Gorman, *Whig Party*, pp. 13–14, 15–18; NRO F(M), 37, Sinclair to Fitzwilliam, 26 May 1784; Black, *Association*, p. 217.

[40] SCC:LAI: WWM, F34/136; Smith, *Whig Principles*, p. 112; Ivon Asquith, 'James Perry and the *Morning Chronicle*', unpublished Ph.D. thesis (University of London, 1973), p. 38 n. 1.

in York Castle prison, donated 20 more to clothe female convicts about to be transported, and discharged the debts of three prisoners languishing in the local gaol on Ouse bridge. On 2 September a fete took place at Wentworth Woodhouse, including a ball and a dinner with 'every delicacy the world could produce' for 247 guests indoors while 20,000 engaged in sports and drank 55 hogsheads of ale in the park.[41]

The collapse of the Yorkshire Whigs had made Wilberforce a national figure, but he still had to establish himself securely with the county's potentates and as he devoted himself for the next 28 years to his constituents' interests, whatever the demands of the great causes he took up – abolition of the slave trade and the reformation of society – he won the respect of Yorkshiremen in every walk of life. As a friend of Pitt, he could bestow favours. As an abolitionist and an evangelical churchman, he attracted Friends and Methodists. His ties with the landed class were always more tenuous. When a partnership in the family business in which he had never been involved was offered him he hesitated, for although it would add £500 or more to his annual income and reinforce his link with the trading areas, 'might not the squires deem the County of York degraded by having a merchant for its representative?'.

Keenly aware where his strength lay, in 1787 he proposed that he and Duncombe – 'a double headed shot that came out of the piece together' – perambulate the West Riding. Their jaunt should not smack of a canvass or it might inspire competition. In the event, he took his mother and sister along on the pretext of mending the latter's health with travel. With Duncombe he visited the Halifax Piece Hall and attended a meeting on a wool bill at Bradford. 'You can scarcely imagine how warmly this cause is taken up,' he reported to Wyvill. 'I really believe that no more effectual way of securing their esteem and good offices can be devised than a marked attention to their wishes.'[42]

A year later his chronic digestive troubles, symptomized by agonizing piles and constipation, reached a crisis. Rumours raced through Yorkshire that even if he survived, he would not keep the county seat and Fitzwilliam cast about for a candidate for a possible by-election. By autumn, thanks to the remedy of opium, Wilberforce had recovered his normal fragile health and signalled he would be on the hustings in any future election.

In the general election called in 1790, the Whigs gained ground in Parliament, but much as those in Yorkshire would have liked to get rid of

---

[41] Smith, *Whig Principles*, pp. 103–8; Allen, *History of York*, vol. 1, pp. 122–3; *Annual Register* (1789), *Chronicle*, p. 221.
[42] Furneaux, *Wilberforce*, pp. 95–6; BOD: AWP, d.56, Letterbook, fols 10v–13v, Wilberforce to Wyvill, 25 July 1787.

Wilberforce, they put up no opposition to him and Duncombe. The crusade to abolish the slave trade, led by Thomas Clarkson in the country and Wilberforce in Parliament, was enhancing Wilberforce's stature as a moral leader and independent legislator even though he no longer paid the county such small attentions as appearing at the races, assemblies and theatres. He was not, however, oblivious to political organization and with William Gray prepared a county election book which he sent to William Hey at Leeds for additions. It had spaces for the names of all persons with real property of £100 a year or more or a minimum of £2,000 in personal property. The extent of each one's influence was to be indicated – little, middling, great or very great – and under 'observations' Wilberforce wished such data as 'whether he likes the leg or wing of a fowl best, that when one dines with him one may win his heart by helping him, and not be taken in by his "just which you please, sir"'.

In York, however, Lord Galway did not stand in 1790 and Fitzwilliam's agents, in covert negotiations, arranged that Sir William Milner be returned with Richard Milnes. At Hull, 'judicious corruption' frightened off Spencer Stanhope and brought in Lord Burford in the Fitzwilliam interest, while other seats were re-taken by Whigs at Beverley and Hedon.[43]

The revolution which burst in 1789 in France effected a kind of civil war in Britain, exciting libertarian yearnings in some and fears of a republican uprising in others. Everything that happened for a generation was coloured by the French overthrow of the monarchy and the long wars which followed. Fox and Pitt personified the cleavage. Pitt, in office through almost all the period, sacrificed the freedom of public dissent to what he and, apparently, the majority of people regarded as the national security. Fox championed liberty. The very word reform became confused with revolution. Corporation and Test Acts remained in force. Combinations of workers were outlawed and *habeas corpus* was suspended. Political argument never died, but it was hushed.[44]

In August race week of 1791, thanks to Fitzwilliam's assiduous attention to the county, Fox was received in York with acclaim. Like the Prince of Wales, he was drawn through the streets amid rapturous cheers and handed the freedom of the city in a fifty-guinea gold casket by a Corporation loud in its praise of his 'brilliant and unrivalled abilities, in support of the British constitution, upon the true principles of the glorious revolution; of the just

---

[43] SRRC: Corbett of Longnor Papers, 1279/47, Corbett to Plymley, 21 September 1789; Furneaux, *Wilberforce*, pp. 76, 78, 96; Pollock, *Wilberforce*, pp. 78–91, where ulcerative colitis is diagnosed; Bod: AWP, d.56, Letterbook, fols 17v–18v, Wilberforce to Wyvill, 9 August 1788; Wilberforce, *Correspondence*, vol. 1, pp. 74–6; Smith, *Whig Principles*, pp. 95, 99–100, 109–11.
[44] For background here, see especially O'Gorman, *Whig Party*; M.I. Thomis and P. Holt, *Threats of Revolution in Britain, 1789–1848* (Macmillan: 1977), pp. 1–2.

rights of every degree of citizens, and the peace, liberty, and happiness of mankind'.[45]

But the Glorious Revolution of happy memory and a century before was a modest assertion of the supremacy of Protestant propertied people over the divine right of kings when compared with current events across the channel, although some – Fox being one, at least at first – saw in the French convulsion a continuation of the unfinished work of 1688–89. He and Fitzwilliam were soon painfully divided.

Happily, it is evident in hindsight that the British trend towards greater civil rights was not stopped by the tide of suppression although it was measurably slowed. The state treason trials of 1794 resulted in acquittals. Other prosecutions were few. The 'English Reign of Terror' reflected the government's panic and its pragmatism, for the repressive acts were not – nor could they be, given the decentralized local government of the time – uniformly or universally enforced. Indeed, in the first years of the revolution, reformists regrouped and flourished in spite of the limits put upon public meetings and the broadened definition of treason. The single most decisive event was the execution of Louis XVI and the Queen. From then on, sympathy for the revolution cooled and 'lamentation over the fate of the French King was as common and as necessary an introduction to a pamphlet or a speech, as an overture to an opera, or grace to a dinner'.[46]

As a body, the Whigs suffered. Enough of them favoured parliamentary reform, had fought for Catholic relief, or admired the ideals if not the acts of the French revolutionaries, to tarnish them all in the patriotic public mind. From being a recognizable party they dissolved into factions. Even though by 1792 Fox was distressed at the drift of the revolution, he held fast to the old faith. 'You seem to dread the prevalence of Paine's opinions (which in most parts I detest as much as you do),' he wrote Fitzwilliam, 'while I am much more afraid of the total annihilation of all principles of liberty & resistance … We both hate the two extremes … but we differ … with respect to the quarter from which the danger is most pressing.'

The two aristocrats were equally firm on religious liberty, above all the necessity to reduce the legal disabilities of Catholics and dissenting Protestants, so many of whom lived in the growing but unrepresented industrial towns. Without great hope that it would transform Parliament for the better, Fox consistently supported reform: only an extended franchise would return the Whigs to power. But here Fitzwilliam was adamant, an 'inveterate Enemy of

---

[45] Allen, *History of York*, vol. 1, p. 123; Whellan, *History of York*, vol. 1, p. 273.

[46] C. Emsley, 'An aspect of Pitt's "Terror": prosecutions for sedition during the 1790s', *Social History* 6:2 (May 1981), 155–84; *Appeal to the Nation*; *Memoirs of the Whig Party During My Time*, ed. Henry Edward, Lord Holland, 2 vols (Longmans: 1852, 1854), vol. 1, p. 28.

all Innovation. ... Though having no dislike to the check on publick men by popular discussion.' And on abolition of the slave trade, which Fox regarded as more important than any other measure before the country, Fitzwilliam, like Portland, felt no commitment.[47]

Fitzwilliam chose 'establishment against innovation, monarchy & aristocracy against the inroads of sans-culotism' and with Portland and several other Whig leaders joined Pitt's government. Fitzwilliam hoped the war with France would end in the restoration of the French monarchy. Of France's tumult he said, 'it is not the red-hot balls of her cannon ... but the red-hot principles with which she charges them ... I dread'.[48]

His price for supporting Pitt, in the attendant distribution of jobs and honours, in which his brother-in-law Sir Thomas Dundas became Baron Dundas of Aske, was the lord lieutenancy of Ireland. Not only did he own 66,000 acres of County Wicklow, but he had also an inherited concern for Ireland's good government and for improving the status of its Catholics. A substantial number of Irish Whigs looked to their British counterparts for emancipation, and Fitzwilliam's appointment was bound to stimulate their hopes. He arrived at Dublin Castle with no special instructions from Pitt, whose energies were swallowed by the war, and, assessing the situation independently, decided not to intervene in a Catholic relief bill then before the Irish Parliament and on the advice of Irish Whigs replaced certain high-handed officials without asking advice from the cabinet. As London's dismay percolated through to him – cries from his own Whig friends included – Fitzwilliam, hurt, explained that his actions had been essential to restore confidence and dignity to Protestant rule from Britain. 'Single, naked, and unsupported, I tremble not,' he declaimed heroically. His was the 'cause of the whole people of Ireland', he told Burke.[49]

The Irish loved him. Pitt, with Portland's assent, recalled him in March 1795. On the day he sailed, Dubliners drew his carriage followed by silent crowds to the quay while houses and shops all over the city were shuttered in mourning. Cruikshank caricatured the 'Journey from Dublin' with a print of Fitzwilliam perched on a pallet borne by priests and surrounded by a ragtag Irish mob. In the foreground, a man crammed implements of torture (for the

---

[47] NRO: F(M), 44/9/1, Fox to Fitzwilliam [16 March 1792]; SCC:LAI: WWM, F32/24, Fitzwilliam to Burke, 30 August 1796.

[48] SCC:LAI: WWM, F32/17, Fitzwilliam to Adair, 12 September 1795; NRO: F(M), 44/5/12, Fitzwilliam to Carlisle, 31 October 1792; Smith, *Whig Principles*, pp. 143–74.

[49] *Manuscripts of the Earl of Carlisle*, pp. 704–5; Maccoby, *English Radicalism*, pp. 89–90; Smith, *Whig Principles*, pp. 174–212; Thomas Pakenham, *Year of Liberty: the Story of the Great Irish Rebellion of 1798* (Hodder & Stoughton: 1969), p. 33; *Correspondence of Edmund Burke*, ed. T.W. Copeland, 10 vols (Cambridge University Press: Cambridge, 1958–78), vol. 8, p. 223.

'conversion of protestants') into a chest: they must be laid aside a while. The title was 'An Irish Howl or the Catholics in Fitz!'. His short, controversial and consequential stewardship, destroyed by the gulf between his forward views and a wartime cabinet's expediency, led to six years in the political wilderness. He rejected any further connection with Portland and supported Pitt only when he believed the war obliged him to, but he also kept aloof from the Foxites 'till such time as all the leaven of sans-culotism is work'd out of their composition'. Fox was warm in Fitzwilliam's defence, however, and on questions concerning Ireland they were one.[50]

Fitzwilliam's bitterness towards Pitt was unbounded: 'under no circumstances whatever will I be in connection with Mr. Pitt – it is sufficient for a mans life to have been duped once … shd circumstances ever present me the opportunity of doing essential injury to Mr. Pitt's power, or of doing essential service to Mr. Fox, I will not fail to seize it.' In 1801 the two old friends were reconciled on virtually every issue as Fitzwilliam became more critical of the conduct of the war and even the necessity of continuing it after Bonaparte's 'monarchy under republican forms' came in and his fears of British jacobinism subsided.[51]

Both before and after his Irish tour, Fitzwilliam maintained a close watch on fringe political activities in Yorkshire. He raised and armed volunteers and led his yeomanry in putting down the occasional disturbance. He was aware that the causes of mob action were more often the scarcity and price of food or low wages than radical opposition to government. A series of bad harvests from 1793 intensified the hardships and chafing restrictions of wartime. The brief peace of 1802–03 brought no relief to the textile industry: 'All their golden expectations have fail'd,' said Fitzwilliam after a visit to Leeds. Trade was dull and he predicted it would get worse. The working men who had banded together for social and political ends and who had supported the parliamentary reform movement did not lose their zeal for change as fast as some of the gentrified leadership when faced with the example of French extremism, but their meetings now were apt to be held in secret and stories abounded that they were arming, drilling and producing pikes for an English revolt. Thomas Paine's visions 'holding out … the prospect of plundering the rich' jeopardized the moderate demands of the Yorkshire Association. 'Nothing can be done upon Republican ground,' Wyvill insisted, 'or ought to be wished.'

But Wyvill himself was blamed in some quarters for coining 'watch words'

---

[50] *Public Characters of 1799–1800* (R. Phillips, 1799), pp. 352–67; O'Gorman, *Whig Party*, pp. 218–32; Smith, *Whig Principles*, pp. 210, 219ff, 251, 263; SCC:LAI: WWM, F32/17, Fitzwilliam to Adair, 12 September 1795; Holland, *Memoirs*, vol. 1, pp. 75–6.

[51] SCC:LAI: WWM, F32/24, Fitzwilliam to Burke, 30 August 1796; Smith, *Whig Principles*, p. 255.

which had led to the overthrow of France's ruling classes. Leading men inspired by John Reeves's Association for the Preservation of Liberty and Property Against Republicans met to counteract these sentiments with pledges of support to the government against all discontent and Fitzwilliam associated himself with the Earl of Effingham, Foljambe, Samuel Tooker, Robert Athorpe and many others 'including a great number of the lower classes … who joined us most Cordially' in a loyal demonstration at Rotherham, in whose neighbourhood every village seemed to have a shrewdly managed club in touch with societies at Sheffield and London 'if not with Paris'. 'They [now] … say they only meant reform which I consider as an insidious manoeuvre tending to the same mischief,' Foljambe informed Fitzwilliam.

As a reward for his diligence, Fitzwilliam in 1798 was to be offered the lord lieutenancy of the West Riding and, after satisfying himself that Pitt had nothing to do with it, Fitzwilliam accepted. The post was taken from the Duke of Norfolk who was unwise enough to have proposed at a birthday dinner for Fox, 'Our Sovereign – the Majesty of the People'.[52]

Wartime tension had reached a peak in October 1795 when, after a huge mass meeting of the London Corresponding Society, the King was jeered and stoned on his way to open Parliament and pursued by a hissing mob back to the palace. The deepest fears of riot and civil war drew people close in manifestations of affection and loyalty, and bills prohibiting large public meetings without approval of a magistrate and extending the definitions of treason and sedition were rushed through. Wilberforce backed Pitt in this 'temporary sacrifice' of liberties to stem the advance of radical imported philosophies.[53]

Wilberforce was by nature cautious about any extra-parliamentary activity, even in the campaign against the slave trade, though he continued to press for abolition in the Commons throughout the unfriendly 1790s. Although he has been called the 'first of the Pittites', and his friendship for the prime minister never faltered, Wilberforce never saw himself as any party's man. He supported the repressive acts because levelling or republicanism were as abhorrent to him

---

[52] NRO: F(M), X515/156, Fitzwilliam to Laurence, n.d.; Smith, *Whig Principles*, pp. 242–7; Parsons, *History of Leeds*, vol. 1, pp. 70–1; D.L. Linton (ed.), *Sheffield and Its Region* (British Association: Sheffield, 1956), p. 145; Wyvill, *Political Papers*, vol. 1, pp. 51–2; Black, *Association*, pp. 233, 237, 248; NRO F(M), 45, Foljambe to Fitzwilliam, 13 January 1793 and 20 December 1792; NRO: F(M), 44, handbill 17 December 1792; Holland, *Memoirs*, vol. 1, p. 131.

[53] Furneaux, *Wilberforce*, pp. 135–9; William Wilberforce, *Substance of the Speech … at the County Meeting … on the First of December, 1795* (Thomas Wright: Leeds [1795]); Maccoby, *English Radicalism*, pp. 92–5; J. Barrell, *Imagining the King's Death. Figurative Treason, Fantasies of Regicide, 1793–1796* (Oxford University Press: Oxford, 2000), pp. 551–603.

as to Fitzwilliam and furthermore would imperil the orderly society in which Christianity could flourish. Radicals marvelled that the advocate against the slave trade could enforce the 'slavery of silence' at home. He was embarrassed when the French Convention bestowed honorary citizenship upon him, in company with Thomas Clarkson, Jeremy Bentham, Benjamin Franklin and the evil genius Paine, and the compliment did not go down well with some of his Yorkshire supporters. But in 1794 and 1795 he had courageously urged peace negotiations, which Pitt opposed as premature. Yorkshire also was said to be hostile to peace at the time, and events showed that it was impossible of achievement. In the summer of 1795 Wilberforce made a conciliatory tour of his constituency, staying with families of rather too jolly habits for his taste but, as usual, inspiring affectionate regard for himself.[54]

The latest sedition and treason acts had excited the fears of some moderates, however, foremost among them Wyvill and the other county MP, Henry Duncombe, and once more Wilberforce was called upon to hold Yorkshire for Pitt. Wyvill believed that such electors as the Yorkshire clothiers would rally against the 'gagging bills', even though the causes of West Riding unrest, as Fitzwilliam realized, were usually much more mundane, and the issues had crystallized into a crude choice between the King and the mob. Wyvill's request to the high sheriff to call a county meeting to protest against the extreme acts was refused, so he and his friends circulated invitations for a meeting on Tuesday 1 December 1795 in what were believed to be sympathetic areas such as the cloth district, summoning the weavers to 'come forth from your looms ... and show you deserve to be free'. Wilberforce received a warning from William Hey and William Cookson at Leeds as he was setting out for church on the Sunday and by afternoon he was headed north in Pitt's borrowed carriage.

Meanwhile, thousands of clothmakers, later dubbed 'Billymen' for their enthusiasm for Pitt, were making their way to York in quite a different mood to that Wyvill had anticipated and at the Guildhall on Tuesday government supporters outnumbered the organizers by three to one and forcibly ejected Wyvill's chairman, Sir Thomas Gascoigne. Wilberforce's carriage swept up to the hall to a great roar from the crowd outside. Taking charge of the milling government forces, he led most of those present to the more spacious Castle Yard where, after speeches from Ralph Creyke, Spencer Stanhope and Wilberforce at his oratorical best, a King-and-Constitution petition was adopted with scarcely a dissenting vote. Seven thousand signatures were

---

[54] Furneaux, *Wilberforce*, pp. 19, 107, 114, 130–3; Reginald Coupland, *Wilberforce* (Oxford University Press: 1923), p. 20; *Edinburgh Review*, April 1838, pp. 167–8; Wilberforce, *Life*, vol. 2, pp. 98–108, 434–7; Jephson, *Platform*, vol. 1, p. 268.

collected. The opponents of the acts could muster only some 300. At Leeds the bells rang merrily at the news, and the cry went round 'Twenty King's men to one Jacobin'.[55]

For this hearty loyalty, some credit must go to the sweeping inroads of Methodism in the West Riding. As a body the Methodists have sometimes been viewed as preventers of an English revolution – supposing the threat of one ever existed – or at least as a steadying influence. In their own organization, they enjoyed a form of democratic government which served as an outlet for expression. United spiritually in a new style of disciplined living, they had the strength to absorb the rapid changes of the period and the all too frequent hard times. John Wesley's example had initially kept the great majority within the Established Church and loyal to the King and the government of the day. Even after his death in 1791, Methodists continued to honour the King, officially submitted to the law and resolved never to speak lightly or irreverently of the government. At the height of the jacobinical scares, they undoubtedly felt it necessary to quiet the worries of their brother churchmen that Methodism, with its lay and itinerant preachers represented unregulated and levelling sentiments. Some, it is true, were sympathetic to the current radicalism but until Alexander Kilham and his 'Tom Paine Methodists' were expelled in 1796, the Methodists did not split into the Old and the New Connexions and the latter was never very large.[56]

Henry Duncombe's defection from Pitt on this and other wartime measures would have doomed him to retire from Parliament even if he were not, as was the case, ready to do so when the general election of June 1796 was called. Wilberforce's seat was 'as secure as if the county were your own private borough', he was assured. But a contest loomed for the other seat and Wilberforce would have had to stand his share of that dreaded expense if it came. Three men had volunteered their services: Charles Duncombe of Duncombe Park, Henry's nephew; Walter Fawkes, a wealthy Whig proprietor and moderate reformer whose seat was at Farnley Hall; and, new to county politics, Henry Lascelles, second son of Edward who in 1795 had inherited the Harewood estate from his cousin Edwin (who had been routed as a county MP in 1780 by the Yorkshire Association and created a peer a decade later, though the title died with him). Henry's elder brother had an aversion to public life and although invited to do so by the leading men of Leeds had declined to stand. All three promised their second votes to Wilberforce. All three also

---

[55] Gooder, *Parliamentary Representation*, pp. 110–11; Furneaux, *Wilberforce*, pp. 137–9; Pollock, *Wilberforce*, pp. 133–6; W.L. Mathieson, *England in Transition, 1789–1832: A Study of Movements* (Longmans: 1920), pp. 52–3; Thomis and Holt, *Threats of Revolution*, pp. 129–32; Wilberforce, *Life*, vol. 2, pp. 112–32; Dinwiddy, *Wyvill and Reform*, pp. 9–10.
[56] Teale, 'Methodism', pp. 26, 32, 71, 163, 168, 109–12, 157, 161, 162.

canvassed Fitzwilliam's support for the nomination but the earl appeared content to sit this one out.[57] He wished Fawkes success and did not go to the nomination meeting. His friends were chiefly for Fawkes. The show of hands, as so often happened, was inconclusive. Duncombe withdrew and the struggle lay between Fawkes and Lascelles. Pressure was put on Wilberforce to form a ticket with Lascelles, which had a certain logic since both drew strength from the commercial areas and the popularity of Pitt. Wilberforce, however, prized his freedom above all and insisted that he stood alone. Fawkes's support was apathetic. He wanted to 'prevent a Sale of ye Representation of the County' to Pitt 'or making it a perpetual appendage of Harwood House'. Richard Milnes scented a bargain was being struck between Pitt and Lascelles but few seemed to care. Fawkes consulted such prominent men as were in York and not already pledged to Lascelles and found them 'unripe for his purpose'. Thus when Lascelles declared his willingness to stand a poll, Fawkes had little choice but to withdraw. 'So Pitt has got ye County by purchase,' Robert Sinclair told Fitzwilliam.[58]

Only afterward did it leak out that Fawkes might have prevailed had not one of his committee 'mislaid' a letter promising him the substantial support of Fitzwilliam and the dukes of Norfolk and Devonshire. Sir George Armytage, who told Wilberforce about the incident, blamed 'Harewood's long purse'. On 7 June Wilberforce and Henry Lascelles were elected in the Castle Yard, almost exclusively packed with freeholders from the West Riding. Unnerved by the tumultuous chairing and an indecent toast at the celebration dinner, Wilberforce retired early, prayed 'and shed many tears'. On 18 June Henry Lascelles's father accepted a barony.

The next general election took place in the summer of 1802. Pitt had resigned, unable through the King's obduracy to keep promises given to the Irish Catholics in return for their support for union with Britain. Unrest continued in the populous areas among workers beleaguered by low wages, high prices and the slump in trade, and the workers' revolt against mechanization in the West Country had spread to the Yorkshire cloth districts. There were issues in plenty but public debate was subdued under repressive laws and party disarray. Some of the arguments were aired, however, in the six counties and

---

[57] Wilberforce, *Life*, vol. 2, p. 150; SCC:LAI: WWM, F34/198, Beckett to Fitzwilliam, 22 May 1796; WYAS(L): WYL250/6/3/8, copy of letter to Beckett; SCC:LAI: WWM, F34/187, Lascelles to Fitzwilliam, 20 May 1796; F34/199, Fawkes to Fitzwilliam, 24 May 1796; F34/202, Duncombe to Fitzwilliam, 24 May 1796; F34/201, draft Fitzwilliam to Fawkes.

[58] Wilberforce, *Life*, vol. 2, pp. 152–4; SCC:LAI: WWM, F34/205, Sykes to Fitzwilliam, n.d. [1796]; Furneaux, *Wilberforce*, p. 147; SCC:LAI: WWM, F34/204, Sinclair to Fitzwilliam, 31 May 1796; ERALS: DDGR/38/60, handbill.

The Political Past: Reform and Reaction

62 boroughs which produced contests. The rowdy one at Windsor delighted Lord Viscount Milton, Fitzwilliam's 16-year-old son then at Eton. He rushed through his lessons to join the crowd at the hustings and tricked himself out in enormous bunches of Opposition ribbons. The government side had let it be known that the King would go mad, should his man lose, Milton gossiped in letters home.[59]

But in Yorkshire the 1802 election was a model of untaxing decorum with next to no expense, as thoroughly agreeable as any resort to the 'sense of the people' could be. Wilberforce had some anxiety because he had neglected to visit the county more than usual and rumour again had it that he might retire. Indeed, he had contemplated it: 'to be active in preserving my situation seems like labouring to be permitted to tug at the oar like a galley slave,' he once remarked to his friend William Hey. 'I pant for quiet and retirement.'

By now he had no ambition for high political office and hoped by independent example alone to further his moral and religious causes. Parliament was dissolved on Tuesday 29 June and on the 30th Wilberforce set out from Broomfield, his house at Clapham since his marriage five years earlier, for the North. Nomination day was fixed for 12 July. Henry Lascelles left his Hanover Square house for Harewood on 30 June, too, departing at 3.30 a.m. to reach his destination on the Thursday.[60] He quickly arranged visits to the various towns according to their market days and sent word of his plans to Wilberforce. Notwithstanding the fact that no new candidate had emerged, neither member could avoid paying courtesy visits to as many of their constituents as time allowed. However peculiar it might have seemed to some, the abolitionist and the man enriched by slavery were congenial colleagues. Probably abolition was their single serious difference, and there is no surviving evidence that they discussed it. Wilberforce, in fact, rarely referred to abolition in his Yorkshire appearances, preferring, as any canny politician, topics of local importance such as (in 1802) the drawback on soap, the duty on flax or the stagnant state of trade.

So Wilberforce and Lascelles in 1802 appeared together almost everywhere on their obligatory tour. They met near Leeds on Saturday 3 July and proceeded to Halifax where they were greated by thirty leading citizens. After breakfast at the Talbot Inn, they toured the Piece Hall without experiencing 'one unpleasant circumstance', then dined with sixty friends who rose to the toasts of 'unanimous Election to our late Members, with thanks … for their honest and upright conduct in Parliament' and 'may [they] be returned for the

---

[59] Harvey, *Britain*, pp. 88–91; Jephson, *Platform*, vol. 1, pp. 301, 302; NRO: F(M), 61, Jenkins to Fitzwilliam, 5 July 1802 and Milton to Lady Fitzwilliam, 6 July 1802.
[60] Wilberforce, *Life*, vol. 3, pp. 50–2, 60; WYAS(L): WYL250/6/3/8, Lascelles's notebook, 'Election June 1802'.

County of York as long as They live'. After spending a quiet Sunday in Halifax, they dined on Monday with the aldermen of Leeds and Lascelles returned to Harewood for the night. Deputations of Methodists called upon each of them to offer full support, which was particularly gratifying to Wilberforce who had incurred their wrath for opposing repeal of the Test Act.[61] On Tuesday they walked through the Leeds cloth halls, observing 'no symptom whatever of dissatisfaction'. Similar welcomes were forthcoming during their pleasant journey at Huddersfield, Sheffield, Barnsley, Wakefield, Bradford, Pontefract and Doncaster. Only at Rotherham was there an unexplained 'want of cordiality'.

Wilberforce fell ill at North Cave, where they spent the night of 9 July en route to Hull, and he returned to York but Lascelles, speaking for them both, visited Hull and Beverley before reaching York. On Monday 12 July Wilberforce and Lascelles rode to the Castle Yard, were nominated, spoke, declared elected and chaired to the York Tavern for the election dinner. Each donated £100 to the county hospital.

Afterwards, Wilberforce left William Gray's house for a visit to Henry Duncombe, whose property Gray now managed in the county, and then travelled on 15 July to Harewood House where he had a very good time. He toured the grounds with the landscape designer Humphrey Repton and wrote to his wife, 'This is really one not only of the most magnificent, but of the finest places in England. Great natural beauty, vast woods, expanses of water, a river winding through a valley portioned into innumerable enclosures. Within the house, perfect ease and great good-humour without the smallest mixture of pomp and parade, except in the rooms themselves, which are too gaudy for my taste.'[62]

---

[61] Wilberforce, *Life*, vol. 2, pp. 117–18.
[62] *Ibid.*, vol. 3, pp. 55–6.

CHAPTER FOUR

The Election of 1806: A Rehearsal

ALTHOUGH the general election of November 1806 passed off with deceptive ease in a canvass, on closer examination it proves to be a worthy forerunner to the legendary battle of 1807. The preceding twelve months had been a year of lost heroes. Nelson's funeral on 9 January was followed on 23 January by the death of Pitt at the early age of 46. Hardly eight months later Fox too was dead. Pitt, who had been restored as prime minister in 1804, probably died of stomach cancer (Fox spoke of 'gout in the stomach' as the cause) but it was the popular and entirely plausible belief that the burdens of wartime office had exhausted him. 'Pitt was killed by the enemy as much as Nelson,' Wilberforce commented.[1]

Both Wilberforce, carrying Pitt's crested banner ahead of the coffin, and Lascelles, a flag bearer behind, took part in the majestic public funeral which closed with Pitt's burial in Westminster Abbey. But it was a controversial as well as a solemn occasion. The move for a state funeral and monument hailing Pitt as 'that excellent statesman' had originated with Lascelles on the day after Pitt's death, an unusual – to say the least – leap into the limelight for a man who had served such a quiet ten years on the back benches. He had not consulted Wilberforce beforehand and he misjudged completely the sensitivities within the House in this crisis. Pitt's friends were sorry, but the motion could not be withdrawn. Fox, although a lifelong foe of Pitt, had been 'very sorry, very, very sorry' to hear of his death. 'This is not a time to lose talents like his,' Fox had said. Yet he and other Whig leaders could not vote for the motion even though it might mean the King's displeasure and a veto upon their taking office in future. Not only was Pitt in Whig eyes a disastrous war minister, but to lavish praise upon his entire record would be to endorse policies which they had fought against relentlessly. But Lascelles's motion passed by 258 to 89.[2]

---

[1] Furneaux, *Wilberforce*, p. 237; Derry, *Fox*, pp. 419–20.
[2] [Gower], *Private Correspondence*, vol. 2, pp. 167, 169; Pollock, *Wilberforce*, p. 199;

Pitt's surviving ministers resigned in the face of growing dislike of the conduct of the war, and a new government, again a coalition, took office, the 'Ministry of All the Talents', with Lord Grenville at its head and Fox as Foreign Secretary. Fitzwilliam was made Lord President of the Council. Most of the Talents were Whigs, but Addington (now Lord Sidmouth) was the Tory Lord Privy Seal and he gave notice before joining that he would never accept any measure for Catholic relief. The presence of Fitzwilliam discouraged the parliamentary reformers. A bill which would have prohibited the conveyance of voters to the polls by the candidates was denounced by members on both sides as a form of disenfranchisement and soundly beaten.

But better fortune attended another hoary cause. The government now favoured the abolition of the slave trade and on Fox's motion Parliament committed itself to ending the traffic soon. To Wilberforce this first victory in a crusade which had begun for him in 1787 was bittersweet, for only the loss of Pitt and a change of government had made it possible. 'How wonderful are the ways of God!' he mused, and wrote in his journal, 'I quite love Fox for his generous and warm fidelity to the Slave Trade cause.'[3]

Much of the time of the two Yorkshire members during the 1806 session was occupied with the wool inquiry. The pros and cons of factory production had seized the attention of the woollen district of the county. Wilberforce's masterly committee report managed to praise the old domestic system of manufacture while unleashing the 'enterprising capitalist' to embark upon factories. Lascelles earned 'very great Credit from all the Mercantile & Leading People' in the West Riding for his unabashed support of the factory system, but the slowness of Parliament to repeal the restraints that protected the clothiers bewildered the county's merchants. They could not easily prove that working men were illegally combining to make themselves the 'paramount Masters over their Employers' but they were sure that the 'Lower Class of Clothiers require that no Man who has Capital, Enterprize & ability ... shall be allowed to exercise them in Yorkshire', an agitated William Cookson advised Wilberforce. Cookson pointed out that master clothiers were increasing at least as fast as the objectionable factories and now hired out much of their work, bought their materials (at inflated prices), were dragged from their homes twice a week for the cloth markets 'and far too commonly spend too much of their time and money in public-houses'. How much better would be a system under which an 'opulent manufacturer' would hire father, mother

---

Hobhouse, *Fox*, pp. 256, 258–9; *York Herald*, 1 February 1806; John Ashton, *Dawn of the XIXth Century in England* (T. Fisher Unwin: 1886), pp. 120, 126; *Parliamentary Debates, House of Commons*, vol. 6, col. 31 (24 January 1806); cols 41–73 (27 January 1806).

[3] Wilberforce, *Life*, vol. 3, pp. 259, 261, 268.

and all children above nine years for six days a week at better pay, 'and the alehouse only is the loser'.

As a friend to factories, Lascelles in the summer of 1805 was the target of insults in certain villages by a 'few Lads & Blackguards' acting with the silent consent of their masters and was burnt in effigy in half a dozen other places.[4]

Although Fitzwilliam was again in the cabinet, his appointment in February 1806 occurred while his son lay gravely ill at Milton House where Fitzwilliam remained, absenting himself from the decision-making that followed Pitt's death. Lord Milton made a full recovery by March, thanks to his 'uncontaminated habits' and the attentions of several highly paid physicians, and was married on 8 July 1806 to his cousin Mary, daughter of Lord Dundas of Aske Hall and Fitzwilliam's sister Charlotte. Milton was 20, his bride 17. Both families were overjoyed, and the new Lady Milton seemed to charm everyone she met.[5]

Milton that year took on other manly offices such as a steward for Doncaster races and commander of the Wath troop of the West Riding Yeomanry Cavalry. Even without the lively interest in electioneering he had shown when a schoolboy, Milton could not have escaped his political destiny. His father was one of the country's eight first-rank political peers. He could dispose of two seats at Malton, the single seat at Higham Ferrers and both seats at Peterborough in Northamptonshire and both from County Wicklow in Ireland. He had a strong if not always decisive say in the Yorkshire and York elections and influence in several of the county's boroughs. He could seat seven MPs in any election; with luck, more. Clearly a place could be found for his son.

It is unlikely that the earl needed reminding but soon after Milton's marriage William Elliot, MP for Peterborough, called his attention to the fact that 'Lord Milton ... is on the point of coming of age, and this circumstance must of course make a great change in the distribution of your parliamentary interests'. There need be no scruple about using his seat at Peterborough, he added. Dr French Laurence, the Oxford legal authority whom Fitzwilliam had adopted on Burke's advice for the other Peterborough seat, had taken a close interest in the education and well-being of the heir. Milton had 'from his birth & rank in society a weighty obligation of publick duties upon him', Dr Laurence observed at the end of 1805. As he was likely to leave a long

---

[4] *Ibid.*, pp. 264–7; BOD: AWP, c.45 fols 75–6, Cookson to Wilberforce, 5 February 1805 (printed in Wilberforce, *Correspondence*, vol. 2, pp. 8–10) and fols 77–8, Cookson to Wilberforce, 19 March 1806; Wilson, *Gentlemen Merchants*, p. 169.
[5] NRO: F(M), 68a, Jan.–Mar. correspondence; SCC:LAI: WWM, F127/75, 76, 6, correspondence with physicians, Dundas to Fitzwilliam, 15 November 1805; Stirling, *Letter-Bag*, vol. 1, p. 113.

posterity (being already engaged at 19) Milton 'should so much the more feel an incentive to aim at transmitting to them with his & your titles & estate, a constitution & system of polity, which may give lustre to the one, & security to the other'.[6]

Charles Fox's death on 13 September 1806, aged 58, was the cruel stroke which brought Milton into parliamentary politics earlier than could have been anticipated. Utterly dissimilar in temperament, unevenly matched in talent, Fox and Fitzwilliam had been intimate friends since their Eton schooldays. Fox was painfully ill with dropsy throughout the summer of 1806 and the entire nation followed his decline. Fitzwilliam was summoned from Yorkshire to share his friend's final hours. 'Those who have known him longest appear to have loved him best; and ... those who attended and wept round his death bed, had been ... the companions of his youth, and the friends of his whole life,' the *Leeds Mercury* reported in a column-long obituary heavily bordered in black.

When Fitzwilliam reached the bedside Fox could not speak but stretched out his hand. He died hardly two hours later, in the arms of his nephew Lord Holland, and Fitzwilliam collapsed in a faint. For a time it was feared that he, too, would die. There was no state funeral for Fox but it was a conspicuously public occasion with a cortège travelling to Westminster Abbey through streets lined with soldiers and mourners. The chief mourner, Lord Holland, was accompanied by Earl Fitzwilliam and Lord Howick (lately Charles Grey). A memorial service attended by the lord mayor and Corporation was held at York Minster on 12 October for this 'ever-to-be-lamented ... valued Friend of Liberty and Mankind'.[7]

Lord Grenville's decision to seek a general election was intended to strengthen the Foxite dominance in the cabinet before the warmth for Fox's memory had cooled. There also was a chance to capitalize on the recent scandal over Pitt's intimate Lord Melville (formerly Henry Dundas) who was impeached for speculating with the Admiralty's money but found not guilty by his peers. Both Wilberforce and Lascelles had voted for the impeachment. There was widespread public resentment, akin to that in the early days of the agitation for parliamentary reform, over 'peculation', abuse of royal

---

[6] *York Herald*, 27 September 1806; *Doncaster Gazette*, 16 October 1806; SCC:LAI: WWM, F64/4, Elliot to Fitzwilliam, 14 July 1806; Laurence to Fitzwilliam, 31 December 1805 in Harvey, *Britain*, p. 17.

[7] NRO: F(M), 69/36, 41, 43, letters on Fox's illness; X512, Fitzwilliam to Lady Fitzwilliam, n.d. [Sept. 1806]; *Journal of Elizabeth Lady Holland, 1791–1811*, ed. Earl of Ilchester, 2 vols (Longmans: 1908), vol. 2, pp. 180–1; *Leeds Mercury*, 30 September 1806; *Halifax Journal*, 18 October 1806 (one of many accounts of the funeral in the Yorkshire press); *York Herald*, 18 October 1806.

privilege (large increases in royal family incomes having been voted) and the hated wartime income tax. It may also have seemed to Grenville necessary to demonstrate that the King, in agreeing to the dissolution, supported the government in spite of his antipathy to Fox's peace overtures and the abolition of the slave trade. Grenville got his dissolution but the King withheld for the first time in his reign the £20,000 he habitually gave his prime minister for the administration's election expenses. In spite of this and a poorly mounted campaign, Grenville did gain more than 40 parliamentary supporters.[8]

News of the October dissolution took the old members for Yorkshire by surprise. Wilberforce had left London in August for the 'snug and retired harbour of Lyme, for the purpose of careening and refitting' and to compose a treatise on the slave trade. He was startled to receive the announcement in a letter from Grenville on 15 October. He directed that a handbill be issued confirming his intention to stand again and on the 21st was on the road to Yorkshire. At Blandford he saw an advertisement dated 18 October that Walter Fawkes was a candidate; a contest was possible! His anxious friends at York inserted a notice in the Yorkshire papers under the date of 20 October urging freeholders not to give their votes 'to any interest adverse to that of ... Mr. Wilberforce'. From Nottingham Wilberforce sent a declaration to the gentlemen, clergy and freeholders that he was hastening to pay them his respects and beseeching their continued support. At Rotherham he learned that Lord Milton had already successfully canvassed that town and Sheffield for Fawkes while Wilberforce's local friends remained confused over the perennial rumour that he might retire. A letter from Cookson caught up with him; the clothiers were exasperated with both him and Lascelles. Those who had appeared as witnesses before the wool committee were 'violent beyond all conception'. Fawkes would get plumpers if Wilberforce joined Lascelles in the canvass. In Leeds, Lascelles would not have 10 votes in both cloth halls. 'A contemptuous expression that he is said to have uttered is bandied about with great effect. Many are very sore against you, and all the Presbyterians are with Fawkes. Mr. Lascelles has the unqualified support of all the landed gentry and nobility. The intent is certainly to affright you into giving up. But I see no reason why you should suppose that your old friends would desert you.' Cookson, himself, still supporting both old members, was sorry for Lascelles but argued that Wilberforce must think of self-preservation as well as friendship. The clothiers 'to a man' were against Lascelles but Wilberforce might obtain their second votes. Lascelles had been making a neutral canvass for nearly a week before Wilberforce reached Yorkshire and was apparently equally cool to a coalition himself. But from the East Riding contradictory

---

[8] M.G. Hinton, 'General Elections of 1806 and 1807', vol. 2, p. 94.

advice reached Wilberforce. Sir Mark Masterman Sykes reported that the Driffield Hunt was firmly behind both old members and believed they should canvass together.[9]

Wilberforce reached York on Saturday 25 October and, working until past midnight, scrawled seventy letters with the help of William Gray and Dr Burgh. His supporters, chiefly leading men from the East and North Ridings, collected on Monday. After dinner, Wilberforce wrote another seventy letters, then drove to Leeds where he stayed with William Hey who later remembered the three days his house served as Wilberforce's headquarters as among the most agreeable of his life.[10]

Leeds merchants escorted Wilberforce to the cloth halls the next day and the clothiers received his address warmly, according to the reports sent to the press, unharnessed his horses and hauled his carriage to an inn for dinner before dragging him to Hey's home where the cloth hall trustees called and agreed to canvass for him. But Wilberforce was plainly told that if Lascelles had come with him, the clothiers would have let Wilberforce enter and then would have 'shoved cloth in his way' to keep Lascelles out. One trustee (Robert Cookson) said that Wilberforce had treated him like a gentleman; Lascelles had 'us'd him like a Dog'. Lascelles's agent in Leeds, Lucas Nicholson, reported, 'You will be much surprised to hear Wilberforce never once adverted to the misstatements amongst the Clothiers or even mentioned your name. The Committee which has for several days been sitting in the united Interest of yourself & Mr. Wilberforce, I consider at an end.' He was organizing another for Lascelles alone.[11]

The East and North Ridings were left to Wilberforce's friends and agents to secure while he made a canvass of the West Riding. His progress was much the same everywhere – at Bradford, Wakefield, Dewsbury, Heckmondwike and Huddersfield he was 'dragged and speechified'. One night on the dreadful roads his carriage grazed a loaded wagon and was nearly upset. At Sheffield he was the guest of the Company of Cutlers (who also supported Lascelles) and was thanked by them for defeating the pig iron tax. He used this as an example of his independence – for Pitt had proposed it – and recalled that he had never exploited his seat for personal advancement. 'I can affirm, that

---

[9] Wilberforce, *Life*, vol. 3, pp. 273, 275, 278–9; *York Courant*, 20 and 27 October 1806; Wilberforce, *Correspondence*, vol. 2, pp. 100, 102.

[10] Wilberforce, *Life*, vol. 3, p. 280; John Pearson, *Life of William Hey* (Hurst, Robinson: 1822), pp. 164–5, 166–7.

[11] Wilberforce, *Life*, vol. 3, p. 281; WYAS(L): WYL250/6/3/9, Cookson to Lascelles, n.d.; J.F. Hirst, 'William Wilberforce, A Commemorative Sketch', *Yorkshire Notes and Queries*, new series 2 (Bradford, 1905), p. 148; WYAS(L): WYL250/6/3/9, Nicholson to Lascelles, n.d. [28 October 1806].

The Election of 1806: A Rehearsal

I am at this hour neither a richer nor a greater man than I was when I first became an object of your choice,' he declaimed from the Sheffield Town Hall steps. 'Did I say neither richer nor greater? – I beg permission to correct my words; I am richer, I am greater now ... richer in the continued possession of your confidence and esteem for twenty-two years; and greater for having been four times elected ... for the County of York.' The 'loudest acclamations' burst from the sea of faces before him and his carriage was dragged around the Sheffield streets among applauding thousands, '(several run over, but not much hurt)', to the Angel Inn.[12]

Halifax provided him with a cavalcade of a hundred gentlemen on horse-back and a band of music to escort him from John Edwards's house, Pye-Nest, to the multitude gathered at King Cross, from where his carriage was dragged to the Piece Hall for his speech. Afterwards he was chaired to the Swan Inn – all proper civilities, as the *Halifax Journal* stated, for 'that old and faithful servant of the public, who has, for so many years shone with distinguished lustre in the British Senate'. Wilberforce, however, noted a few hisses and cries of 'Fawkes for ever', which he took the trouble to find came from bellringers who, through the over-zealousness of the vicar, the Rev. Dr William Coulthurst, had been forbidden to ring when Fawkes visited the town. And during his chairing someone pelted him with something 'happily not hard'. It was at Halifax late that Saturday afternoon that Wilberforce learned Lascelles had given up. Wilberforce earlier had predicted to Lord Grenville in a confidential 'whisper' what 'I cannot be as glad of as you, from my personal goodwill to Mr. Lascelles, though I am most scrupulously and conscientiously neutral' that Fawkes would be so far ahead that Lascelles would withdraw. He wrote to his wife that he would come first on a poll but, he was sorry to say, Fawkes second. 'Some of Mr. Lascelles's friends have been in a degree the bringers-on of this business, from over-estimating their strength, and thinking they could turn me out without great difficulty; whereas almost all the respectable people who are not connected with great men when it comes to the point of choosing between Lascelles and me, give him up without hesitation.' Wilberforce carried on writing letters and meeting supporters (with a Sunday pause to hear Dr Coulthurst preach) until Tuesday 4 November when he headed contentedly for York and the now pro-forma nomination meeting set for the 6th.[13]

---

[12] Wilberforce, *Life*, vol. 3, p. 281; WYAS(L): WYL250/6/3/9, Cookson to Lascelles, n.d.; J.F. Hirst, 'William Wilberforce, A Commemorative Sketch', p. 148; WYAS(L): WYL250/6/3/9, Nicholson to Lascelles, n.d. [28 October 1806].

[13] *Halifax Journal*, 8 November 1806; WYAS(L): WYL250/6/3/9, Bernard to Harewood, 26 October 1806; Wilberforce, *Life*, vol. 3, pp. 282–4; Pollock, *Wilberforce*, p. 207; Furneaux, *Wilberforce*, pp. 261–2.

Halifax provides a typical example of Lascelles's disastrous canvass. A Wilberforce-Lascelles committee, headed by John Edwards, as early as 20 October had urged the voters to re-elect the old members and had arranged for their joint appearance on 1 November. Two days before the event, Dr Coulthurst, for the committee, discouraged Lascelles from coming on the feeble pretext that Halifax's leading gentlemen would be too busy with Wilberforce to give Lascelles their 'full respect and attention' on the same day. Lascelles politely accepted the rebuff, saying he had to be in Bradford that day anyhow, but one Halifax advocate stood up on the day to praise him publicly and ask the embarrassing question of why Lascelles was not present to speak for himself.[14]

Lascelles appeared to take politics lightly, in spite of his reputation for arrogance. He was dilatory in getting underway and after two easy elections, the second carried in companionable partnership with Wilberforce, he approached the 1806 canvass complacently 'probably from his own Weight of Metal (if there should be a Contest) & the former mad Aristocracy of the Times', a Fitzwilliam ally conjectured. Wilberforce never took his seat for granted and had a happy faculty of convincing audiences of all stations that he could be trusted to look after their interests. Lascelles had this empathy only with the landed proprietors and wealthy merchants and he suggested in his starchy applications for votes from others that it was a rather distasteful duty. He was lazily inclined to leave critical decisions to his supporters, who often failed him. He was accused of having more writers of squibs and letters than voters.

Wilberforce had needed only a whiff of Lascelles's unpopularity to distance himself from his colleague although he much preferred Lascelles to Fawkes and often mentioned the former's 'manly and independent' conduct. Indeed, 'manly' and 'independent' or 'upright' were the adjectives most commonly found for Lascelles by his admirers.[15]

Lascelles's friends at first were unconcerned whether Wilberforce held or Fawkes took the second seat. Wilberforce was weak where Lascelles and Fawkes were strong, with 'noblemen in general & most of ye foxhunters'. Some of Fitzwilliam's friends, too, thought this might be a good time to throw Wilberforce out and dignify the county with another landed MP for 'he's poor & durst not contend', as Tom Scatcherd of Wyton in Holderness put it. Harewood House would be satisfied to let in one Whig member if Wilberforce retired. John Lister Kaye was equally blunt: Wilberforce's 'Family & Property

---

[14] *Halifax Journal*, 1 November 1806; WYAS(L): WYL250/6/3/9, Coulthurst to Lascelles, 30 October and Edwards to Lascelles, 31 October 1806; Wilberforce, *Life*, vol. 3, p. 284.

[15] For the moral and political significance of such terms, see McCormack, *The Independent Man*, pp. 1–55.

do not entitle him to represent the County; & to my thinking no Dissenter to our established Church ought to be a member of the British Parliament.' (Wilberforce was often mistaken for a Methodist.) Many of the gentry actually believed that because of the friendship between the families at Harewood House and Farnley Hall and with Fitzwilliam behind the latter, Wilberforce would see that the sensible thing to do was bow out. Equally it must be said that Wilberforce and his allies accepted second votes for either Lascelles or Fawkes impartially. Lascelles's partisans believed that the merchants 'alarm'd for their darling Wilberforce' at first coupled his name with Lascelles to help him and then when they found it expedient abandoned Lascelles for Fawkes. 'The whole from beginning to end has been carried on in a Mercantile way – First Lord Fitzwilliam & Fawkes have taken advantage of your unpopularity with the Clothiers, & the Merchants whose cause you was fighting. Deserting you is no more than what one might expect from a Merchant, all of whom have sacrificed you for Wilberforce,' said George Bernard.[16]

That there was a genuine desire among a substantial number of electors to reward the two old members is beyond doubt. Try as either might to avoid it, they, as Pittites, were fused in the minds of those who shared their views. And as one freeholder asserted, the voters had a right to join any two names they wished. What had the present members done to forfeit the county's good opinion, asked A Freeholder in one of the many widely printed letters? Well, what Lascelles had done was to offend the clothiers.

He was at Harewood House when he was alerted to the dissolution by Edward Wolley, his agent in York, and he announced on 18 October that he was willing to serve again. Many supporters had begun to canvass even before hearing from him but repeatedly he was told that Fawkes's forces were on the move 'teazing people so much' that they promised their votes just to 'get rid of the solicitors'.[17]

No one put the case for Lascelles to make haste more pointedly than the numerous family of the octogenarian Archbishop Markham of York. 'Pray take a lesson in Caesar from your eldest boy,' the archbishop's son, William Markham, importuned. 'You will find his success depended almost entirely

---

[16] SCC:LAI: WWM, E209a, Armytage to Fitzwilliam, 25 October 1806; *Leeds Intelligencer*, 10 November 1806; Wilberforce, *Life*, vol. 3, pp. 279, 282; KINCM: Wilberforce letters, Wilberforce to Montagu, 3 November 1806; NRO: F(M), 69/16, Scatcherd to Fitzwilliam, 25 July 1806; SCC:LAI: WWM, E 209a, Carlisle to Fitzwilliam, 21 October 1806; WYAS(L): WYL250/6/3/9, Kaye to Lascelles, 21 October, Belasize to Lascelles, 28 October and Bernard to Lascelles, 4 November 1806.

[17] *York Chronicle*, 23 October 1806; WYAS(L): WYL250/6/3/9, Wolley to Lascelles, 16 October, Lascelles to Wolley, 18 October 1806, and other correspondence including A Freeholder to Lascelles.

on his celerity in execution.' William's brother, Robert, Archdeacon of York, reported that charges of Lascelles's neglect abounded: he was letting his own votes be snatched by the first canvasser to come round; he was not getting out enough to set an active example; he had failed to write letters to some people and they were offended. 'I have already tired my horse,' Robert declared, 'but not myself. ... if you lose your Election, it will be your own fault.' The Dean of York, their brother George, was actively canvassing Lascelles votes also and, while the Archbishop himself kept to Bishopthorpe Palace, his interest in the Harewood family was manifest, but Fawkes secured the Markhams' second votes, for the evangelical Wilberforce was not a favourite of the church.[18]

All three candidates knew they must concentrate their short time on the West Riding towns and here Lascelles's efforts collapsed under the weight of the clothiers' anger. Leeds was a disaster for Lascelles. Wilberforce on 27 October rejected his invitation that they walk the halls together the following day and went alone instead. Mayor Richard Ramsden Bramley refused to attend Wilberforce's solo performance and suggested that Lascelles come to the following week's market, promising to do everything he could to get a good attendance. Meanwhile, Lascelles's case was put to the Leeds Cloth Hall trustees by William Cookson who stressed the agreement of the old members on the wool committee report of which Fawkes had 'exprest compleat aprobation. ... But they would not Hear Reason.' From Leeds to Saddleworth, Lascelles suffered from 'Brutal unpopularity', deserted, when he deserved the kingdom's praise. 'Most certainly there never was an Instance of a Member of Parliament ... being so shamefully Treated,' Cookson said.

From Bradford on 26 October Lascelles's staunch friend, Samuel Hailstone, expressed surprise that Lascelles had not already come and told him a 'set of Miscreants' were his only serious opponents. But his agents there were saying that his canvass had become a 'very unpleasant task indeed among the Manufacturers'. Lascelles expected insults at Huddersfield and Joseph Radcliffe, a leading local landowner, volunteered to be at his side in his role as a magistrate 'to see no harm happens to you, or to anyone else'. But more personal appearances, however belated, a Wakefield friend wrote regretfully afterwards, would have allowed his supporters to drown 'by a torrent of applause the paltry disapprobation of an ungrateful & ignorant rabble'.[19]

---

[18] WYAS(L): WYL250/6/3/9, W. Markham to Lascelles and R. Markham to same, 23 October; Gilby to same, 26 October 1806; SCC:LAI: WWM, E209c, William Ebor to Fitzwilliam, 21 October 1806; Wilberforce, *Life*, vol. 3, p. 280.

[19] WYAS(L): WYL250/6/3/9, Nicholson to Lascelles, 27 October; Bramley to same, 28 October; Cookson to same, Thursday eve, n.d.; Hailstone to same, 26 October; Radcliffe to same, 29 October; Naylor to same, 31 October; anon. to same, 7 November 1806.

The Election of 1806: A Rehearsal

The *Leeds Intelligencer* tried to carry Lascelles's voice to the public he could not reach in person. In a purported letter from Your Brother Freeholders, it traced the controversy over the future of wool manufacture and asserted that Lascelles had devoted his whole time to the county's commercial interests. The evils of attempting to control the free use of capital were so obvious that laws passed in the infancy of the trade were silently flouted. If the restrictive laws were enforced foreign countries would dominate the industry. Living as he did in the heart of the wool district, Lascelles knew better than Wilberforce how destructive the continuation of the mis-named domestic system would be and 'firmly but temperately' did his parliamentary duty, heedless of popularity. Lascelles's success at ferreting out the secret workmen's combinations, 'a conspiracy at once unconstitutional, dangerous and destructive – unparalleled in the manufactories of Great Britain' was what really cost him his election, a body of Halifax boosters argued.

The clothiers retorted through the *Leeds Mercury* that the delegates whom Lascelles had despised would now exert their influence to remove him. As for Wilberforce, they were his ardent friends 'when he stands alone'.[20]

In previous elections, abolition of the slave trade had scarcely figured. With the victory for the abolition resolution that spring, abolitionists were concerned to make certain that the final step was taken in the 1807 session. Newspapers everywhere carried advertisements cautioning electors to support only those men who favoured abolition. The Society of Friends and other dissenting Protestants who seldom stirred during elections in Yorkshire were united for Wilberforce and many for Fawkes too, or to be more precise, against Lascelles whose family owned slaves. A letter signed by William Tuke, Thomas Priestman and Lindley Murray, prominent York Quakers, cited Wilberforce's peculiar claim to their votes because of his long dedication to the 'cause of the African race' which had engaged their Society for half a century.[21]

If the foxhunters preferred their own kind, the Methodists did also, and in Wilberforce's personal character and piety they found the nearest to their own image. The Methodists were a powerful force now in the industrial towns and they set up their own committee, directing strenuous efforts for Wilberforce

---

Radcliffe was later to earn himself a baronetcy and popular hatred for his anti-Luddite activities.

[20] *Leeds Intelligencer*, 27 October and 3 November 1806; *Leeds Mercury*, 28 October 1806.
[21] BI: Tuke 110, Circular letter of Tuke and others, printed in *Report of the Proceedings Relative to the Election for Yorkshire* (York, 1806), pp. 29–30; and *Hull Advertiser*, 1 November 1806 (among other papers). See also WYAS(L): WYL250/6/3/9, printed and manuscript address and signatures.

from the York Tavern. Like the Quakers they worked for a massive attendance on nomination day to guarantee Wilberforce's return and to deflect a contest.[22]

As if he were not hurt enough by the wool and slave trade issues, Lascelles suffered from the limited exertions of his principal agent in York, Edward Wolley who, before hearing from Lascelles, had accepted the agency for the Hon Lawrence Dundas in the York city election. This son and heir of Lord Dundas, like all the family, was actively promoting Fawkes wherever he went. Wolley had been retained to handle the organization in the North and East Ridings from York for Lascelles at the last two elections and should have expected to be called upon again, yet he coolly informed Lascelles that he was having such uphill work for Dundas he could give Lascelles only advice until the York election was over. He did order 4,000 handbills, printed and distributed, and engaged the George Inn in Coney Street as a headquarters. In one of his reports, Wolley lumped the York citizens in the Fawkes column. The memory of Fox, 'our Brother Freeman', plus the determination of the Fitzwilliam party elected Dundas and Sir William Milner without a contest. 'Whigs are triumphant here – never to be defeated,' exulted Robert Sinclair, the Recorder.[23]

Even – perhaps especially – in the pre-reform days, electioneering needed personal warmth and open-handedness, neither a Lascelles characteristic. Henry Cholmley of Howsham Hall replied frigidly to Lascelles's letter requesting his presence and vote on nomination day. The letter surely was meant for someone else since 'for the last five years you have hardly deigned to Honour me with a Nod, and that coldness should extend to your Lady, who neither returned my Wife's Card or her Call the last Winter in London – I shall neither attend your Nomination or your Election.' The injury done one Charles Holmes of Leeds dated back even further: 'In 1796,' he replied, 'I was called upon … for my Voate for you and I gave it them thay towld me all my Expences would be paid I Got a Horse and went to York and stayd Till Mr. Fawkes Gave it up and never Got nothing It Cost Me – £3 8s. 0d. Now I am Calld upon a Gain for my Voate But I shall not Give it Till I Get Paid the Last Expences.'[24]

---

[22] WYAS(L): WYL250/6/3/9, Wolley to Nicholson, 24 October 1806; and printed and manuscript address and signatures from the Leeds Circuit.

[23] WYL250/6/3, Wolley to Lascelles, 19, 20, 24 and 26 October 1806; *York Herald*, 25 October 1806; SCC:LAI: WWM, E210, Sinclair to Fitzwilliam, endorsed 1 November 1806.

[24] WYAS(L): WYL250/6/3/9, Chomley to Lascelles, 23 October 1806; Holmes to same, 29 October 1806; Bethell to same, Friday, n.d. References to money are in pre-decimal sterling (pounds, shillings and pence) in which 12 pennies (12d.) = 1 shilling (1s.) = 5 pence (5p.); and 20s. = £1. So £3 8s. 0d. = £3.40. A guinea was worth £1 1s. 0d. (i.e. £1.05).

By 30 October, Lascelles was being pressed to deposit something equal to the £5,000 Fawkes's committee had banked for current expenses and he was told that his adversary's subscription now totalled £76,000 (a wild exaggeration, as it turned out) while Wilberforce was assured of ample funds from London and Yorkshire. An appeal dated 30 October urging his friends on, picturing himself as unable to believe that they would desert him simply because another had applied to them first, was published on the following day as Lascelles penned a dignified withdrawal statement. The editor of the *Leeds Intelligencer* thought he quit from disgust at the ingratitude of a 'certain class'. The final straw may have been a letter from Robert Markham in York disclosing that a joint meeting of Lascelles's and Wilberforce's most influential supporters had concluded on 27 October that Fawkes was sure to be elected and, having to give up one old member, had abandoned Lascelles to press for single votes for Wilberforce. From this day, Wilberforce had canvassed alone. Markham mentioned the names of those at the meeting, labelling them 'Wilberforce first' men. Lascelles's resignation released a flood of flattering and sorrowful addresses from all the places where unmentionable circumstances had prevented him from 'personally consulting the sentiments of the county'.[25]

The versatile Walter Ramsden Hawksworth Fawkes (his father had taken the last of these names when he inherited the Farnley estate in 1786) presented himself in 1806 as a 'plain and independent Country Gentleman' who was 'tired of "crawling between Heaven and Earth" without Occupation'. 'I pant for Employment,' he proclaimed on the hustings. But there was nothing rustic about the man who discovered J.M.W. Turner sketching in the park which overlooked lovely Wharfedale, invited him in and gave him a second home and ample patronage for the next 17 years. Fawkes was descended from an old Yorkshire family, came down from Cambridge in 1788 and gave himself to country pursuits, including duties as a magistrate. He spoke out as occasions offered for moderate parliamentary reform (he became more passionate about that issue as the years passed) and for abolition of the slave trade. He was worth an estimated £7,000 to £8,000 a year, among the county's wealthiest, if not at or near the level of the Wentworth Woodhouse or Harewood families.[26]

---

[25] WYAS(L): WYL250/6/3/9, Wolley to Nicholson, 30 October; Markham to Lascelles, 27 October; Cookson to same, n.d., and Lascelles's draft reply, 5 November 1806; *York Herald*, 1 and 22 November 1806; *York Courant*, 3 and 24 November, 15 and 22 December 1806; *Leeds Intelligencer*, 3 November 1806; *Doncaster Gazette*, 14 November 1806; *Halifax Journal*, 8 November 1806.

[26] *York Courant*, 3 November 1806; *Report of the Proceedings*, pp. 34–8; *Halifax Journal*, 25 October 1806; Turner anecdote from the late C.E. Wrangham; *Turner in Yorkshire*, ed. D. Hill *et al.* (York City Art Gallery: York, 1980); Fawkes, *Speech ... on Parliamentary Reform*; R.W. Smith, 'Political Organization and Canvassing', p. 1550.

Fawkes became a notable agricultural improver, a successful breeder of shorthorns and founder of the Otley Agricultural Society. In the lean 1790s he distributed 20 loads of wheat each week around his neighbourhood and encouraged the millers to grind it free of charge. He was a patriot – a point frequently mentioned in his 1806 electioneering – and served as colonel in the West Yorkshire militia and leader of the Wharfedale Volunteers. At a huge county meeting in York on 28 July 1803, during the French invasion scare, Fawkes delivered a rousing speech for a loyal address, which outshone the orations of Wilberforce and Lascelles. That harangue (too florid for Wilberforce's taste) was celebrated for years and recalled in the 1806 canvass. There were those who thought that in Parliament he could rival Pitt or Fox. His tastes for history, art and literature led in 1810 to publication of an ambitious *Chronology of the History of Modern Europe From ... 475 ... to 1793* and a magnificent two-volume edition of Horace.[27]

Only in 1796, however, had he stepped forward as a county candidate, and met a discouraging response. In 1806 the climate was different. Earl Fitzwilliam had resigned from the government to make room for Lord Holland, but he was still a member of the cabinet without portfolio. With Grenville at Fox's funeral, the talk had run to regaining Yorkshire, and Lascelles's known unpopularity provided the opening. Fitzwilliam's big battalions organized by his Yorkshire agent, Charles Bowns, were quickly alerted and Fawkes was 'Mounted – armed cap a pied (the Training complete), & ready to start' before Wilberforce or Lascelles knew that the election was imminent. With some trepidation, Fawkes had left London on 14 October and on the 18th he sent a messenger with a letter to his Wharfedale neighbour Lascelles and sent out an address to the freeholders as well as letters to 'every man of [£]100 per. an. in the West Riding'. Good care also was taken of the other two Ridings. 'The Die is thus cast, my D[ea]r Lord – & we must stand the hazard,' he wrote to Fitzwilliam.[28]

---

[27] R.V. Taylor, *Yorkshire Anecdotes* (Whittaker: 1887), pp. 105–7; *Proceedings of the County Meeting ... 28 July 1803* (A. Bartholoman: York, 1803) (reprint of *York Herald* article of 30 July 1803); Wilberforce, *Life*, vol. 3, p. 111; [Joseph Farington], *Farington Diary*, ed. James Grieg, 8 vols (Hutchinson: 1922–28), vol. 4, p. 108; James Hamilton, 'Fawkes, Walter Ramsden Hawkesworth (1769–1825)', *Oxford Dictionary of National Biography* (Oxford University Press: Oxford, 2004); W. Stokes and R.G. Thorne, 'Fawkes, Walter Ramsden (1769–1825), of Farnley Hall, Yorks' in *The History of Parliament: the House of Commons, 1790–1820*, ed. R.G. Thorne, vol. 3, pp. 730–1.

[28] SCC:LAI: WWM, E209a, correspondence before Fawkes's announcement; Smith, 'Yorkshire Elections', p. 69; WYAS(L): WYL250/6/3/9, Cookson to Lascelles, Saturday, n.d., and Thursday evening, n.d.

To Lascelles (and as soon to everyone) he revealed the hitherto unsuspected fact that to be a county member was the great aim of his life and this time 'my friends have ... so numerously & so powerfully called upon me that it is vain for me any longer to resist'. One circumstance only pained him – that he and Lascelles would meet again in the Castle Yard. He prayed the contest might be conducted 'without a shadow of asperity on our parts'. To which Lascelles replied, 'It is equally painful to me that there should be even a Prospect of our being obliged to meet in hostility ... But ... I hope & trust the Castle Yard will be the only Place where any degree of enmity may prevail'.[29]

Anyone who forced a contest had to answer the serious charge of 'disturbing the peace of the county'. 'Some demon of prodigious vanity and vast ill nature must have taken possession of the Gent[lema]n that moves him to kick against his Neighbour, and without cause to disturb the peace of this large County,' one outraged opponent declared. Walter Spencer Stanhope was both irate and astonished that Fawkes 'has been gulled into a Resolution to disturb the Peace of the County. He will find the Fruit sour that was ripening for his Mouth.' Fawkes, of course, used the time-worn plea that he had succumbed to 'most flattering Promises of Support from a very numerous Body of Freeholders', and the *Leeds Mercury* indignantly defended the right of any county to seek talent such as Fawkes possessed in a time of crisis. 'Let those then, who boast of long and tried services, recollect, that it is not the length, but the importance of the service rendered, which can justly claim to be remunerated with the gratitude ... of the Country.'[30]

Canvassers, both gentleman friends and hired agents, usually attorneys, scattered in every direction to seek single votes for Fawkes at first, hinting that there would be no contest since neither of the old members had yet been heard from. Even without the King's usual assistance, the government had influence to bring to bear and Fitzwilliam solicited Lord Grenville for 'at least the countenance of government' for Fawkes, citing his early spectacular success in the cloth district canvass. Which of the two sitting members would go to the wall he did not know; he thought Wilberforce the stronger in numbers, but not in purse. Grenville replied with an urgent request that Wilberforce be supported along with Fawkes. 'Independently of my own long friendship and sincere regard for him, I really think that his character is such as would render his rejection much to be lamented,' said Grenville. 'Lascelles, though undoubtedly a man of fair, and honourable character, is a decided political enemy. ... Both the sentiments and conduct of Wilberforce have been

---

[29] SCC:LAI: WWM, E209a, Fawkes to Fitzwilliam, Saturday [18 October 1806]; WYAS(L): WYL250/6/3/9, Fawkes to Lascelles and draft reply, 18 October 1806.

[30] WYAS(L): WYL250/6/3/9, Cooke to Vavasour, 29 October and Stanhope to Lascelles, 20 October 1806; *York Courant*, 20 October 1806; *Leeds Mercury*, 25 October 1806.

uniformly friendly to the present Government; and in the last session, he gave us active and useful assistance ... on the military questions. It would give me great pain if he had reason to think that there was any slackness on the part of Government in giving him in return such aid as is in our power; and it would certainly be very impolitic to suffer, if we can prevent it, the election of Lascelles.'

To this Fitzwilliam replied that Fawkes's friends already were more inclined to Wilberforce than Lascelles, but that they would have to act in the way best calculated to avoid a poll which might cost each side some £50,000 to £60,000. Fawkes might get off lightly, because so many clothiers were willing to pay their own way to York and many of them would give their second votes to Wilberforce anyhow.

So far (this was 30 October) Wilberforce and Lascelles stood alone, wrote Fitzwilliam, 'But I am much afraid the private convesation of W will not do much to strengthen the favourable disposition of Fawkes's friends ... To a particular friend of mine ... he acknowledged a preference for Lascelles. ... what must be his language to a friend of Lascelles?' It was part of the general treachery, a friend warned Lascelles: 'even Ld. Fitzwilliam, who was said ... to favour your Interest after Mr. Fawkes's, is now understood to have signified to his friends in the East Riding that his real wish is to support Fawkes & Wilberforce.' The ubiquitous William Cookson had some explaining to do to Earl Fitzwilliam after bandying it about that the earl had promised to support Wilberforce if he stood aloof from Lascelles. Fitzwilliam firmly assured him that his concern was confined to Fawkes. Fitzwilliam did not enjoy helping Wilberforce.

Some landed men refused to bend to Grenville's pressure. In 1784, one protested, he had thought Wilberforce an improper representative for the county and he thought so still. Robert Sinclair, however, agreed with Grenville. 'I by no means like Wilberforce,' he wrote. 'There can be little doubt however but that it is of infinitely greater consequence as well to the Independence of the County as to the strengthening of the present Administration that we get rid of Lascelles instead of him.' For his part, Lascelles could scarcely believe that the Government which had supported the better regulation of the woollen trade would take advantage of the unpopularity he had incurred 'to promote a third candidate'.[31] Everywhere Lascelles was shunned Fawkes was welcomed with open arms and encouraged to expect that he would take 90 of every 100

---

[31] *Report on the [Grenville] Manuscripts ... at Dropmore*, Historical Manuscripts Commission, vol. 8 (HMSO: 1912), pp. 392–3, 406, 412; WYAS(L): WYL250/6/3/9, Whiteley to Lascelles, n.d. [28/29 October 1806]; SCC:LAI: WWM, E209, Lee to Fitzwilliam, 31 October, Cookson to same, 11 November, Fitzwilliam to Cookson 14 November, Cookson to Fitzwilliam [16 November] 1806; E209a, Mackenzie to Fitzwilliam, 23 October and

votes in the West Riding. He could hardly credit his own reception and it startled his supporters and opponents alike. Leeds, Bradford, Wakefield, and Halifax fell in his circuit of the towns. With a promise in advance of support from the Cloth Hall trustees, he walked the halls at Leeds on 21 October to the 'unbounded acclamations' of an estimated 10,000 freeholders, and his carriage was dragged through the streets. In his speech in the yard of the Coloured Cloth Hall, he rejected accusations that he was a mere puppet of the Whig party: he was no man's tool. When he vowed strict attention to their industry in Parliament, his civilities 'jerk'd them out of their particular alienation against Foxites', Lascelles was told.[32]

'Yesterday was a glorious day for our cause,' Fawkes reported to Fitzwilliam. 'I shall go and administer another dose to our adversaries at Bradford 'tomorrow' (23 October), which he did. On the 24th he visited Wakefield where the *Star* that morning had carried the 'news' that 'Colonel Fawkes has entered upon his canvass with spirit, and we hear with a success highly flattering to him and his friends'. The next day, Saturday, was Halifax market and Fawkes expected some trouble on the 'no popery' front because a 'priest has been busy there with my character'. But he was given an ecstatic welcome, dragged a mile into town, addressed a multitude in the Piece Hall and was carried on the shoulders of a crowd to the Talbot Inn. 'I really was quite afraid for him,' his brother, Francis Hawksworth, confessed to Fitzwilliam, adding his certainty that Fawkes 'has won your battle'.[33] Sir George Armytage of Kirklees, who canvassed the Huddersfield and Saddleworth clothiers and collared nearly 500 votes in the latter place alone, let Joseph Radcliffe and other Wilberforce partisans go round the Huddersfield cloth hall first and watched them emerge 'with despair on their countenance'. Both old members were disliked; he could not tell which was the most unpopular. Lascelles's friends who saw the Huddersfield turnout thought that Fawkes was strong only with '*second rate* merchants, small freeholders & nobility'. Many gentlemen were not there. 'It is with sincere regret that I mention my opinion that Mr. Wilb. has preserved the good will of the people about Huddersfield by some speeches in favour of the Domestic System of Manufacturing whilst the more manly part acted by you has exposed you to the ill will of a numerous sett of freeholders whose

---

Sinclair to same, 22 October 1806; WYAS(L): WYL250/6/3/9, Lascelles to Rose, 12 November, same to Bernard, 2 November 1806.

[32] *Leeds Mercury*, and *York Herald*, 25 October 1806; SCC:LAI: WWM, E209e, Fawkes to Fitzwilliam, 20 October, and Hawkesworth to same, 20 October 1806; *York Courant*, 27 October 1806; WYAS(L): WYL250/6/3/9, Cookson to Lascelles n.d.

[33] SCC:LAI: WWM, E209e, Fawkes to Fitzwilliam [22 October] 1806; *Wakefield Star*, 24 October 1806; SCC:LAI: WWM, E209e, Hawkesworth to Fitzwilliam, 25 October [1806].

enthusiasm ... cannot be corrected ... by any means possible,' a Huddersfield correspondent reported to Lascelles.³⁴

Fawkes was ushered into York on 29 October with a band leading his carriage and the crowd to his headquarters at Etridge's Inn in Lendal.

During his canvass, Fawkes exploited the slave trade controversy in handbills and letters to the press but ignored it in his public appearances, as did Wilberforce, and, of course, Lascelles. As soon as the issue was raised by the Quakers and abolitionists on Wilberforce's behalf, Fawkes's posters and paragraphs appeared to tell the public that he as well as Wilberforce 'has ever held, the SLAVE TRADE in the deepest abhorrence, and that he has solemnly pledged himself to make every exertion in his power, whether in or out of Parliament, for the purpose of disburthening this Nation of the sin of that most abominable traffic'.

His canvass returns before nomination day on 6 November showed 9,056 votes: 6,582 in the West Riding, 1,374 in the North and 694 in the East, with another 406 in York itself. His expenses were £1,590 19s. 8d. out of a £27,050 subscription of which £11,000 was pledged by Fitzwilliam and his son.³⁵

The nomination ceremony in the Castle Yard and the ritual of election a week later were colourless affairs. But the revolt of freeholders in the cloth district, previously fervent friends of the King, Constitution and sitting members, shook Pittites generally, encouraged Whigs to dream of resurrection and proved to the clothiers themselves that they could 'throw a rascal out'. Wilberforce, distressed at Lascelles's defeat, paid him tribute from the hustings on election day before politely 'stretching out to [Fawkes] the hand which the County had associated with his own'. Fawkes bowed 'in the most affable manner'.

At Wilberforce's celebration dinner in the York Tavern the party saluted the King, the memory of Pitt and 'Mr. Lascelles, and the grateful remembrance of his services'. The joyous Fawkesites at Etridge's hailed Lord Milton and the election committee he had headed at York, the memories of Rockingham and Fox, liberty around the world – but 'May the Tree of French Liberty be planted in Hell, and those who like it, live under it' – and the abolition of the slave trade. Fawkes proposed a toast to Wilberforce and was himself the subject of a verse:

---

[34] SCC:LAI: WWM, E209e, Hawkesworth to Fitzwilliam, 22 October and Armytage to same, 26 October 1806; WYAS(L): WYL250/6/3/9, Bernard to Harewood, 24 October 1806; Kaye to Lascelles, n.d.; W.Y. to Lascelles, Tuesday, n.d.

[35] *York Courant*, 3 November and *York Herald*, 1 November 1806; *York Courant*, 27 October 1806; SCC:LAI: WWM, E226, Report of the State of the Canvass; Peter Jupp, *British and Irish Elections, 1784–1831* (David & Charles: Newton Abbot, 1973), p. 40.

> Here's a Health to the Man who is loyal and brave,
> The Protector of Freedom, the Friend of the Slave,
> The Scourge of the Despot where Tyranny walks,
> Here's a Health, brother Whigs, to the Patriot Fawkes.

The re-election of Wilberforce inspired a lengthy poem which was published in the *York Chronicle* a month later. The opening lines will indicate its message:

> Hark! in the land where Slavery's galling chain
> Scorn'd by the free born mind gives millions pain,
> What gratulations rise! – Again they cry,
> While Hope's gay visions light the tear-dimm'd eye
> Hear Yorkshire, hear! – to you the praise we owe,
> That, list'ning to the voice of Afric's woe,
> You gave her cause its Advocate once more,
> To tell the horrors of this hated shore …[36]

Young Milton's plunge into county politics at this premature opportunity has been mentioned in passing. He was chairman of the Fawkes committee, made a vigorous canvass in the West Riding, and travelled with Fawkes to various towns. He also canvassed York for his cousin, Lawrence Dundas. 'Lord Milton exerts himself much in politicks, his only forte perhaps, however, that is better than if it were his only foible,' remarked Marianne Stanhope.[37] Several of Fitzwilliam's friends, observing Milton in action, wished that he were 21 and eligible to take Lascelles's seat himself – or be a second Whig for the county. 'He is fully equal to it,' said Sir William Milner.

But at 20, the best the earl could do was to give him a seat at Malton where no one would have the temerity to raise the question of the legal age for members. Bryan Cooke kept the other seat there and Henry Grattan, the Irish politician, whom Fitzwilliam had installed at Malton only the year before, accepted the Chiltern Hundreds. Grattan, too, admired Milton's precocious talents.[38]

Milton and Cooke dashed to Malton on 2 November and were elected the following day by the dutiful voters. William Carr, a York alderman, brother of the architect and an old hand in politics, travelled with them and was

---

[36] *York Herald*, 15 November 1806; *York Chronicle*, 20 November 1806; *York Courant*, 17 November 1806; *York Chronicle*, 1 December 1806.
[37] Stirling, *Letter-Bag*, vol. 1, p. 113.
[38] SCC:LAI: WWM, E209a, Denison to Fitzwilliam, 23 October 1806; NRO: F(M), 70/10, Milner to Fitzwilliam, 1 November 1806; [Gower], *Private Correspondence*, vol. 2, p. 65; SCC:LAI: WWM, F127/66, Grattan to Fitzwilliam, 1 May 1805.

delighted with the heir. 'Lord Milton promises well to make a good Canvasser, he shakes by the hand Men and Women smiles at them and they seem pleased with him,' he wrote to Fitzwilliam shortly before the election feast which he dreaded: 'I can't drink any more than Lord Milton – however we must do as well as we can –.'[39]

---

[39] NRO: F(M), X1636, Carr to Fitzwilliam [3 November 1806]; *Leeds Intelligencer*, 24 November 1806.

CHAPTER FIVE

A Note on Contests and Factions

WHAT by clever means or foul had been so successfully dodged in general elections for more years than most Yorkshire electors had lived came to pass in 1807 when three stubborn contenders presented themselves for the county's two seats. Yorkshire's immensity – the distances which had to be covered to reach York by the 20,000 or more electors, most of whom would require free conveyance and refreshment – gave peculiar authority to the preference among weighty men to decide on their representatives in smoke-filled dining rooms after a swift canvass of preferences among those voters who mattered most. In the century beginning in 1732 and ending with the Reform Act twenty general elections and five by-elections occurred but only four polls were taken in Yorkshire: in 1734, 1742 (for one seat), 1807 and 1830. On nine occasions, however, including 1806, disputing interests had to conduct spirited canvasses and in half of the total there were challenges of some kind.[1] What with speeches by the MPs, whom their constituents rarely saw between elections, newspaper advertisements, handbills, posters, cockades and musical bands, there was enough commotion to excite interest even when the ultimate crime of disturbing the peace of the county was averted.

These 'bloodless contests' could be brutal, and Beilby Thompson of Escrick Hall retired not just from a contest at Hedon in 1784 but 'from the World', for 'my Spirits are broke – & I wish *never more* to see the face of *any one* of the Sons of Adam – except those that live in my own Village'. But a political grandee such as the Duke of Norfolk, proprietor of lands, mines and ironworks at Sheffield, relished the battle: 'what greater enjoyment can there be in life than to stand a contested election for Yorkshire, and to win it by one?' It was a sport akin to racing which fitted into the national craze for gambling.[2]

---

[1] R.W. Smith, 'Political Organization', pp. 1539–40, 1560.
[2] SCC:LAI: WWM, F34/95, Thompson to Fitzwilliam, 28 March 1784; Joseph Grego, *History of Parliamentary Elections and Electioneering from the Stuarts to Queen Victoria* (Chatto & Windus: 1892), p. 324; Furneaux, *Wilberforce*, p. 17; Halevy, *History*, p. 198.

Contested elections, in fact, although widely deplored, horrified chiefly those who had to pay the final bills and that larger number – but still a minority – of virtuous persons who were appalled at the bribery and corruption, the free spending and beer swilling that inevitably attended them. Some tradesmen also feared the effect of tumult and venom on business in general and on the reliability of their workmen in particular, for rioting seemed part of the English political tradition.[3]

Where a relatively large electorate existed, nothing was more unpopular than a polite agreement between power brokers to divide the representation and certainly few freemen in York, which existed on patronage of its shops, craftsmen, races, balls and theatre, could ignore the prosperity a lengthy poll would bring. In 1780, Lord John Cavendish and Charles Turner, returned unopposed, placated the people by giving the money that might have gone into 'Balls or Treats' to the poorer freemen. York candidates must needs be admitted freemen by the Corporation as well, with attendant expenses of some £320.[4] The usually disappointed lust of the common voters for a third (even fourth) man to raise the passions and the bidding was exhibited in the farcical events at Beverley and Hull when, during the autumn election of 1806, two men with no slightest idea of seeking that honour found themselves elected to Parliament. Mind you, it was not the first time the worthy freemen of Beverley had refused the offer of only two men for its two seats. Oldfield reports that they actively urged an opposition in 1774 and again in 1780 for fear that if the Pelham interest met no competition 'the loaves and fishes, if not the liquor they swam in, might escape from their possession'. Left to themselves, voters would seek a candidate who was rich, generous and not too inquisitive 'as to the course his money ran', as a Yorkshire historian phrased it.

In 1806, certain Beverley electors unhappily learned that only John Wharton and Lt General N.C. Burton were to stand and, let down by one Alderman Prinsep who preferred Colchester, they literally scoured the countryside until they came upon Lt General Richard Vyse at the head of his volunteer brigade and with his passive consent nominated him. He won – with Wharton – hardly aware that he was a candidate. General Vyse died before the spring election of 1807 and his son topped the poll in another three-cornered single day of balloting.[5]

---

[3] Read, *English Provinces*, pp. 23–4; Halevy, *History*, p. 196.

[4] Collyer, 'Politics in York', p. 15; *Pick's Edition of the State of the Poll for Members of Parliament, to Represent the City of York* (W. Pick: York, 1807), p. 61; William Camidge, *York: Parliamentary Old Time Elections* (York, 1907), p. 14.

[5] *Doncaster Gazette* 14 November 1806; Oldfield, *History*, vol. 2, p. 282; Camidge, *York*, pp. 12–13; H.S. Smith, *Parliamentary Representation*, p. 11; 'Beverley, 1700–1835: Parliamentary Elections' in K.J. Allison (ed.), *A History of the County of York East Riding: Volume 6: The*

Hull's representation traditionally was shared between the mercantile community and the Rockingham or Savile interest, the latter figures having been made honorary high steward and governor, respectively. The mercantile interest had been manifested since 1780, first in Wilberforce and after 1784 by Samuel Thornton. The town had a large and 'undependable' electorate, however, and in 1806 it was avid for the stir and spending of a contest.

William Joseph Denison, a London banker and Foxite who had tried for a Hull seat to no avail in 1802, decided four years later that he did not want to offer again and Fitzwilliam, who had had a run-in with the Pittite John Staniforth over a local appointment, was reconciled to standing aside and letting the two old members – Thornton the Saint and Staniforth the Tory – be returned peacefully. Fitzwilliam's local friends accepted his decision somewhat grudgingly, and plain-speaking Tom Scatcherd told him how much he hated both MPs' principles and how easily Denison could eliminate either one. As the Prince of Wales was expected in the county, Scatcherd added that he would dispatch some potted shrimps to Wentworth House and Denison, serene in London, sent a small turtle for his royal highness.[6]

Daniel Sykes of the commercial branch of the Sykes family reported no sign of an opposition and Samuel Thornton, seeking Fitzwilliam's backing to add to the good wishes of Lord Grenville's administration, made it clear that, like his brothers in Parliament, he could be relied upon to give the administration 'a general & fair support'. In the county, Thornton promised to ignore the candidacy of Lascelles since he was a consistent opponent of the Talents government and to work for the return of Wilberforce and for Fawkes.[7]

Thornton prudently donated 50 guineas towards a charity school but he hardly bothered to canvass. The 'lower sort' among the 1,400 electors were not content with this tidy arrangement and hankered for Denison's known generosity – or at least the liberality which the threat of Denison might stimulate in the others. Only an hour before the nomination meeting outside the Guildhall, Joseph Corfield and his cohorts, canvassing for Prinsep for Beverley at the time and decked in their candidate's pink, rode into Hull and word flashed through the town that Denison (who had chosen pink in

---

borough and liberties of Beverley (1989), pp. 126–31. http://www.british-history.ac.uk/report.aspx?compid=36430 [accessed 31 July 2013].

[6] Gordon Jackson, *Hull in the Eighteenth Century* (Oxford University Press: 1972), p. 302; Hinton, 'General Elections of 1806 and 1807', pp. 121–3; *Report on the [Grenville] Manuscripts*, vol. 8, p. 392; SCC:LAI: WWM, E210, Scatcherd to Fitzwilliam, 19 October and Denison to same, 22 October 1806.

[7] SCC:LAI: WWM, E210, Sykes to Fitzwilliam, 19 October and Thornton to same, 20 and 25 October 1806.

1802) had arrived on the scene. As the nomination speeches began, the crowd bellowed for Denison and the Whigs were 'forced' (in the capable person of Daniel Sykes) to make an energetic nominating speech for him. By the time Samuel Thornton arose on the hustings, the clamour drowned his every word. The balloting, with Thornton trailing from the start, continued until the following midday, when Thornton withdrew. Staniforth and Denison were elected and, as the latter was comfortably distant in London, his delighted supporters chaired 'Honest Tom Scatcherd' in his place.[8]

'We have obtained a signal Victory without giving any Liquor, any Ribbands, or having made any Canvass,' the Rev. Richard Sykes, Daniel's brother, wrote wonderingly to Fitzwilliam. The earl disclaimed any responsibility for the electors' revolt and it was generally conceded that he had not interfered personally. The Whig candidate had won by the voters' ardour plus 'some Dexterity in taking advantage of it', was Daniel Sykes's sly boast.

The happy freeholders were regaled with ale, dispensed without 'riot or confusion' after a celebratory dinner for Denison, who did not come down for that, either. Richard Sykes presided, Daniel spoke for the absent hero and host, and the company toasted the lamented Fox, Earl Fitzwilliam, Sheridan and the proxy candidate, Scatcherd.[9]

The unpredictability of the outcome with a large electorate was a trenchant reason for avoiding a poll if a truce could possibly be arranged. Devonshire and Lincolnshire were the nearest county comparisons to Yorkshire for geographical size and consequent travelling expenses, though neither county had more than about a third of the Yorkshire numbers. Until 1807 Lincolnshire had not seen a contest in 80 years. On the last previous occasion when a sitting MP was challenged by the richest man in the county, the old member had to decide whether to 'part with his seat or his fortune' and wisely chose the former course. Yorkshire with 20,000 or more electors would be the most costly battlefield of all. The 1807 Lincolnshire contest was settled with only a fifth of the qualified voters polled, but nearly all of the Yorkshire electorate would have to be transported, bedded and fed, coming and going over longer distances before the result was determined, for influence was much more diffuse and great numbers were independent of any landlord who might be counted upon to pay their expenses. These would fall upon the candidates.

---

[8] *Hull Advertiser*, 25 October and 1 November 1806; *Doncaster Gazette*, 14 November 1806.
[9] SCC:LAI: WWM, E210, R. Sykes to Fitzwilliam [31 October] 1806; SCC:LAI: WWM, 209b, Etherington to Fitzwilliam, 1 November 1806; *Report on the [Grenville] Manuscripts*, vol. 8, pp. 420–1; NRO: (F(M), 70/25, D. Sykes to Fitzwilliam, 13 December [1806]; *Hull Advertiser*, 22 November 1806.

An extraordinary number of paid agents also would be required simply to cover the ground.[10]

It would make the politics of 1807 much easier to talk about if we could fairly use the terms Whig and Tory as representing then the party system entrenched today, espousing (to oversimplify) broadly liberal and conservative philosophies embodied in party manifestoes. But it would be misleading for, in the early nineteenth century, parties as such were in embryo and although the labels were used – often obliquely – and the attitudes of each body of shifting alliances well understood, the great thing was to claim to be independent. Party designations were considered abusive, although the Whigs, represented by their opponents as a collection of petty cliques, thought of themselves as a body acting as custodian of the 'true national interest' and were more willing to use their historic title than were the Tories who were reluctant to revive memories of their 'traitorous' opposition to the first two Georges. In truth, the politicians and their followers were only groupings, the chief ones having for their now lost leaders those bitter enemies Fox and Pitt. The shield of independence was often a ruse to escape responsibility but self-styled independents held the balance of power in Parliament. The true independent MP was not merely too financially secure in his own property to be tempted by honours or offices; he was also the embodiment of manly virtue and was ambitious for neither wealth nor office. The notion of 'independence' carried with it 'self-mastery, conscience and individual responsibilty'; it conveyed that a individual was 'disinterested, incorruptible and impartial'. Such a representative could be trusted to be bound only by the interests of his constituents.[11]

The party names date to the late seventeenth century when Tories became identified with hereditary monarchy and an exclusive Established Church, while the Whigs stood for a limited monarchy, shutting out Catholic James II, and toleration of Protestant dissent stemming from their historical association with the Scottish Presbyterians. Restraints upon the Crown had been imposed successfully in the Glorious Revolution, and Nonconformists were accepted in general by the first two Hanoverian kings, so as the initial distinctions blurred, current issues came to be decided by groups formed by patronage, family relationships, or constituency interests. George III's open desire to revive the Crown's authority kindled the very party spirit that he – and all 'right minded' politicians – affected to deplore.

He supplied the key issue which now identified the two broad sides: the use or abuse of the royal prerogative, but a better electioneering handle

---

[10] Oldfield, *History*, vol. 3, pp. 280–1; *York Courant*, 25 May 1807; Smith, 'Yorkshire Elections', pp. 63–4.
[11] McCormack, *Independent Man*, p. 2.

for his supporters was found in the pervasive distrust of Catholicism. The Whigs, proponents of tolerance and individual liberty with responsibility, were lumbered with Catholic emancipation: it gave their opponents a unifying and vote-winning slogan – 'No Popery'. Whereas around three-quarters of Yorkshire clergymen of the Established Church voted 'Whig' in 1742, in 1807 the proportions were reversed.[12] Among the followers of the late William Pitt, Church and King were now defining the Tory position much as defence of the Revolutionary Settlement (with its symbolic colour of Orange) rallied the followers of the late Charles James Fox.

Accepting that organized, centralized political parties did not exist as early as 1807, it may be less misleading to speak of the government of the day and the opposition, or, as the *Annual Register* called them, the 'OUTS and the INS'. Systematic opposition, however, was frowned upon if not considered actually disloyal. All legislators were supposed to be serving the King. Frequent changes of ministers were to be deplored. The desirable state was stability. Under George I and George II, from 1714 to 1760, the taint of disloyalty to the House of Hanover (real or imagined) had been used to keep Tories in almost permanent opposition. But under George III and IV, from 1760 to 1830, the leading Whig aristocratic groups were the ones to find themselves out of royal favour for much of the time, not least because of their position on the Catholic issue. Perhaps for this reason they began to develop some of the characteristics of a political party such as emerged in the generation after the reform of Parliament in 1832. But the words 'Tory' and 'Whig' were used at the time, if only as terms of abuse in the heat of an electoral contest, including that of 1807, such that historians have felt justified in employing party terminology, setting down Lascelles and Wilberforce as Tories and Fawkes and Milton as Whigs. Only Wilberforce, who, although a follower of Pitt, did assert his independence on a number of questions and honestly deprecated partisanship, might seriously have quarrelled with this.[13]

---

[12] R. Hall and S. Richardson, *The Anglican clergy and Yorkshire politics in the eighteenth century* (Borthwick Institute: York, 1998), pp. 14, 27–9.

[13] For this section, see A.S. Foord, *His Majesty's Opposition, 1714–1830* (Clarendon Press: Oxford, 1964), pp. 299–466; B.W. Hill, *British Parliamentary Parties, 1742–1832* (Allen & Unwin: 1985), pp. 111–94; F. O'Gorman, *The Emergence of the British Two-Party System, 1760–1832* (Arnold: 1982), pp. 3–80; F. O'Gorman, *The Long Eighteenth Century: British Political and Social History, 1688–1832* (Arnold: 1997), pp. 277–86; *Annual Register* (1807), History of Europe, p. 235.

PART II

THE CONFRONTATION OF 1807

CHAPTER SIX

The Dissolution

WHETHER styled the 'Ministry of All the Talents' or the 'broad-bottomed' cabinet (from the Grenville family's pear shape) the coalition government was an easy mark for satirists. Its peremptory dismissal by George III on 24 March 1807 prompted Gillray to draw the King kicking Lord Grenville from his presence, grasping the hapless peer by the pigtail and raising his sceptre to strike, while ministers fled, rubbing their own backsides. From his majesty tumbled the words 'what! – what! – bring in the Papists! – O you cunning Jesuits, you!' Falling from Grenville's hand is a 'Catholic Bill – for bringing the Papists into Power'. Even ruder is another print in which the King extends his hand to the elderly Duke of Portland to be kissed upon his appointment as the new prime minister while he contemptuously raises the skirt of his royal coat to the departing old ministry.[1]

The King's action was immensely popular and his reputed answer to Lord Grenville when presented with the Catholic bill – 'My Lord, I am one of those who respect an Oath; I have Firmness sufficient to quit my Throne, and retire to a Cottage, or place my Neck upon a Block or a Scaffold, if my People require it; but I have not Resolution to break that Oath which I took in the most solemn Manner at my Coronation' – was emblazoned on huge handbills entitled 'TRUE PATRIOTISM'. Inevitably the 'No Popery' cry was exploited relentlessly by his supporters during the spring election. In Yorkshire the *Leeds Intelligencer* printed a metaphorical jest: 'A bay colt, *All the Talents*, got by *Obstinacy*, out of *Pride*, and bred by *Opposition*, a year, a month, and a day old, was lately *knocked down* to an agent of the POPE, who thought him a fit *back* for his Holiness's *rump*. He made one desperate attempt to throw his late master, but was defeated by that admirable breaker-in, JOHN BULL; and

---

[1] M.D. George, *Catalogue of Political and Personal Satires ... in the British Museum*, vols 5–11 (British Museum: 1935–54), vol. 8 (1947), pp. 410, 516–17 (she calls Gillray a pensioner of Pitt's), pp. 518–19. See Plate 3: 'A Kick at the Broad Bottoms'.

as no fresh jockey presides over the mews of the POPE, we tremble for his Holiness's neck.'[2]

The establishment of the Church of England was settled in the Glorious Revolution of 1688 but the 'Catholic question' lingered on. Both Catholics and nonconforming Protestants were given the right to worship under the 1689 Toleration Act but excluded from holding public offices or military commissions. They adapted surprisingly well, existing and even flourishing alongside their politically acceptable neighbours. Many were of the middling classes and shared the established order's reverence for property and stable government, and Baptists, Presbyterians and Quakers in particular released their energies in business, philanthropic and educational pursuits. During the period of the American and French revolutions, many rejoiced in the destruction of church establishments abroad. Several attempts to lift legal restraints on Nonconformists were made but the harsh climate created by the prolonged French wars favoured the narrow-minded. Besides, the Test and Corporation Acts which technically deprived all Nonconformists of full citizenship were not uniformly applied or enforced. It was an unhappy circumstance, however, that persons such as Sir John Lawson of Brough Hall could employ a blacksmith or a stableman who could vote in Yorkshire while he could not. He believed he 'shou'd be placed in a Situation Equal to theirs, being an Englishman, from my property fully entitled to expect ye same priviledges in point of Loyalty yeilding to no Man'.[3]

Roman Catholics were in many ways a special case. The hostility to them was rooted in English nationalism for it was a widely held conviction that their primary allegiance was to Rome. In 1778 Parliament legislated to allow them to inherit property and because he proposed that bill, Sir George Savile's London house was looted in the Gordon riots of 1780. As the Whigs were identified with sympathy for Catholics, the Marquess of Rockingham was garrisoned during those turbulent days by a justice of the peace and a hundred armed tradesmen, as well as servants and friends who sought refuge with him.

Another advance was made in 1791 when Catholics were permitted to attend mass openly in registered chapels, although marriages by priests were still invalid, funds provided for religious purposes could be confiscated and Catholic soldiers and sailors were compelled to attend Anglican services. Like everyone else, Catholics were taxed to support the state church.

---

[2] One such handbill in SCC:LAI: WWM, E221; *Leeds Intelligencer*, 13 April 1807.

[3] John Bossy, *English Catholic Community, 1570–1850* (Darton, Longman & Todd: 1975), pp. 5–7, 391–3; Read, *English Provinces*, pp. 21–2; David Bogue and James Bennett, *History of Dissenters, from ... 1688, to ... 1808*, 4 vols (Williams & Smith: 1808–12), vol. I, pp. 146–205; Maccoby, *English Radicalism*, pp. 20–37; WYAS(L): WYL250/6/3/9, Lawson to Lascelles, 29 October 1806; SCC:LAI: WWM, E225, Lawson to Fitzwilliam, 10 June 1807.

But Catholics in England were a relatively small body and could safely be ignored when it suited a government to do so. In occupied Ireland, however, they formed the majority and the 'Catholic question' as it affected British politics around the turn of the century was another way of referring to the 'Irish problem'.[4] Needing manpower, the government in 1793 made a few more concessions: Irish Catholics could become commissioned officers but if their troops were stationed, say, in England, they could not command them and 40-shilling freeholders were allowed to vote for members of the Irish Parliament but not to sit in it. Under the threat of Irish unrest – notably a savage peasant revolt in 1798 – and the possibility that France would exploit the Irish sense of injustice, Pitt effected a parliamentary union with an understanding that this would be accompanied by full religious toleration. George III rejected the terms. Pitt was obliged to resign in 1801. The King was promised that the subject would never again be raised while he lived. The vast majority of his subjects, venerating this ailing, aging, upright but determined monarch, thought that this was no less than he deserved.[5]

When All the Talents formed the government after Pitt's death, Ireland impatiently looked to the Whig members – especially Fox and Lord Grenville – to fulfil the Act of Union agreement. There were tentative proposals, discussions, delays and talk of Irish petitions for relief. The cabinet was divided and the King remained obdurate. When Fox died, the Catholics lost their finest spokesman. Grenville and Viscount Howick, now leader in the Commons, intended, however, to move some way towards rectifying the Irish anomalies.

Early in 1807, a bill to provide an extra £5,000 annually for Maynooth College (founded in 1795 so that Irish priests could be trained at home rather than on the continent) came before the Commons and, although assailed by royalists and anti-Catholics led by Spencer Perceval, it passed. Wilberforce risked losing government support for abolition of the slave trade by speaking against it. He confessed that he entertained no 'large and liberal views on religious subjects', even though he agreed that Ireland had been the victim of much bad policy. The important object to Wilberforce was to encourage the spread of Protestantism in Ireland and expansion of priest training would not

---

[4] Belsham, *History*, p. 16; *Georgiana, Extracts from the Correspondence of Georgiana Duchess of Devonshire*, ed. Earl of Bessborough (J. Murray: 1955), p. 47; Bernard Ward, *Eve of Catholic Emancipation*, 3 vols (Longmans: 1911–12), vol. 1, pp. 2–4; M.R. Leys, *Catholics in England, 1559–1829* (Longmans: 1961), p. 140; Bossy, *English Catholic Community*, pp. 5–6, 100.
[5] Leys, *Catholics in England*, pp. 204, 142–3; J.H. Plumb, *First Four Georges* (Batsford: 1956), pp. 141–2. For George III's increasing popularity, see L. Colley, 'The Apotheosis of George III: loyalty, royalty and the British nation, 1760–1820', *Past & Present*, 102 (February 1984), pp. 94–129.

achieve that end. Too soon afterwards, Howick introduced a bill to broaden the 1793 Act which had permitted Irish officers to rise to the rank of colonel in Ireland. The new measure would cover Catholics (and all Nonconformists) in England and the navy as well as the army. Any officer who could take the oath of allegiance could reach the top ranks and there would be freedom of worship in the forces. Confusion surrounds the short history of the 'Catholic bill' as it was called but ministers appear to have thought that the King had reluctantly consented to it, ostensibly swayed by arguments that it would produce needed recruits. They were mistaken or misled. When the King realized that he might find Catholics among his staff officers, he refused to let the bill proceed on the grounds that his coronation oath forbade his consent. The ministers retreated but reserved their right to express their views in Parliament and to re-open the issue at a future date. The King demanded a written pledge that they would never lay before him this bill or anything like it. Grenville, in what a fellow peer termed an act of suicide, refused to surrender the ministry's right and duty to advise the Crown. 'We did not resign but left it to the King to consider whether he chose to change his government,' said Grenville. 'He said he would look about him.' Encouraged by Pittites hungry for office, by the church hierarchy and the defection from the cabinet of Lord Sidmouth, the King asserted his prerogative and in a week the Talents were turned out.

The King called upon the old reliable Duke of Portland – 'infirm, diseased, exhausted – "kept up" in busy times only by laudanum and cordials, and apt to fall asleep over the most important letters' – at the head of what by consensus was a weak and probably temporary government. It included Perceval and Sidmouth.[6]

'It cannot last,' predicted the Rev Francis Wrangham of Hunmanby in a letter to the Earl Fitzwilliam, 'or we shall have a substantial proof, that states like Clocks may be wound up by Blockheads. The cry in "the low prints" has been strong against "All the Talents": we are now, it seems, to try what can be done by the total want of them.'[7]

Defending his attempt to strengthen the welfare and security of the empire, Grenville in the Lords delineated the question before the country as the scope of the King's prerogative. Ministers, he declared, were constitutionally bound

---

[6] *Leeds Intelligencer*, 6 April 1807; Maccoby, *English Radicalism*, pp. 213–21; Ward, *Eve of Catholic Emancipation*, vol. 1, pp. 44–6; *Diary and Correspondence of Charles Abbot, Lord Colchester*, ed. Charles, Lord Colchester, 3 vols (1861), vol. 2, pp. 92–3; *Diaries and Correspondence of James Harris, First Earl of Malmesbury*, ed. 3rd Earl of Malmesbury, 4 vols (R. Bentley: 1844), vol. 4, p. 376; SCC:LAI: WWM, F64/33 and 35, Howick to Fitzwilliam, 17 and 19 March 1807; SCC:LAI: WWM, F64/34, Grenville to Fitzwilliam, 18 March 1807; Harriet Martineau, *History of England, A.D. 1800–1815* (1878), pp. 240–1.

[7] NRO: F(M), 71/45, Wrangham to Fitzwilliam, 28 March 1807.

to advise the King – this was an issue larger than the safety of Ireland. In the Commons, Lord Howick echoed these arguments: it would be criminal in a government to offer anything but the best advice it could frame. Harriet Martineau, the near-contemporary historian, wrote pithily, 'the bigoted and irritable sovereign, while so alarmed for the Protestant Constitution, forgot this great constitutional principle'.[8]

The Whig opposition hoped, with the aid of independent members, to win this point in Parliament and on 9 April Thomas Brand put down a motion that it was contrary to their primary duty for servants of the Crown to promise not to offer any advice they deemed necessary. The newly installed ministers and their friends countered that this was a matter for the King and his government and not a fit subject for public discussion. Walter Fawkes was among the leading advocates for Brand's motion, arguing that the old ministers had paid due deference to the King's august person by discreetly withdrawing their 'Catholic bill' but that to have accepted the fetters of a pledge on future conduct would have been dangerous as well as unconstitutional. Since the debate had widened to consider the whole record of the Grenville administration – with charges that it had promised much but had done nothing – Fawkes pointed to such achievements as avoiding new taxes, abolishing the slave trade, curtailing patronage, reforming Scottish law and attempting to heal the wounds of Ireland. These were issues which, the opposition expected, would bring the independents to their side, but Brand's motion lost by 32. Wilberforce was ill and absent; 42 independents (including nearly all the rest of the Saints) abstained and 59 voted with the King and his new government. The list of the minority was advertised prominently in the provincial press. Fawkes, of course, appeared in it with both the York city members, Dundas and Milner. Milton, still underage, could not vote. In the Lords, where a similar motion was lost by an even greater margin, Fitzwilliam's name appeared in the roll of constitutionalists or Papists, depending upon the point of view.[9]

Press comment was predictably florid and set the tone for the election ahead. The Tory *Leeds Intelligencer* reported gleefully that Brand's motion was *branded* with the fate it deserved for trying to arraign the King in Parliament. 'Nine-tenths of the public have long been aware that the late contemptible Administration did NOTHING, or NOTHING BUT MISCHIEF!' and could not even claim passage of the abolition act since it was not enacted as a government-sponsored measure but by a Commons elected in 1806 on pro-abolition promises. The fallen Talents 'remain in history as *an ambitious*

---

[8] *Parliamentary Debates, House of Lords*, vol. 9, cols 231–44 (26 March 1807); *Parliamentary Debates, House of Commons*, vol. 9, cols 261–80 (26 March 1807); Martineau, *History*, p. 244.
[9] *Leeds Intelligencer*, 13 April 1807; *York Chronicle*, 16 and 23 April 1807; Hinton, 'General Elections', pp. 293–304.

imbecile faction'. The liberal *Sheffield Iris* jumped on the legislators who had caved in before a threat from George Canning (Foreign Secretary) that Parliament would be dissolved and would faced a third election in five years if Brand's motion passed. Canning was twitted as 'a pretty little pocket-politician, who if he had been born a mouse, would probably have seconded the motion in council for belling the cat, though he certainly would not have had the heart to make it'.

The government won a series of subsequent divisions but the margins were too small for comfort and Canning's threat came true: Parliament was dissolved on 29 April by the King's proclamation. The Duke of Portland could be sure of a majority of only 23 in the Commons 'and with that there was no going on'. An election might bring in another 150 to 200 supporters. No government, backed by the King's patronage and purse, ever lost ground in these pre-reform days.[10]

As the voting was to demonstrate, the effort to shift the focus from the controversial 'Catholic bill', the immediate cause of the King's rage, to his demand for pledges – a threat to constitutional liberty – was a total failure. Because even such mild concessions to Catholics alarmed the King, his intensely loyal subjects were equally angered and legalistic arguments over the proper relationship between sovereign and Parliament induced little but yawns. George III had no doubt that he held a veto power over his ministers and when he prorogued Parliament on 27 April, his words were directed over the heads of the politicians to his people. He was anxious, he said, to recur to their sense while recent events were still fresh in mind. He had reigned for 47 years and had fully proved his indulgence and tolerance towards his Roman Catholic subjects as well as others. The proposals brought to him were unfortunate, uncalled for and uncongenial to his people. When the agitation they had aroused passed, all Britain could unite behind the constitution to bring an honourable end to the great war with France.[11]

Everyone but 'partisans of the Papists', according to the *London Courier*, would read the King's speech with pleasure. The people would now determine whether to uphold the 'old Protestant Constitution' or open the door to Catholic principles. No matter how hard the 'Papists' strove to substitute other grounds, 'let us be unanimous in echoing the patriotic cry which has proceeded from the Throne – "No Popery, no Popery"'. The Whiggish *Morning Chronicle* deplored an election based upon the 'senseless and wicked' cry of popery. Ministers themselves did not believe the disputed bill would

---

[10] *Leeds Intelligencer*, 13 April 1807; *Sheffield Iris*, 14 April 1807; *Diaries of Malmesbury*, vol. 4, p. 385.
[11] *Yorkshire Election*, pp. 6–7.

in any way weaken the Established Church, 'Yet such is the shamelessness of political prostitution that they are determined to have a new election ... when religious zeal and bigotry will, it is thought, prove beneficial to Ministerial Candidates'.[12]

Another subject – corruption in high places – briefly distracted the public as Parliament rose. The government was accused of seeking dissolution not just to increase its numbers but to conceal the contents of the report of a select committee on finance. The committee had been set up by the Grenville administration to investigate sinecure offices and Crown placemen. Hints were thrown out that the inquiry would expose the misuse of sums up to £100,000. 'It is absolutely necessary for *certain persons*, that inquiry should be quashed,' the *Morning Chronicle* claimed. Some of the ministers' 'dearest friends and connections' were implicated, but if the dissolution was a part of a conspiracy 'no Court intrigue will secure the peculators from punishment', said a report in the *Hull Advertiser*. The committee was dealing with, among other cases, charges against Thomas Steele, paymaster of the forces under Pitt in 1800, who allegedly diverted £16,000 to the purchase of a private estate. Opposition scribblers were not slow with their broadsides:

> From the friends of the Court
> All your votes and support
>   You cannot in *justice* withhold!
> For so *clever* are they
> As to find a new *way*
>   Of converting their STEELE into GOLD.

The committee's report was ready on the very day – 27 April – that Parliament was prorogued. The opposition insisted, indeed, that its chairman was about to deliver his dreaded message when Black Rod summoned the members to the Lords. The government had acted like a 'gang of pickpockets, who raise a false cry ... to enable a detected accomplice to escape'. It was reasonable to ask why had taken the committee so long to report? One member let slip that only the rumour of a dissolution had stung the members into action.[13]

The trusty device of the 'loyal address' in support of the good old King was used as never before to whip up public passion and 197 declarations were gazetted, all praising the King for upholding the Protestant faith. Thirty-one issued from county meetings. It was exceedingly awkward to object to these

---

[12] *Courier*, 27 and 28 April 1807; *Morning Chronicle*, 27 April 1807.

[13] *Morning Chronicle*, 27 and 28 April 1807; *Hull Advertiser*, 2 May 1807; SCC:LAI: WWM, E150, handbill; *York Chronicle*, 25 June 1807; *Leeds Intelligencer*, 18 May 1807.

expressions of fealty without being perceived as more Catholic than the quiescent English Catholics.

Yorkshire did not send an address but most of its towns did. For some time Leeds, the most important one, had seemed to be hanging back, to the annoyance of the *Intelligencer*. The higher classes in society might be apathetic, but those in inferior circles were fully sensible of the dreadful effects of Catholic relief, thundered the editor. 'No sooner is the question started than the general cry is "We'll have no Catholics! no Popery! Protestants for ever!!!"' A meeting of inhabitants on 2 May at the Moot Hall finally saved the Corporation's face by adopting a suitable testimonial of 'Ardent Zeal for your Majesty's just authority'.[14] Sheffield, Scarborough, Hull, Bridlington, Halifax, Pontefract, Ripon and Wakefield followed suit.[15] The public meeting at Hull can serve as a sample of the public debate. A meeting was called by Mayor R.W. Moxon at the behest of adherents of the Pittite MP, John Staniforth ('a mob of the lowest Mechanicks', said opponents). Orbison Kirkbride, clerk to a Baptist meeting house, circulated the opposition petition but it would not have helped even if it had been called for by fully respectable gentlemen since, as Samuel Martin, a Fitzwilliam friend, admitted, 'our side the Subjt is certainly the unpopular one'. On the day, opposition supporters were loudly heckled and when the question was called, the address, declaring the town's gratitude for the King's paternal care and fortitude was adopted by a 'considerable majority'. It was the sense of the gathering that Hull was not commenting upon the dismissal of certain ministers and the appointment of others but on the dangers lurking in the 'Catholic bill', but opponents saw in the event a highly partisan intention to discredit the old ministers on the eve of the election.[16] Led by the Rev. Richard Sykes they argued that the church stood in no danger in a nation governed by Protestants where almost all landed property was in Protestant hands and Protestants dominated seats of learning; that ancient persecutions had best be forgotten, and that Rome's 'absurd tenets' would gradually vanish in the general diffusion of knowledge. But such opinions were unavailing before speakers such as the Rev. T. Dykes who insisted that the intolerant 'Popish religion' was unchanged since James II attempted to re-establish it, as witness the national catechism recently published by Bonaparte. Qarton Levitt, a merchant, thought the elevation of Catholics in the navy especially sinister for a Catholic captain could establish 'Popery' on board his ship.

---

[14] *Leeds Intelligencer*, 13, 20 and 27 April, 18 May 1807.
[15] *Sheffield Iris*, 5 May 1807; *Hull Packet*, 19 May 1807; TNA: HO, 43/16, Domestic Letter Book, July 1806–June 1808.
[16] SCC:LAI: WWM, F36/23, Martin to Sykes, 26 April 1807; SCC:LAI: WWM, E171/4, Sykes to Fitzwilliam, 28 April 1807; *Hull Advertiser*, 2 May 1807, for a full report of the meeting.

Of all the national issues aired in the general election of 1807 this was the most potent. But had 'No Popery' dictated the Yorkshire result, as it did in many of the county's boroughs, Wilberforce and Lascelles would have coasted to an easy victory. Yet though this did not happen the prediction of Tom Scatcherd that the 'cursed crye of "No Popery" will do our [Whig] cause serious mischief amongst ye *unthink*[*in*]*g* and lower orders of people' did prove accurate.[17]

[17] SCC:LAI: WWM, E177, Scatcherd to Fitzwilliam, 30 April 1807.

CHAPTER SEVEN

The Adversaries

'CONCEIVE the bustle which prevails thro'out this great town,' Marianne Spencer Stanhope wrote to her brother John from Grosvenor Square as Parliament rose. 'The gentlemen are in agonies for their purses, and the ladies for their parties, which must either be postponed or destitute of beaux.' Every post horse was requisitioned as MPs fanned out to their constituencies.

The Duke of Portland had reached his final decision to seek a dissolution on 25 April and sent word to 'confidential friends of Government' that night. The King's proclamation would be delivered on Wednesday 29 April and, following an election, the new house would assemble on 22 June.[1]

The abrupt nature of the election call guaranteed that the canvass would start in disarray. Although Lascelles may have been planning to make a comeback and Wilberforce certainly intended to retain his seat, the sudden withdrawal of Walter Fawkes took the Earl Fitzwilliam entirely by surprise. He received Fawkes's message at Milton in Northamptonshire on Monday the 27th. Fawkes disclosed that he had found Parliament 'profaned by the wicked men who have now got possession of power – The K. to save an illustrious character from impeachment will be advised to go all lengths. The Church & King cry is with him – & our liberties are in jeopardy ... the people have abandoned their rights & are prepared for servitude,' he wrote despairingly. Fawkes's public announcement skirted specifics to say only that after recent Commons events a seat 'which was the first wish of my heart, has ceased to be the object of my ambition'.

Fawkes was not only disillusioned by the rough and tumble of politics but concerned at the cost of another election, his obligations to a large family and his genuine preference for life at Farnley Hall. He was not fond of constituency duties; he had spoken of the alarm he felt when his servant 'brought up a tray full of [Yorkshire] letters in a morning'. More than that, he was tarred by the

---

[1] Stirling, *Letter-Bag*, vol. 1, p. 136; *Courier*, 28 April 1807; *Diaries of Malmesbury*, vol. 4, p. 385.

'No Popery' brush, an early victim of 'that foul, unprincipled, and sanguinary cry', as Sheridan was to say in a public tribute. Fawkes protested to no avail that he had not opened his mouth on the 'Catholic bill' as the pro-government press in Yorkshire alleged.[2]

Shocked, but generous in his response, the earl had only hours to find a candidate or 'the county was to be surrendered into the hands of the Enemy'. It was agreed between them that his son would stand. 'A more vexatious event could not have been imagin'd, being one that all circumstances consider'd placed me in the most awkward situation & involved me in the greatest perplexities,' Fitzwilliam told Dr French Laurence. 'No opportunity for consultation, no means of canvassing the sentiments of others: We had to decide for ourselves, whether after having so lately rescued the county out of hands so hostile to us, we should suffer it to fall back again, without a struggle.'

The leader of the coalition which had crushed Fitzwilliam's designs in 1784, Christopher Wyvill, now sent his good wishes from far-off Torquay. Wyvill steadfastly refused his vote at county elections because the Association compact of 1780 bound him to support only parliamentary reformers. But he was outraged that the present ministers 'have come into Power on the principles of Intolerance, & on a system of unqualified Prerogative. Detesting those principles & that system,' he replied to a letter from Lord Milton, 'I rejoice that You have determined to resist them, by opposing … those candidates who are the Supporters of both. … & although a senseless clammour may mislead a numerous portion of the Electors in some of the Great Towns, it is my hope & very earnest wish that your exertions may completely succeed.' Recent events, he added, only proved that unless county representation could be strengthened at the expense of the 'obnoxious boroughs', the nation's rights and liberties would be sacrificed to the 'enormously increased, & still-increasing Influence of the Crown'.[3]

Lord Milton set out for Yorkshire and his address to the gentlemen, clergy and freeholders was sent from Wentworth on 28 April.

'I take it for granted,' Fitzwilliam had said to Laurence, 'that Lascelles will stand again, & circumstanc'd as things now are, & if he finds a strength

---

[2] SCC:LAI: WWM, F41/34, 35, Fawkes to Fitzwilliam, 25 April 1807; E177/25, 26, same to same [28 April 1807]; *Yorkshire Election*, pp. 7–8; *Sheffield Iris*, 5 May 1807; Baines, *Life*, p. 63; Smith, 'Yorkshire Elections', pp. 57, 73; SCC:LAI: WWM, E173/17, Wrangham to Fitzwilliam, 3 May 1807; Wrangham's notes on Sheridan's words at three public dinners, pasted in Walter Fawkes's *The Chronology of the History of Modern Europe* (York, 1810), copy seen in the possession of the late C.E. Wrangham; *Leeds Mercury*, 11 April 1807.

[3] NRO: F(M), X515/2/1–3, Fitzwilliam to Laurence, 29 April 1807; X515/23/1–3, Fitzwilliam to Baldwin, 1 May 1807; SCC:LAI: WWM, E223, Wyvill to Milton, 3 May 1807.

that will justify his proceeding, I have no doubt of Wilberforce joining with him covertly, if not openly – this makes the undertaking the more arduous, but it must be gone through with – Had we had a little more time, & a fore knowledge of Fawkes's intention, measures might have been taken to fight the battle on more equal terms –.'

From Harewood House on 28 April came Henry Lascelles's address to the electorate. Wilberforce, closer to government councils, was ahead by a day. The 'smart contest' so long avoided was on foot. Fitzwilliam was prepared to spend and Lord Harewood did not ignore the probable cost: the former was prepared to spend £150,000 and expected his future income would be cut by some £4,000 to £5,000 a year and Harewood was ready to invest in the battle the whole of his Barbados property which has been estimated as being worth £97,776 at this time. By one story, Lord Harewood had held up his purse at a public gathering and threatened to use it to crush anyone who blocked Henry's path to the Commons. The story-teller could think of no other qualification for the son with his 'common-rate talents' and poor manner of public speaking.

There was first the delicate problem of Milton's age to be got over. He would not be 21 until 4 May. The first accusation his rivals circulated was that Fawkes had been put up the previous autumn merely to keep the seat warm for his lordship. Fitzwilliam directed that the central committee at York should be composed differently from the one which had served Fawkes and that agents be appointed swiftly to counteract the insinuations. Fawkes, pledging Milton his hearty support, would keep out of the way until Milton and Lascelles were 'fairly pitted'. Those who in 1806 had toiled for Fawkes murmured that his conduct was 'unfortunate'.[4]

The Hon. Henry Lascelles

In spite of a creditable if not a conspicuous ten-year parliamentary career (Pitt himself had said there was no better county member), Henry Lascelles gave an unfortunate impression of being a ditherer and, it may be, slightly penurious. His somewhat precipitate withdrawal from a potential fray in 1806 was fresh in memory and the address with which he launched his candidacy in April 1807 appeared diffident to some. Fitzwilliam had predicted that Lascelles would put himself forward tentatively, to test the breeze. 'It is wholly repugnant to my disposition & habits to enter into the intrigues & cabals of a contested

---

[4] Wilberforce, *Life*, vol. 3, p. 315; Smith, 'Yorkshire Elections', p. 73; Smith, *Slavery*, p. 243, Table 8.4; SCC:LAI: WWM, E177/58, Fitzwilliam to Carr and Nicoll, 1 May 1807; E173/1, Milton to Carr, 25 April 1807; E177/58 and E173/132, Fawkes to Milton [1 May 1807] and 29 April 1807; E170/5, Nicoll to Fitzwilliam, 2 May 1807; *Leeds Mercury*, 31 May 1807; Farington, *Diary*, vol. 4, p. 145.

election,' Lascelles had written after leaving the stage in 1806. He was unsure of Fawkes's intentions the following spring but at least one of his friends doubted that Fawkes would long forego his 'social Comforts, all his Leisure for so many Months in the Year'. Others expected the clothiers to petition again and fail again, with Fawkes this time taking the same unpopular position as Lascelles and Wilberforce and suffering the same discomfort.[5]

The convention of yielding to the demands of admirers was particularly congenial to Lascelles. A substantial body of landed aristocrats, gentry and men in commerce wanted him back as they had made clear in their tributes the previous autumn. They regretted the loss of 'so constitutional a character'. The county's ingratitude mortified them. Now that a more sympathetic, predominantly Pittite administration had returned to power and the country was aroused to defend King and Church, his value and his chances were much enhanced. He was still loathed by the clothiers, of course, but it was deemed unlikely that they could prevail against weightier interests.

His address touched upon the recent 'important and interesting circumstances' which prompted him to think again of a Yorkshire seat because they raised questions of the very security of 'our Constitution and our Establishments'. 'I should act unworthily towards you,' he said, 'if I did not avow my grateful approbation of the firmness with which this Constitution and these Establishments have been lately protected and maintained; and if your sentiments should agree with mine … I cannot forbear hoping I may receive your support.'

Robert Sinclair was not impressed by this 'strange jesuitical address – He seems to throw out Innuendos without having the courage to avow anything explicit – He wishes to set people by the Ears about he knows not what – He wishes to feel the pulse of the county, and afterwards be ready to proceed as the fever may arise – and according to symptoms there is no knowing what may be its paroxisms.' Sinclair believed that if the crunch came, Lascelles would not undertake the expense of a contest for he had learned from Lascelles's agent that he had sent no instructions to begin a canvass or employ agents. 'I cannot see that Lord Harwood's second Son has any right to encourage any such expectations, or that his Services or importance should warrant such vanity,' he added.

The response among Leeds merchants, whom Lascelles met at the Rotation Office on 28 April, was hearty, however; news of Fawkes's withdrawal

---

[5] WYAS(L): WYL250/6/3/9, Rose to Lascelles, 7 November 1806; draft Lascelles to Frank, 12 November 1806; Cookson to Lascelles, n.d., and 2 November [1806]. See Plate 4 for a portrait of Lascelles.

spread and soon Lascelles stood revealed as an 'avowed and unconditional Candidate'.[6]

Lascelles was born on Christmas day 1767 at Stapleton Park to Edward Lascelles (afterwards Baron Harewood) and his wife Anne Chaloner of Guisborough whose father, William, was chairman of the first public meeting of the Yorkshire Association in 1779. Henry is the least known of the 1807 contenders. He attended Harrow School. The opposite in temperament to his elder brother, Edward ('the Beau'), he developed an abiding love of the country and was to die in 1841 from a ruptured blood vessel after a run with the Harewood Hunt. In 1794 he married Henrietta, eldest daughter of Sir John Saunders Sebright of Flamstead in Hertfordshire. Of their engagement, Queen Charlotte wrote, 'The younger Lascelles, *Alias* Cupid, is to marry Miss Seabright. The Gay Lothario is to Wed the Sedate & retired Wife; how they will suit, time will shew; for Beauty there is none, nor Fortune on the Female side. I do not mean by that, that much of either is necessary for real Happiness; but as on the one side there has always been so much pretension to Beauty, I wish there was more Money on the other side. She has been well Educated; as I hear, is possessed of many Talentts, & has behaved with great attention to her Mother; I hope she will be happy.' In marriage Henry shed his playboy reputation thoroughly. By 1807 the couple had seven boys, the youngest only five months old, and two daughters. Another son, a twin, had died soon after birth and two daughters were to be added to the brood.

As the *Gentleman's Magazine* reported solemnly, Lascelles was a 'bright example of a rigid discharge of "home duties"'. As husband, father, charitable squire and friend, he was 'truly great, though unostentatious to simplicity'. He was a faithful public servant, deputy lieutenant of the West Riding from 1796 (until in 1819 he was made lord lieutenant when the Earl Fitzwilliam offended the government by taking part in a public protest against the Peterloo massacre) and an officer in the West Riding militia. His elder brother who properly should have carried the Harewood colours in Yorkshire sat perfunctorily for the family borough of Northallerton.[7]

The Lascelles family was one of Yorkshire's oldest but not until the early

---

[6] *Yorkshire Election*, p. 4 (and all the county press); SCC:LAI: WWM, E170/6, Sinclair to Fitzwilliam, 30 April 1807; *Sheffield Iris*, 5 May 1807.

[7] W.A.J. Archbold, 'Lascelles, Henry, second earl of Harewood (1767–1841)', rev. H.C.G. Matthew, *Oxford Dictionary of National Biography*; R.G. Thorne, 'Lascelles, Hon. Henry (1767–1841), of Harewood House, Yorks' in Thorne, *History of Parliament. The House of Commons, 1790–1820*, vol. 4, pp. 377–80; Mary Mauchline, *Harewood House* (David & Charles: Newton Abbot, 1974), pp. 116, 122; J.W.E. Doyle, *The Official Baronage of England*, 3 vols (Longmans: 1886), vol. 2; Edward William Harcourt (ed.), *Harcourt Papers*, 14 vols (Oxford University Press for private circulation: 1880–1905), vol. 6, pp. 44–5; *Gentleman's*

eighteenth century one of its richest. Picot de Lascelles arrived from Normandy in the train of a nephew of William the Conqueror and was rewarded with land in Richmondshire. The family fortunes were transformed in the eighteenth century through trading, finance and finally plantation ownership in the Caribbean sugar islands. When the slaves were emancipated in 1838, Lord Harewood owned 1,277 slaves on six estates in Barbados and Jamaica.[8]

Their deep Yorkshire roots gave many generations of Lascelles local political prominence. The West Indies wealth extended their influence and allied them with commerce. A succession of Lascelles served in Parliament as members of the West Indies bloc which opposed heavy taxation and restrictions on the slave trade, sought government contracts and assured that the islands were protected in wartime. The West Indies members totalled 169 between 1734 and 1832 and eight of them were Lascelles, up to and including Henry. The anti-slave-trade agitation led by Clarkson and Wilberforce from 1787 onwards had latterly made this lucrative connection something of a political embarrassment. The Lascelles MPs almost always sat for pocket boroughs, almost never spoke in the House, and never figured in national administrations.[9]

They had a long record, however, in the national legislature. Roger de Lascelles was summoned to Parliaments called by Edward I in 1295 and 1296; later heads of the family were a high sheriff and member of the first Elizabeth's Council of the North, and Francis Lascelles, MP for Thirsk, commanded the parliamentarian troops at the siege of Scarborough Castle in 1645.

With the acquisition of the Barbados estates, members of the family began to live on the island. Henry, a son of Daniel born in 1690, was notably successful there. He became Collector of Customs, married a Barbadian heiress and figured in colonial politics. In 1730 he transferred the customs post to a brother Edward but continued to reside in Barbados as planter and merchant until he returned to England permanently in 1743.[10] West Indian

---

Magazine, 17 (1842), pp. 96–8; John Jewell, *Tourist's Companion, or the History and Antiquities of Harewood* (Leeds, 1819); NRO: F(M), 72/10, Fitzwilliam to Lady Fitzwilliam, 9 May 1807.

[8] Smith, *Slavery*, p. 252, Table 8.9.

[9] G.P. Judd IV, *Members of Parliament, 1734–1832* (Yale University Press: New Haven, 1955), pp. 67–8; L.M. Penson, 'London West India Interest in the Eighteenth Century', *English Historical Review*, 36 (1921), p. 380; L.J. Ragatz, *Fall of the Planter Class in the British Caribbean* (Century: New York, 1928), p. 52. English, 'Harewood Mss', p. 14.

[10] Family history drawn from C.J. Davison Ingledew, *History and Antiquities of North Allerton* (Bell & Daldy: 1858), p. 311; John Jones, *History and Antiquities of Harewood* (Simpson, Marshall & Co.: 1859); Jewell, *Tourist's Companion*; R. Rutherford, 'A Distinguished West Indian House', West India Committee *Circular*, 21:172 (5 January 1906), pp. 10–11; Bean, *Parliamentary Representation*; Namier and Brooke, *History*, vol. 3, pp. 22–3; Porritt, *Unreformed*

repatriates were both admired and resented. The story is told that George III and Pitt, on a visit to Weymouth, spotted a recently arrived Jamaican whose carriage with outriders was truly regal. The King was not pleased: 'sugar, sugar, eh?' he is supposed to have said to his prime minister, 'all *that* sugar! How are the duties, eh, Pitt, how are the duties?' No motive other than to acquire the most money in the shortest possible time is known to have actuated those who settled in the Caribbean.[11]

Henry's father died in 1734 and he, the second son, inherited, for his elder brother had died five years earlier. With his now vast fortune, Henry bought the Harewood and Gawthorpe estates in the West Riding to add to the family's Yorkshire holdings. In London he became a director of the East India Company and founded Lascelles & Maxwell, sugar factors, a firm which arranged loans for planters, filled their orders for English goods, and sold their sugar, rum, ginger and cotton. The firm owned shares in ships and handled insurance and investments for its clients. As Whigs devoted to Sir Robert Walpole, the Lascelles lost their patronage in the island when Walpole fell, but to protect their interests Henry in 1745 bought the borough of Northallerton for under £13,000 and was returned at a by-election.

He died in 1753. Of his property, valued at £284,000 plus annuities, £53,000 represented the Yorkshire property while the remainder was in public funds and Barbados plantations. His eldest son, Edwin, inherited most of the estate but one-third went to Daniel, the son to whom he had already transferred his partnership in Lascelles & Maxwell.

Although Edwin held a seat in Parliament for Scarborough, Northallerton and the county for 46 years – from 1744 to 1790 – he is not known to have uttered a word except for one contribution to a debate on a Selby canal bill in 1768. He was usually in the Whig division lobby until he swung over to Pitt in the American war and lost his county seat as a consequence. However, in 1790 he gained a barony. Edwin is remembered chiefly as the builder of Harewood House. He commissioned John Carr of York to erect the mansion on a hill above old Gawthorpe Hall out of locally quarried golden stone in an 1,800 acre park. The young Scot, Robert Adam, was brought in to do the interiors. 'We tickled it up so as to dazzle the eyes of the squire,' said Robert's brother. By 1771, Harewood House was finished and furnished and here Edwin dwelt as an archetypal lord of the manor only twenty miles from the county social capital of York and eight from the industrial centre of Leeds. House and

---

House, pp. 243–4; Richard Pares, *Historian's Business and Other Essays* (Clarendon Press: Oxford, 1961), pp. 199–223.
[11] L. Ragatz, *Old Plantation System in the British West Indies* (Educational Research Bureau: Washington, DC, 1953), pp. 50, 3.

pleasure grounds were open to 'tourists, and all persons of decent appearance' on Saturdays.¹²

Edwin married twice but died childless in 1795 at the age of 82 and the estate (but not the title), conservatively estimated at £50,000 a year, devolved to his cousin Edward, now 55, who had been born in Barbados to Edward Lascelles and Frances Bell, daughter of a member of the Barbadian council. Edward had married Anne Chaloner in 1761 and was the father of four children. He and his elder son and namesake shared an interest in the fine arts. The son studied watercolour painting with Thomas Girtin and patronized Turner extensively. He collected the famed Harewood House Chinese and Sèvres porcelain, hurrying to Paris in 1802 during the Peace of Amiens to buy pieces auctioned by penniless aristocrats. Plump and pretty, 'the Beau' was occasionally mistaken for the Prince of Wales, who resentfully referred to Lascelles as 'the Pretender'.¹³

Between 1761 and 1796, Edward Lascelles spent 19 years in Parliament, even more reticently than his cousin Edwin whose lead he followed in the divisions. He represented Northallerton. From the record, it cannot have been a passion for politics that possessed him to put forward his second son for a county seat in 1796 (Henry's success, and that of the Pitt government that year did, of course, net him a title) or to finance the momentous contest of 1807. But the Lascelles were by now the natural opponents of the Fitzwilliam interest in Yorkshire. This plus the fact that the family was entrenched with the merchants and tradesmen of Leeds and vicinity, a class proportionately unrepresented, must have brought about the decision. Hardly less important was the fact that Lord Harewood was one of the very few rich enough to risk a head-on clash with Fitzwilliam. His total annual income in the years 1799 to 1805, for example, ranged between £51,614 and £64,136, including between £10,695 and £23,217 from the West Indies. At the beginning of 1807 he owned nine plantations in the sugar island of Barbados (two of which

---

¹² Earl of Harewood, 'Harewood House', *York Georgian Society Annual Report* (1970), p. 40; Allen, *History of York*, vol. 3, p. 388; Mauchline, *Harewood House*, pp. 2, 15; Bigland, *Beauties XVI Yorkshire*, pp. 716–17. For a discussion of Henry Lascelles' wealth at the time of his death in 1753, see Smith, *Slavery*, pp. 86–7.

¹³ *Leeds Intelligencer*, 2 February 1795; Gooder, *Parliamentary Representation*, pp. 108–9; Earl of Harewood, 'Harewood House', p. 41; Mauchline, *Harewood*, p. 114; G.E. C[ockayne], *Complete Peerage of England, Scotland, Ireland, Great Britain and the United* Kingdom, 8 vols (1887–98) revised edn, ed. V. Gibbs *et al.*, 14 vols (St Catherine Press: 1910–59), vol. 6 (1926); Tancred Borenius, *Catalogue of the Pictures and Drawings at Harewood House* (privately published by Oxford University Press: 1936), pp. 262, 329, 330; Richard Buckle, *Harewood* (English Life Publications: Derby, 1950; paperback edn [1959]), pp. 2, 20; Hugh Tait, 'Sèvres Porcelain in the Collection of the Earl of Harewood', *Apollo*, June 1966, p. 437.

were disposed of in 1807), two in Jamaica and four in Tobago, all acquired between 1773 and 1787. When slavery was finally abolished in 1838, Henry Lascelles, then the second Earl of Harewood, received £26,309 compensation for the 1,277 slaves on the four Barbadian and two Jamaican estates which were still in his possession at abolition. In the run-up to the 1807 election, perhaps as a precaution in case of failure, or simply to increase his influence, Lord Harewood bought the borough of Westbury in Wiltshire for a reported £10,000 and Edward stood for Parliament there as well as for Northallerton.[14]

Henry Lascelles did two things as an MP that attracted notice beyond his home county or the sugar islands. As we know in 1806, he moved for a state funeral for Pitt. Four years before that he had the honour of seconding the nomination of Charles Abbot (later Lord Colchester) for Speaker, not then quite the impartial office it has become. ('I perceive they have chosen that fool Abbott Speaker without any opposition,' young Lord Milton wrote to his mama.) The year 1806 was a busy one for Lascelles, for during the session he also was heard on the pig iron tax and the wool bill.[15] His votes and his views usually coincided with Wilberforce's. Lascelles opposed Catholic relief, supported restricted corn imports to protect British agriculture, and on issues affecting the wool trade reflected the views of the rising merchants. He was a firm believer in the wartime suspension of *habeas corpus*. Speaking in 1799, he argued that the repressive measures had brought general tranquillity; all 'well affected' people should be protected against the 'disaffected'. He was a steady supporter of Pitt's war policies, agreed to the peace in 1801 and in 1803 backed the resumption of the conflict and expansion of the military forces. Like Wilberforce, he was much occupied in preparing and seeing through Parliament such purely local bills as those to authorize new court houses in the West Riding, enlarge the Scarborough harbour, establish a judges' lodging in York, repair old roads or build new ones, permit enclosures or raise money for canals.[16]

When George Rose commiserated with Lascelles over his 'retirement' in 1806 – 'What a Conduct on the Part of your late Constituents!' Rose had

---

[14] Collyer, 'Rockingham Connection', p. 263; Smith, *Slavery*, p. 241, table 8.3; p. 250, table 8.7; p. 252, table 8.9; *Leeds Mercury*, 16 May 1807; Ragatz, *Fall*, p. 277; SCC:LAI: WWM, E177/2, Baldwin to Fitzwilliam, 1 May 1807.

[15] *Diary of Charles Abbot*, vol. 1, p. 411; O'Gorman, *Whig Party*, p. 24; NRO: F(M), 61, Milton to Lady Fitzwilliam, 19 November 1802.

[16] *Gentleman's Magazine*, 17 (1842), pp. 96–8; W.A.J. Archbold, 'Lascelles, Henry, second earl of Harewood (1767–1841)', rev. H.C.G. Matthew, *Oxford Dictionary of National Biography*; *Cobbett's Parliamentary History* (1796–1803) – see 19 February 1799, col. 1472 for *habeas corpus*; 4 November 1801, cols 85–6, for attitude to the Peace; and 25 May 1803, col. 1492 for resumption of war; see also, 25 April 1800, col. 116; 28 April 1800, col. 123; 1 May 1800, cols 125–34, 142–3; *Journals of the House of Commons*, vol. 61 (1806).

written, 'and what an Encouragement to a Representative to do his Duty with Firmness' – Lascelles agreed completely that it was his 'strict ... discharge of my public duty' which had caused the quarrel with the clothiers. 'I consider your removal ... as one of the most effectual Blows they have aimed at the Friends of Pitt,' another comforter, Lord Mulgrave, declared. Lucas Nicholson, the Leeds town clerk and Lascelles's agent for the West Riding, assured him that his services would never be forgotten and that he daily heard those 'who most shamefully deserted you, confess their Error'.[17]

Charles William Wentworth Fitzwilliam, Viscount Milton

The Earl Fitzwilliam and his countess, Lady Charlotte Ponsonby, youngest daughter of the second Earl of Bessborough, had been married for 16 years before their only child, Charles William, was born on 4 May 1786 at the town house in Grosvenor Square.[18]

'Ly. Fitzwilliam & Ld. Milton are perfectly well,' a delighted aunt reported two days afterwards. 'She has suckled him several times without the least pain, one could hardly have conceived it possible she could have been so well after what she has gone through, & I think in my life I never saw so happy a creature as Ld. Fitz. He really is almost out of his senses with joy, & can see, think & talk of nothing but his child.'

The example of the Fitzwilliams' tardy parenthood was trotted out many years later by Sydney Smith to illustrate the folly of despair over the delayed advent of children: 'the old Lady Fitzwilliam was 22 [*sic*] years in Composing the present Lord Fitzwilliam the excellent and original Simon Pure of the House of Lords. The surgeons not having the smallest idea of her real situation were just about to Tap her for the Dropsy when Praise God Barebones made his appearance.'[19]

One of Lord Milton's ancestors, reputedly an officer in the army of the Conqueror, for it was fashionable to find a link to the Norman invaders, was said to have been so brave at the Battle of Hastings that William unwound

---

[17] WYAS(L): WYL250/6/3/9, Rose to Lascelles, 7 November and reply 12 November 1806; Mulgrave to Lascelles, n.d.; Nicholson to Lascelles, 15 November [1806].

[18] G.B. Smith, 'Fitzwilliam, Charles William Wentworth, third Earl Fitzwilliam in the peerage of Great Britain and fifth Earl Fitzwilliam in the peerage of Ireland (1786–1857)', rev. H.C.G. Matthew, *Oxford Dictionary of National Biography*; R.G. Thorne, 'Fitzwilliam, Charles William Wentworth, Visct Milton (1786–1857)' in Thorne, *History of Parliament. The House of Commons, 1790–1820*, vol. 3, pp. 769–74. See Plate 5 for a portrait of Lord Milton.

[19] *Lady Bessborough and Her Family Circle*, eds Earl of Bessborough and A. Aspinall (J. Murray: 1940), p. 38; *Letters of Sydney Smith*, ed. Nowell C. Smith, 2 vols (Clarendon Press: Oxford, 1953), vol. 2, p. 750.

the scarf from his own arm and tied it around his; later it became a family christening mantle. As a baptismal present for Milton, Lady Godolphin, one of his sponsors, restored to the family a watch given in 1587 by Mary Queen of Scots to the third Sir William Fitzwilliam who then held the sinecure office of gaoler at Fotheringay Castle, as well as being lord deputy of Ireland.[20] The family indisputably was securely linked to glory, but its fortunes were founded by the first Sir William, wool stapler and merchant tailor, who became Cardinal Wolsey's treasurer. He was the only Fitzwilliam who really made money; his income in the 1530s was reckoned at a fabulous £400 a year. It was he who invested in land, first in Essex and later in Northamptonshire with its splendid pastures for sheep. He bought Milton and other manors in 1502 for £800. The estates were later expanded by purchase, marriage and inheritance to make the family one of the largest landowners in Britain. In 1620 the son of the fourth Sir William was made an Irish lord. Advancement to the English peerage followed in 1742. Thus the Lord Fitzwilliam of 1807 was the second earl in the English and the fourth in the Irish peerage. The first (English) earl in 1744 married Lady Anne Wentworth, eldest daughter of the first Marquess of Rockingham and sister of the Whig leader upon whose death in 1782 that enormous fortune came to Milton's father.[21]

The Fitzwilliam family seat was Milton House west of Peterborough and it remained a favourite residence, although after Rockingham's death, Wentworth Woodhouse, four miles from Rotherham, was the base for lordly entertainments and administration of political, agricultural and industrial affairs. By the early nineteenth century, these reached well beyond farming into coal and ironstone mining, pottery making and canal building – a veritable business empire. The houses were almost equally splendid, Milton an imposing combination of long, low Tudor battlements and classical Georgian 'improvements', Wentworth, after its reconstruction in the mid-eighteenth century, boasting a palatial east front 606 feet long.[22]

---

[20] J.T. Ward, 'The Earls Fitzwilliam and the Wentworth Woodhouse Estate in the Nineteenth Century', *Yorkshire Bulletin of Economic and Social Research*, 12 (1960), p. 19; Smith, *Whig Principles*, pp. 1, 2, 25 n. 4; Taylor, *Yorkshire Anecdotes*, vol. 2, p. 110; Christopher Hussey, 'Milton, Northamptonshire', *Country Life*, 18 May 1961, pp. 1148, 1151.

[21] Smith, *Whig Principles*, pp. 1ff; Ward, 'The Earls Fitzwilliam', pp. 21–2.

[22] Nikolaus Pevsner, *Buildings of England: Northamptonshire* (Penguin Books: Harmondsworth, 1961); Christopher Hussey, *English Country Houses: Early Georgian, 1715–1760* (*Country Life*: 1955), pp. 147–53; Hussey, 'Milton', *Country Life*, 129:3350–3352 (18 and 25 May, 1 June 1961), pp. 1148–51, 1210–13, 1270–4; R.M. Milnes, 'Wentworth Woodhouse and Its Owners', *Yorkshire Archaeological and Topographical Journal*, 6 (1881), pp. 344–65; Bigland, *Beauties XVI Yorkshire*, p. 834.

The life led in such magnificence is difficult even to imagine. At Wentworth, for example, there was a household staff of 100. Milton's father was an energetic man, attractive and popular with his contemporaries. Among his recreations, hunting stood first and racing a close second. The pack of the Fitzwilliam Hunt was housed at Milton in a romantic eighteenth-century folly meant to look like a ruined castle, and cost £1,000 a year. The racing stables at Wentworth took another £1,500–£3,000 annually. It was not all outgoings, of course. In 1807 the earl won £2,822 at the York and Doncaster race tracks, a net, after subscriptions, of £2,045.[23]

Lord Milton was from birth a great object of attention. When the Prince of Wales visited Wentworth in 1789, he held the 3-year-old in his arms before a charmed crowd thronging Wentworth park. Adored by his parents, Milton grew into an affectionate son in return. His mother preserved a quantity of his childish letters which seem to have been composed almost daily: 'Dear Mama, I hope you are better. I am just going to Breakfast. Love to Papa. Milton,' and others in that vein. His letters from Eton, where he went with his tutor at 10, were almost equally brief but more interesting. His tutor, Edward Jenkins, thought at first Milton was too meek for boarding school (he picked up a nickname, 'Old Lady Milton') but he soon got the hang of it and Jenkins could report the lad 'fights his way among the boys much better now' and shared the new rage for football.[24] Milton did not proceed to university, but his education was encouraged not only by his parents, both grounded in the classics, but by Dr French Laurence who set him a study of English constitutional history. Because of the French war, he did not make a leisurely grand tour as his father had done and his interests turned early to politics and economics. He developed a wide-ranging intellect and keen curiosity about natural history and scientific developments. In time he became a fellow of several learned societies and the first president of the British Association. Because of his lanky physique, earnestness and disapproval of reading novels or wasting time, Milton earned from Creevey the nickname 'Praise God Barebones' which Sydney Smith borrowed. He had shiny carroty hair. He, too, loved hunting and riding, but he grew up to be more solemn and less grandiloquent than his father.[25]

---

[23] *Farington Diary*, vol. 8, p. 98; Juliet Smith, *Shell Guide to Northamptonshire* (Faber: 1956), p. 78; Thompson, *English Landed Society*, pp. 147, 97; SCC:LAI: WWM, F130/1, Payments and Accounts Doncaster and York Racing Stakes.

[24] NRO: F(M), 44, Milton to Lady Fitzwilliam, 27 September 1792 and others; NRO: F(M), 50, Jenkins to Fitzwilliam, 10 and 14 November 1796, and others; Stirling, *Letter-Bag*, pp. 1140.

[25] Smith, *Whig Principles*, pp. 223–4; Graham Mee, *Aristocratic Enterprise: The Fitzwilliam Industrial Undertakings, 1795–1857* (Blackie: Glasgow, 1975), p. 7; David Spring, 'Earl

On his trial run in Yorkshire politics in 1806, Milton had shown an aptitude that delighted those with the old Whig interest at heart. He gave his maiden speech in Parliament on 23 February 1807 in favour of the abolition of the slave trade. Lord Howick congratulated Lord Fitzwilliam: 'Without any previous preparation, & occasioned only by the state of the debate, all he said was in point, sensible & animated & his delivery very good.' Lord Dorchester could never forgive himself for missing the debut, but he heard Milton's praises sung on all sides. Milton, underage, could not vote on the bill and Fitzwilliam was confined with a cold when the vote came in the Lords. He had once opposed abolition, ostensibly for commercial reasons, but in 1806 supported the resolution which committed Parliament to end the trade.

Dr Laurence was astonished at the eloquence he discerned in a printed account of one of Milton's electioneering addresses. When Milton had to say something twice, the fond friend commented, he always improved or adorned the thought. 'He was marked almost as a special gift of providence ... & he seems destined to be a prodigy,' said Laurence proudly. Milton clearly enjoyed public speaking. Edward Baines, the Leeds editor, was to recall Milton on the hustings 'erect as a dart, his fine eye dilating, and a smile of proud honour upon his lips, whilst his voice rose under emotion to a Stentorian compass, and he thundered forth his denunciations of whatever he deemed unjust and wrong. He was not eloquent ... but so noble was his spirit ... he produced a popular effect upon his audience which few orators could surpass.'[26]

Milton was also forward in love. He married on 8 July 1806 his 17-year-old cousin, Mary, fourth daughter of the first Lord Dundas. The Duchess of Devonshire thought Milton was lucky for, although clever and sensible, 'so odd in person and so unlike other people it was a great chance against him ever finding any woman who liked him for himself'. However, she added, 'he is so steady there is no fear of his finding out in a few years that he likes many better than her'.[27] Mary was pregnant and remained in London during the hectic election of 1807. Milton's views at this time were essentially those of his father, with whom his relations were always close and trusting. With Fox dead, Fitzwilliam invested his public ambition in his son and to him as to others of the new Whig generation he became counsellor and

---

Fitzwilliam and the Corn Laws', *American Historical Review*, 59:2 (1954),), pp. 289–90; NRO: F(M), X1636, lock of Milton's hair sent by his mother to his father; *Letters of Sydney Smith*, vol. 1, pp. 418, 419–20.

[26] NRO: F(M), 71/28, Howick to Fitzwilliam, 26 February 1807; NRO: F(M), 71/29, Dorchester to same, 27 February 1807; *Doncaster Gazette*, 13 February 1807; Smith, *Whig Principles*, p. 286; SCC:LAI: WWM, F48/23, Laurence to Fitzwilliam, 6/7 June 1807; *Leeds Mercury*, 6 October 1857.

[27] Quoted in Smith, *Whig Principles*, p. 283.

conciliator. Milton imbibed his father's opinions on free trade, anti-jacobinism, aristocratic obligations to society, Catholic emancipation and parliamentary reform. On the last, Fitzwilliam believed that the interests of the landless poor were best served by enlightened paternalism, not a form of democracy. Father and son were benefactors of hospitals, infant schools, friendly societies and needy individuals as well as thoughtful caretakers of their tenants. Both were orthodox Anglicans but subscribed to certain evangelical good works and were patrons of the Bible Society. But the Society for the Suppression of Vice, of which Wilberforce was a founder, seemed to Fitzwilliam a profoundly mistaken attempt to legislate morals. Penal laws enacted to purify manners would be absurd or a worse shame because of the 'time-serving and hypocritical motives' which prompted them, he wrote to Wilberforce in 1787. 'Having seen London in flames only seven years ago, we do not wish to put the potent and zealous arm of enthusiasm under the guidance of hypocrisy so soon again.' Wilberforce respected Fitzwilliam in spite of the fact that he did not know the 'true religion' and was to write of the earl years later as 'all benevolence; really there is a seraphic benignity about him ... a finer gentleman cannot be conceived.'[28] Sons of peers were not always welcomed as candidates for the Commons and until 1549 heirs apparent were specifically excluded. As they were en route to the Lords, even after that time some felt that they should settle for a nomination borough and leave the county representation to others.

> Let the Peers know their Place, and from us keep their Distance
> Let their Rank meet Respect, their encroachment Resistance:
> Let them have in *their* House, their due check on the Commons,
> But no Pow'r o'er the Choice, no Control o'er the Summons.

ran a ballad which greeted Lord Althorp's 1806 candidacy in Northamptonshire.[29] The most severe criticism against Milton, however, was his youth, still six days short of 21 when he addressed the freeholders. Even Wilberforce, elected for the borough of Hull six weeks after his 21st birthday, disapproved. He had little doubt that 'Mr. H. Lass & myself will be returned. Without prejudice, Lord M is really too young ... I cannot think it right to treat ye County of York as if it were a petty Borough.'[30]

Milton's 21st birthday parties at Wentworth Woodhouse, Milton, Higham

---

[28] *Ibid.*, pp. 283, 287; Mee, *Aristocratic Enterprise*, pp. 9–22; Forrester, *Northamptonshire Elections*, p. 131; Ford K. Brown, *Fathers of the Victorians, the Age of Wilberforce* (Cambridge University Press: Cambridge, 1961), pp. 256, 241–2 nn. 2, 58; Smith, *Whig Principles*, p. 34.
[29] Forrester, *Northamptonshire Elections*, p. 108.
[30] BL: Add Ms 45,130A, Wilberforce to Acklon, 4 May 1807.

Ferrers and Malton on 4 May 1807 were unavoidably political occasions. The main event was at Wentworth and the county had seen nothing like it since the Marquess of Rockingham came of age in 1751. In spite of rain, an estimated 10,000 people collected in the park to feast on two oxen roasted whole (weighing together 3,360 pounds), 20 sheep and bread made from 240 bushels of wheat, along with 10,000 gallons of ale most of which had been brewed in 1786. The proceedings opened with cannon fire 'whose thunder the soft strains of music succeeded, and the bells of neighbouring churches rung merrily'. There were pony, foot and sack races before at noon the oxen were drawn from the fire, carved and served with the roast mutton and bread at long tables sheltered by the garden terrace wall. The ale flowed from hogsheads into troughs where it was dipped out so freely that a few intemperate guests 'made beasts of themselves'. Indoors, nearly 1,000 tenants and local worthies sat down to loaded tables in the great hall and dining room with the earl and his chaplain, the Rev. John Lowe, as hosts. The 'Bill of the Fare' included 56 dishes of roasted and boiled beef, 42 dishes of roasted and boiled mutton, 7 dishes of lamb, 10 of ham, 6 of calf's head hash, 18 of fowl, 12 of veal, 12 pigeon pies, 40 mutton pies and 75 puddings all washed down with strong ale, small beer and more than 500 bottles of wine, rum, brandy and rum shrub. Lord Milton thanked everyone for coming and then excused himself to hurry to Leeds on his canvass. At Malton the bells rang, a fat ox, its head garlanded and horns tipped in gold, was roasted and 3,000 gallons of ale were poured for a crowd 'representing all the beauty and fashion of the surrounding neighbourhood'. The Higham Ferrers populace feasted on roast ox and fine ale while nearly £400 was spent on grander festivities at Milton House. Ten days later came the finale, a 'grand entertainment' regaling the county's nobility and gentry at Wentworth.[31]

William Wilberforce

Of the trio vying for the two county seats, Wilberforce at 47 was the senior compared with Lascelles, 39, and Milton scarcely 21. So much has been written of Wilberforce, in his own time and ours, that anything but a sketch would be superfluous here. Leader of the parliamentary struggle against the slave trade and influential moral reformer, he attracts continuing study partly because of his immense gifts and complex personality, capable of arousing

---

[31] *Doncaster Gazette*, 8 May 1807; *Sheffield Iris*, 5 May 1807; *Hull Advertiser*, 16 May 1807 – examples of the county press; NRO: F(M), 72/2, Bill of the Fare; *York Herald*, 9 May 1807; Thompson, *English Landed Society*, pp. 78–9; *Northampton Mercury*, 9 and 16 May 1807.

emotions ranging from near worship to disgust with his 'canting hypocrisy' – a 'treacherous subject' indeed for any biographer.

Yorkshire may have been the 'blue ribband' of county seats, but it has sent no one to Parliament of world stature except Wilberforce. In 1980, the 200th anniversary of his first election at Hull, the Anglican Church voted him on to its roll of saints and a biography appeared entitled *God's Politician*.[32] And it is as a moral man in a corrupt society that he is perhaps best remembered. His 1797 book, *A Practical View of the Prevailing Religious Systems of Professed Christians, in the Higher and Middle Classes in this Country, Contrasted with Real Christianity*, became a runaway best seller and the bible of the Evangelical revival. Wilberforce practised – he would say, imperfectly – what he preached. He was an MP for 45 years and in the last 38 of them was guided by no other power than his own conscience,[33] thus often maddening both friend and foe who could not always comprehend its turns. The abolition of the British slave trade (and in his dying year, colonial slavery) was the most important political expression of his evangelicalism. Wilberforce devoted himself to this legislative campaign against powerful court and commercial interests from 1787 until his retirement from Parliament in 1825. Another achievement was the assembling around his frail self of a body of 'independent' MPs, derided as the Saints, who tended to back the ministry of the day but were not 'party' men.

Wilberforce's political views ripened during the period of the French Revolution and war and in this climate he put a premium upon order and looked upon 'party' as its enemy. The chief effect of a party system was that half or more of the country's talents were occupied in thwarting the other half, 'in fomenting discontent, in damping ardour, in checking public spirit', he argued. This created a set of false principles under which party zeal was an excuse for anything. 'I hate it just in proportion as I love my country,' he declared.[34]

Revered for his virtue in his own time and in all classes, if not by all persons, Wilberforce might be assumed to be an easy victor at the polls once his reputation had been established. But that was not the case. As was the

---

[32] White, *Age of George III*, pp. 225–6; Pollock, *Wilberforce*, p. xv; Gash, 'Brougham', p. 77; Garth Lean, *God's Politician* (Darton, Longman & Todd: 1980). See Plate 6 for a portrait of Wilberforce.

[33] Yvette Wilberforce, *William Wilberforce, An Essay* (C.E. Wrangham: 1967), foreword by C.E. Wrangham, p. viii.

[34] Furneaux, *Wilberforce*, p. 49; Brown, *Fathers*, p. 91; Wilberforce, *Life*, vol. 2, pp. 452–9; John Wolffe, 'Wilberforce, William (1759–1833)', *Oxford Dictionary of National Biography*; R.G. Thorne, 'Wilberforce, William (1759–1833)' in Thorne, *History of Parliament. The House of Commons, 1790–1820*, vol. 5, pp. 557–73; W. Hague, *Wilberforce*.

custom, he had bought his way in for Hull in 1780 and acquired his county seat in 1784 by deft manipulation of Pitt government support in combination with the reform movement. He survived intervening elections partly because the Fitzwilliam interest was too shattered to put up any effective opposition. Wilberforce also worked hard for his constituents. In each election, however, many of the great men of Yorkshire would have preferred someone other than Wilberforce. There was always a risk that the first merchant's son to be elected for a county would be replaced by someone more acceptable to the principal landed families. Wilberforce was well aware of this, as he was of the price he paid in some quarters for his leadership in such controversial causes as abolition, the suppression of vice, or the Bible Society, but these activities also brought him adherents. He was a consummate politician; he hated to offend people and he had invincible charm. He preferred to carry a point by persuasion; he had not the ruthlessness for high office. His political life he believed to be an outward manifestation of his religion. He said he did not like electioneering or the bustle of Parliament, but he was good at both.

Wilberforce was born at the High Street house (now the Wilberforce House Museum) in Hull on 24 August 1759, the only son of Robert Wilberforce and Elizabeth Bird, and grandson of Alderman William Wilberforce, twice mayor of Hull, whose ships carried goods between Britain and Russia. Two of William's three sisters died young and in 1768 he lost his father. Wilberforce attended the Hull Grammar School and a boarding school at Putney when, after his father's death, he was sent to live with his Methodist-inclined uncle and aunt. Soon elements of Methodism were detected in the boy's letters home and his shocked mother brought him, heart-broken at 12, back to Hull and entered him at Pocklington School. Said his grandfather, 'if Billy turns Methodist he shall not have a sixpence of mine'. A quarter century later, Wilberforce philosophically viewed his rescue as providential; had he remained with Uncle William, 'I should probably have been a bigoted despised methodist', instead of a useful figure in the highest circles.[35]

Hull was a socially lively town, the family rich and well connected and Wilberforce had the engaging nature to relish society. In 1776, he entered St John's College, Cambridge, where, 'With a great Yorkshire pie crowning his table, and with wit, drollery, and song ever flowing from his lips', he idled away four happy years, a centre of attraction in a fellowship of carefree young gentlemen.[36] The decisive experience in Wilberforce's life was his religious conversion which began in the winter of 1784–85 when the new member for

---

[35] R.W. Smith, 'Political Organization', pp. 1549–53; on Wilberforce's early life, Wilberforce, *Life*, vol. 1; Furneaux, *Wilberforce*; Pollock, *Wilberforce*.

[36] James Stephen, *Essays in Ecclesiastical Biography*, 2 vols (Longmans: 1849), vol. 2, p. 206.

Yorkshire was travelling on the Continent with the Rev. Isaac Milner. In 1787, after intense inner turmoil, he embarked on the serious objects which filled the rest of his life. At 37 Wilberforce married Barbara Ann Spooner, daughter of a well-to-do Birmingham businessman (a merchant, country banker and ironmaster) and by the time of the 1807 election they had completed a family of four sons and two daughters. The baby, Henry, was born at the time the slave trade was abolished. The Wilberforces lived at Broomfield House near Clapham Common, a pleasant villa built by Wilberforce's cousin, best friend and neighbour Henry Thornton. They also had a town house in Palace Yard, Westminster. In 1808 they gave up both and leased a mansion (where the Albert Hall now stands) in the rustic suburb of Kensington.

Wilberforce was well furnished financially though never so wealthy as the 'world imagines'. He was heir to land and money from his father, grandfather and uncle and in 1784 was believed to be worth £2,000 a year with a ready fortune of £25,000. Barbara's marriage portion was a relatively modest £5,000. These figures appear in modern biographies of him. A contemporary thought him worth rather more, setting his income when he came of age at a handsome £10,000 a year. He spent nearly £18,000 on his first two Hull elections but his family was not large and although his eldest son's disastrous speculation later cost him some £50,000, Wilberforce ought to have been able to take such a loss and preserve his station had he husbanded his resources properly, this censorious observer insisted.

Here, then, was a man of the highest motivation, dedication to public service, parliamentary skill, happy family life and 'incomparable readiness to give pleasure, and to be pleased', yet he troubled some constituents and critics elsewhere because he lacked a country seat, took scant interest in his property and gave (too) unstintingly to charity. The Wilberforce family, settled in Yorkshire before the Conquest, had acquired only pieces of farmland. Wilberforce, instead of attending to what contemporary critics regarded as the primary duty in life of superintending, conserving and enhancing his inherited wealth, threw away his life in a 'quixotic crusade against public wrongs and remote injustice'. His mind, it followed, lacked firmness, steadiness and a knowledge of men and the world 'of which he died – at the age of seventy-four – as ignorant as a child' and in a 'borrowed house', as well. The high Tory who reviewed his sons' biography of Wilberforce in 1838 continued incredulously:

> He changed his places of residence as if they were lodging houses ... living successively in every point of the whole circuit of London, and spending his summers in any part of England, in preference to his native and electoral county. His life was that of the Arabs, who spend their existence in wandering and squandering, and think they have

fulfilled their duties, provided they turn themselves to the east at the prescribed hours and say their prayers three times a day.[37]

In his person, Wilberforce was as uncommon as in his attitudes. A foreign visitor, seeing the famous figure for the first time from the gallery of the House of Commons, was astonished by the little man, 'thin as a shadow', moving awkwardly, but graceful in his speech. 'Nothing can surpass the meanness of his appearance, and he seems half-blind,' he recorded in some dismay. He was indeed myopic. The grey eyes, so bright in conversation, had to peer through an eye-glass at papers held at nose length and were a constant source of annoyance to him. One eye finally failed entirely. He was barely five feet tall and weighed about eight stone in his prime. He never knew what it was to feel well and the worst of his afflictions – 'my constitutional complaint', he called it – was the bowel disorder that nearly took his life in 1788. One doctor spoke of his 'calico guts'. Opium pills brought the only relief and Wilberforce took a controlled dose of them daily the rest of his life. For a long debate he would carry a box of sandwiches to restore his energy. The food served in the extravagantly disordered Wilberforce household was awful by any standard but the head of the family was oblivious to any shortcomings in his beloved wife.[38]

Given his place in the forefront of so many sober undertakings, Wilberforce's vivacity must have been another surprise to those who met him for the first time. He was playful, endearingly kind and unaffected. Invited to dine at Sir Richard Hill's, and having no time to dress, he took along a clean shirt, changed there, then bounded into the drawing room with a dancer's leap, crossing his legs in mid-air and ending with a low bow to the company. Mme de Staël dubbed him 'the best converser I have met with in this country'. During lengthy, solemn conferences with Thornton and others of what later was called the Clapham Sect, Wilberforce would get restless, toss a ball or a

---

[37] BOD: AWP, d.56, Letterbook, fol. 44r, Wilberforce to Wyvill, 5 March 1807; Hague, *Wilberforce*, pp. 294–5; Pollock, *Wilberforce*, pp. 157, 318 n. 3; Furneaux, *Wilberforce*, p. 165; *Quarterly Review* (1838), pp. 215–79, review of Wilberforce, *Life*; *Autobiography of the Rev. William Jay* (eds), George Redford and John Angell James (Hamilton Adams: 1854), p. 300; Dr Williams's Library, London, HCR Diary 17, Henry Crabb Robinson MS diary, 22 August 1837–26 October 1839 (22 June 1838).

[38] [Simond], *Journal*, vol. 2, p. 161; SRRC: Corbett of Longnor Papers, Katherine Plymley Ms diary, Book 43 (1796); Furneaux, *Wilberforce*, pp. 10, 76, 78; Stephen, *Essays*, vol. 2, p. 222; Mary Carr, *Thomas Wilkinson, A Friend of Wordsworth* (Headley Bros: 1905), p. 36; Henry, Lord Brougham, *Historical Sketches of Statesmen Who Flourished in the Time of George III*, second edn, 6 vols (C. Knight: 1845), vol. 1, p. 100; Pollock, *Wilberforce*, pp. 76, 78–81; Joshua Wilson, *Biographical Index to the Present House of Commons* (Thomas Goddard: [1808]), p. 680.

flower to the adoring Marianne, Thornton's eldest daughter, or race her across the lawn to warm his feet. He always dressed, however, as a gentleman of the old school, complete with powdered hair.

Farington likened him to a 'Bird which hops from sprig to sprig. ... He talks, reads, is grave, sprightly, playful, absorbed, light & free in such quick succession that unless something of moment fixes His attention ... no hold can be had of Him.' Sydney Smith said, 'He looks like a little Spirit running about without a body'. Out of this fragile being emerged a melodic voice which made occasions of his frequent contributions to Commons debates. He recognized that God had given him a 'certain natural turn for public speaking' and that it was his duty to cultivate it. But he spoke from knowledge, diligently attending committees and steeping himself in his subject beforehand.[39]

What has troubled students of Wilberforce's career is the seeming contradiction put by Eric Williams: he was 'familiar with all that went on in the hold of a slave ship but ignored what went on at the bottom of a mine shaft'. Hazlitt refrained from calling Wilberforce a hypocrite only to damn him as a fine 'specimen of *moral equivocation*', carefully selecting the ground on which he would fight for humanity while guarding his Yorkshire seat.

Each age has its priorities and Wilberforce was not unique in his time for what now would be branded in any public figure as indifference to many distressing problems. The charge in fact is that he did not crusade against all the evils of corruption, gross inequality and cruelty in a day when these were tolerated by the great majority and even defended by many. As Ford K. Brown points out, the Evangelicals were not concerned with what we mean by freedom or reform. The Saints were not secular humanitarians but harbingers of true religion for all.[40]

During the precarious 1790s, Wilberforce steadfastly supported and even initiated repressive acts. Many of his abolitionist colleagues and numbers of Nonconformists found the draconian measures against free speech or assembly unwarranted and some were bitterly disappointed that the champion of liberty, as they had regarded Wilberforce the abolitionist, should lack a 'principled attachment to the civil and religious rights of Men – They cannot suppose him that Foe to Oppression and Slaughter which they once consider'd him.'

---

[39] Harford, *Recollections*, pp. 2,3, 44–5; [Benjamin Silliman], *Journal of Travels in England* (T.B. Wait & Co.: Boston, 1812), p. 197; SRRC: Corbett of Longnor Papers, Katherine Plymley MS diary, Book 43; E.M. Forster, *Marianne Thornton, 1797–1887* (Arnold: 1956), p. 42; Wilberforce, *Life*, vol. 4, pp. 167, 169; vol. 3, p. 59; *Farington Diary*, vol. 8, p. 23; *Letters of Sydney Smith*, vol. 1, p. 469.

[40] Eric Williams, *Capitalism and Slavery* (University of North Carolina Press: Chapel Hill, 1944), p. 182; William Hazlitt, *Spirit of the Age* (Oxford University Press: 1825), pp. 219, 220; Brown, *Fathers*, pp. 376–83, 91, 155.

Wilberforce asked his friend, the Rev. William Jay, the dissenting minister of Bath, to explain to those puzzled or grieved by his support of Pitt's gagging bills that 'times were peculiarly perilous, and it was necessary to support the Government generally, when there were so many tendencies to anarchy and confusion'.[41]

Wilberforce celebrated his 25th birthday in 1784 at York races, attended the seasonal ball and even sang in public. From the time of his conversion, however, he dropped out of the county's social life and was forever grateful that his constituents continued to return their eccentric member:

> In former times the county members displayed their equipages annually at the races, and constituted a part of the grand jury at the summer assizes; the latter indeed I should have been glad to attend but for the unseemly festivities which commonly take place at that period,

he commented, looking back in time.

> I could not consistently with my principles frequent the theatre and ball room, and I knew that I should give offence by staying away were I actually at York; but no discontent was ever expressed at my not presenting myself to the county on these occasions. My friends appeared tacitly to admit my claim to the command of my own time during the recess, satisfied with my attending to their and the public interest during the session of parliament. In fact no man I believe was ever more punctual in his attendance on the House of Commons than myself. I was always in my place on the first day of the session, and I do not remember having been ever absent on the last, excepting once when I was drawn [away] ... by the illness of some of my family.[42]

His loyal Yorkshire friends set his campaign in motion spontaneously in late April 1807, as they had done so many times before. Wilberforce had only just got round to thanking personally Messrs Russell & Bourne of Hull, his agents, for their exertions in 1806 when they were wanted again. They happened to be in London as Wilberforce learned of the impending dissolution. He had been notified early, by the 24 April at least, and the agents set out post haste for Yorkshire. His York committee was at work by the 27th when Wilberforce's address to the freeholders was released and he arrived in York himself on

---

[41] Wilberforce, *Life*, vol. 2, pp. 434–7; vol. 3, p. 269; Pollock, *Wilberforce*, p. 168; Hague, *Wilberforce*, pp. 227–57; SoF: MS vol. 337/15: Gibson MSS, IV fol. 15, Matthews to Phillips, 19 January 1796; *Autobiography of Jay*, p. 317.
[42] Harford, *Recollections*, p. 210; Wilberforce, *Life*, vol. 1, pp. 382–3.

the 30th. In the address, typically, he warned: 'While I express my deep and unalterable gratitude for all your past kindness, let me assure you that should I again receive from you the important Trust which you have Five Times conferred on me, my Conduct will continue to be governed by those Constitutional and Independent Principles, which have been sanctioned by your Approbation during three and twenty years.'[43]

---

[43] StJC: GBR/0275/Wilberforce/5, Wilberforce to Russell and Bourne, 7 March 1807; YA: Acc. 5, 6, 24, 235, Gray Family Papers, J13, Gray to Mrs Gray, 24 April 1807; *Yorkshire Election*, pp. 3–4.

CHAPTER 8

The Canvass, 27 April–13 May

No general election campaign in the modern hybrid region of Yorkshire and Humberside could match in intensity the canvass that swept the old county in 1807. It was accomplished by men (and a few remarkable women) travelling at the pace of horses and scratching out letters with quills, but no one in the most remote dale was left unaware that a titanic struggle was afoot.

Personal approaches to the electors by the candidate or some notable surrogate were indispensable. Calling for a list of friendly nobles and gentlemen, Milton's Beverley agent, Samuel Hall, explained, 'in general the first Question that is asked … [is] by whom is he supported'. The candidates' own overtures had no real substitute, however. Speaking of an influential neighbour who in 1806 was inclined towards Lascelles but was a resolute anti-Pittite, a friend notified Lascelles, 'if you can spare time his vanity I think may be tickled by your thanks. … As he is a friend to Fawkes I was obliged to excite his aversion to Wilberforce & to celebrate you as a sportsman which has more weight with him than any political conduct.'[1]

Both Lascelles and Milton could rely on their fathers as valuable supplicators, and both parents were prime movers behind the scenes. Neither came into the committee rooms or was seen on the hustings but both made strategic decisions and dispatched shoals of letters. The Countess Fitzwilliam also was busy with her pen. It was a tedious business to write hundreds of missives and not one dared be delegated to a secretary.

It was not easy either for the high born to curry favour. Wilberforce, when a novice in politics, 'rather shrunk' from shaking the hand of Johnny Bell, a butcher: 'I thought it going rather too low for votes.' But picture the discomfiture of an earl! When Fitzwilliam requested his old schoolfellow, the Earl of Carlisle, to use his influence in the area around Castle Howard, he

---

[1] SCC:LAI: WWM, E172/10, Hall to Milton committee, 2 May 1807; WYAS(L): WYL250/6/3/9, Bethell to Lascelles, 30 October 1806.

was told, 'My dear Fitzwilliam, whatever votes I can command you shall have; but I could not stoop to ask a favour of any plebian.'

Their ladies were not very pleased with the imposed hospitality of electioneering. 'Our doors are Open to every dirty fellow in the country that is worth forty shillings a year,' complained one reluctant hostess, 'all my best floors are spoiled by the hobnails of farmers stamping about them; every room is a pig-stye, and the Chinese paper in the drawing-room stinks so abominably of punch and tobacco that it would strike you down to come into it.'[2]

Landlords canvassing their tenants sometimes were carried too far in their zeal. 'I heartily wish some friend of Mr. Belasyse would advise him not to incur such odium as he does from his Tenants, by calling upon them for their rents *before they are due*,' an agitated Sir Thomas Frankland of Thirkleby wrote to Lascelles. Absentee proprietors depended on their stewards or land agents to spread the word and at times failed to get the message across. Lady Julia Petre was aghast to learn from Milton that votes for opposition candidates were being collected on her estate near Selby. She gave orders that 'any tenant that refuses to give his Vote or interest for [Lord Milton] shall have immediate notice to give up his Farm, if not on Lease, and also to inform any Lawyer or other Persons that may have been employed by me that if they act contrary to my wishes ... I shall immediately withdraw my Business.' She had only 36 tenants qualified to vote but her agent collected 187 promises for Milton.[3]

Fitzwilliam soon realized that he could not count on the landed interest as much as in 1806 because of the change in government. There were refusals from 'many of the Non-Resident Courtiers' but as they *were* non-resident, and their properties old, their influence was limited to actual tenants for 'they have swallow'd up their small freeholds in the course of time'. Rebuffed by the Earl of Lonsdale on his 1806 application, Fitzwilliam left it to Milton to appeal for his interest in 1807, but the answer was the same. Such 'mortification' in elections was nothing new, Fitzwilliam replied to Lonsdale's letter. 'I am not come to my time of life without having experienced many, many heartfelt disappointments.'

Some respondents provided abundant aid and advice. William James Aislabie, claiming to be the oldest living male of the family influential at both Studley Royal and Pontefract, offered his name and as many pledges from 'outvoters' as he could find from his parsonage in Huntingdonshire and revealed that the Dean of Ripon was against Wilberforce for banning Sunday

---

[2] Furneaux, *Wilberforce*, p. 14; E.D. Cuming (ed.), *Squire Osbaldeston: His Autobiography* (John Lane: 1927), p. 15; Mingay, *English Landed Society*, p. 124.

[3] WYAS(L): WYL250/6/3/9, Frankland to Lascelles, 20 October 1806; SCC:LAI: WWM, E223, Petre to Milton, 6 May 1807; E226, Petre to Fitzwilliam, 11 May 1807; E178/224, Harper to Bowns, 28 May 1809.

newspapers and would therefore be useful in winning over Pittites. Gentlemen away from home with their troops rapidly canvassed for Yorkshire votes among their officers and men.

Haste in getting about the county was absolutely vital, not only from the recurring hope that a show of strength would stave off a contest but also because Yorkshire had an unusual number of freeholders who were 'under no Influence and first come first served'. Whatever his cohorts, the candidate had to exhaust himself in meeting or being seen by as many electors as he could, making himself agreeable and convincing to them, submitting gracefully to criticism or insult.[4]

Certain components were common to the organizations deployed by each of the candidates. Yorkshire was divided for election purposes into 29 districts based on the wapentakes, and each canvass was planned in terms of these territorial divisions. Professional men, usually attorneys, were retained in key towns and they with their clerks were expected to give themselves full time to the canvass, recording the information brought in, spying on the enemy's manoeuvres, chasing up overlooked prospects and finally recruiting manpower for the polling stations. Wherever feasible, a local committee of eminent men was set up to stage triumphal entrances by the travelling candidates, to wine and dine them, to produce and distribute handbills and squibs and to send observations almost daily to the York headquarters. When balloting actually began, the combined local forces would get the voters to the polls.

Each candidate had a skeleton plan left over from previous canvasses. There was no precedent, however, for a fight waged through the full legal allotment of 15 days. The last occasion Yorkshire went to the polls was in January 1742, to choose one of two men for one vacant seat. That contest lasted nine days and 15,049 votes were counted. No one concerned with the running of the 1807 election knew anything more than that about the 1742 events. Scarcely any of the qualified voters of 1742 would still be alive. They would have to be 86 or above, and a handful did emerge, notably Thomas Wade, yeoman, aged 101, who gave Lord Milton a plumper. It was necessary to bone up on the law regarding voter qualifications and bribery and to teach the electors along the way. Many did not know, for example, that each man could cast two votes, one for each of two candidates, or a single vote, a 'plumper', also aptly known as a bullet, for one man only.

In spite of inexperience, the 1807 Yorkshire election was managed so successfully, according to Mr Serjeant Heywood, the Welsh judge who served

---

[4] NRO: F(M), 72/3, Fitzwilliam to Wentworth, 4 May 1807; SCC:LAI: WWM, E226, Fitzwilliam to Lonsdale, 12 May 1807; E178/26, Aislabie to Milton, 11 May 1807; E222, Dixon to Fitzwilliam, 2 May 1807; E173/25, Gossip to Milton, 5 May 1807; E160/3, Allen to Milton committee, 10 May 1807.

in it as a sheriff's assessor, that officials in other counties clamoured to know how it was done. Building on an account that Heywood added to the second edition of his *Digest of the Law Respecting County Elections*, Jonathan Gray, the undersheriff on whom the heaviest burden fell for arranging and supervising the poll, published a handbook, *An Account of the Manner of Proceedings at the Contested Election for Yorkshire, in 1807, Chiefly Relating to the Office of Sheriff*.[5] Gray, the 27-year-old son of William Gray who had so ably directed the Yorkshire Association's activities, had been undersheriff since 1803. Despite the friendship between the Grays, and Wilberforce, there were no complaints about Jonathan's neutrality in his official capacity.

The King's proclamation calling for a new Parliament to be elected was published in London on 29 April and was followed immediately by the dispatch of a writ to every county sheriff who, in turn, had to notify enfranchised boroughs and towns. Within two days of receiving the writ, the sheriff was obliged to announce a county election date, on any day but Sunday and within 10–16 days of the date of the proclamation. Yorkshire's writ was dated 30 April and could have reached Gray the following night. The statute governing the delivery was vague and this bit of paper fell into the hands of a Milton agent who, to gain time, held it up until 4 May, much to the distress of the waiting county and borough officers. Afterwards, perhaps as a result of such interference, the law was changed and thereafter the Postmaster General sent the writs directly to the various postmasters.

Gray lost no time when the belated notice reached York. Acting for the high sheriff, Richard Fountayne Wilson, Gray and the county clerk marched to the Castle Yard to read the proclamation that a 'special county court' would be convened on Wednesday 20 May to elect two knights of the shire. On the same day, Wilberforce's committee formally requested a meeting of freeholders to nominate candidates, and the sheriff's office fixed that event for 13 May.

Wilberforce entered the lists under the neutral colour of pink. Lascelles's champions wore blue, the traditional Tory colour and, incidentally, the choice for the 'blue-cockade banditti' who stormed London in the anti-Catholic riots of 1780. Milton's men paraded in orange, also a symbol of Protestantism, the 1688 revolution and the premier British Orangeman, William III, and probably chosen for these reasons to deflect the charge of 'popery'. The Whigs' usual colours in these days were buff and blue – those of George Washington's army.

Canvassers and candidates still sport rosettes but electioneering now is far drabber than it was in 1807. Then everyone wore a rosette or tucked a

---

[5] Jonathan Gray, *An Account of the Manner of Proceeding at the Contested Election for Yorkshire* (J. Wolstenholme: York, 1818).

cockade or tinted card into a hatband. Horses were arrayed in coloured silks, houses flew the flags of their favourites, and ladies trimmed their bonnets and shawls with appropriate ribbons.[6] Colours were the subject of propaganda, as a Milton handbill shows:

> ORANGE
> Our Gracious Sovereign
> Is Descended from the
> Illustrious House of *Orange.*
> The Ancestors of Lord Milton
> Strenuously assisted in placing
> His Majesty's August Family
> Upon the Throne,
> And are the True Supporters of the
> *King and Constitution*
> Upon its genuine principles.

> BLUE
> This is the constant distinguishing Colour of
> THE TORIES
> who supported the
> Pretender and CIVIL WAR,
> Against those good and virtuous KINGS,
> GEORGE THE FIRST,
> and
> GEORGE THE SECOND.

This was answered by a splashy Lascelles broadside announcing on election day that ORANGES would be auctioned at the 'sign of the Cradle in Lendal' (Milton's headquarters at Etridge's hotel), the damaged remains of a cargo of the 'ship BRAG, direct from *Spain*, on account of the *Inquisition*', which would not keep, 'being *decayed at the heart*'.

To this Milton scribblers rejoined with a poster announcing the auction of some damaged 'SUGAR-CANE of a blue colour, tinctured with a few *red* spots resembling drops of African blood'. The cane 'being *hollow within*, will not bear ... examination'.[7]

---

[6] Navickas, '"That sash will hang you"', pp. 540–65.
[7] *Yorkshire Election*, pp. 78, 42 – copies in SCC:LAI: WWM, E221, and YML: Y/H 8.421, Election Squibs, 1807.

Wilberforce Goes to the County

Spencer Perceval's timely warning of an approaching dissolution enabled Wilberforce to send express messages to his Yorkshire stalwarts and he himself headed down the Great North Road on Tuesday 28 April. He crossed into Yorkshire on the Wednesday and stopped long enough at Doncaster to change horses and confer briefly with supporters. 'Heard for certain Lord Milton standing. But I doing well in Doncaster,' ran his diary entry. He drove away towards York heartened by the cheers of the 'surrounding populace' and reached the haven of William Gray's house at midnight. For another hour he talked over his prospects with Dr Burgh, chairman of the committee already at work for him.[8]

Wilberforce's pre-nomination day canvass was in many of its elements unprofessional but it was not a weak and amateurish operation as it has sometimes been depicted. He saw no need for a large organization. He depended more upon volunteers than hired agents, in comparison with his wealthier rivals, but these unpaid friends were substantial citizens and office holders, wise in local political intrigue and imbued with an enthusiasm money could not buy. Foreseeing a contest, they were busy by Monday 27 April, a week before the first public meeting of a Wilberforce committee took place. William Gray's 'Hints for conducting the Business of a Contested Election', set down in 1784, were dusted off, and the committee had published Wilberforce's election address and sent circular letters to all who had been active in his behalf in 1806 before their candidate arrived.[9] Wilberforce on this occasion may have felt an uncommon over-confidence. No MP at the moment had greater prestige and he was convinced that his record entitled him to re-election. In the autumn canvass of 1806 he had aroused adulation. *The Times* had reported then that the 'ardent and general affection' shown Wilberforce had no parallel. 'He has passed in a kind of triumphant procession, preceded by bands of music, his carriage drawn by multitudes ... and great numbers of gentlemen of the first respectability in carriages, and on horseback, attending their old and beloved representative.' Truly in many parts of Yorkshire no amount of organized effort or free spending by adversaries could dislodge Wilberforce from the hearts of his constituents. As one refrain read:

---

[8] Wilberforce, *Life*, vol. 3, pp. 315–17; *Doncaster Gazette*, 1 May 1807.

[9] R.W. Smith, 'Political Organization', p. 1555, which relies on Wilberforce, *Life*, vol. 3, ch. 21; Furneaux, *Wilberforce*, p. 263; Smith, 'Yorkshire Elections', p. 77; ERALS: Grimston Papers: DDGR/43/27, Burgh to Grimston, 27 April; WYAS(L): WYL250/6/3/9, Dickinson to Wolley 11 May; YA: M90, Election Papers, 52, Hints for a Contested Election; KINCM: 1982.895.409, An Account of the Proceedings relative to the Election for Yorkshire.

> Again your hands, your hearts, your voice,
> Shall fix on WILBERFORCE your choice:
> And to your King return again
> A Man whose conduct knows no stain.[10]

Wilberforce was the only one of the aspirants who could credibly claim independence of party, for Lascelles was backed by the sitting ministers and Milton made no secret of his Whiggery. Until the heat of battle dissolved most restraints, Wilberforce's reputation was left unsullied. To publish anything reflecting on him would only damage his enemies, Samuel Martin of Hull warned the Milton committee as he got rid of some handbills they had sent him. A poster bearing an open letter to Wilberforce from A Yorkshire Freeholder dated 11 May was, however, a signal from the Whig camp that not even he would escape censure in what promised to be a bitter election. It was reprinted in the *York Herald* in the closing days of the poll. In it Wilberforce's record was questioned sharply. If he were a true Christian why not a 'Friend to Peace'? Blinded by affection for Pitt, his voice was only once feebly raised against the war and he had refused to present a Yorkshire peace petition in 1801 for fear of catching cold in court dress. 'Negroes' alone, it seemed, excited his compassion. In his praise of Pitt, did Wilberforce include approval of profligate public spending and grinding taxation? Some men now believed, he was warned, that 'popularity has been your polar star; that … instead of attempting to enlighten and direct the public mind you have taken the easier course of gliding down with the current of popular opinion.' With the clothiers Wilberforce had 'encouraged hopes which you intended not to gratify'. 'Have you not thus transferred your share of the odium on your late colleague, Mr. LASCELLES, who has offended more, because he was too manly and too honest to disguise his sentiments?' As for the abolition question, if Wilberforce laboured for Africans and not just for popularity, 'it must surely surprise every one to see you … appearing to unite your interest with that of Mr. LASCELLES'.

Nonetheless, a Milton committee could not even be established in Whitby, and many a plumper obtained during the canvass for his lordship was transformed into a split vote for Wilberforce as businessmen, Friends, and Methodists rallied to him.[11]

Lascelles's friends and agents bumped into the same stubborn wall. Such was Wilberforce's appeal that progress could be made only by asking for

---

[10] Quoted in Smith, 'Yorkshire Elections', p. 72; Election Squibs, 1807.
[11] SCC:LAI: WWM, E221, handbill; *York Herald*, 30 May 1807; ERALS: Grimston Papers, DDGR/43/27, Thorpe and Gray to Grimston, 1 May 1807; SCC:LAI: WWM, E171/8, Martin to Milton committee, 8 May 1807; E164/1, 3, Hunter to Milton committee, 9 and 13 May 1807.

second votes, Archdeacon Charles Baillie reported during his North Riding canvass. Scarborough was solidly for Wilberforce first, with Lascelles ahead in the race for second place, he thought. Repeatedly, emissaries for both opponents discovered that the electors would 'see him safe' before they would promise their second votes.[12]

The Wilberforce spell was strong in the North Riding and more especially in his home base, the East. This left him relatively free to devote his personal time to the West Riding towns before nomination day. Here, too, his friends were alert and the press friendly. The only subject on which the bitterly opposed *Leeds Intelligencer* and *Leeds Mercury* agreed was that Wilberforce deserved to keep his seat. The *Intelligencer*, whose proprietors sat on the Corporation, was the voice of the merchant class and churchmen and was Lascelles's chief spokesman. Griffith Wright Jr, the printer, endorsed Wilberforce in the expectation that he would unite with Lascelles and together they would recover for Yorkshire its 'wonted respectability'. The *Mercury* was printed by Edward Baines, who had taken it over in 1801 with the help of loans from Unitarian and reform-minded merchants and squires who regarded the *Intelligencer* as 'contemptuous, virulent, and insulting' towards their concerns. Baines's enemies were to call him the 'great liar of the North' and claimed his paper was read only by the 'disaffected and illiterate'. Baines was one of the first provincial editors in the modern sense, airing his reformist-Foxite-abolitionist views regularly, and fully equal to the slanging match with the other Leeds weekly which he referred to as 'that tissue of scurrility and folly'. Although Milton was his preferred candidate, Baines called for Wilberforce's re-election out of fear that the new government, given a Parliament 'packed the same way', would try to repeal the abolition act.[13]

The York Tavern, Wilberforce's headquarters, was a major coaching inn located between St Helen's church and the stately Mansion House and next door to the post office. The mails started from the Tavern which had stabling for 150 horses. From there his lively committee applied for copies of land tax assessments (the nearest thing to a voters' register); employed a corps of writers,

---

[12] WYAS(L): WYL250/6/3/10, Baillie to Wolley, 9 May 1807; Travis and Woodall to same, 9 May 1807; Codd and Garland to same, 8 May 1807; Cater to same, 10 May 1807; SCC:LAI: WWM, E223, Cholmley to Milton [7 May 1807]; E165/3, Hastings to Milton committee, 16 May 1807.

[13] SCC:LAI: WWM, E173/37, Popple to Milton [6 May 1807]; Wilson, *Gentlemen Merchants*, p. 172; *Leeds Intelligencer*, 4 May 1807; Baines, *Life*, pp. 25, 27, 45, 47, 49, 50, 57; M.A. Gibb and F. Beckwith, *Yorkshire Post: Two Centuries* (Yorkshire Conservative Newspaper Co.: Leeds, 1954), pp. 5, 6; Read, *Press and People*, pp. 76–8; D. Thornton, *Mr Mercury: The Life of Edward Baines, 1774–1848* (Merton Priory Press: Chesterfield, 2009); *Leeds Mercury*, 2 May 1807.

appointed messengers and hired the horses to carry them; distributed the 1806 canvass lists to be validated; and bought ruled canvass ledgers, paper, pens and minute books and buckled down to correspondence. At a formal meeting on 4 May, with Bacon Frank of Campsall in the chair, the committee decided to rely on local volunteer committees instead of professional agents to save money and because hired help was not believed to be necessary. The canvass would be carried out by gentlemen resident in each wapentake. The weakness of this plan of trusting the 'irregular zeal of his friends' was conceded afterwards by David Russell, Wilberforce's agent. In the most populated areas, the gentlemen did not cover all the ground; local committees were not always large enough and some participants, instead of staying usefully at home, came to York to enjoy the excitement. Some also had divided loyalties and instructions meant for their eyes only reached Lascelles or Milton workers. By the time around 8 May that the committee decided to employ canvassing agents, most of the available solicitors had been snapped up by the others. Not until the poll was underway did the Wilberforce team have a reasonable field of agents, and some of these were operating in unfamiliar territory. At least a dozen professionals, some with the resources of a partnership, appear to have been employed, but additional agents, especially in the West Riding, worked for Wilberforce and Lascelles at the same time. The York committee might also be faulted for tardiness in engaging inns and vehicles.[14]

The local committees had impressive memberships, however. Supporters in and near Hull met on Saturday 2 May to promote the re-election of this MP of 'transcendent talents' with Robert C. Broadley in the chair and Col. Henry Maister and William Jarratt prominent in the proceedings, an account of which was sent to every paper. At Ripon Mayor Peter Wright was joined by the Recorder and the Dean on a nineteen-member committee which met on 30 April. In the East and North Ridings the Sykeses of Sledmere, Humphrey Osbaldeston of Hunmanby, John Graeme of Bridlington, Col. Ralph Creyke of Marton, Thomas Grimston of Kilnwick Hall and his brother Henry of Etton, Charles Duncombe of Duncombe Park, Digby Legard of Ganton and Henry Yarburgh of Heslington were among the eminent squires who served.

In the West Riding, Wilberforce had the backing of leading merchants and many landlords. Thomas Atkinson was chairman of the Huddersfield committee which was studded with such names as Radcliffe, Armitage and Horsfall. They met as early as 28 April to endorse both old members. The Sheffield committee for Wilberforce convened on 30 April under Samuel

---

[14] Tom Bradley, *Old Coaching Days in Yorkshire* (Yorkshire Conservative Newspaper Co.: Leeds, 1889), pp. 65, 67; KINCM:1982.895.409, Account of Proceedings, fols 24, 30–2, 36, 38, 61, 62; SCC:LAI: WWM, E178/209, Nicoll to Bowns, n.d.

Walker, the ironmaster. On the committee arranging the canvass in and around Leeds were William Cookson, Walter Spencer Stanhope and Benjamin Ferrand of Bradford. The Wakefield area was represented by personages such as John and Joseph Naylor, Richard Henry Beaumont and the Rev E Kilvington. Halifax canvassers included the vicar, the Rev Dr Coulthurst (of course), and such local magnates as John Bramley, John Edwards, William Rawson and William Rothwell. Nearly a fifth of the first eighty committeemen enlisted were Church of England clergymen, in spite of the hierarchy's coolness.[15]

Canvass books are rare in the surviving Wilberforce papers but one Wakefield return showed overwhelming support for him, mostly in plumpers, among the commercial classes. Wilberforce gave his own first days to a rapid tour of the industrial towns, his visits often coinciding with Lascelles's, where he received reassuring acclaim, but he took little personal joy in the familiar exercise and was 'sickened' at the prospect of a contest.

Until 12 May, his and Lascelles's arrangements seemed to be coordinated; at least they appeared together on the hustings. At Halifax on 2 May they shared the crowd at the Piece Hall. Although it was Wilberforce's first public address since the passage of the abolition act, he did not mention it, though the subject 'has peculiarly endeared him to ... the Freeholders of Yorkshire'. The *Wakefield Star* did not pursue this point but the *Leeds Mercury* added that as he was accompanied by Lascelles 'his omission may ... be excused; yet we do confess that in our opinion, Mr. Wilberforce would have acted more worthy himself, not ... to have lost sight of this great object through courtesy to any man.' He came to Leeds on 5 May but postponed a speech and proceeded to Huddersfield where Lascelles followed him. On the 8th he and Lascelles addressed a thronged market place at Wakefield, Wilberforce speaking first with his 'usual fluency and elegance', winning the loudest applause. At Sheffield they breakfasted separately then were escorted together by the Master Cutler, John Sorby, and the Company to the Town Hall where, in defiance of rain, a 'vast concourse' had gathered. Wilberforce touched here on the dignity of representing Yorkshire and his independence in judging the merits of issues. It was, he said,

> peculiarly gratifying to me that whenever I have come into this part of the kingdom, where the minds of men are more especially engaged in the pursuits and speculations of trade, I have observed, that the cares of business do not prevent you from attending to your political rights and privileges. ... you have heads to understand and hearts to feel what is due to the interest and honour of your country. For her you have sacrificed your personal comforts; you have contributed services as well

---

[15] *York Courant*, 4 May 1807; KINCM:1982.895.409, Account of Proceedings, fols 34–6, 426; *Sheffield Iris*, 12 May 1807.

as money to her necessities. ... we have differed in opinion concerning some things, but I have not even once ... given you either wilful or accidental offence ... I need only to assert that as you have hitherto proved me, so shall you always find me a firm, decided, and unalterable friend to the British Constitution, with its laws and establishments, both in Church and State.

Every sentiment, the *Iris* noted, was loudly applauded.[16]

In his major appearance at the Leeds cloth halls on 12 May, and at the request of the trustees, Wilberforce explicitly dissociated himself from Lascelles, as charges of a coalition between them were raising what was to be for Wilberforce the most damaging issue of the campaign. He would not think it right, he said, to influence anyone's second vote. It was only after the nomination meeting on 13 May had guaranteed that there would be a contest that Wilberforce visited the East Riding and spent several hours in Hull where a warm welcome was laid on for its native son. He alighted from his carriage at Thomas Thompson's High Street house and, surrounded by admirers, proceeded to the Sessions Hall to address a crowd from the steps. His speech ('one of the most impressive ... ever delivered') brought a hail of applause and cheers. He reminisced about his birthplace and his first election in 1780 and emphasized his untiring interest in the port's shipping trade. His recollections of Pitt were applauded heartily 'but', Wilberforce added, 'I never addicted myself to him so closely as not to consider every question and every measure with impartiality and freedom'.[17]

The Return of Lascelles

Henry Lascelles was dogged and dependable in performing whatever duties fell to him but had not much stomach for political combat. 'Lord Harewood and the Beau [Henry's brother, Edward] are eager for the Contest and support the spirits of their champion, which are wavering and irresolute,' the Fitzwilliams were told.

As in the previous campaigns, Lascelles was only yielding to popular demand when he 'disturbed the peace of the county' by announcing his candidature before Fawkes's decision was known. On the day (28 April) of his tentative offer, 200 members of the Leeds establishment met to endorse him at

---

[16] JGW: POLITICAL, Yorkshire Election, 1807, Canvass Returns; Wilberforce, *Life*, vol. 3, pp. 317–18; *Wakefield Star*, 15 May 1807; *Leeds Mercury*, 9 May 1807; *Sheffield Iris*, 12 May 1807; *Doncaster Gazette*, 15 May 1807. For a cutler's workshop, see Plate 1.

[17] *Hull Packet*, 19 May 1807; *Leeds Mercury*, 16 May 1807; *York Chronicle*, 21 May 1807; *Hull Advertiser*, 23 May 1807; Wilberforce, *Life*, vol. 3, pp. 319–23.

the Rotation Office with Mayor Richard Ramsden Bramley in the chair. This 'most numerous and respectable gathering' of merchants and manufacturers included William Cookson, the Gotts, Wormalds and Marshalls and such other dignitaries as William Hey, the doctor, philanthropist and leading Methodist who, like many of the others, was also close to Wilberforce. Lascelles gave them a 'manly' and much applauded speech and issued a statement that this flattering reception had convinced him to stand. His Leeds friends resolved that the immense county should not be confided to a young nobleman in need of experience.[18]

The *York Chronicle* learned of his decision with 'the highest satisfaction'. The *Halifax Journal* printed a paragraph declaring that 'All Friends to the Constitution and Commerce of this country will hail with pleasure the opportunity of again restoring to its Parliamentary Service that most active, able, and disinterested Representative'. Addresses from citizens flowed in with surprising speed and committees were functioning in a very few days. This burst of activity was markedly intense in the West Riding where the battle for second place to Wilberforce would be won or lost.

In Halifax the merchant John Edwards and the bustling Dr Coulthurst with 127 others similarly attached to Wilberforce adopted on 28 April an address approving Lascelles's 'upright and disinterested Conduct in Parliament'. The committee had William Greenup in the chair and Edwards and Coulthurst among its members who also included Col. Thomas Horton, chairman of a meeting which had produced a loyal address to the King shortly before, John Waterhouse, a prominent Methodist merchant, and 22 others from important commercial families. The Huddersfield committee was organized on the same day, as we have seen, to work for Wilberforce and Lascelles.

At Sheffield a separate Lascelles committee was formed under James Stuart Wortley with the Rev. Thomas Sutton, chairman of an earlier loyal address meeting, the Rev. Stuart Corbett and George Bustard Greaves among other distinguished old friends. The Cutlers Company, a prestigious body even if, as Lord Fitzwilliam alleged, it could not deliver a dozen votes, advertised its unanimous view that Wilberforce and Lascelles deserved support for their attention to Sheffield's special interests, and the Master Cutler introduced them at their joint appearance there. Wakefield friends of Lascelles called a meeting for 30 April and 57 men pledged themselves to elect him. The Rev. Dr Richard Munkhouse took the chair and 'firm and hearty' support was voted by, among others, John and Jeremiah Naylor and their prosperous fellow citizens, many of whom were also friends of Wilberforce and signers

---

[18] NRO: F(M), 72/10, Wentworth to Lady Fitzwilliam, 9 May 1807; *Yorkshire Election*, pp. 11–12, 100; *York Chronicle*, 7 May 1807; *Leeds Intelligencer*, 4 and 11 May 1807.

of previous loyal addresses and anti-sedition resolutions. Bradford's meeting with William Pollard as chairman appointed a committee to work for both Wilberforce and Lascelles and sent a special address to the latter.[19]

The case for Lascelles almost always was linked to the experience and views he shared with Wilberforce, 'the old and much respected members ... the tried and steady friends of the best of Kings, and the Protestant Religion', as it was put in paragraphs sent to the papers. In the tug-of-war between Lascelles and Milton, a vote for the former was portrayed as a vote against an 'insolent and despotic oligarchy'. Lascelles would preserve the prerogative of the Crown and the superiority of the Established Church.

A Brother Freeholder who on 8 May summarized the choices in a handbill distributed at Wakefield eulogized Wilberforce, the 'Hireling of no Party', and lauded Lascelles as equally independent, 'of noble Extraction, and of respectable Connexions', whose 'unwearied Diligence and Attention to the Interests of your Trade, to which no Man has more confined his Study, (and for which no Man has been so ill requited) entitles him to the Attention of every liberal-minded Man: he is a Man of unshaken Integrity, and unbiassed Judgment' who, like Wilberforce, 'never cringed as a Courtier for the Sake of Power or Emolument.' Milton was dismissed as a stripling with no views but those borrowed from his father or Walter Fawkes.[20]

Who can now say with certainty how Lascelles and Milton compared in their organizations? From this distance they seem broadly similar in tactics and expenditure. If Milton's machine appears in retrospect more spirited and coherent, this may be partly thanks to the fact that its surviving records are by far the best of the lot. Edward Baines spoke of Lascelles as 'an experienced electioneering general' and pointed out that he had marshalled a 'large proportion of the principal law agents in every part of the county' well before Milton.

Lascelles did not have the advantage of a parent who commanded a network of political and party connections but the ministers of the day backed Lord Harewood's son and Lascelles even stamped the royal arms on his election cards. Though never far from Harewood House, Lord Harewood took an active part in the contest and it was a measure of his influence that he was exposed to personal vilification. The *Leeds Mercury* reprinted from the *Morning Chronicle*, well fed by Whigs in London, a poem, 'The Price of the County',

---

[19] *York Chronicle*, 30 April 1807; *Halifax Journal*, 2 and 9 May 1807; *York Courant*, 4 May 1807; NRO: F(M), 72/3, Fitzwilliam to Wentworth, 4 May 1807; *Sheffield Iris*, 5 and 12 May 1807; TNA, Home Office 43/16, Domestic Letter Book; *Wakefield Star*, 1 May 1807; *York Chronicle*, 7 May 1807; *Leeds Intelligencer*, 4 May 1807.

[20] Election Squibs, 1807, King's Appeal to His People; *Yorkshire Election*, pp. 5–6; SCC:LAI: WWM, E221, A Brother Freeholder handbill.

which recalled that he had won his title when Henry was elected in 1796 and pictured him now thirsting for an earldom:

> Said old L—c—s to P-tt, on a sunshiny day,
> 'Ev'ry man has his price, I have heard the folks say:
> And since men are purchased and sold for a bounty,
> Pray tell me, friend P-tt, what's the price of a county?'
>
> Quoth P-tt, 'sure a Gentleman's never the worse
> For lacking of wit, if he owns a long purse:
> So to cut matters short, we'd engage at a word,
> You carry the county, I'll make you a Lord.'
>
> An arduous task, then by both 'twas agreed:
> For money, alas, will not always succeed
> So to cozen poor Yorkshiremen thinking no evil,
> 'Twas P-tt and the K—g, and Charles Fox and the Devil.
>
> Then Honour and Honesty pleaded in vain,
> Not virtue, nor true independence remain
> A cry was excited inviting the gold,
> And P–tt bought the shame, which old L—c—s had sold.
>
> A title thus gain'd which to heroes was due,
> By cheating the many and courting the few;
> Gaunt Harry clapt on the bright armour of glory,
> And entered the lists an unspeakable Tory. ...
>
> One effort alone, to secure their applause,
> He deigned to exert, in his countrymen's cause,
> When the Workmen's petition was brought to his hand,
> He damn'd the plain sense, he could not understand.
>
> No longer in senate, and almost benighted,
> The dreams of past consequence make him short-sighted;
> And H—w—d, once more, at the Treasury porch,
> Asks the price of the county, for Hal and the Church.
>
> Says P[ort]l[an]d, I'm not a political churl,
> Make sure of proud Yorkshire, I'll make thee an Earl,
> The Pope at thy elbow, throws dust in their eyes,
> And Liberty, Britain's inheritance, dies! ... [21]

---

[21] *Yorkshire Election*, pp. 101–2; *Leeds Mercury*, 16 May 1807; *Morning Chronicle*, 11 May 1807.

The canvass books and papers collected by Edward Wolley of Fulford Grange, the York attorney who served Lascelles, if not single-heartedly, supplied the framework for the 1807 canvass. Closer to Harewood and considerably more diligent was Lucas Nicholson, Leeds town clerk and head of a firm of solicitors whose particular assignment was the contentious West Riding. Both men were enlisting local agents by 29 April and canvass results were reaching them a week later. At York an impressive central committee was ensconced for the duration at the George Inn, Coney Street, under the chairmanship of Sir Thomas Turner Slingsby. The George was an ancient inn and the principal posting house, remarkable for its magnificently carved doorway and gables where a life-size Bacchus surveyed the passing scene.[22]

Lascelles employed at least 63 individual agents or firms, 13 in the East Riding, 18 in the North and 32 in the West. Nearly all were solicitors but the Rev. John Headlam of Greta Bridge earned £474 17s. 0d. for his agency. These appointments were lucrative: the partial accounts in the Harewood archives show that Rimington & Wake of Sheffield collected £1,703 4s. 6d. to cover their retainer and expenses; Codd & Garland of Hull earned £1,112 2s. 5d. with another £227 15s. 11d. paid to Stephen Dickinson of Sculcoates, while £822 14s. 5d. went to Travers & Woodhall of Scarborough and William Lockwood Jr of Easingwold was paid £667 16s. 0d. In the less populated areas the costs of agents might range from £40 to £400. Upton, Nicholson & Hemingway of Leeds sent in a modest bill for £496 since Nicholson made no charge for his own services. As Lascelles and Milton raced to sign up the leading attorneys in the towns, many were applied to by both. Some came forward on the first inkling of the dissolution; others, out of old attachment, declined the opposition's bids even though they arrived first and, in the case of Thomas Knaggs of Whitby, 'tho' handsome Terms were offered'. Stephen Dickinson received an invitation on 30 April at 8.00 a.m. from Lascelles and accepted it. At 11.45 the same morning a request was delivered and declined from the Milton committee. A less scrupulous few arranged to work for both Lascelles and Milton, among them Joshua Crosland of Huddersfield, John Piper of Pickering (also helping Wilberforce), Thomas Rylah of Dewsbury, and Thomas Sawdon of Whitby who, although engaged by Lascelles, spent some of his time canvassing for Milton. David Taylor, appointed at Bridlington for Milton, sought second votes for Lascelles. In hindsight, the failure of Lascelles's campaign was blamed by a Yorkshire clergyman on the 'shocking mixture of treachery and imbecility' shown by some agents, as well as by what he took

---

[22] WYAS(L): WYL250/6/3/9, Wolley to Lascelles, 2 November 1806; WYL250/6/3/10 and WYL250/6/3/30, canvass reports; WYL250/6/3/10, Lascelles to Wolley, 30 April 1807; Bradley, *Old Coaching Days*, pp. 65–6, 77; Whellan, *History of York*, vol. 1, p. 349.

to be the 'indolence and supineness in the whole Harewood family', but these seem extreme judgments born of frustration.[23]

Agents not only received retainers but were the conduits for payments to others. They canvassed personally, especially among the lesser freeholders who would be satisfied without an approach from some noble or gentleman; they composed or commissioned local squibs and paragraphs, posters and handbills; they circulated the material sent them, ordered ribbons, booked inns, hired horses and vehicles, lined up cargoes of voters for York, attended committee meetings, copied out the returns and eventually served as clerks in the polling booths. Sending word of the foe's activity was an important function. William Ward notified Wolley of Lord Dundas's pre-emptive strike in the Richmond area where it would take quick work to find unattached votes. The North Riding in general was difficult canvassing ground for Lascelles, although in the end he carried seven of its twelve wapentakes. William Chaloner's interest at Guisborough was not, as might have been hoped, entirely at his grandson's disposal but 90 votes were divided between Lascelles and Milton. The Dowager Lady Amherst of Leven Grove near Stokesley produced 103 votes but divided between Lascelles and Wilberforce. Archdeacon Baillie canvassed vigorously in Yarm and Stockton and managed only 20 plumpers against the antagonism of such landowners as John Wharton of Skelton Castle, Sir Charles Turner of Kirkleatham, William Ward Jackson of Normanby, Thomas Hustler of Acklam Hall, Bartholomew Rudd of Marton Lodge and the Rev. Henry Hilyard of Stokesley. Though none commanded a formidable number of votes, they could enforce attendance at York. Another 100 would split between Wilberforce and Lascelles, Baillie reported, but those willing to appear in the Castle Yard on nomination day would put up their hands for Wilberforce only, so it was no use encouraging them to join 'Mr. Wilberforce's Phalanx' at Lascelles's expense. The good news was that Baillie had met with only eight voters for Milton on his rounds. Thomas Knaggs of Whitby called a meeting for Lascelles and almost nobody came. A strange set of people, he commented, many refusing to give their names to any canvasser. Sawdon sent Lascelles thirty promises from Whitby but none would go twice to York (for both nomination and election days). Expert use was being made of Milton's alleged support of 'Catholicks & his youth has had a good effect

---

[23] WYAS(L): WYL250/6/3/17, Robert Cattle's account; WYL250/6/3/10 and WYL250/6/3/13, letters and election account; SCC:LAI: WWM, E176, Dickinson to Carr, 30 April 1807; WYAS(L): WYL250/6/3/10, Dickinson to Wolley, 7 May 1807; Knaggs to same, 1 May 1807; Piper to same, 3 May 1807; Nicholson to same, 6 May 1807; Sawdon to Sinclair, 6 May 1807; Sawdon to Wolley, 1 May 1807; Smith, 'Yorkshire Elections', pp. 79, 80, 81; SCC:LAI: WWM, E179/38, Dawson to Strickland, 18 September 1807; E163/6, Tottie to Milton committee, 16 May 1807.

in favor of Mr. Lascelles', Sawdon added. Robert Clarke, chairman for the Cleveland district, sent welcome tidings that all of Lord Bridgewater's tenants and friends would be shepherded to York by his land steward on nomination day at his lordship's expense to raise their hands for Lascelles alone.[24]

In the East Riding, Wilberforce's popularity was again an obstacle and several great families were helping Milton, although their second votes were for Lascelles. In Hull, Milton's numbers looked impressive at first glance, but many supporters were barely qualified and probably unable to get to York for the first hurdle of the nomination. 'Ours are a superior sort,' boasted Stephen Dickinson, who could pay their own way.

Richard Bethell of Rise in Holderness was active on behalf of both Wilberforce and Lascelles and so was the steward of the Constable family of Burton Constable, Catholics who would be unable to vote themselves but whose tenants had the franchise. At Beverley the canvass produced figures of 222 for Wilberforce, 146 for Lascelles and only 33 for Milton. But both Dickinson and the agents Codd & Garland cautioned that Milton's party 'are now at the old Subject of the Slave Trade which has great Weight with many & Hand Bills ... are now publish[in]g to give effect to the idea that Mr. Lascelles is an Enemy of the Abolition'. If Lascelles would, in fact, oppose repeal of the abolition act, he should say so.

Because distant voters showed understandable reluctance to journey to York twice and the candidates had no wish to promise double expenses, Nicholson pressed Wolley to make strenuous efforts in the City and Ainsty of York, as 'a great deal will depend upon the shew of strength' on nomination day.[25] We shall look presently into the delicate business of assisting voters to perform their civic duty without actually violating the laws on bribery and treating; it was one which touched all parties. But here the general point can be made that Lascelles was careful with his father's money, doling it out to his agents only as it was asked for and fearful of any spent to bring in votes not absolutely needed or of doubtful validity, in contrast to Milton who appeared willing to pay now and worry later, or Wilberforce whose known poverty, compared to the riches at the others' disposal, spared him many demands on his election purse.

When Lascelles publicly lamented the necessity of disturbing the peace of the county, opponents mocked him in a broadside signed 'H–L of H–R–D'

---

[24] WYAS(L): WYL250/6/3/10, Ward to Wolley, 1 May 1807; Newton to same, 1 May 1807; Amherst to Lascelles, 9 May 1807; Baillie to Wolley, 9 and 12 May 1807; Knaggs to same, 10 May 1807; Sawdon to same, 6 May 1807; Clarke to same, 9 May 1807

[25] WYAS(L): WYL250/6/3/11, Dickinson to Wolley, 11 May 1807; 1/10, Codd and Garland to Wolley, 8 May 1807; Shepherd to Wolley, 11 May 1807; Nicholson to Wolley, 7 May 1807.

which declared he was too mean to face the costs and expected his supporters to pack sackfuls of bread and cheese for their journeys to York and to take a bit extra for others 'trudging on Foot and fainting in the Way'. The treasury of the Lascelles committee room at Leeds was derided as the 'Harewood Poor Box'.[26]

Money, however, was among the least of Lascelles's worries in the West Riding where the clothiers – the 'Billymen' once so boisterously behind Pitt, the King and Church – supported the Whigs in 1806 to advertise their indignation at Lascelles's attitude towards them. They had not yet returned to their old loyalties. West Riding canvass returns showed that in the clothing districts he and Wilberforce shared much of the support of the gentry, merchants, shopkeepers and farmers but that both were displaced by Milton in the affections of most of the workers connected with the cloth trade. In one report from Wakefield Westgate, where business and professional men outnumbered craftsmen voters, Milton trailed with 21 promises to 39 for Lascelles and 60 for Wilberforce. In the clothworking villages of Heckmondwike, Liversedge and Cleckheaton, Milton led in each, with a total of 119, to 71 for Wilberforce and 69 for Lascelles.

Important West Riding proprietors such as John Lister Kaye of Denby Grange and James Lane Fox of Bramham Park were staunch for Lascelles, and his Doncaster agent said he could count on Lady Irwin of Temple Newsam, the Earl of Egremont whose seat was at Wressle near Selby and Lord Grantham of Newby Hall. But in some places, the agent added, Milton was so popular that 'were he even but 15 instead of 21 there are many who w[oul]d vote for him'.[27]

Lascelles began his inevitable confrontation with the clothiers in a published address on 3 May. He relied on the sensible Yorkshire freeholders not to be led astray by the clamour of one group irritated with him for 'strenuously and conscientiously promoting the general prosperity of the Country; and (when justly estimated) their own real interests'. He was instantly taunted in a fake circular letter calling attention to his ten years '*mis*representing' the county by caring exclusively for the merchants. He began his West Riding circuit at Halifax on a Saturday market day, appearing on 2 May with Wilberforce at the Piece Hall, but his speech went unreported because 'efforts to get the substance of it were ineffectual'. It was not said in so many words that the audience was unruly when he spoke, but Wilberforce had got a hearing.

---

[26] YML: Y/H 8.421, Election Squibs, 1807; *Yorkshire Election*, p. 43.
[27] Wilberforce, *Life*, vol. 3, p. 329 and my analysis of the poll book; JGW: POLITICAL, Yorkshire Election; SCC:LAI: WWM, E176, Kaye to Milton, 2 May 1807; E223, Fox to Milton, 5 May 1807; Peel, *Spen Valley*, pp. 305-7; WYAS(L): WYL250/6/3/10, Stocks to Wolley, 9 May 1807; SCC:LAI: WWM, E223, Grantham to Fitzwilliam, 5 May 1807.

Leading citizens of the Halifax neighbourhood were stout friends of both old members. William Walker of Crow Nest told Fitzwilliam that the canvass for them had begun as early as 27 April 'with the most astonishing Success' and that the 'Tide is universally against us'. An item in the *Halifax Journal* declared there was little chance for a third candidate, so great and general was Lascelles's popularity. At Huddersfield the merchants were equally busy although their techniques for compiling the excellent canvass report were open to question. The Milton agent at Huddersfield claimed that some whose names were put down for Lascelles 'did not give Consent, others that they were not consulted, and a considerable part ... assert they will not vote for him at all'. At their joint Wakefield appearance, where Lascelles, but not Wilberforce, met some 'symptoms of disapprobation', Lascelles appealed for support for the King. 'The measure which has led to the present dissolution ... was the same as that which produced the revolution of 1688,' he declared. At Sheffield on 9 May, after seeing handbills linking him to slavery, Lascelles publicly vowed to oppose any attempt to repeal the slave trade abolition act but this declaration did not stop the jibes that he had never voted for abolition and that his brother Edward had voted against. His Leeds committee issued a formal statement of the pledge on 11 May. In his Sheffield speech, Lascelles related how he had agreed to become a candidate at the call from the 'principal commercial quarters, and invitations from immense landed interests' in the belief that a more auspicious climate for his principles prevailed now than last autumn. He was pleased that Sheffield approved his resistance to the pig iron tax, a stand not taken out of local interest, however, but because the tax would not have helped the war effort. His conduct in the cloth trade issue had been less fairly judged; it involved the question of *'restricting the use of great Capital in the improvement and extension of manufactures,* and of reducing an immense staple trade to the condition in which it was in the reign of Queen Elizabeth!' The wool inquiry committee and the Commons had agreed with him. 'Respectful attention' greeted these remarks, with some cheers, but his postscript about the slave trade produced loud applause.[28]

Lascelles attempted the obligatory tour of the Leeds cloth halls on 5 May, the day also fixed for Milton's appearance. The White Cloth Hall, built in 1774, contained five 'streets' of facing stands used by up to 1,300 clothiers through which the candidates strolled before addressing a crowd in the courtyard. The Mixed (sometimes called the Coloured) Cloth Hall built 70 years earlier in a large U around an open space, provided six covered aisles

---

[28] *Yorkshire Election*, p. 13; KINCM:1982.895.409, Account of Proceedings, fols 346–7; *Wakefield Star*, 8 and 15 May 1807; *Halifax Journal*, 9 May 1807; SCC:LAI: WWM, E222, Walker to Fitzwilliam, 1 May 1807; E223, Radcliffe to Milton, 5 May 1807; E156/2, Allison to Milton committee, 8 May 1807; *Sheffield Iris*, 12 May 1807.

with 1,770 stands. On the day appointed, Lascelles and his party had to fight their way into the White Cloth Hall and on to the hustings prepared for Milton, accompanied by shouts of 'Out, out', 'No Lascelles' and 'No Slavery'. His appearance had been preceded by a papering of the town with handbills run off by the opposing side with the result that a swell of indignation had been aroused against him. A Yorkshire Clothier had pointed out, in a poster printed by Baines at the *Mercury*, how avidly the town's ruling merchants were trying to foist upon them the very man they had so firmly rejected six months before. From Lascelles clothiers could expect nothing but '*supercilious disregard*'. Their numbers would win the day, they were told; if they failed this election test, no man hereafter would be hardy enough to 'attempt our Delivrance from the abject State of Bondage to which we shall be reduced'. Whatever the outcome of the issue before Parliament, the clothiers must elect MPs who would listen to them civilly. Milton was such a man.

A Freeborn Briton countered in a handbill from the *Intelligencer* shop that the clothiers were fooling themselves if they thought Fawkes had or Milton would espouse their cause. 'Remember in what shoals, and with what ardour, you flocked to York, on the Glorious First of December, 1795, to avow your abhorrence of the Foxites' *sedition-bill*. ... if you have any spark of loyalty ... you cannot ... hesitate to say *We'll have no Foxite, no Milton, but* WILBERFORCE AND LASCELLES, *And the King and Constitution for Ever!!!*'

John Grant and Robert Cookson, the Cloth Hall trustees who had served as delegates to the parliamentary inquiry, promptly published a reply that Fawkes had been 'most attentive, gentlemanlike and encouraging' towards them. The answering salvo raged against Milton's 'puny Character' and asserted it was not in Lascelles's nature to treat anyone with contempt. Then, searching for more fruitful ground, this handbill dragged in the emotive issue of 'popery' to demand,

> will You ... for the sake of indulging an undeserved revenge ... support the avowed Abettors of those Men who have dared to DICTATE A MEASURE most repugnant to the conscience of the King. The Men who would with impious and sacrilegious hands have ... torn down that BARRIER which for Ages past has stemmed the torrent of POPERY, SUPERSTITION, and FANATICISM.[29]

---

[29] *Leeds Guide*, pp. 50–7; E.M. Sigsworth, 'Leeds and Its Industrial Growth: 8. The Leeds Cloth Halls', *Leeds Journal*, 25 (1954), p. 416; *Leeds Mercury*, 9 May 1807; *Yorkshire Election*, pp. 103, 8–10, 10–11; SCC:LAI: WWM, F42/58, A Yorkshire Manufacturer, 4 May 1807; E221, handbills; Election Squibs, 1806–37.

After the event, Lascelles's friends published their 'heartfelt satisfaction' at his 'highly flattering reception' in the Leeds cloth halls, but the opposition was right when they circulated a report of 'The Speech and Reception of the Hon. H. Lascelles' which insisted that the hoots and hisses were so loud and long that his entire speech consisted of:

> Silence, Gentlemen, Silence,
> Pray Gentlemen, do be Silent.

The hooting and hissing, retorted Lascelles's writers unwisely, issued from a 'parcel of DISAFFECTED RAGAMUFFINS, hired for the purpose'.

> We have no doubt [the Miltonites crowed] that these 'Disaffected Ragamuffins', will, on the Day of Election, convince the County, that they have more weight ... than the Son of a Barbadoes Planter. But Mr. Lascelles having told the Clothiers of Yorkshire that he did not care a *D—n for them all*, it is perfectly in character for his friends to call the Clothiers at the Cloth-Hall 'A parcel of *Disaffected Ragamuffins*'.

Lascelles's friends retreated rapidly, denying that they had called the clothiers ragamuffins. The epithet applied solely to the 'prevaricating partizans of Lord Milton'. At Bradford, they trumpeted, Lascelles was received with the largest meeting and most thunderous applause ever recalled. But this or any other success could hardly compensate for the humiliation at the woollen capital. The *Mercury* at least gave Lascelles credit for having the courage to walk the halls and try to speak. If an MP insults his constituents, Baines opined, he must expect to be insulted in return. 'The reception of Mr. Lascelles was ... so ignominious, as to extort pity from his bitterest enemies.' Lascelles claimed the merit of independence for his behaviour towards the clothiers' concerns but 'he has no claim whatever ... the cause he espoused has always been considered the cause of the *strong* against the *weak*. He courted ... the men of large property, but the manufacturers, who, till the last election, had always been considered subservient to the merchants, he treated with indignity, contempt, and even with personal insult.'

The Cloth Hall Trustees now reprinted the address they had issued during the 1806 election promising to 'prevent the Re-admission of that Man to Parliament, who had the imprudence to say to 19,000 Clothiers ... 'you may hoot me, or scout me, or do what you please, I don't care a d—n for you all'.[30]

As Wilberforce had done, Lascelles reserved the week between nomination

---

[30] *Yorkshire Election*, pp. 17–19, 55; SCC:LAI: WWM, E221, handbill; *Leeds Mercury*, 9 May 1807.

and election for paying his personal calls on more reliable parts of Yorkshire. His reception at Hull was quieter than Wilberforce's but he was gratified with his meeting at the Neptune Inn. Knowing Wilberforce's special claims on this region, he prudently sought only second votes. Again, in response to requests for his views, he declared that should any attempt be made to repeal the abolition act, he would oppose it. His East Riding friends were well aware of the clothiers' animosity. As Ralph Creyke had told him, they did not understand the wool trade but as in other areas they depended upon its prosperity. Creyke had studied the evidence before the committee in 1806 and concluded that Lascelles had acted properly in supporting the committee's recommendations. This rural Riding could provide noble backing for him, 'but alas! we are lost & hurried away by the tempestuous torrent of the traders of the West'.[31]

Milton, the 'Infant Candidate'

Once the decision was taken to place Lord Milton in Fawkes's empty seat, the Fitzwilliam party went on the offensive with gusto. There was none of Lascelles's ambivalence or Wilberforce's agonizing in these proceedings. It was assumed at once that this would be a fight to the finish, for Wilberforce was simply too popular to be pushed or to stand aside, and Lascelles, having been bluffed out once before, clearly now believed he had sufficiently strong support to take back his seat. For Earl Fitzwilliam the stakes were high. It was not only a question of family pride but of helping to retrieve Whig fortunes nationally. All eyes were on the Yorkshire conflict. Milton, too, was on his mettle for the single most worrying fact about him was his youth. There were few other reasons for personal attack. 'Surrounded by wealth and power and grandeur ... and at the Time, when the generality of young Men are engaged in the fashionable vices of the age, we see L[or]d Milton quietly settled with an amiable wife and living the life of a domestic man,' said one who knew him.[32] Objections thus boiled down to his father's ambition and Milton's age (his red hair also seemed to be an offence) but these meagre grounds were fertile enough for lampoons.

> Poor little Fitz,
> Has lost his Wits,
> And can't tell where to find them;

---

[31] *Hull Packet*, 19 May 1807; WYAS(L): WYL250/6/3/10, Lascelles to Wolley [15 May 1807]; *Hull Advertiser*, 23 May 1807; WYAS(L): WYL250/6/3/9, Creyke to Lascelles, 2 November 1806.

[32] Wrangham MSS, Robert Grimston's account of the election.

> Let him alone
> Till F–w–s comes home,
> And brings his Votes behind him

sang the 'Wet Nurse lately hired by Lord F–z–m for the Infant Candidate'. Walter Spencer Stanhope, a Lascelles volunteer, whiled away a few moments composing an election ballad which ran

> Wave the flag, hoist the pennant,
> Hear our great Lord Lieutenant
> Who would save us the trouble of choice.
> 'Let not Lascelles content you, Milton *shall* represent you,
> And in the House guide his voice!' …
> What a lordling it is,
> With his carrotty phiz,
> So cried up, so flattered, so built on.
> You may oft take a rule
> From a nickname at School
> And the boys named him
> Old Lady Milton' …

'WANTED,' one advertisement ran, 'A young Woman to superintend the care of a grown baby. Apply at W–ntw–rth–House. If Irish and Roman Catholic will be preferred. No objection to Presbyterian.'

In his speech at Leeds on 5 May Milton deftly used an idea contributed by a Wakefield friend that since the clothiers were trying to preserve apprenticeships Milton might 'in a jocular way' point out that he was young enough to learn, and the clothiers on nomination eve trumpeted

> Our MILTON, as Apprentice, has begg'd us to Elect him,
> And the Merchants *on this account* may wish us to reject him;
> But *without their kind assistance* on Wednesday we'll venture
> To sign and seal *for seven years* YOUNG ROCKINGHAM's *Indenture.*[33]

But doubts about the 'baby lord', heir presumptive to a frequently ailing earl, were not confined to partisans of Wilberforce and Lascelles, such as the *Leeds Intelligencer*, which in one of its kinder references attributed Milton's reckless candidacy to the fact that he had not yet arrived at the age of discretion. Henry Galley Knight at Cambridge tried to get his father's Yorkshire vote for

---

[33] *Leeds Intelligencer*, 11 May 1807; Stirling, *Letter-Bag*, vol. 1, p. 140; *Yorkshire Election*, p. 34; SCC:LAI: WWM, E177/67, Heywood to Milton, 2 May 1807; Election Squibs, 1807.

his friend Milton and had to report his father would not support his own son for Parliament at 21. Sir George Cayley of Brompton earnestly believed it was unconstitutional for the heir of a peer to represent commoners, yet, he added sadly, so many conventions had been overturned lately that he was inclined to commit a 'political crime' and give the country the benefit of Milton's ability. This he did, canvassing actively and casting a plumper.

The scribbling committees industriously circulated items about men who had entered Parliament early and turned out well, such as Wilberforce, the Earl of Chatham and his son Pitt. One anecdote popular with the printers told of an elderly MP who objected to Henry Lord Falkland's arrival in the House before he had sown his wild oats. 'Then I am come to the proper place, where there is a goose to pick them up,' Falkland retorted. That Milton was no longer a minor, dependent on his father, but the head of his own family was essential to his appearance before the electorate as an independent man. Conversely, his opponents' stress on his youth was meant to undermine his claim to independence.[34]

Milton's canvass had the benefit of two talented organizers. The chief one was Charles Bowns, now Fitzwilliam's Wentworth estate agent and financial officer who lived at Darley Hall near Barnsley. The other was Thomas William Tottie of Leeds. S.W. Nicoll, William Carr and the Recorder Robert Sinclair were the York core of Milton's central committee as they had been of Fawkes's. As soon as word of Milton's intentions reached the city, they began to line up agents in the North and East Ridings. They prepared a circular letter to electors and canvassed freeholders in the city who had a county vote, as well as those in the villages for some twelve miles around, since 'votes in the neighbourhood are useful & cheap'. Fitzwilliam acted as chief of staff from Wentworth Woodhouse and from both York and Wentworth the first 107 letters went out to gentlemen whose aid was particularly valuable. Bowns had begun with the West Riding and, together with Francis Maude, Recorder of Doncaster, Tottie of Leeds and John Schofield of Horbury, had by the night of 2 May divided it into numbered canvassing districts with many agents assigned or being approached.[35]

One problem to which Milton's campaign had to address itself was the position of Fawkes. The West Riding clothiers' revolt had upset Lascelles, to their delight, but now only months later the beneficiary of their successful exercise

---

[34] *Leeds Intelligencer*, 4 May 1807; SCC:LAI: WWM, E177/56, Knight to Milton [5 May 1807]; E177/101, Cayley to Milton, 22 May 1807; *Leeds Mercury*, 9 May 1807; *York Courant*, 11 May 1807; McCormack, *Independent Man*, pp. 19–20.

[35] SCC:LAI: WWM, E170/6, Sinclair to Fitzwilliam, 30 April 1807; E177/44 [2 May 1807]; E177/43, Maude to Milton, 3 May 1807; E150, List of Gentlemen Wrote To, 2 May 1807; E177/36, Tottie to Fitzwilliam, 30 April 1807.

had left the field. They were still opposed to Lascelles but disgruntled that their recent effort had now to be repeated. Milton could 'overpower the mercantile votes' only with their vigorous assistance and to assure that it was now essential to employ more agents than had been needed in 1806. This was the considered opinion of Tottie, who was to be Milton's adviser for the next 25 years. He rode out himself to select agents in the towns and to canvass spots on his map which his clerks, fellow attorneys or friends had missed. He employed four writers just to copy land tax lists. Richard Lee, one of those Leeds wool merchants who had backed Baines and the *Mercury* and who was popular among the clothiers, sat on the Leeds committee, sometimes serving as chairman.[36]

Favourable responses came from many West Riding proprietors including the Earl of Thanet, the Duke of Devonshire and his heir the Marquess of Hartington at Barden Tower; Lord Stourton of Allerton Mauleverer, the Earl of Mexborough whose son, Lord Pollington, rounded up votes near Methley Park, the Earl of Darlington of Ackworth Moor Top near Pontefract, Lord Hawke of Womersley, Conyers Norton of Scawley Hall near Ripon, the Earl of Effingham of Thundercliffe Grange near Rotherham, Henry Vernon of Wentworth Castle near Barnsley and the Duke of Leeds whose holdings were extensive in the North Riding as well.

The agents' initial canvassing reports, arriving by 1 May, showed that the clothing districts were holding reasonably firm, that Milton's second votes were usually for Wilberforce and that in Wilberforce territory Milton appeared to be ahead of Lascelles for second place.

If Milton had a livelier political organization, Lascelles had the advantage of getting to many places first. Repeatedly Milton's agents reported that votes had been promised before their appointments and briefing instructions had arrived. In much of the East Riding, Milton canvassers were two or three days behind Lascelles's, in some cases 'criminally tardy'. Edward Dyne Brisco of Wakefield regarded the election result as requiring 'next to a miracle', considering the time lost at the beginning; Lascelles had more than a week's head-start there. But it was hoped that in such places as Barnsley where merchants had sent out their clerks to seek Lascelles votes, spreading word that Milton would not really stand, many would retract their promises. After a harsh denunciation of the clothiers by Lascelles's friend Col. Thomas Horton in the Halifax Piece Hall one day, the Milton committee picked up 300 'retractors'.

When an agent turned out to be a bad choice, as did Taylor of Bridlington, work did not begin until the mistake was corrected, and in this case George

---

[36] SCC:LAI: WWM, E177/36, Tottie to Fitzwilliam, 30 April 1807; E163/2, same to same, 4 May 1807; E163/5, Tottie to Milton committee, 16 May 1807.

Dawson who took over found himself riding from 5.00 a.m. to midnight to make up for lost time. Wilberforce was no small threat either, for by 30 April his 'Methodistical friends' were 'active and indefatigable' all over the county.[37]

The canvass books preserved in the Wentworth Woodhouse archive show the care with which each prospective voter was recorded, a method similar to that used in all three campaigns. Agents were instructed to obtain a list of freeholders from the land tax records, to request of each 'the favour' of his 'vote and interest', and to ask for which of the other two the man might vote. The freeholder also was asked where the property on which his qualification was based was located. The information gained was transmitted to the York committee where it was compiled into ledgers. Doubtful voters or persons requiring special persuasion were given additional attention.

In the 'observations' column are such telling phrases as 'rather Insane', 'won't promise till he arrives at York', 'an Idiot', 'will not attend unless conveyance sent', 'won't stir', 'at sea', 'Papist', 'undecided not Lascelles', 'needs personal visit', 'not 12 mo. in possession', 'won't say', 'won't vote for anyone', 'goes with [naming an important person]', 'abroad', 'assessed at only 30/', 'dead', 'don't pay land tax', 'obliges the Dean of York'. In the case of certain freeholders at East and West Ayton in the North Riding: 'These 5 would come if absolutely necessary but being very ancient or ill, would prefer not going.' Four of the five did make it to York and gave Milton their plumpers: a publican, a farmer, a yeoman and a gentleman. Of William Langstaff, shopkeeper, and Edward Weddall esq. of Bubwith in the East Riding, the canvasser said, 'two independent gentlemen & will vote accordingly if wanted may be applied to' (both, at the poll, gave single votes for Milton) while the Rev. George Ion of the same community 'obliges Ld Egremt with all the Votes he can get' for Wilberforce and Lascelles.

The rights of many potential voters were disputable. Whether they could slip by the scrutineers had to be weighed. Observations: 'if not objected to', 'If Mr Crowther, Agent for the Crown does not Interfere', 'has received coals once', 'a Catholic, think he will vote for Ld M if he votes', 'objects to taking the oath of supremacy'.[38]

---

[37] SCC:LAI: WWM, E156/54, 133; E158/1, 2, 5; E163/49; E171/6; E172/11,12, canvassing reports; E225, Brisco to Fitzwilliam, 15 June 1807; E151, circular to agents, 2 May 1807; E173/79, Ion to Milton, 12 May 1807; E225, Scatcherd to Fitzwilliam, 17 June 1807; E159/3, Keir to Milton committee, 12 May 1807; E159/1, Jackson to same, 10 May 1807; E177/112, Walker to Milton, 30 April 1807; E156/69, Alexander to Milton committee, 16 May 1807; E179/38, Dawson to Strickland, 18 September 1807; E170/6, Sinclair to Fitzwilliam, 30 April 1807.

[38] SCC:LAI: WWM, E221, Instructions for canvassing; E41, 51, 52, 59, canvass records.

Plate 1 'A Sheffield Cutler'.
(*Source*: George Walker, *The Costume of Yorkshire* (1885); photography © University of York)

Plate 2 'The Cloth Makers'.
(*Source*: George Walker, *The Costume of Yorkshire* (1885); photography © University of York)

Plate 3

'A Kick at the broad-bottoms! – i.e. – Emancipation of "All the Talents"'. The subject is the dismissal of the Ministry of All the Talents by George III (hidden behind the pillar), which precipitated the general election of 1807.

(Etched by James Gillray, print (1807); © The Trustees of the British Museum. All rights reserved.)

Plate 4
The Hon. Henry Lascelles (1767–1841), later second earl of Harewood.
(By Thomas Goff Lupton, after Sir Thomas Lawrence (1823), print (1828); © National Portrait Gallery, London)

Plate 5
Charles William Wentworth Fitzwilliam, Viscount Milton (1786–1857), later third Earl Fitzwilliam in the peerage of Great Britain and fifth Earl Fitzwilliam in the peerage of Ireland.
(By William Ward, after John Raphael Smith, print (1808); © The Trustees of the British Museum. All rights reserved.)

Plate 6
William Wilberforce, (1759–1833).
(By James Heath, after John Russell, print (1807);
© The Trustees of the British Museum. All rights reserved.)

Plate 7
The White Cloth Hall, Leeds.
(By Percy Robinson [1926], drawing reproduced from Thoresby Robinson Prints 7;
© The Thoresby Society, the Leeds Historical Society)

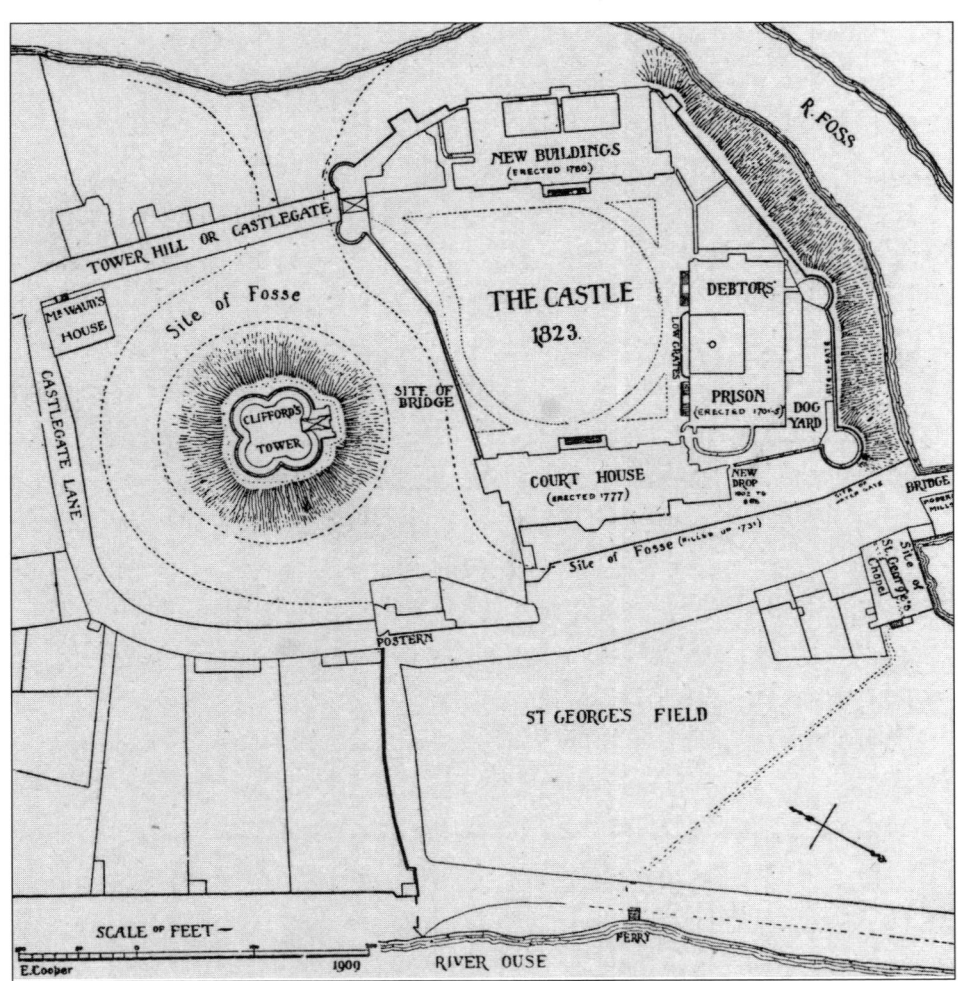

Plate 8 A Plan of York Castle.
(From T.P. Cooper, *The History of the Castle of York* (1911); photography © University of York)

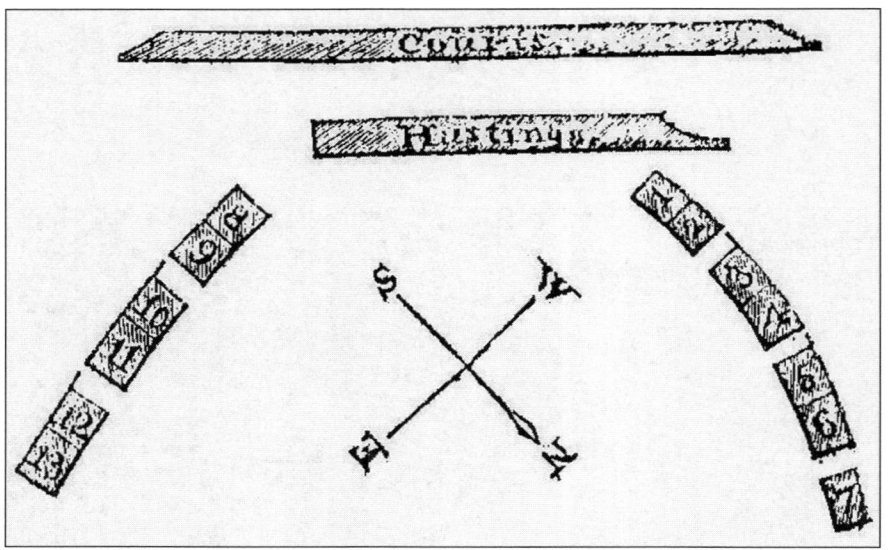

Plate 9 The arrangement of voting booths in Castle Yard.

Six booths were placed on one side of the castle-yard, and seven on the other. They began from the hustings, and proceeded right and left, extending wider as they approached the extremity, as represented in the sketch above.

The following is the plan is of two booths, as they appeared after some minute subsequent improvements and alterations

Key:
- A   admission bar
- B   second bar
- C   voter stands here
- D   tables, numbers for authorised persons
- E   rear exit
- H–h   rail outside crowded booths to form a 'pen like those for cattle'
- h–g   entrance to this 'pen'

(From Jonathan Gray, *An Account of the Manner of Proceeding at the Contested Election for Yorkshire, in 1807* (1818))

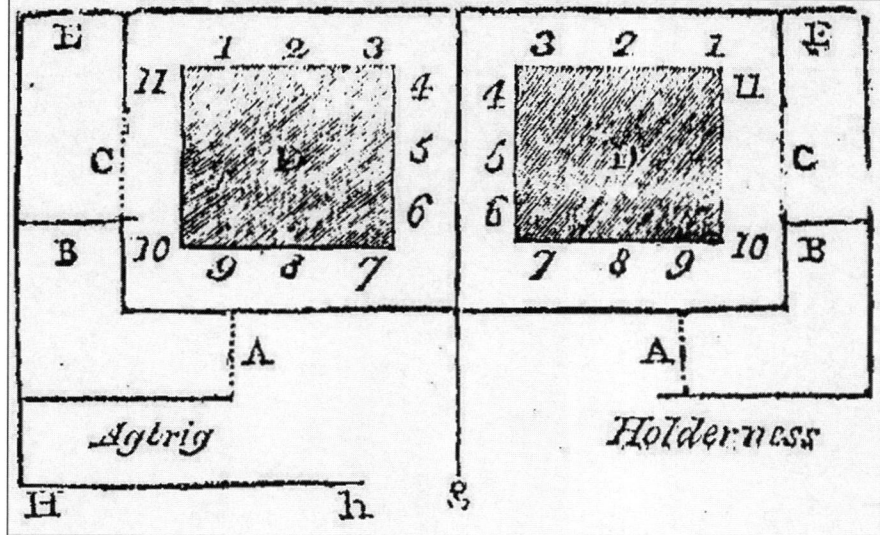

Plate 10 James Gillray, 'Orange Jumper'. This shows a 'character' in the Milton camp, standing in front of a hoarding covered with election posters near Milton's headquarters at Etridge's Hotel.
(By James Gillray from a drawing by Francis Hawkesworth, print (1809); © The Trustees of the British Museum. All rights reserved.)

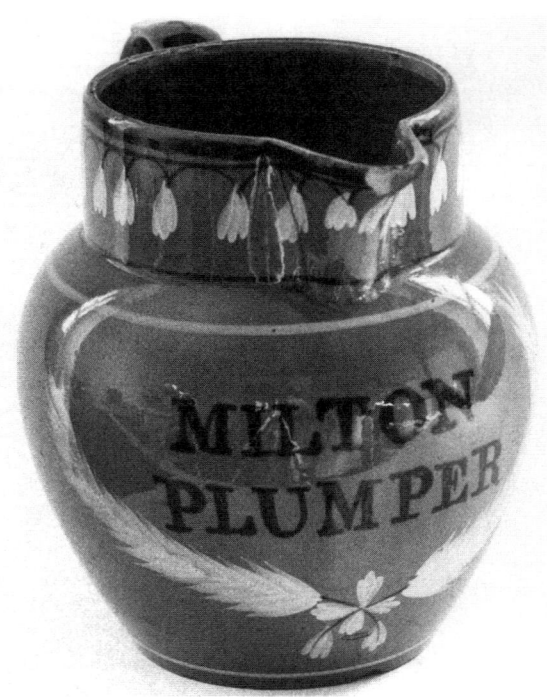

Plate 11
A Milton plumper jug.
(KINCM:1971.17; © Hull Museums: Wilberforce House)

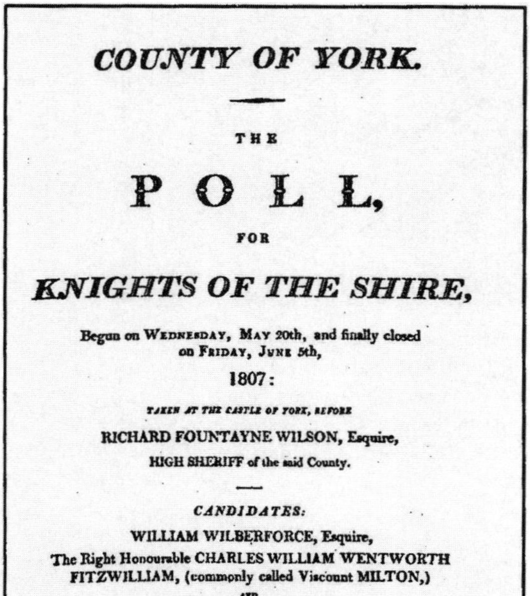

COUNTY OF YORK.

THE

POLL,

FOR

KNIGHTS OF THE SHIRE,

Begun on WEDNESDAY, MAY 20th, and finally closed on FRIDAY, JUNE 5th,

1807:

TAKEN AT THE CASTLE OF YORK, BEFORE

RICHARD FOUNTAYNE WILSON, Esquire,

HIGH SHERIFF of the said County.

CANDIDATES:

WILLIAM WILBERFORCE, Esquire,

The Right Honourable CHARLES WILLIAM WENTWORTH FITZWILLIAM, (commonly called Viscount MILTON,)

AND

The Honourable HENRY LASCELLES.

ARRANGED FROM

The Sheriff's POLL BOOKS, under the DIRECTION and INSPECTION of the UNDER SHERIFF.

YORK:

Printed by T. WILSON and R. SPENCE, High-Ousegate:

For J. MAWMAN, No. 22, Poultry, London; and for J. TODD, WILSON and SPENCE, and J. WOLSTENHOLME, York.

1807.

Plate 12
Title page from the County of York 1807 Poll Book.

The Canvass, 27 April–13 May

'The Fair Sex, as the best canvassers, were distinguishable in a high degree' in the Yorkshire election, said chroniclers at the time, and at least two women deserve special notice. Lady Elizabeth Laetitia Strickland of Boynton Hall near Bridlington, acting for the ailing Sir George, exercised the family's important interest for Lord Milton. It delighted her that her sons and daughters were also enthusiastic Miltonites: 'the latter', she wrote to Lady Fitzwilliam, 'could not have been surpassed even by Mrs. Osbaldeston in their activity and exertions, altho' they did not make themselves so conspicuous on their canvass'. Sons William and Arthur sat on the Milton committee in York and Henry had collected more than a hundred promises for Fawkes before they knew their candidate was Milton this time round.[39]

It was no use Lady Strickland trying to equate with motherly pride her daughters' efforts with those of the redoubtable Jane Osbaldeston of Hutton Buscel. She was the *non pareil* of the 1807 election, the toast of Milton dinners from Yorkshire to London, 'The Female Patriot'. One gala was staged entirely for her, at Malton on 6 June, the day after the poll closed, as she was driving home from York. Outside the town, the horses were taken from her carriage and she was drawn behind a band of musicians and a small forest of gold-fringed banners. Bells rang and 'a thousand acclamations' arose. 'Never was such an honour conferred on any person at Malton,' said the account in the *York Herald*, as for this 'worthy and strenuous advocate in Lord Milton's interest.' The cavalcade carried her to the Head Inn for an 'elegant refreshment' while the band played popular airs on the terrace. On her departure, Mrs Osbaldeston's carriage was dragged as far as Norton where the ladies in her party 'stripped themselves of their orange coloured ribbands and handkerchiefs to adorn the surrounding multitude'.[40]

Mrs Osbaldeston will be remembered now if at all as the mother of Squire George, who was admired in his prime as the 'best sportsman of any age or country'. He was just over 5 feet tall and looked like a fox cub, an acquaintance recalled, and he lacked entirely his mother's love of society and bustle. In particular, George did not care for politics. He was a few months younger than Lord Milton but inherited little of his own father's interest in public affairs. His mother persuaded him, on Fitzwilliam's recommendation, to stand for East Retford in 1812 and he never could remember how long (actually five years and nine months) he represented the constituency although he could recollect every detail of any hunt he had ever been on. He made one appearance in

---

[39] *York Herald*, 6 June 1807; SCC:LAI: WWM, E225, Lady Strickland to Lady Fitzwilliam, 22 June 1807; E222, same to same, 30 April 1807.
[40] *York Herald*, 13 and 20 June 1807; *Sheffield Iris*, 18 August 1807.

the House. 'I did not consider it an honour at all,' said George. 'I thought it a great bore.'

George's father, an MP for Scarborough, died in 1793, leaving his only son, then 6, large estates which, with the help of greedy trustees, his mother's extravagances and his own susceptibility to swindlers, diminished steadily. Of his mother, the former Jane Head, daughter of Sir Thomas Head of Langley, he was to write, 'a cleverer woman never existed, nor a better mother. None of her children have inherited half her intellect.' From friendship and distant kinship to the Fitzwilliams, she was devoted to Milton's cause and canvassed in person every voter within 25 miles of Hutton Buscel. 'Perhaps no lady ever performed such a feat, or even attempted it,' said George.

Poor George was dragged into the fun but, deciding that his efforts would only interfere with his mother's, he drifted off to York races. One day, he rode there on a 'fidgety hack' which slipped on Ouse bridge and rolled over him. A corkcutter carried his unconscious form to his shop where the young Osbaldeston took nearly a fortnight to recover.[41]

In 1806 Mrs Osbaldeston had flung herself with Sir George Cayley into the canvass of their Pickering Lythe wapentake and gained several hundred votes for Fawkes. She was in Sussex and in poor health in April 1807 when she read of Milton's candidacy and instantly offered to send George, then at Oxford, to the nomination meeting. She herself would return home and meanwhile her eldest daughter would alert their agents.[42]

The canvass books for Pickering Lythe wapentake, a stretch of vale and moorland which ran from west of Pickering to Scarborough on the sea and north as far as Goathland, show that it was painstakingly covered and largely by volunteer friends. W.B. Smart, the Hutton Buscel apothecary whose services Mrs Osbaldeston obtained by promising to send her own emissaries to all far-away points, testified that her direct efforts 'to serve the good old Rockingham cause can hardly be equalled not only by agency, but personal application'. The expenses for the wapentake amounted to £1,065 11s. 10d., of which £285 3s. 9d. was paid to the Scarborough solicitor Robert Smith Robson and £63 9s. 9d. to Mr Smart while entertainment and conveyance provided by innkeepers and publicans took £743 13s. 1d. But in spite of strenuous endeavours, Milton came in third, for the 1,035 electors gave 698 votes to

---

[41] Cuming, *Squire Osbaldeston*, p. 16; Smith, 'Earl Fitzwilliam and Malton', pp. 61–2; Smith, *Whig Principles*, p. 327. A less than flattering portrait of George Osbaldeston is reproduced in W.M. Ormrod (ed.), *The Lord Lieutenants and High Sheriffs of Yorkshire, 1066–2000* (Wharncliffe Books: Barnsley, 2000), p. 180.

[42] SCC:LAI: WWM, E209a, Denison to Fitzwilliam, 30 October 1806; E210, J. Osbaldeston to same, 20 October 1806; E222, same to same, 30 April 1807.

Wilberforce, 546 to Lascelles and 443 to Milton. Hutton Buscel bucked the trend: every one of its 16 resident voters cast a bullet for Milton.[1]

On Boxing day in 1807 George Osbaldeston came of age and his mother gave a party for 3,000 tenants and yeomen who feasted on roasted ox and sheep with plenty of ale. The spectacle of the booths and the crowd on the lawn of the mansion reminded many of the Castle Yard at York during the election and George proposed a toast to Lord Milton and the independence of the county while every bosom heaved 'with emotions of patriotism'. George remembered that more than half of the guests got 'beastly drunk' and space had to be cleared for them in the stables.[2]

The Milton expense accounts indicate (in all three Ridings it is impossible to be more specific because of the inconsistencies of reporting and the dearth of complete records) that he had around 65 paid agents in the field, like Lascelles with the major thrust in the West Riding where 37 were employed.[3] The East Riding was covered by 10 and the North by 17 with one other stationed in York. As usual, most were solicitors, but the Fitzwilliam estate agent at Malton, William Hastings, and Bowns's steward at Darley Hall, William Newman, also were drawn in. One surgeon, W. Royston of Wetherby, also turned his hand to the game.

The common retainer was five guineas a day. The Fitzwilliam accounts help more than the Harewood archive to clarify somewhat how much went to or through the agents and what was spent for committee activities. For example, Lewis Alexander of Halifax was paid £1,514 18s. 6d. and the Halifax committee spent another £295 18s. 2d. Top spender among the agents was H. Candler of Tadcaster at £2,602 1s. 9d. At Leeds the committee made use of £3,211 1s. 11d. while Tottie's firm received £484 12s. 11d. The Sheffield committee accounted for £3,385 4s. 3d. and the agents, Messrs Rogers & Shearwood, another £662 9s. 3d.

Double agents also turned up in the Milton camp, an outstanding one being William Iveson, the attorney and patron of Hedon, who was retained to cover Holderness for Milton but who ('a great traitor') worked for Lascelles. One agent for Keighley, Cuthbert Metcalf, did more harm than good, complained the other agent in the town, Thomas Delaface, for he was not on his horse a half dozen times and employed Joseph Sharp, an avowed enemy of Milton, to get votes. Sharp instead solicited for Lascelles. It had not been simple to recruit Delaface who had got 550 votes for Fawkes, spent 15 guineas out of his own pocket and never was recompensed. This time he had warned

---

[1] SCC:LAI: WWM, E59, 106, 166/1,2, Pickering Lythe returns; E179/23, J. Osbaldeston to Bowns, 17 August 1807; E166/4, Smart to Milton committee, 10 May 1807; E91, accounts.
[2] *Rockingham*, 2 January 1808; Cuming, *Squire Osbaldeston*, pp. 16, 212.
[3] SCC:LAI: WWM, E114, Payments to Agents; E83, Agents and Districts.

he would have to know who was paying before he stirred. Shepley Watson of Barnsley, another Milton agent, collected split votes for Lascelles. Stumped for an agent around Northallerton, Lascelles country, a supporter came up with the name of a clerk with one of the 'inferior attorneys' whose father was the parish clerk. This young Bray could collect local information but was not 'suffic[ientl]y respectable to put in the foreground'.[4]

The leading men who served on Milton's committees compared well to Lascelles's although there seemed to be fewer such bodies and no meetings were called anywhere to implore Milton to stand. Rather, the Milton gatherings publicly lamented the loss of a 'virtuous and economical administration' which had sacrificed office for duty and distinguished itself in detecting public defaulters, reforming public spending and abolishing the 'Diabolical SLAVE TRADE'. The Rev. Richard Sykes was the indefatigable chairman in Hull. Col. George Wroughton of Adwicke Hall, working with Bryan Cooke of Alverley Grange, the sitting MP for Malton, was tireless at the head of the strategic Doncaster committee. Hugh Parker of Woodthorpe headed the committee in Sheffield where members included the Duke of Norfolk's agent, Vincent Eyre; Samuel Shore, the ironmaster who had entered politics with Wyvill and the Yorkshire Association; and the Revs Wilfred Huddleston and James Dixon who were among the relatively few Anglican clergymen to figure in the Milton campaign. He had, of course, the useful support of Mr Lowe at Wentworth and such others as the Rev. James Bailey, vicar of Otley, home parish of Francis Hawksworth, Fawkes's brother, who reported that 55 of the 58 voters there would plump for Milton. No churchman applied himself more heartily than the Rev. Francis Wrangham of Hunmanby who had signed up 200 promises by 30 April. 'We go on swimmingly,' he reported with justifiable satisfaction.[5]

At York, the central committee was headed by William Wrightson of Cusworth Hall, outside Doncaster, and took over Etridge's Hotel (formerly Bluitt's) in Lendal, the 'exclusive resort of the nobility and country gentry'. Instead of building its business on stage coaches and mails, Etridge's provided relays of horses for those travelling in their own equipages. The proprietor, Thomas Etridge, was a freeman and familiar figure whose 24 stone bulk filled the gig in which he drove around the city each day.[6]

---

[4] SCC:LAI: WWM, E179/40, Delaface to Bowns, 2 May 1807; E163/13, Wates to same, 2 May 1807.

[5] SCC:LAI: WWM, E173/71, E156/68; *Hull Packet*, 5 and 19 May 1807; *Sheffield Iris*, 12 May 1807; E177/122, Bailey to Milton, 1 May 1807; E173/3, Wrangham to Nicoll, 30 April 1807.

[6] Bradley, *Old Coaching Days*, pp. 66, 68, 79; YA: M22, Robert H. Skaife, 'Catalogue of Lord Mayors and other Civic Officials of York (1895)'.

Like his rivals, Milton's first concern was to make his obeisance to the industrial West Riding, with particular attention to the clothiers. He would be 'universally supported by the *Manufacturing* Body – the Merchants are generally against him ... but the manufacturing body will turn out 10, 20 – 100 to 1 in numbers of Freeholders', Fitzwilliam calculated. At Birstall, Dewsbury and Bradford the clothiers took Milton's horses from their traces and dragged his carriage, but such effusions although heartening should not be boasted about for fear of prodding the enemy to stir more. Instead the papers were informed that Milton had been 'politely received'. Speaking for Pudsey with its concentration of cloth makers, William Stowe noted that most men entertained Whig principles but all opposed Lascelles because he had objected to their petition.[7]

Milton's speech at the Leeds White Cloth Hall on 5 May was a cloudless triumph in complete contrast to the rough handling of Lascelles, and a tribute to the careful arrangements of the clothiers. His speech was reprinted all over the county and in London as well. At a stroke, he seemed to destroy the doubts about his youth, his ability and his doctrines. After his Leeds speech, he became, to his own father's surprise, 'the popular Candidate'. Lord Fitzwilliam had never been optimistic. At Leeds, he had predicted, Milton 'must fail: there is an antient ill-will to the House of Wentworth prevalent in the Corporation ... it is Lascelles's Hd Qrs, but carried little with it on the last Election.'[8]

The clothiers left nothing to chance. The trustees met on 2 May and arranged to bring in Milton supporters from every manufacturing district on the following Tuesday market day. 'Your Lordship will meet with a most flattering reception,' promised Richard Lee. John Heywood at Wakefield urged Milton not to exhaust himself before Leeds as so much depended upon that performance. The chief criticisms he would meet were his age, the alleged 'juggle with Fawkes' and the 'general nonsense of No Popery'. Milton followed the hapless Lascelles on the hustings in the Cloth Hall yard before the crowd of nearly 5,000. Waves of applause welcomed the platform party. Fawkes first, in a sparkling speech, denied any deal had been made between him and Milton, who added his own word of honour that the accusation was totally false. As Milton concluded his address, '*The Air was rent with continued acclamations*'. His 'manly sentiments, delivered in a firm and powerful voice, electrified the assembly'. The crowd then drew his 'chariot' to Richard Lee's house by a roundabout tour of Leeds to huzzas of '*Milton for Ever*'.

---

[7]   NRO: F(M), 72/3, Fitzwilliam to Wentworth, 4 May 1807; SCC:LAI: WWM, E178/7, Stowe to Milton, 30 April 1807.

[8]   SCC:LAI: WWM, E226, Fitzwilliam to Lonsdale, 12 May 1807; E225, Peckover to Rawnsley, 9 May 1807; NRO: F(M), X515/23/1–3, Fitzwilliam to Baldwin, 1 May 1807.

That, at least, is what happened according to Baines's *Mercury*. Griffith Wright and the *Intelligencer* put it rather differently. An 'immense rabble ... evidently hired for the purpose of insulting Mr. Lascelles' had taken possession of the yard early in the morning and to cheer for Milton when he arrived with Fawkes and 'no less than SIXTEEN *interested* gentlemen'. Milton, however, was not Wright's chief target this day. That was Fawkes, Milton's *'prompter'*, who was accused of using 'Dr. W-ng-m' [Francis Wrangham] as a speech writer, the opening shot in what was to be a persistent onslaught against Milton through Fawkes. A Quaker from Bradford who witnessed Lascelles's visit to the hall said 'the Mayor Corporation nor the Merchants put together could ever procure [Lascelles] a hearing Tho' much strugling & many blows were given & rec'd by the latter'. Some merchants declared that they would buy no more cloth from anyone who was for Milton, 'and I believe Cloth was actually taken back ... for this reason'.

Milton's seven-minute cloth hall speech, prolonged by eight bursts of applause, regretted the dissolution of a Parliament whose greatest achievement was the abolition of the slave trade and he praised Wilberforce for his long service to that cause. The manner in which that Parliament had been ended was 'unprecedented since the Revolution' and gave reason to suspect the 'most corrupt motives have led to this profligate act'. He recalled that at the moment Black Rod summoned the Commons to the Lords for the prorogation, the finance committee was ready to report that a man [Steele] entrusted with public money had diverted thousands to his own use. Without naming him, Milton implied that Lord Melville was 'lurking behind the curtain' of the new administration 'not the prow of the vessel which first presents itself to one's sight, but the rudder which directs its motions'.[9] This oratory generated 'thunders of applause'. As did every candidate, Milton claimed to stand independently, pledged to no man or set of men. 'The party, with whom I act, I will abandon as soon as they abandon the interests of their country,' he declared. He denied charges that he wished to overthrow the Constitution. The hallmark of political independence was not freedom from party principles but patriotic citizenship and commitment to the common weal. He believed the country would benefit by relaxing some laws against 'DISSENTERS of all descriptions, both Protestants and Catholics', although he was personally attached to the Established Church. 'But such is the malice and the imbecility of my enemies, that they roundly assert, that I maintain in my house a Popish Priest.' This brought cries of indignation.

---

[9] Henry Dundas, Lord Melville, was in 1806 the last person to be impeached (unsuccessfully) in Britain for the misappropriation of public money.

The accusation that he was young was true, but it gave him the advantage of not being 'confirmed in error, or grown old in prejudice'. His friends could attest that from an early age he was accustomed to habits of industry and application to business. He turned to some of these friends on the platform, who nodded 'Yes! Yes!' 'Besides, Gentlemen, it must surely be proper that the Representative for the County of York should serve a regular Apprenticeship. (*Plaudits*).'

As an MP, said Milton, he would be a trustworthy guardian of the public purse. Above all, he would pay the greatest attention to the wool trade; 'I will observe the strictest justice, and the most perfect impartiality between the merchant and the manufacturer,' he said. The prosperity of the British Empire depended on his auditors, who clothed half the world. 'You, Gentlemen, are the most industrious, the most useful of his Majesty's subjects,' he added, a sentiment with which they could not disagree. And with confidence in the outcome based upon assurances from a 'very great majority of the landed interest' and 'aided by your exertions and your enthusiasm', the weedy, red-haired young candidate promised to stand a poll.

A song, 'British Clothiers', circulated widely afterwards to commemorate this conquest of the cloth halls. It ran, in part:

> Sit down, Neighbours all, and hear with Exultation,
> The Victory we've gain'd o'er the mighty Corporation!
> The BRAMLEY's and the NICHOLSON's would fain have chosen Harry,
> But COOKSON *and his Coffee-room this point shall never carry!*
>
> This HARRY was a staunch Friend to GOTT and to his factory;
> He call'd the poor Croppers, 'Disaffected and refractory':
> He slander'd British subjects with the title of *Sedition*,
> *Because we sent to Parliament a dutiful Petition!!*
>
> To enrich individuals with HARRY we will all agree,
> There is nothing in the world so *useful* as Machinery:
> But surely, Mr. L–sc–lles, there is very little reason
> Why all who have not *Gig Mills*, are guilty of HIGH TREASON![10]

---

[10] SCC:LAI: WWM, E177/45, Lee to Milton, 2 May 1807; E177/67, Heywood to Milton, 2 May 1807; E177/43, Maude to same, 3 May 1807; *Leeds Mercury*, 9 May 1807; *Leeds Intelligencer*, 11 May 1807; SCC:LAI: WWM, E225, Peckover to Rawnsley, 9 May 1807; *Yorkshire Election*, pp. 14–17; Election Squibs, 1807; *Sheffield Iris*, 19 May 1807.

Even among his well-wishers, Milton's reference to the dissolution as a 'profligate act' caused unease, for it seemed to be a direct criticism of the King. At least two supporters deserted him because of it. But he was showered with compliments. Lord Dundas ordered 500 copies of the speech to distribute in the North Riding and told Milton, 'I think you now have the game in your Hand'. 'Fore God you are not mealy-mouthed, but I declare to God you sometimes take away my breath,' Lord Dorchester glowed.[11]

Fawkes who had at one time hoped to sink into oblivion, was pressed into service to accompany Milton on parts of the West Riding circuit to pacify the supporters whom he had let down by his speedy abdication. But, as it happened, he was not of the party with Milton at Halifax where he would have seen black handbills ridiculing him in some of his own ringing phrases from the previous autumn. 'so, POOR WATTY ... is compelled to accompany and proclaim from Town to Town, those eminent Qualities of his strippling Successor, which may indeed be found in Watty's Oratory, but will be inquired for, in vain, in Parliament. Poor Watty has been made the *Stalking Horse* of the Wentworth-House Faction, his Popularity amongst disaffected Foxites and a Jacobin Rabble was made use of ... till the Heir ... might be of Age to take his Place.' The posters promised that a great crowd of 'Croppers and Rabble' would turn out on 9 May to see the 'Mountebank and the Merry Andrew' whose speeches were cranked out by 'Parson Wrangham with more than his usual Pomp and Felicity'.[12]

The *Leeds Intelligencer* asserted that because Milton had too few friends in Halifax to put on a good show, a rabble – there was no other kind of Milton audience – was brought in from the country and promised free meat and ale. The 'tumultuous and expectant beef-eaters and drinkers' engulfed the candidate's carriage and drew it to the Piece Hall where Milton was hoisted on their shoulders and borne to the 'place of harangue', said that paper. The *Leeds Mercury* denounced this 'outrage on truth and decency' by the *Intelligencer*'s 'scribbling Junto' and reported, with others, that Milton's Halifax reception was one of the grandest manifestations yet seen. A 'mob' hired to hiss, cut his carriage ropes and slash the drumheads had succeeded only in getting thrashed. Milton's Halifax agent, Lewis Alexander, managed to get the *Intelligencer* to print a letter correcting its account. From other sources, it appears that Milton's carriage was met two or three miles from town by several hundreds on foot who unhitched his horses, fastened on ropes and

---

[11] SCC:LAI: WWM, E224, Cooke to Fitzwilliam, 16 May 1807; E178/42, Hewgill to Milton committee, 16 May 1807; E117/13, Dundas to Fitzwilliam, 7 May 1807; E173/45, Dorchester to Milton; McCormack, *Independent Man*, p. 3.

[12] SCC:LAI: WWM, E222, W. Fawkes to Fitzwilliam [30 April 1807]; F. Fawkes to same, 5 May 1807; E173/15, Lee to Milton committee, 3 May 1807; E221, poster.

drew him towards Halifax. A mile out they were joined by 62 gentlemen on horseback, a large band and the drums and fifes of the volunteer corps. 'The Bells rang merrily' as the carriage was dragged to the Piece Hall where 20,000 (it was claimed) had gathered. The speech was much like his Leeds address except that Milton dwelt on his party connections with Frederick Lumley of Tickhill Castle, nephew of Sir George Savile, standing near him. 'I am ... what my enemies have insinuated – a party man,' Milton asserted, and his references to Whig principles and to Savile were loudly applauded. Afterwards Milton dined at the Talbot with about 60 prominent men, and was dragged out of Halifax as he had been brought in.[13]

At Huddersfield a Lascelles supporter was seen desperately ripping Milton posters from a wall with a cowl rake before his appearance there on 12 May, the day before the nomination meeting at York. It was reported as another joyful occasion. Milton was escorted into town by a band amid the usual 'acclamations of thousands'. After visiting the cloth hall he was introduced by the Rev. John Lowe from a window of the George Inn to the people crammed into the market place and exploded, so it was said, all the allegations levelled against him and exhibited a 'maturity greatly surpassing his years'. 'Instead of a papist they found a member of the church of England, and a friend to toleration: – instead of disaffection, they found loyalty: instead of a *dealer in blood*, the advocate for the abolition of slavery, a truly independent character.' This last phrase was important. To be of independent character implied virtue, manliness as opposed to effeminacy or childhood. Milton had only just reached legal manhood, so to assert his independence was to reinforce the message of maturity.[14]

Milton's last important appearance in the county's industrial heartland was at Sheffield. Hugh Parker, his chairman there, had reported a highly favourable canvass and his visit on 16 May was expertly staged. Once more the entrance procession was led by musicians and his carriage drawn by partisans to the Tontine Inn where he breakfasted with several hundred supporters. To an overflow audience at the Town Hall, Milton delivered an energetic defence of his views, echoing his Leeds speech, but was more precise in blaming the 'profligate act' of dissolution on the King's advisers, not His Majesty. Of allegations that he would subvert the Constitution or the Church, he declared he had been 'taught from infancy to revere the Constitution, as established in the Revolution of 1688 ... educated in the tenets of the Church of England

---

[13] *Leeds Intelligencer*, 11 May 1807; *Leeds Mercury*, 16 May 1807; SCC:LAI: WWM, E178/180, Talbot to Fawkes, n.d.; E173/31, Lumley to Milton, 6 May 1807; *Halifax Journal*, 16 May 1807; *Leeds Intelligencer*, 18 May 1807.

[14] *Sheffield Iris*, 19 May 1807; *Leeds Mercury*, 9 May 1807; McCormack, *Independent Man*, p. 5.

... and embraced its doctrines from conviction'. 'But because I venerate the Church of England, am I to withhold all toleration from others who dissent from it and from me? No! I must be allowed to plead for privileges which in my soul I am convinced ought to be extended to every class of His Majesty's subjects, at a time when all their hands and all their hearts are required to support the glory, independence and power of the Country.' 'Perhaps there was never an occasion in Sheffield,' said the *Iris*, 'on which so much popular joy was expressed in favour of any visitor [as] towards the illustrious heir of the HOUSE OF WENTWORTH' to whose beneficence Sheffield could testify.[15]

---

[15] NRO: F(M), 72/3, Fitzwilliam to Wentworth, 4 May 1807; SCC:LAI: WWM, E224, Parker to Fitzwilliam, 4 and 9 May 1807; E224, Browne to same, 12 May 1807; KINCM:1982.895.409, Account of Proceedings, fols 354–5; *Sheffield Iris*, 19 May 1807.

CHAPTER NINE

Nomination Day in York

O N a wet Wednesday 13 May the candidates girt their swords; and their musicians, banner bearers and retinues emerged from their respective inns to lead separate processions through the winding ways of the mellow city of York and into Castlegate, which led through a portal into the walled greensward of Castle Yard. This space, from its oval shape, was called the 'eye of the county' and all great public meetings for Yorkshire assembled here. Here, too, royal proclamations were read and convicted criminals hanged. Between events, deer fed on the grass and visitors strolled along the gravelled walks, sometimes chatting through the windows with friends temporarily incarcerated in the commodious debtors' prison, one of the tasteful new buildings on the perimeter of the yard. The others were John Carr's impressive assize courts, with its broad stone steps leading into a columned portico under a pediment where Justice held her scales and spear, and the elegant female prison opposite. Looming romantically over all on its massive Norman motte was the derelict white stone keep of Clifford's Tower, sprouting trees and shrubs.

In 1807, York, although spoken of as England's second city, had a population of fewer than 19,000, most of them packed inside the medieval walls which ran for two and three-quarter miles around the centre. Four battlemented gates, protected by barbicans, led in and out: Micklegate, facing the direction of London; Bootham, from which ran the road to Newcastle and Edinburgh; Monk, leading towards Scarborough and the coast, and Walmgate, the exit or entrance for Beverley and Hull. Six posterns guarded the only other openings in the wall. The city was built on a peninsula formed by the confluence of the Ouse and Foss rivers, a site chosen by Roman invaders in the year AD 71. The streets outside and inside each entrance gate (or bar, as York people knew them) were lined with inns. Extensive rebuilding in dignified brick and stone in the eighteenth century had not eliminated all of the overhanging timber-framed houses that, in various stages of dilapidation, edged the tangled streets. York had reached its peak in the fifteenth century when it was a port for wool sent to the Continent. It revived in the eighteenth century as a market town and northern social capital. Country gentry built town houses in it to enjoy more comfortably the markets and fairs, the races, assizes, Theatre Royal and Assembly Rooms. Its workshops produced small quantities of linens, gloves, flint glass, livery lace, wigs, combs, books, chemicals, flour and sweets, and its craftsmen were renowned for their work on some of the finest houses in the kingdom. The Ouse, crossed by one medieval bridge, was crowded with sloops and barges carrying grain, butter and coal. There were pastures and orchards within the walls. The drains emptied into the streams. A visitor was wise to beware of the 'vile York water affecting the lower organs'. Except for Pavement, the streets were atrocious to walk on and so narrow that 'air cannot purify nor smoke rise'. 'A lady is in some danger should she meet a chimney-sweeper,' one observer commented, and from the leaning garrets lovers 'might steal a kiss across the street at mid-day'. The lofty towers of York Minster soared above the huddled roofs, a gigantic landmark for miles across the flat surrounding plain.[1]

The spring of 1807 had brought tempestuous weather with sudden changes from winter to midsummer temperatures. Violent storms had caused floods in the West Riding where a woman, four children and many beasts were drowned. Torrential rain had washed out some fields of corn, but on nomination day in York it was just quietly drizzling on the several thousand electors and onlookers who filled the Castle Yard. It was, as always, a theatrical event and had been advertised as such by Lascelles and Milton wits:

By desire of the Right Hon. Earl F–tz–m,
On Wednesday, May the 13th, 1807, at the Theatre, Castle-Yard, York,
his Majesty's late servants will perform a grand melo-
drama, (never acted here before) called,
'OF AGE TO-MORROW' …
To conclude with the popular farce of
'WHO IS THE DUPE?'

Tickets to be had of the Managers, at Etridge's.
By desire of the Worshipful the Company of Merchants

---

[1] Royal Commission on Historical Monuments (England), *Inventory of the Historical Monuments in the City of York*, 5 vols (HMSO: 1962–81), vol. 2, *The Defences* (1972); [Stillman], *Journal*, vol. 2, pp. 243–8; Bigland, *Beauties XVI Yorkshire*, pp. 231, 237–40; Hutton, *Tour*, pp. 47–58, 61; M. Hallett and J. Rendall (eds), *Eighteenth-Century York: Culture, Space and Society* (Borthwick Institute: York, 2003); WYAS(L): WYL250/6/3/9, Frankland to Lascelles, 20 October 1806.

trading to Africa, on Wednesday the 13th of May instant, his Majesty's present Ministers will present
a new Tragedy, called the
WEST INDIAN: or *Slavery revived ...*

The Manager being disappointed of the assistance of
the YORKSHIRE CLOTHIERS, their places will be supplied
by a company of NEGRO DRIVERS, whom the Manager has
lately engaged at a great expence.[2]

The stage was the hustings, erected in front of the assize courts and big enough to hold 100 men, about eight feet above the ground and roofed against inclement weather (see Plate 9).

High Sheriff, Richard Fountayne Wilson, opened the proceedings at 11 o'clock and Wilberforce was nominated by Sir Robert D'Arcy Hildyard who had put his name forward on five previous occasions.[3] The nomination was seconded by Bacon Frank, giving Wilberforce two highly respectable sponsors, landowners respectively in the North and West Ridings. Except for deploring the prospect of a contest and recognizing Wilberforce's dedicated service to the county, neither took much time about his task. Frank paid a brief tribute to Wilberforce's tireless work for abolition of the slave trade.

Lascelles was nominated by John Bacon Sawrey Morritt, who declared roundly that it was a stain upon the county's character that Lascelles had not been adequately supported in the autumn election. Morritt emphasized Lascelles's maturity, contrasting it with Milton's inexperience, and endorsed the King's action in dismissing the previous administration, concentrating in his remarks on the risks that lay in Catholic emancipation. The Leeds Recorder, John Hardy, seconded the nomination and it signified the growing political power of the industrial parts of Yorkshire that Lascelles's proposers had strong Leeds, rather than country, connections, for Morritt, although his seat was at Rokeby Park near Greta Bridge, was the father of William, a Leeds merchant and hearty friend of Lascelles.[4] Probably in response to placards exhibited that day around town, Hardy pledged that, if the slave trade question were revived, Lascelles would 'not only vote for the Abolition of the Slave Trade, but even for the Abolition of Slavery itself', something the leading slave trade abolitionists had never promised. When Lascelles later

---

[2] *Leeds Mercury*, 9 May 1807; *Wakefield Star*, 15 May 1807; *Yorkshire Election*, 34–5.
[3] For the proceedings, *York Herald*, 16 May 1807; *Sheffield Iris*, 19 May 1807; *York Courant*, 18 May 1807; *York Chronicle*, 21 and 28 May 1807; *Doncaster Gazette*, 15 May 1807; *Leeds Intelligencer*, 18 May 1807; *Leeds Mercury*, 16 May 1807; *Hull Advertiser*, 16 May 1807.
[4] Wilson, *Gentlemen Merchants*, p. 171.

spoke for himself he was more circumspect. 'It might be supposed from his being unfortunately connected with West Indian property, that he should vote for measures tending to impede the Abolition ... but he pledged himself to resist any such attempts to the utmost of his power,' the papers reported.

Lord Milton was nominated and seconded by chief proprietors, according to convention, both resident in the West Riding, but Walter Fawkes, who proposed him, was in the unique position of having to defend his own conduct while recommending his successor. Sir Francis Lindley Wood of Hemsworth seconded the nomination, calling attention to Milton's political descent from Rockingham and Savile. Fawkes was given more space than the candidates by both friendly and antagonistic editors who reflected the public curiosity about his startling withdrawal. He told the crowd he believed it unfair to his large family to fight a 'powerful opposition' in 'the peculiar circumstances of the times'. After the political practices he had witnessed at Westminster he knew he could not continue there with 'satisfaction to myself or advantage to you'. He defended his parliamentary votes, praising the previous government for its opposition to 'public plunder' and added taxes and as the 'Deliverer of Africa'. As for its alleged attempt to introduce 'Popery', some of the same ministers the electors were now called upon to support 'to secure you from monkery and mummery – from the cowl and the cope, and the crucifix – from fire and faggot', who were to 'serve as a sort of oilskin case to protect you from Holy Water', had resigned with Pitt when the King refused their own Catholic relief proposals in 1801. The Duke of Portland, George Canning, Lord Castlereagh and Lord Cornwallis were named as having at one time or other taken a pro-Catholic (or pro-Irish) position.

'What then, Gentlemen, is the main difference between the late and the present administration? Why the former dared to perform the unpleasant and dangerous task of acquainting the King with what they thought necessary for the safety of his dominions – while the latter have smothered their sentiments and agreed never to talk to him of anything unpleasant.' This, Fawkes averred, was novel and unconstitutional conduct.

This opinion led him to oppose Lascelles, although there was no more amiable or active man in public life, and to recommend Lord Milton, who was diligent, knowledgeable beyond his years, anxious to serve and a powerful advocate of independent principles. Fawkes had a warm word for Wilberforce, too.

The *Leeds Intelligencer* claimed that most of Fawkes's address was drowned in shouts from the rain-soaked crowd, and the *Hull Advertiser* referred to 'loud clamours' when the Catholic question was raised. In fact, Lascelles's friends had flooded early into the Castle Yard to take up the space in front of the hustings and heckle Fawkes and Milton. Besides those who had been entreated to come from outside the city, there was a substantial segment of York citizenry. Having heard rumours that Lascelles was 'half sick of the business already', they were afraid they would be cheated out of a contest and crowded 'in shoals' to the Castle Yard to cheer his 'drooping spirits'.[5]

The candidates spoke in the order of their nomination, Wilberforce first 'with that easy flow of eloquence so natural to him', as the *Sheffield Iris* related. He made one of his infrequent references in county electioneering to his own great achievement in the abolition of the slave trade and promised that so long as Spencer Perceval, a friend for 25 years, led the administration, any effort to repeal the abolition act would be stoutly opposed. Wilberforce conceded freely that without the support of the dismissed ministers the act could not have carried. To his regret, however, he had to oppose them on other measures. He believed that the King in the dispute over the Catholic bill had been treated disrespectfully and had a perfect right to dissolve Parliament. But his tone was conciliatory and he clearly wished to avoid becoming entangled in national arguments: it was his conduct as their representative he wished them to judge. He had been elected as a private man, almost unknown to them. He had not sought personal riches or aggrandizement at the expense of their welfare or the country's. It was gratifying to 'think that amidst every political difference of opinion, they all knew the value of liberty, and the blessings of our free constitution'. In all the jewels that adorned the crown of the sovereign, 'the brightest was the love and gratitude of a free people'.

To W.N.W. Hewitt, a Fawkes committeeman in 1806, who shouted a question on Wilberforce's relation to the other candidates, Wilberforce declared that he stood 'perfectly unconnected' with either one. He put himself into the hands of his friends and would not presume to dictate how they disposed of their second votes.

Lascelles confirmed that he and Wilberforce had not joined forces. He stood as a public duty, impelled by many solicitations. Most of the rest of his speech was devoted to his stand on the woollen bill. The prejudice against him because of it could only stem from ignorance. To fetter capital would deprive all parties of prosperity. He had been concerned not with popular outcry but with the general interest of the country and Wilberforce had agreed with his position, but no clamour had arisen against him. Why should he, Lascelles, alone be blamed for it? The answer was because the criticism had arisen from a 'polluted source'. The York press represented Lascelles as saying that the domestic system was 'expiring … almost … extinct' but Lascelles complained to his agent later that this was a gross falsehood, probably put in mischievously. He concluded by commending the King for dissolving Parliament 'for the safety of our Constitution'. Pitt, he observed, had never dragged his sovereign

---

[5] SCC:LAI: WWM, E224, Scatcherd to Fitzwilliam, 15 May 1807; *Yorkshire Election*, p. 66.

'to the bar of the people'. Lascelles spoke, according to most accounts, in a 'firm and manly' way and was both audible and impressive. He ended to loud applause.

Milton spoke last, and from the printed reports, least. He made the points he had laid out in his Cloth Hall speech, citing once more the frustrated finance committee report and inferring again that it was Lord Melville and not Perceval as Wilberforce would have it who 'conducted the vessel of State'. Milton presented himself as a candidate eager to investigate public affairs, watchful of the public spending and imbued with the principles of his ancestors, although he stood, of course, as an independent. He recalled to their minds the popular Savile as one of his models – not that he could equal him in ability, only in integrity. He declared his attachment to the Established Church but was also a believer in 'enlightened toleration'. As their member, he would promote Yorkshire's wool and shipping.

Col. Horton of Halifax stepped forward on the hustings to belabour Milton as a disciple of Fox and friend to Catholics but the dripping crowd 'did not seem anxious to be detained any longer' so the high sheriff called for a show of hands. Wilberforce's friends thought it looked like 7 to 1 for him and Lascelles, with an almost universal vote for the former.[6] Lascelles's people estimated it at 10 to 1 against Milton. Sheriff Wilson contented himself with declaring a 'considerable majority' for the old members. Lord Milton then announced that, since a show of hands was not an accurate reflection of opinion in all the county, he would on election day demand a poll. The meeting broke up at 2 p.m.

Wilberforce's judgment of the day's oratory was 'Morritt's excellent. ... Lord Milton pretty well. I but middling.' A retired Leeds innkeeper, John Hick, told friends Milton had been a joy to see, speaking 'bold as a Lyon' and bringing tears to the eyes of those who remembered the great days of Rockingham and Savile. A bit of horseplay indulged in by Lascelles to ridicule Milton's youth was adroitly turned against him, to the crowd's amusement. Lascelles stepped across the hustings and handed Milton a child's whip and a top. Unruffled, Milton threw the top into the audience and returned the whip, suggesting Lascelles's father might find it useful to flog his slaves.[7] Milton had not tried to procure a big turnout on nomination day. Those of his supporters who could go to York without inconvenience were encouraged to do so but at their own expense. Heartened by his canvassing results, especially in the West Riding, he expected to win through a poll. Wilberforce likewise had exerted little pressure to bring his followers in for the preliminary formality. But Lascelles, in the

---

[6] KINCM:1982.895.409, Account of Proceedings, fol. 6.
[7] Wilberforce, *Life*, vol. 3, p. 318; SCC:LAI: WWM, E225, Hick to Crofts, 16 June 1807; Stirling, *Letter-Bag*, vol. 1, pp. 138–9; *Halifax Journal*, 30 June 1807; Clarkson, *Memories*, pp. 185–6.

forlorn hope of settling the election on the day, had stirred mightily. Friends and tenants had been called from as far away as Stockton-on-Tees and he let it be known that if he did not make a good showing on 13 May he would be weary of the business. His worried supporters in the Castle Yard, to bolster his nerve, had held up both their hands, the *Leeds Mercury* jeered.[8]

Fitzwilliam's allies in Hull had made one overture to avoid the staggering cost of an election, but without success. The Rev. Richard Sykes had conveyed to Wilberforce's friend, the banker Thomas Thompson, an offer to bring in Wilberforce, who was known to be much alarmed at the thought of a county contest, 'free of all expence' at Hull if he would relinquish his county seat. Thompson reportedly wished Wilberforce would agree, but doubted, rightly, that he would.[9]

In the post-nomination debating, the *Intelligencer* indulged its appetite for Fawkes-baiting by charging, among other things, that his address was composed by Francis Wrangham, but the latter denied he had ever suggested a single word for Fawkes whose eloquence was entirely his own.[10] But this minor feud was of dwindling interest as the election contest got underway in earnest. Fawkes returned to London where his wife was expecting another baby. He carried excellent reports of her husband's performance to Lady Milton, who also heard from another spectator that Milton had astonished him with the strength of his voice. 'They told us he was a boy, but this is not the voice of a boy & he don't speak like one,' people had commented.[11]

Milton's report to his father recommended that they accept a proposal from Wilberforce committeemen that, as Wilberforce seemed safe, both Lascelles and Milton should give him their second votes to save him the cost of the contest. It might be unpopular to drive Wilberforce out of the race, Milton thought. To Fitzwilliam's relief, the committee under William Wrightson turned the proposition down. 'There may attach some unpopularity from the appearance of distressing Wilberforce at the expence of a contest: but ... what mischief must have ensued from ensuring him his election, & placing him in a situation, that would enable him to throw much of his own interest into the scale of Lascelles, without the least risk of suffering himself,' the earl told Wrightson.[12]

---

[8] SCC:LAI: WWM, E151, Wrightson's circular letter, 7 May 1807; NRO: F(M), 72/13, Fitzwilliam to Wentworth, 12 May 1807; *Leeds Intelligencer*, 11 May 1807; *Leeds Mercury*, 16 May 1807.
[9] SCC:LAI: WWM, F36/33, Sykes to Fitzwilliam, 30 April 1807; E177/4, same to same [5 May 1807].
[10] *Leeds Intelligencer*, 18 May 1807; *York Courant*, 18 May 1807; *York Chronicle*, 28 May 1807.
[11] NRO: F(M), 72, Lady Milton to Lady Fitzwilliam, 18 May 1807.
[12] NRO: F(M), 72/16, Milton to Fitzwilliam, 13 May 1807; SCC:LAI: WWM, E178/215, Fitzwilliam to Wrightson [14 May 1807].

The Miltonians were damaged by the results of elections at York and Malton which preceded the county contest, set to begin on 20 May. In York where the poll began at the Guildhall on 7 May and continued for six days, Sir William Milner, who had represented the city since 1790, and Lawrence Dundas, elected by acclamation with Milner in 1802, were candidates, as expected, but Sir Mark Masterman Sykes, an old Fitzwilliam adversary, sensing in the political atmosphere created by the controversial Catholic bill a chance to challenge his interest, entered his own name on nomination day and with Milner won the show of hands. Dundas demanded a poll and when it closed had been soundly beaten. The figures were Milner 1,454; Sykes 1,316 and Dundas 967, with 2,238 freemen taking part.[13] Dundas had been late in starting his canvass and Sykes was a dangerous and powerful opponent who waved the 'No Popery' banner shamelessly. The local Tories and Methodists were incited to bitter attacks on Dundas for his support of the dismissed ministers and Dundas had to fight a lonely battle, constantly denying that he was a 'Papist', while Milner and Sykes competed for the title of which was the more devoted to the King and Constitution.

The contest had been soured by deteriorating relations between the Milner and Dundas factions. When Dundas stood in 1802, after the resignation for health reasons of Richard Milnes, his committee and Milner's, despite the candidates' identity of views, did not join forces, at the insistence of Milner's group. Their coalition would have barred future rivals. Milner was particularly popular with the city's common men, and the freemen who had been denied the rewards of a contest gradually cooled towards Dundas who did not, in any case, give the city the attentions his untamed constituents thought they deserved. At the 1806 election Milner and Dundas were returned unopposed in a deceptively easy fashion, but their relative popularity was made all too clear when their committees dined in the same room at separate tables, Milner's full and Dundas's embarrassingly half empty.

Only a combined effort could have beaten Sykes in 1807 and Milner carefully kept his distance from Dundas, making much of his opposition to certain clauses in the Catholic bill. On his canvassing rounds, Dundas found many voters not at home. 'No Popery' won the day. The victorious Sykes sent each of the freemen who had plumped for him (there were 593) a fine hare, ticketed with the date it had been killed on his East Riding estates and tied with a blue ribbon on which 'No Popery' was printed. The York butchers seriously considered sending him a petition protesting at this 'new mode of feeding his volatile constituents'.[14]

---

[13] *Pick's Edition of the Poll*; 'Members of Parliament for York, 1713–1832', *Yorkshire Notes and Queries* (Bingley, 1888), vol. 1, pp. 20–3.

[14] SCC:LAI: WWM, E170/2, Rhodes to Fitzwilliam, 27 April 1807; E222, Wentworth to Lady Fitzwilliam [30 April 1807]; E170/5, Nicoll to Fitzwilliam, 2 May 1807; E177/8,

A much more humiliating blow to the Fitzwilliam interest occurred at Malton, however, where Milton had been put in so effortlessly in the previous autumn. Of the 500 voters in Malton, 438 were Fitzwilliam's tenants, tenants of his tenants or dependent in some way on him as lord of the manor. Usually his parliamentary candidates were obediently approved. There had not been a contest in Malton since 1730. Some small unrest had been evident about Burke in 1789 and Grattan in 1805, but there was no reason to expect trouble in 1807. The earl, however, rarely visited Malton which had no house suitable for him, and he and his son were now absorbed in the county contest. His agent, William Hastings, was cordially disliked by almost everyone. He was of humble origin but arrogant ways and so irritated the electors that Fitzwilliam's enemies saw an opening. Lord Headley, MP for Ripon in 1806, was diverted by Sykes from standing at York and Isaac Leatham of Barton-le-Street, a leading and benevolent landowner, offered themselves against the sitting members, Col. Bryan Cooke and the hastily recruited replacement for Milton, Robert Lawrence Dundas, another son of Lord Dundas. Headley let it be known that he had brought £10,000 with him and could find as much again if he needed to. Lord Milton did not take the challenge seriously at first, predicting that Headley would not get 50 votes, and urging Hastings to spend his time on the county contest. Cooke canvassed on 6 May for himself and Dundas and obtained 200 promises for himself and 204 for Dundas with 125 supporting Leatham and 90 Headley. However, 99 were 'doubtful'. The poll opened on 11 May and the candidates at the end of the day stood in this order: Dundas, Headley, Leatham and Cooke. Malton dissidents wanted, above all, to elect one MP of their own choosing, a kind of declaration of independence. At this point Leatham stepped down in Headley's favour (in return for his election expenses, it was rumoured) and on 12 May Dundas and Headley were elected. The result was decided by 154 voters who gave one vote to each side, and of these, 113 were tenants or undertenants of Fitzwilliam. Leatham's recommendation had carried weight for he had endeared himself to Malton families when during a severe food shortage in 1800 he had brought extra corn to the market and sold it cheaply, while Fitzwilliam had sought to relieve the widespread distress with a 'soup shop' retailing broth at a penny a quart and cut-price potatoes and salted herrings, and none of these dishes was as relished as wheaten bread. Headley (who was a member of Wilberforce's county committee and had been encouraged by Wilberforce to stand at Malton) employed the 'No Popery' rhetoric which was becoming a hallmark of the pro-government campaign, but the women's

---

Croft to same, 4 May 1807; *York Courant*, 4 and 11 May 1807; Smith, *Whig Principles*, p. 65; SCC:LAI: WWM, E170/1,6 Sinclair to Fitzwilliam, 26 and 30 April 1807; J. Fairfax-Blakeborough, *Sykes of Sledmere* (Allan: 1929), p. 66 and note.

derisive shouts of 'sawt fish and taties' directed at Cooke and Dundas probably did more damage to the Fitzwilliam cause.

To lose a seat at Malton outraged Fitzwilliam but he waited until after the county election to redress the insult. In an excess of joy, Malton's defectors celebrated by giving Leatham a silver cup and declaring the 12th of May as independence day to be commemorated annually by a dinner.[15] A Lascelles poet made use of both defeats in a ribald new song, 'To Quiet a Baby':

> To quiet a baby that cried for the County
> 	The old women of Yorkshire were called in to try,
> Whoever would attend him was offer'd a bounty,
> 	His Irish wet nurses were lately run dry.
>
> At Malton his rattle was stole by the Freemen
> 	The go-cart at York slipt from under his feet
> So they came in a body, and all the old women,
> 	Are hushing the baby and wiping him sweet.
>
> Lords, Clothiers and Jacobins bow at his levee,
> 	And Sycophants hail him the County's best hope;
> While the old Whore of Babylon, heading the bevy,
> 	Proclaims him the Friend of her darling, the Pope;
>
> When you meet 'em you smell the true Nursery's savour,
> 	At LASCELLES's name all the Host are dismay'd;
> What they get on their fingers, they wear as a favour,
> 	And club every night for a *yellow* cockade. ...
>
> But now we're aware of the shallow Deceiver,
> 	So send back the Child to his Play-things and Tarts,
> And let us proclaim as our motto for ever,
> 	Independence and LASCELLES, the man of our Hearts.[16]

Hull always presented an instructive portrait of venality at elections but in 1807 the freemen were cheated out of a contest. William Denison discovered

---

[15] Smith, 'Earl Fitzwilliam and Malton', pp. 57–61; Smith, *Whig Principles*, pp. 303–5; M.A. Huddleston, *History of Malton and Norton* (Scarborough, 1962), p. 155; R.G. Thorne, 'Malton' in Thorne, *History of Parliament. The House of Commons, 1790–1820*, vol. 2, pp. 452–4; SCC:LAI: WWM, F72, Fitzwilliam correspondence with Hastings, Cooke and Cleaver, May 1807; Hinton, 'General Elections', pp. 464–9; *Hull Packet*, 19 May 1807; *York Chronicle*, 21 and 28 May 1807; *The Times*, 3 June 1807.

[16] Election Squibs, 1807.

that his agent had prematurely dispensed 2,000 guineas among the burgesses and declined to stand again, before any more harm could be done to his fortune. Daniel Sykes believed that Denison's motives went deeper. Denison, not unlike Fawkes, appeared to suffer a 'sort of despair about the country & a weariness of the tiezing Requests of his Constituents'. Determined to keep out the Thorntons, the Fitzwilliam interest brought in Lord Mahon, an early parliamentary reformer and abolitionist, to stand with the other MP John Staniforth. 'Our *Worthies*,' observed the *Hull Advertiser*, 'were greatly disappointed at not having a *Third Man*' when John Thornton, son of Samuel, refused an invitation to be a candidate as well. 'There are some customs prevalent at Elections in Hull, which, however sanctioned by time … would alone be sufficient to deter me,' Thornton had replied diplomatically.[17]

---

[17] SCC:LAI: WWM, E222, Foljambe to Fitzwilliam, 28 April 1807; F36/32, Denison to same, 28 April 1807; E171/2, same to same, 30 April 1807; F36/20, Sykes to same, n.d.; *Hull Advertiser*, 9 May 1807.

CHAPTER TEN

Preparing to Poll

As in Biblical times the people of the house of David had to make their way to Bethlehem to pay their taxes, so were the electors of Yorkshire required to journey to York to exercise their franchise. Arrangements to cope with this flood of purposeful visitors could not be left until election day, 20 May. Shortly after the committees had dined on nomination day, their representatives conferred with the undersheriff, Jonathan Gray, and lodged their formal requests that the sheriff erect voting booths. Gray brought along his father's plans for 1784 when a contest had last seemed probable. Edward Wolley, representing Lascelles, arrived with calculations of the potential vote in each wapentake and the joint committee adopted regulations signed by him and the other two agents, John Brook of Huddersfield for Wilberforce and Charles Bowns for Lord Milton.

Fifteen booths were permitted by law. In 1784, seven had been judged sufficient; now 13 were agreed. The remaining permitted space was assigned for handling disputed cases, but in the event these were dealt with in the court house before assessors appointed by the sheriff and legal counsel representing the candidates.[1] The 13 May conference decided that a sheriff's deputy (the deputies to be selected from among those few county attorneys who had not yet been engaged as agents) and a poll clerk would be delegated to each voting booth. Each candidate might have one scrutineer (or cheque clerk) and one agent per booth to challenge dubious voters whose cases would then be referred to the assessors or commissioners for oaths (for example, if a Roman Catholic attempted to vote). Each committee could employ a messenger who would be allowed into the booth to copy the poll results for his committee. By mutual connivance the messenger was usually a second agent who often stayed

---

[1] For arrangements, Male, *Treatise*, pp. 19–72; Gray, *Account of Proceedings*, pp. 6ff; WYAS(L): WYL250/6/3/10, Gray to Lascelles committee, 11 May 1807; YA: M90:49 and 50; KINCM:1982.895.409, Account of the Proceedings, fols 14–18; SCC:LAI: WWM, E150, agreement of three candidates, 19 May 1807.

in the booth. Each committee could station a porter at the booth's back door to run the polling figures to headquarters. The sheriff set the polling hours at 9 to 5 without a break. Gates to the Castle Yard would open at 8 a.m.

Percival Watson and Samuel Green were appointed commissioners of oaths, administered in practice only after an opponent's challenge. The law provided for a freeholder's oath (or affirmation in the case of Friends), oaths of allegiance, supremacy and abjuration and a declaration or test of religious belief. The assessors were Samuel Heywood, the Welsh judge, and John Bayley, later Sir John and a King's Bench judge, both serjeants-at-law. Wilberforce engaged two barristers as counsel: William Reader of London and Robert Osborne, Recorder of Hull; Lascelles three: George Courthope of London, John Hardy, the Leeds Recorder, and Henry John Dickens of York; and Milton six: Robert Sinclair, the York Recorder; J.P. Heywood of Wakefield, Thomas Clifton, Daniel Sykes, S.W. Nicoll and Francis Maude of Wakefield, the Doncaster Recorder.

Costs of polling had to be borne by the candidates until 1832 and were considerable although a fraction of what each had to spend to transport and entertain their voters and pay to their agents and other workers. The two assessors received £630 each and their clerks were paid 15 guineas. The 112 constables (appointed to keep order by the sheriff from names supplied by the candidates) were paid 5 shillings a day and their bill came to £441. Poll clerks, of whom there were 14, were paid two guineas a day and their bill totalled £449 8s. 0d. The 13 'gentleman deputy sheriffs' earned five guineas a day and cost £1,134. There were additional bills for board and lodging, and poll books, ink stands, pens and paper accounted for another £28 14s. 0d.²

The hustings, or speakers' platform, had been built by William Halfpenny for £35 14s. 6d. He also was the principal joiner for erecting the voting booths, which cost £352 13s. 7d. Another joiner was paid £9 14s. 0d. for constables' staves and inscription boards on which the names of the wapentakes were painted for an extra £3 16s. 8d. The candidates gave £105 to the undersheriff and 15 guineas to his clerk, plus 20 guineas for the county clerk. All in all, the bill for staging the election came to £4,088 17s. 11d., and each candidate was bound to pay his third.

With only the hustings ready and just a week to go, the Castle Yard became a scene of frenzied activity. The hustings, under an oil cloth roof, stood in front of the assize courts. Now the 13 booths were constructed, in pairs but for one, to form with the hustings a semicircle on the grass. The law was interpreted by the sheriff's office to mean that no wapentake could be split into

---

² Gray, *Account*, pp. 40–2; WYAS(L): WYL250/6/3/17, Robert Cattle's account; SCC:LAI: WWM, E151, report of agents' meeting, 6 June 1807.

two booths, but that it was legal to combine less populous districts. Milton's voters were concentrated in the three heavily peopled West Riding wapentakes of Strafforth and Tickhill, Agbrigg, and Morley and, as his representatives predicted, these booths were swamped while voters were swiftly dealt with at booths for the sparsely settled North and East Ridings. The 29 wapentakes were assigned booths thus: (1) Agbrigg, including Wakefield and Huddersfield among its centres; (2) Morley, including Bradford, Halifax and Dewsbury; (3) Strafforth and Tickhill, including Sheffield, Rotherham and Doncaster; (4) Skirack, including Leeds; (5) Staincliffe, including Keighley, combined with Ewecross, which included Sedbergh and Dent; (6) Staincross, Osgoldcross and Barkston Ash, the latter including Pontefract; (7) Ainsty, outside York, and Claro, including Ripon; (8) Holderness; (9) Harthill, including Beverley; (10) Ouse and Derwent, Howdenshire, Buckrose and Dickering; (11) Allertonshire, Bulmer, Birdforth and Gilling East and West; (12) Hang East and West, Halikeld and Ryedale; and (13) Langbargh, Pickering Lythe and Whitby Strand. Hull and York freeholders were 'outvoters' so far as the county went, each being a county of its own, and with others from beyond Yorkshire voted in the booths where their freeholds lay.[3]

Voting was public but the Miltonites protested that the booths did not allow it to be public enough so that any observer, suspicious of a voter's qualifications, might 'give the alarm'. The York booths were square with wooden walls, roofed with tarpaulins so that rain or cold weather would not interrupt the polling, and lined with matting. The electors were admitted at a bar attended by two constables and progressed through a dog-leg passage to a second bar, again guarded by constables. This led them – one at a time – into a railed enclosure where stood a green baize-covered table around which sat the deputy sheriff, his poll clerk and the inspector, agent and messenger for each candidate, an audience of 11. The voter stood at the railing and was asked by the deputy sheriff if he were a freeholder, his name, residence and occupation; where his freehold was located and who occupied it (while agents riffled through their land tax lists to confirm or challenge his voting right), and finally whether there were any objections to his vote. If none, he was asked for whom he voted and his one or two choices were recorded in the poll book. The elector then was released through the back door.[4]

How severely the voters were interrogated was left to the discretion of the returning officer and the candidates' spokesmen.[5] The oath of allegiance posed problems for few subjects:

---

[3] Gray, *Account*, pp. 7, 10–12.
[4] *Ibid.*, pp. 16, 19–20. For the arrangement of the voting booths, see Plate 9.
[5] Male, *Treatise*, pp. 111–14, Appendix, xxiii–xxvi, xiv–xviii.

> I, do sincerely promise and swear, That I will be faithful, and bear true allegiance to his Majesty King George. So help me God.

The more vehement supremacy oath required one to swear that

> I do from my heart abhor, detest, and abjure, as impious and heretical that damnable doctrine and position, that Princes excommunicated or deprived by the Pope, or any authority of the See of Rome, may be deposed or murdered by their subjects, or any other whatsoever. And I do declare, that no foreign prince, person, prelate, state or potentate, hath, or ought to have, any jurisdiction, power, superiority, pre-eminence, or authority, ecclesiastical or spiritual, within this realm.

The lengthy and archaic oath of abjuration committed one to declare 'before God and the world, That our Sovereign Lord King George is lawful and rightful king' and that the pretender (claiming to be James III) had no right to the crown. Allegiance was sworn to King George against all 'traitorous conspiracies', and a promise was made to disclose all such treason, and support was pledged to the descendants of Princess Sophia of Hanover, 'being Protestants'.

These oaths could be distasteful or objectionable to Catholics but the declaration of test, when employed, was meant to disfranchise them, for under it one had to endorse the tenets of the Church of England and declare that transubstantiation, adoration of the Virgin Mary or any other saint and sacrifice of the mass as in the Church of Rome were 'superstitious and idolatrous'.

The laws against bribery and treating (or entertaining) of voters were almost impossible to enforce. Rarely did a defeated candidate petition against an election on such grounds for fear that this would provoke inquiry into his own activities. Every candidate had to contend with his electors' expectations and the favourite candidate all too often was the one able to treat the most, particularly in the boroughs. William Cobbett became a radical parliamentary reformer after standing at Honiton, a borough with 400 electors, where he quoted scripture to them on the wickedness of bribery, and was jeered for trying to rob them.

Under the law the voter was guilty of bribery if he asked, received, took or contracted for any money to affect his vote, and the candidate was guilty if he, by any gift or reward or promise 'corrupted' a man to give or refuse his vote. By recent decisions in the House of Commons, it was illegal for a candidate's agent to give so much as a glass of ale to a freeholder whom he was canvassing and he was forbidden to promise anything in the way of food or drink in York on nomination or election days. The candidate or his agent could only provide coach or chaise hire for travelling voters. The candidate's friends, however, could pay voters' expenses – a handy loophole. The Fitzwilliam forces sought the advice of Charles Dundas, a barrister son of Lord Dundas, but he gave them little joy. He had no doubt that, strictly interpreted, the law prohibited candidates or agents from giving freeholders refreshments or beds. Although he believed himself – as did nine-tenths of the bar, in his opinion – that a plaintiff should have to prove that the 'treat' was meant to win a vote and it had in fact influenced it, Commons committees faced with petitions to void elections tended to see proof in the very allegations. Special care should be taken not to treat York residents: there was 'no plea whatever for their having refreshment'.[6] It was common knowledge, however, that the laws were flouted on all sides.

The Saint, Henry Thornton, had been shocked into quitting in his first attempt to enter Parliament in 1782 by the discovery that every burgess in Hull expected two guineas from him, in spite of the bribery law. As Thornton admitted, the voter could truthfully swear he had been given no promise because 'a strict & cautious silence is observed', but silence, by custom, was consent and, by tradition, the candidate deferred his payments until the deadline for filing a petition against his election had passed. That same year Thornton stood for Southwark where the 'evil of the 2 guineas' did not exist. Assisted by a distinguished committee, his family's reputation for charity and a modicum of treating, he won by a large majority and remained MP for Southwark the rest of his life.[7]

A common dodge was to pay publicans and innkeepers, rather than the voters directly, for coaches, refreshments and lodgings for voters. Thus Milton's committees published notices that they would be responsible to innkeepers at the following rate:

	s.	d.
Breakfast	1	0
Dinner	2	0
Supper	2	0
Bed	1	0
Bait	1	0
Horses' bait, including hostler	1	0
Horses, a night	3	0

---

[6] Michael Brock, *Great Reform Act* (Hutchinson: 1973), p. 17; Maccoby, *English Radicalism*, pp. 206–7; C.F.F. Wordsworth, *Digest of All the Election Reports, from the Earliest to the Present Time* (A. Maxwell: 1834), p. 16; *York Herald*, 16 May 1807; SCC:LAI: WWM, E173/19, Dundas to Cooke, 3 May 1807; WYAS(L): WYL250/6/3/17, Cattle's instructions for canvassing.

[7] CUL: GBR/0012/MS, Add 7674/1/N, Henry Thornton, First Vellum Book, fols 16–21.

Each voter had to present a ticket signed by a member of the committee and the innkeeper had to turn over the tickets to collect his bill.[8]

From the surviving records of the great Yorkshire election of 1807, the majority of voters were unable or unwilling to travel to York for nothing. Assuming that the three sides spent the generally accepted rough total of at least £250,000, each vote cost (in post-decimal money) £10.85. In the British general election of 2005 the expenditure on each vote was £3.71, less than half this sum even at current prices.[9]

There was a faint chance that the election might be decided by upraised hands on 20 May. If not, polling would start at once, so in either event, it was important that each side produce a massive demonstration of support on that day.[10] Milton's hawk-eyed agent in Leeds, Thomas Tottie, learning that Lascelles was hiring chaises for the Wednesday only, warned that he would attempt to settle the election there and then. 'I need not tell you,' he added,

> that his having an advantage twice in the shew of hands will be a prejudice to us in the popular opinion, notwithstanding our Declarations to stand a Poll, & I think … we should meet the shew of hands with vigour. Is it not possible for the friends of Mr. Lascelles, unless faced by ours, to get Possession of the Castle Yard to the exclusion of our adherents & thereby support his advocates and & hoot ours as they did last Wednesday … & will it be prudent on the first Day of the Poll to suffer this?' … [He suggested arranging for a] serious Body of Men to make a shew of Hands & a triumphant shout. … Will it not dismay the house of Harewood? Or at any rate it will shew our Spirit, support our friends & dishearten our adversaries.

They should be assembled in York early and take over the Castle Yard. Before he closed his letter, Tottie learned that Lascelles's friends were asking his voters to go to York at their own expense: 'depend upon it that will make a poor show.'[11]

Even before the nomination spectacle, Lascelles's committee had heard that horses and houses were being engaged far and wide by Milton's agents

---

[8] SCC:LAI: WWM, E163/29/1, Rates of Lord Milton's Committee at Leeds.
[9] See C. Rallings and M. Thrasher (eds), *British Electoral Facts, 1832–2006* (Ashgate: Aldershot, 2007), tables 2.03, 5.09, 5.10, pp. 61–2, 117–22 for votes cast, and candidates' and returning officers' expenses in 2005; and http://www.ukpolitical.info/Expenditure.htm [accessed 16 August 2013] for central party expenditure.
[10] KINCM:1982.895.409, Account of the Proceedings, fols 439, 440; WYAS(L): WYL250/6/3/10, Lascelles to Wolley, 17 May 1807.
[11] SCC:LAI: WWM, E163/6, Tottie to Milton committee, 16 May 1807.

for the duration of the contest, including many of the inns on the Great North Road which traversed the county – two at Ferrybridge, a key coaching junction; twelve at Tadcaster through which most of the West Riding electors would pour, and six at Easingwold and nine at Thirsk for those coming from the north, in addition to others in every market town.[12] At Halifax, Lewis Alexander, who had taken up all available carriages for the full two weeks of polling, proposed that wagons and carts fitted up to transport militia men should be used for the 'middling class of Freeholders'. The competition for vehicles was fierce. The joint Wilberforce-Lascelles committee at Huddersfield, for example, had engaged all the carriages at posting houses throughout the Saddleworth district by 15 May and no others were available closer than Manchester. But many clothiers were willing to come to York on their plodding galloways or to walk as far as Leeds or Wakefield for a ride. At strategic Doncaster, Milton's chairman George Wroughton promised ten pairs of horses and four carriages from the Red Lyon Inn, his headquarters, which could make three trips a day with 48 voters as far as Ferrybridge, while three pairs of horses and three carriages at the Reindeer could take another 24 on two trips a day. The voters would be transferred to other conveyances at the Greyhound, Ferrybridge. From Hull, five days before election day, came word that all the coaches were Milton's; if others elsewhere were equally successful 'the *day*, & Road are ours'. In Whitby, on the other hand, Wilberforce's friends left only three pairs of horses and three chaises unengaged before the poll started. At Scarborough Milton's agent resorted to hiring space in the daily mail coach to and from York for the whole of the period.[13]

In the North Riding the large and well known family of Lord Dundas served as vigorous surrogates for Fitzwilliam and Milton. Dundas completed the roster of agents in the Dales and Cleveland district and reported almost daily to Fitzwilliam or Milton. He had some of his tenants alter more than fifty carriages, previously used for the volunteers, which his steward had spotted in the neighbourhood. The bodies were taken off the springs and long boards installed on each side where eight to ten of the hardier voters could sit. The old and infirm would go in chaises and Dundas's breaking carriage. On 16 May he called his tenants together and mustered 78 horses plus 14 of his own

---

[12] WYAS(L): WYL250/6/3/10, Bland to Slingsby, 12 May 1807; Dickinson to Wolley, 15 May 1807 and Atkinson to Lascelles committee, 15 May 1807; SCC:LAI: WWM, E171/13, 15 Martin to Milton committee, 14 and 16 May 1807; E152, Inns Engaged on the North Road.

[13] SCC:LAI: WWM, E156/69, Alexander to Milton committee, 16 May 1807; E178/34, Ainley to same, 15 May 1807; E161/35, Wroughton to same, 19 May 1807; E224, Scatcherd to Fitzwilliam, 15 May 1807; E178/47, Cooke to Milton committee, 17 May; E166/5, Allen to same, 18 May 1807.

farm horses. These were immediately stationed along the road from Stokesley to Easingwold to carry Milton plumpers swiftly to the first day's poll.[14]

The Dundas influence was not enough to carry the rural Langbargh wapentake for Milton. Lascelles came first but Milton trailed by only 32 votes (11 ahead of Wilberforce) in the 1,353 cast, a respectable result. At Marske, the Dundas base, all 22 votes from blacksmith to vicar were Milton plumpers. Lofthouse, Redcar and Skelton were other bastions but in the towns, such as Guisborough, Yarm and Stokesley, Wilberforce and Lascelles scored heavily.

Agents for each side complained of the lack of precise instructions which, one must appreciate, must have been hard to draw up given the ambiguities of the law and seven decades of inexperience. Milton's orders were probably typical. A circular letter first advised agents to tell voters when and how carriages would be provided and that 'all reasonable and legal expences' would be paid. Voters were to be encouraged to make their own way and if they did a 'greater proportion' of the cost would be paid. Printed forms were distributed requesting freeholders to go on specified dates.

Milton's York committee set 6s. a day as the maximum to be allowed for a voter's incidental expenses (the sum allowed to witnesses attending the assizes) but later, in view of living costs at York, the daily allowance was adjusted upwards to 10s. 6d. Those who found their own way to the polls were allowed 9d. a mile each way, while a spokesman for Wilberforce and Lascelles mentioned 2s. a mile for the round trip. Innkeepers, by Milton's records, were to be paid £1 11s. 6d. a day for each pair of horses (with carriage) if the innkeeper kept them exclusively for Milton voters. The horses were expected to cover 42 miles a day at least.[15]

Wilberforce's committee notified innkeepers that it would pay the 'reasonable and necessary' expenses of voters who arrived under an appointed leader or captain authorized to meet the bill. If they came without such an escort, they must pay their own bills and seek reimbursement back home from their local committees.

A row broke out among the three York committees over how to pay the expenses of electors who gave split votes, a dispute which exacerbated the baneful argument over whether Wilberforce and Lascelles were forming a coalition. The fault for the clumsy negotiations lay with the Wilberforce committee which was convinced that nine-tenths of the voters were already for

---

[14] SCC:LAI: WWM, E177, Lord Dundas to Fitzwilliam, 9 May 1807; E173/45, same to Milton, 7 May 1807; E177/33, same to Fitzwilliam, 16 May 1807; E177/31, same to same, 15 May 1807; E224, same to same, 18 May; E173/89, C. Dundas to Milton committee, 19 May 1807; E178/67, Lord Dundas to T. Dundas, 18 May 1807.

[15] SCC:LAI: WWM, E151, circular letter, 14 May 1807, printed notice for voters and private instructions to agents, 18 May 1807; E221, further instructions, 24 May 1807.

him while 'promises upon promises' still poured in. 'He was safe as to Votes but not Money,' so when Milton's chairman William Wrightson suggested that the candidates share equally the burden of transporting electors who would vote for both of them, Wilberforce's friends were frightened at the prospect of the potentially unlimited cost, since they fully expected the second votes of both Milton and Lascelles electors. 'They would have been answerable in their own Pockets to the whole Extent of this immeasurable Engagement,' explained David Russell. The committee reached a complicated agreement with the Lascelles headquarters on 16 May. The pact provided that if the daily voting record showed that Wilberforce was secure in his election (that is, had at least 10,000 votes) on a given day, he would pay one-half of the voter expenses to the end of that day's polling only. Lascelles's supporters were not thrilled at this arrangement, regarding Wilberforce's chairman Dr Burgh and his fellows as very 'shy' about appropriating money for carrying joint votes. Milton's committee wanted no part of a procedure primarily intended to benefit Wilberforce, but Burgh declined the half-and-half proposal for fear Lascelles would want the same arrangement and Wilberforce would, in consequence, be saddled with half the cost of almost every voter, a potential £100,000. By Wilberforce's calculations, more than half of the voters would come after he had been to all intents re-elected. Milton's refusal to accept the same terms as Lascelles 'spread a panic in the whole camp of Mr. Wilberforce; for the powers of his Lordship's purse were tremendous. It was like the news of an invasion by Buonaparte,' one participant recalled.

Emboldened by reports that the spreading rumour of a Wilberforce–Lascelles coalition already was inspiring plumpers for Milton, the latter's committee publicly hailed the failure to come to agreement with Wilberforce on expenses as additional proof of a 'decided Preference' if not a 'Junction', which to 'Men of plain Understanding is the same Thing'. On election day, Wilberforce's committee announced that it would share the expenses of Wilberforce–Milton voters on the same basis as for the Wilberforce–Lascelles men, but many voters were uncertain whether, when they came to vote, Wilberforce would pay.[16] John Benson, Milton's agent at Thorne, declared that the opposing agents there would pay 'not a farthing' for a Milton split. From Hull Robert Sandwith sent a list of Milton plumpers each one of whom had intended to cast a second vote for Wilberforce until it was understood he

---

[16] KINCM:1982.895.409, Account of the Proceedings, fols 172–7, 275–6, 429; SCC:LAI: WWM, E224, Wrightson to Milton, 13 May 1807; WYAS(L): WYL250/6/3/10, Slingsby draft to Milton committee, Wrightson to Slingsby, 15 May 1807, Strickland to Slingsby, 16 May 1807; NRO: F(M), 72/20, Milton to Fitzwilliam, 19 May 1807; WYAS(L): WYL250/6/3/10, Prickett to Wolley, 16 May 1807; *York Courant*, 15 June 1807; *Sheffield Iris*, 2 June 1807.

could or would not pay travelling expenses. 'All the lower orders of Freeholders ... were much disgusted' and Sandwith canvassed them successfully while two of Wilberforce's clerical friends, the Revs T. Dykes and Richard Patrick, 'were running about ... like madmen, using all means in their power to keep the voters to their promises'. But at Doncaster and Sheffield the local supporters of Wilberforce and Milton reached amicable agreement to convey split votes and share the cost.[17]

Wilberforce's precarious financial footing offered some cause for panic. His modest fortune had increased little or nothing since his first election. As he often reminded his constituents, he had not enriched himself in any of the ways open to men in public life. The usual subscriptions raised for candidates were limited to themselves and a small circle of wealthy friends. As a rule, the heaviest burden fell upon the candidate and if he was worried about the cost, he probably couldn't afford to stand. In and out of Yorkshire, however, there were many people who refused to contemplate a Parliament without Wilberforce. Thus there was launched a nation-wide subscription unparalleled in British election annals. Noblemen found a public subscription offensive. 'Was there ever such a miserable *mendicant* as Wilberforce, canvassing in forma pauperis, there are people going about the Country begging Subscriptions, which they accept, tho' ever so small provided it is silver –' Lord Dundas remarked to Fitzwilliam.[18] Wilberforce's subscription drive was aimed at the thousands who had supported the effort to abolish the slave trade. Scarcely any editor could resist the (probably apocryphal) story of the Liverpool fund to which 'a poor African' donated five guineas.[19] And every town had someone like Doncaster's Catherine Wood, a coal dealer, who, upon hearing about the Wilberforce fund, observed, 'I do not know him, but I admire his conduct in Parliament'; pulled out her nutmeg grater, extracted a guinea and handed it in at the Old Bank with the words, 'accept the *widow's mite* towards his success; and God bless him.' '*Bravo!*' added the editor of the *Gazette*.[20]

The subscription opened almost simultaneously in York and London on the eve of nomination day. Wilberforce had made it plain that he would not be put into the position of having to exhaust his own fortune and then

[17] SCC:LAI: WWM, E161/28, Benson to Milton committee, 26 May 1807; E171/18a, Sandwith to same, 19 May 1807; E171/16, Marton to same, 17 May 1807; E224, Scatcherd to Fitzwilliam, 15 May 1807; E161/38,42, Wroughton to Milton committee, 19 and 20 May 1807.
[18] SCC:LAI: WWM, E224, Dundas to Fitzwilliam, 25 May 1807.
[19] African story used, among others, by *York Chronicle*, 18 May 1807, *Courier and Times*, 13 June 1807. No Liverpool gifts are on the lists in KINCM:1982.895.409, Account of the Proceedings, to confirm it.
[20] *Doncaster Gazette*, 29 May 1807.

spend his future parliamentary life repairing it. Promises of support had been given and he called upon them: about £18,000 was pledged at once, and the old Yorkshire Association rule was adopted that he should contribute nothing to the subscription himself. In the end, £64,426 7s. 4d. was raised from 2,587 named donors, some of whom presented collections taken in societies and churches. Collections were also sent from various towns so it seems fair to say that perhaps 5,000 individuals contributed. In Yorkshire the subscriptions totalled £43,944 0s. 11d. London and the south of England produced £20,482 6s. 5d. This 'unexampled liberality' did not alter the 'conscientious frugality' of Wilberforce's committeemen although it probably made them feel much more comfortable. Their final expenditures amounted to only £28,600, a fraction of the dreaded bill. A post-election squabble between the Yorkshire and London committees over which monies should be drawn upon first and in what proportion from each fund does not detract from the magnitude of the undertaking, promises of money in the heat of an election being notoriously difficult to redeem. Forty-six per cent of the Yorkshire subscriptions were returned (the large ones, that is; the small cash offerings were spent) and London subscribers had to pay only half of the sum raised in the first appeal there and none of the subsequent provisional one.[21]

The contribution lists reveal Wilberforce's broad appeal, reflecting the support he had built up across the political board in the campaign for abolition of the slave trade. The fund-raising drew together Whigs, Tories, Friends, Methodists, Anglicans, Evangelicals, abolitionists, and Bible Society and missionary society friends. The Yorkshire fund was opened by the self-styled 'Friends of Wilberforce and the Independence of the County' whose chief concern was to be able to confront the 'well organized, well paid and well fed army' of Lord Milton. The multitude of Wilberforce voters was daunting but as the subscription approached £60,000, the 'Friends' were confident that they could see the election out, however 'trifling' their resources might seem to a Milton. Milton saved them quite a bit of money in the end with his success in winning plumpers (for whom he paid in full) 'by the cry', as the Wilberforce partisans had it, 'partly of no coalition, by inserting Milton's plumper in … every Miltonites Hat, by giving popish absolution to all who had promised Wilberforce, by stirring up the hatred of the Clothiers … and by insisting that Lord Milton was as good a friend to the Abolition … as Mr. Wilberforce'.[22]

The prospect of losing Wilberforce galvanized the Society of Friends to

---

[21] Wilberforce, *Life*, vol. 3, pp. 318–19, 335; Add Ms 35,129, Mr Wilberforce's Election circular, 11 May 1807; KINCM:1982.895.409, Account of the Proceedings, fols 249–50, 252–8. The *Life*, vol. 3, p. 334, uses a figure of £64,455 and Furneaux, *Wilberforce*, speaks of £64,544. My figure is calculated from KINCM:1982.895.409, Account of the Proceedings.

[22] *Ibid.*, fols 177–244, for lists and comments, except as noted.

seek ways to demonstrate their 'grateful attachment' while not contributing to the immorality 'which necessarily attends contested Elections', in the words of Samuel Tuke, secretary for the York Quaker committee. It was decided that all gifts known to come from Friends would be earmarked solely to hire conveyances, not to 'entertain'. In the Yorkshire lists, £1,069 11s. 6d. can be identified as coming from 195 Friends, and more was given through the London fund. Quakers who were freeholders were urged to vote but only at their own expense or with some help from the Society.

For appeals to the political public on Wilberforce's behalf, all restraint was cast aside. An Englishman declared:

> To expatiate on the Brilliancy of Mr. W's Character is needless, His shining talents his unwearied labours in the Cause of Suffering Humanity, his inflexible integrity are too well known ... For three and twenty years this truly great and amiable Man, has done honour to the choice of this extensive and opulent County ... shall it be suffered that an ambitious individual by the power of his riches, shall overwhelm the patriotism, the Sense, the virtue, the affluence, the independence of this great County? Will you submit that a stripling, who cannot yet know, but by hearsay, even the Common forms of bringing a Bill into parliament, shall by the force of his father's wealth, set aside your long tried faithful Friend? ... Bring forward that Treasure, which can alone counteract the Treasure of your youthful Antagonist. Do you look for assistance from the middling Classes of Society? You look in vain, their help would be trifling ... It is those only whose minds are expanded by Education, by Commerce, and by extensive Intercourse with the World, who can feel, and who can make a Sacrifice. Gentlemen, be free, be generous, nay, for once be lavish.

Yorkshire subscriptions of £1,000 were few: Charles Duncombe, Sir Richard Johnson and Samuel Smith being the only recorded ones, but a score gave £500 and more than 40 gave £100 to £300. The most interesting aspects about the contribution lists, however, are not the larger but the smaller donors. Women are conspicuous among them. Lady Johnstone gave £1,000 and a few others, such as Mrs Bethell and Mrs and Miss Buck of Bainton, Lady Irwin and Lady Sykes[23] made handsome contributions of one to five hundred pounds, but most of them shared their guineas or shillings, sometimes anonymously: 'A Friend and Daughter, York', £1 1s. 0d.; 'Ladies at Mrs. Ware's School, Ripon', £1 1s. 0d.; 'sundry subscriptions by Ladies at Burlington', £26 18s. 0d.; or 'Ralph Creyke (for a Lady)', £50. (Creyke and his

---

[23] *Hull Chronicle*, 3 June 1807; *Halifax Journal*, 13 June 1807.

son each gave £100.) Methodists took up collections and turned in £7 10s. 0d. from Beverley and £13 0s. 6d. at Doncaster, for example. Each member of a family seemed to wish to be represented: William Hey and his son at Leeds subscribed £100 apiece and turned in £605 5s. 0d. from anonymous friends while Mrs Hey and their daughter each gave five guineas. Many wives offered a guinea or two to supplement their husbands' offerings. Clergymen gave individually and took up collections and many business firms contributed as companies, especially around Sheffield and in the Quaker-owned iron works at Coalbrookdale in Shropshire. 'An Old Schoolfellow' at Ripon gave £5 5s. 0d. 'A Friend to Freedom and Independence of the County' at Pontefract added £2 2s. 0d. and 'A few poor Wellwishers' six shillings. Fitzwilliam's erstwhile domain at Malton produced £28 0s. 6d. from twelve men and women. At Sheffield several men on the first published list added enthusiastically 'double if wanted' to their subscriptions of £5 or £25.[24]

The London subscription was organized at an illustrious gathering on 13 May at the New London Tavern, Cheapside, with Lord Teignmouth presiding. Henry Thornton was made treasurer.[25] According to the group, Wilberforce's talents served not only Yorkshire but the nation; though he had never stood higher in public opinion than now, he might face 'insuperable difficulties' in the expected contest unless 'powerfully supported', and should the county subscription fall short of the need, the 'privilege of supplying the deficiency could most appropriately be claimed by the Friends of the Abolition of the Slave Trade'.

Seventy-four subscribed on the spot and the list had grown to 317 by the time the report of the meeting was published.[26] Lord Teignmouth pledged £100 and Thornton £800 in two portions while his brothers gave another £700. Many names associated with abolition appeared, among them Thomas Clarkson, Joseph Hardcastle, James Stephen, Thomas Babington, Archdeacon Joseph Corbett, the Rev. Thomas Gisborne, the Hoares and the Grants. Old associates in the Sierra Leone Company were reunited, including three former governors of the West African colony – John Clarkson, Zachary Macaulay and William Dawes – and the onetime chaplains, the Revs Melvill Horne and Nathaniel Gilbert. Macaulay's whole family followed his five guinea contribution with their own, two guineas from Mrs Macaulay and one from each of the children from 'Master T.B.' to 'Miss Jane'. Colleagues in Parliament contributed, including Spencer Perceval, although he was Chancellor of the Exchequer. He said he should not be deprived of a privilege of friendship but

[24] *Sheffield Iris*, 26 May 1807.
[25] Examples, *Leeds Intelligencer* and *York Courant*, 18 May 1807.
[26] BL: Add Ms 35,129, fols 409, 411, 413.

Wilberforce might not like his name published[27] which it was not, unless he was the 'Particular Friend' credited with £200.

Again the 'mites' flowed in – from the three children of the Rev. John Owen of Fulham, £1 1s. 0d.; from the Rev. W. Price of Loudwater 10s. 6d. – to mingle with the gifts of the famous or mighty – the Dowager Countess Conyngham £52 10s. 0d.; Admiral Cornwallis £105; Admiral Gambier £50; Admiral Sir George Young £5 5s. 0d.; Nicolas and George Vansittart £50 each; Arthur Young, the agriculturalist, £15 15s. 0d.; Lady Mary Fitzgerald, £10 10s. 0d.; Lady Waldegrave, £5 5s. 0d.; Dean Milner £200; Lord Muncaster, £500; Sir Richard Hill, £50, and Mrs Hannah More and her sisters a sacrificial total of £60 with the promise of another £50 to the provisional fund which came later. 'These Elections are so impoverishing, that I suppose … we shall hardly have a rag to our backs,' Mrs Henry Thornton, busy at forwarding contributions, confided to Mrs More.[28]

A collection in Oxford raised £36 4s. 0d.; at Tewkesbury £72 9s. 0d.; at Birmingham £300 and at stylish Brighthelmstone £36 9s. 0d. Henry Ellis, Esq. of the British Museum contributed a guinea and so did George Valentine, Esq. of the Bank of England. As in Yorkshire many gave anonymously, often as 'An Abolitionist'. Others called themselves 'An Artillery Officer', 'A few friends in Dover', 'Four female friends', 'A Military Medical Man', usually enclosing the odd guinea, occasionally more. The 'Benefit Society at Upper Ship, Reading' sent a guinea and 'supporters in the West Indies' accounted for another £50.

The London meeting on 13 May was described by Charles Mary Wentworth, a key organizer for Milton in the capital, as likely to raise £100,000 although it came nowhere near that. 'Every Person connected with the Abolition Bill is to be engaged in forwarding the Subscriptions,' he informed the Earl Fitzwilliam. 'It was the general opinion, that Lord Milton will be returned with Mr. Wilberforce.' London newspapers and the provincial press carried articles urging support.[29] 'What will party Rancour say to this?' demanded the account in the *Wakefield Star*. 'Here are the first Characters which the Metropolis of the World can boast of stepping forwards not merely with their good wishes, but with their purses and their Hearts opened.'[30]

York was the nerve centre of each faction and here Lascelles and Milton set up very similar organizations consisting of a core of professional men (often lawyers) surrounded by politically valuable friends. Wilberforce relied more heavily on his volunteers who, more niggardly in their attitudes than

---

[27] Wilberforce, *Correspondence*, vol. 2, pp. 124–5.
[28] WLCT: EHC18/M786, Mrs Thornton to Hannah More, 25 May 1807.
[29] SCC:LAI: WWM, E174/6, Wentworth to Fitzwilliam, 13 May 1807; *Morning Chronicle*, *Morning Post*, *Courier*, all 21 May 1807, as examples.
[30] KINCM:1982.895.409, Account of the Proceedings, fols 179–80.

professionals would have been, probably cost him some votes. But to critics who thought they carried economy to the point of parsimony and 'too much neglected ... the procession, and the music, and the streamers, and all the other purchased decorations, which catch the vulgar eye', Wilberforce replied that it was not *his* money, but that of his public-spirited supporters. Furthermore, it was not to his taste to compete in 'parade and profusion'. Wilberforce, however, recognized faults in his operation. In Milton's and 'in a degree' among Lascelles's forces he saw 'a unity, discipline, and disposition to obey orders and act from a common impulse which belonged to a formed party. ... We had nothing of this; but the exact opposite – a mixture in our cabinet of a number of heterogeneous particles, and no common impulse either felt or obeyed.'[31]

Each of his rivals had a central committee which composed most of the letters soliciting support and answered inquiries, employing a corps of clerks, writers and copyists (for it was not unusual to make 15 or 50 copies of a letter or directive), runners, messengers and postboys. Anyone with a talent for a turn of phrase was put on the 'scribbling committee' to churn out election songs, squibs, epigrams, newspaper paragraphs, handbills, broadsides, advertisements, posters and letters to the papers – serious, funny, scurrilous, high-minded, always anonymous. Walls were plastered with their productions, printers deluged, coffee houses littered with them. Up to a hundred additional men were hired as bodyguards to parade with the candidate to and from his daily appearance at the hustings. The major qualification for this job was to be good in a fight. Each committee also hired musicians who played outside the committee rooms to draw a crowd for some speech or announcement from a first-floor window and who livened up the candidates' processions or torchlight parades to the various inns where voters were staying. The musicians were very well remunerated, at a going rate of a guinea a day. Lascelles's bills for music came to a startling £698 3s. 6d.[32] Street rallies were held at night to inspire the freeholders waiting to poll the next day and, to make the harangues more palatable, barrels of beer were rolled out and tapped.

The printers of weekly newspapers who usually stuffed their columns with foreign strife and London gossip, between advertisements for life-prolonging Balm of Gilead, Prince's Paste Pearls (a do-it-yourself product to replace or conceal decayed front teeth), Welch's Female Pills for the 'Green Sickness', cockfights, auction sales and lettings, now had to cope with heavy local reports and advertising. Weekly they had to postpone the usual 'recapitulations' of

---

[31] Wilberforce, *Life*, vol. 3, pp. 336, 323–4.
[32] SCC:LAI: WWM, E149, joint conference, 21 August 1807; WYAS(L): WYL250/6/3/17 and WYL250/6/3/11, Cattle's accounts.

far-off events, for, in the words of James Montgomery at the *Sheffield Iris*, 'while the civil war of a General Election is carrying on at home, there is no room in the breasts of Englishmen for any foreign favour or animosity: all their love and hatred are cordially exerted towards each other.' [33] The *Iris* carried no partisan material except in the form of advertisements, and if it had any bias it was perhaps towards Wilberforce and Milton in general outlook. The two outright Whig papers, the *Leeds Mercury* and the *York Herald*, now printed by Alexander Bartholoman, communicated regularly with the Milton committees and ran their pieces in preference to – but not the exclusion of – others. The *Leeds Intelligencer* was the most virulent of the Lascelles press and Griffith Wright was a virtual part of Lascelles's organization. The *Wakefield Star* remained fairly cool throughout the election period, continuing its budget of war news, printing political advertisements but only a few contributed squibs and letters and, judging by the selection of the items, moderately behind Milton and Wilberforce. The *Halifax Journal* at first appeared – again from the choice of material, for 'leaders' or editorials were little known outside Leeds – to endorse Wilberforce and Lascelles and to ridicule Milton's pretensions, but it carried everyone's advertising and showed no animosity at the outcome. Hull had three papers, the *Packet*, the *Advertiser* and the *Hull and Lincolnshire Chronicle*, and all three tended to favour Wilberforce and Lascelles but none had a strongly political tone. In addition to the *Herald*, York had the *Chronicle*, published by William Blanchard, and the *Courant*, published by George Peacock. The *Courant* remained relatively impartial. The *Chronicle* – 'your truly Constitutional paper', as one correspondent called it [34] – provided very full election coverage: on Thursdays during the polling it was produced in a second edition with the day's voting tally and it offered mailing franks to gentlemen to send out copies by post. Blanchard 'endorsed' Lascelles, but allowed generous space to other viewpoints. There were no papers in the North Riding at this time.

Both Lascelles and Wilberforce set up sub-committees in York to care for their voters once they arrived in the city. Lascelles's met at the Black Swan, across Coney Street from the George, with Robert Cattle as 'superintendent'. There were sixteen 'regulars' in constant attendance, sometimes working until midnight. The Rev. William Cautley, who was also on Wilberforce's committee, headed this list. Eleven other men gave time occasionally. On a typical evening, they would start their rounds about 9 p.m., take down the names of freeholders staying at the various houses, checking whether they had

---

[33] *Sheffield Iris*, 19 May and 16 June 1807; G.P. Jones, 'Political Reform Movement in Sheffield', *Hunter Archaeological Society Transactions*, 4 (1937), pp. 66–7.

[34] *York Chronicle*, 2 July 1807. The *Sheffield Mercury* began publication in March 1807, but I have been unable to find copies for this election period.

polled and offering protection to promised voters or inducements to wavering ones to vote for Lascelles.[35]

Milton's sub-committee sat daily at Swift's Coffee House, part of the Coach and Horses at the corner of Nessgate and Ousegate. Its purpose was to see that Milton voters reached the Castle Yard in one piece and 'got up with Facility to each Booth'. The Lord Mayor, William Hotham, presided over a group of about 35. Smaller groups were responsible for each of the four wards, Micklegate, Bootham, Monk and Walmgate, and protected Milton voters in their lodging places and escorted them to the poll. In the latter days of voting, committee members were billeted at the various houses in pairs for the further safeguarding of the freeholders from contamination by their adversaries.[36]

Among the vital duties of each central committee and the scattered agents was to weed out doubtful electors and to brief qualified ones on what would be expected of them when they stepped into a polling booth for the first time in their lives. For Lascelles, Wolley sent reasonably straightforward instructions which explained the arrangement of the booths and outlined what to say when the freeholder arrived in the correct one.[37] The printed circular sent to Milton's agents to prevent '*evidently*' disqualified voters from being brought to York was so complex that Thomas Tottie protested 'it will amount to a Scrutiny & we shall never be able to get sufficient Numbers mustered in so short a Time'. He boiled the queries down to five: Are you 21? Have you house, land or rents in this county worth 40 shillings per annum clear? Is it freehold ('copyhold or leasehold wont do')? Have you got a conveyance of it to yourself as of a year ago or did you acquire it as heir, by will or marriage? Is it rated to the land tax in your own name or your tenant's, or is the land tax redeemed? Anyone who could answer all these affirmatively 'may safely be taken to the Poll', Tottie judged.[38]

Arrangements to deliver the voters – often referred to as cargoes or booth fodder – were planned with martial efficiency to make a dramatic early impact, holding in reserve, but ready to march, those cohorts who would be required if the poll ran its permitted fifteen days. Agents were directed to send single votes first. Next, from Lascelles's point of view, should come voters casting second votes for Wilberforce. As the race lay between him and

---

[35] WYAS(L): WYL250/6/3/17 and WYL250/6/3/10, Cattle's accounts.
[36] SCC:LAI: WWM, E147, 148, sub-committee minutes.
[37] WYAS(L): WYL250/6/3/10, instructions to freeholders.
[38] SCC:LAI: WWM, E151 instructions to agents, 15 May 1807; E163/6, Tottie to Milton committee, 16 May 1807.

Milton, 'those who poll for both Mr. Lascelles and Lord Milton are of little consequence', said Wolley.[39]

A march of the Miltonian clothiers was planned at Leeds for the opening of the poll. Tottie promised at least 250 that Wednesday, 20 May, and 300 each for the two following days. The first arrivals would nearly all be Milton plumpers. 'The clothiers will be headed by 14 Gentlemen of whom 12 are Merchants & will march, I conceive in 7 Divisions, two or more Divisions on a Day according to Numbers,' Tottie informed the York committee. Each voter would carry a ticket entitling him to subsistence along the way and at York. The first phalanx of Miltonites was called up from around Leeds: Bramley, Armley, Wortley, Pudsey, Stanningley and Farsley. They would meet at the Mixed Cloth Hall at midday on the 19th and proceed the 15 miles to Tadcaster for the night, continuing the last 10 miles into York the next morning. They would travel in carriages, stage coaches, a hackney coach, three chaises and a light wagon.[40]

The passions excited by electioneering hubbub easily spilled over into violence and Leeds erupted on Tuesday evening, 19 May. The disturbance was sparked off by the appearance in Briggate, where a throng waited to cheer and wave good-bye to the first contingent of Milton voters, of two boys with Lascelles cards in their hats. Yards of orange ribbon had been distributed to decorate the hats of the majority and orange Milton cards were everywhere. The Milton cavalcade was led by a volunteer drum corps and to the *Mercury*'s reporter, 'The populace entered into the scene with hilarity, and felt that elation which the flattering prospects of their favourite Candidate were calculated to inspire, but no disposition to riot any where prevailed; in fact, we never witnessed so much moderation and decorum.' That was until the intrepid Lascelles admirers strolled into the happy scene. They were instantly spotted, hooted and shoved. When Mayor Richard Ramsden Bramley (also Lascelles's local chairman) collared a young Miltonite as he cried 'Milton for Ever' – possibly, as the more agitated onlookers suspected, to carry him off to prison – the mayor himself was heckled and pushed. The *Intelligencer*'s report, predictably, differed from the *Mercury*'s: Milton partisans openly provoked friends of other candidates and they were not simply hissed and pushed but '*pelted* with *dirt* and *stones*'. The people who insulted the mayor were 'pretty well heated with liquor'.[41] Mayor Bramley escaped the clutches of the mob and took

---

[39] WYAS(L): WYL250/6/3/10, Lascelles to Wolley, 16 May 1807; Wolley's instructions to agents, 16 May 1807.

[40] SCC:LAI: WWM, E163/5, 7, Tottie to Milton committee, 15 and 17 May 1807; E157/6, Hunter to Wrightson, 19 May 1807.

[41] *Leeds Intelligencer*, 25 May 1807; *Leeds Mercury*, 23 and 30 May 1807. Accounts in the rest of the county press varied little in details, chiefly resembling the *Mercury* report and

refuge in the Bull and Mouth Inn, where from a window he read the Riot Act ordering the throng to disperse in the name of the King. In twenty minutes (instead of the legally required hour), seeing no slackening in the uproar, the mayor called for the Irish Inniskilling Dragoons who arrived at a gallop and cleared streets, alleys and footpaths with drawn sabres. Some troopers pursued supposed rioters into private houses and churchyards, witnesses claimed. An unknown number of persons was stunned or trampled on by the horses or cut by the swinging swords but, early reports to the contrary, no one was killed.

The next evening, without civil or military orders and alarmed only by a bugle call from a passing stage coach, the troops again raced through the town centre with swords bared 'in the most furious and menacing manner'. Several terrified townsfolk were slashed but, again, there were no fatalities. The troops were confined to barracks and a few men and boys revenged themselves by smashing window panes in Bramley's house. 'Happily the populace had not the Bugbear of "No Popery" in their mouths or it is impossible to say what might have been the consequence, though to do the friends of Mr. Lascelles justice ... they have spared no pains ... to introduce this mischievous cry,' the *Mercury* declared. A versifier wrote:

> 'Tis surely unfair
> In a Protestant Mayor
> And his party must feel very sore
> That he who rails most
> At the Pope and his host,
> Should call out a Catholic corps.[42]

The great numbers demonstrating for Milton set Lascelles's friends 'on the tiptoe & they are bustling about to send off all the voters they can', Lucas Nicholson informed Wolley, warning him to expect double the number promised earlier. But the next day, as the poll booths opened in the Castle Yard, Lascelles's York committee learned from the same source that the Bradford road was 'completely blockaded by a set of Blackguards who assault all the Voters who do not appear to be in the Interest of Ld. Milton'. Voters from Haworth had been dragged from their wagon and beaten. Unless steps were taken to end this 'game', said Nicholson, 'God alone knows where it will end'.[43]

---

possibly from the same hand. Most London papers carried accounts, for example *The Times*, 28 May 1807.

[42] YML: Y/H 8.421, Election Squibs, 1807.
[43] WYAS(L): WYL250/6/3/10, Nicholson to Wolley, 19 May 1807 and same to Slingsby, 20 May 1807.

CHAPTER ELEVEN

The Public Argument

Four issues dominated public debate during the Yorkshire election of 1807. Two also influenced contests elsewhere: the threat of repeal of the slave trade abolition act and, even more highly charged, the question of Catholic relief as encapsulated in the shouts of 'No Popery'. To these were added the question of whether Wilberforce had joined Lascelles in a secret coalition to defeat Lord Milton; and the future of the domestic system of woollen manufacture. It was the controversy over the latter that fatally injured Lascelles's chances but they were also weakened by the abolition argument; Milton was attacked for his father's – and the Whig – stand on Catholic emancipation; while Wilberforce suffered most, in votes and in spirit, from the accusation of a secret coalition with Lascelles. The impact of the Report of the Wool Committee has already been considered. How were the other issues, of slavery, popery and coalition, used to manipulate the numerous and unpredictable Yorkshire freeholders in 1807?

Abolition

Fox's motion in June 1806 to bring in a bill to abolish the slave trade won so heavy a majority (114 to 15) that the passage of an act was a foregone conclusion in 1807. In the Lords, Earl Fitzwilliam rather uneasily supported the 1806 resolution. In 1807 he was not present when the bill was passed. In the Commons, Fawkes argued vigorously for abolition, the first time Wilberforce had had the support and adulation of a brother MP from Yorkshire in this cause. As the underage MP for Malton, Milton, too, denounced Britain's role in 'rapine and murder' and in preventing the progress of civilization in Africa. Whatever the cost to Liverpool merchants, 'let this foul stain be washed from the character of the nation', he had intoned.[1] Lascelles is not recorded

---

[1] *Parliamentary Debates, House of Lords*, vol. 7, col. 809 (24 June 1806); *Parliamentary Debates, House of Commons*, vol. 8, cols 963–7, 972, 994 (23 February 1807).

as having voted or spoken on the 1806 resolution but his brother Edward opposed it. The act passed the Commons by 283 to 16 in the small hours of the morning of 24 February 1807. After an incomparable eulogy from Samuel Romilly for Wilberforce, the little man sat with his head in his hands, the tears streaming down his cheeks, while MPs stood, applauding and cheering him.[2] But it was the Fox–Grenville administration – reviled and dismissed by the King only a month later over the Catholic bill – which had achieved the abolition victory after twenty years before the House.

The slave trade had little economic importance for Hull. No slave ship had ever cleared Hull harbour and although woollens from the West Riding were sold to America and the West Indies, the county's prosperity did not depend upon this part of its trade. No pro-slave-trade body of opinion existed, therefore, to support the Lascelles family interest.[3]

Grateful as he was to the Grenville administration for carrying through the act, Wilberforce on other subjects, such as Catholic emancipation, was much more in tune with the King's new government. He was deeply sensible of the 'importance of not embarking on a Roman Catholic bottom, (if I may so term it) the interest and well-being of our Protestant empire', he wrote to the Rev. Francis Wrangham. In the 1807 election, Wilberforce never exploited his abolition triumph, perhaps from humility, possibly for fear of embarrassing Lascelles. Tales circulated that Wilberforce had married a black woman, and he was amused by a letter from one constituent who had 'lowered' himself by marriage to his cook congratulating the MP on having risen above the 'common prejudices of society'.[4]

The change of government disquieted the abolitionists who feared that the act might be repealed, or at least weakly enforced. As in the 1806 general election, they cautioned electors to choose MPs 'sincerely disposed to the Act's enforcement'. A letter from the 'celebrated Mr. Clarkson' to a Hull resident ('A Detester of Slavery in All Its Shapes') was published in the county press. In it Clarkson spoke of the uneasiness of the anti-slave-trade committee and requested voters everywhere to seek the promises of candidates to oppose any attempt at repeal. Revealing his Whig colours, 'A Detester' then added his own judgment that Wilberforce would say yes, Milton *'Yes, with all my heart'* and if Lascelles said no, 'do you say No, no, no, to him'.

Clarkson did what he could to mobilize support from his wide acquaintance

---

[2] Furneaux, *Wilberforce*, pp. 252–3; Y. Wilberforce, *Wilberforce*, facing p. 1; *The British Slave Trade: Abolition, Parliament and the People*, ed. S. Farrell, M. Unwin and J. Walvin (Edinburgh University Press for The Parliamentary History Yearbook Trust: Edinburgh, 2007).

[3] Jackson, *Hull*, pp. 51, 70.

[4] Wilberforce, *Life*, vol. 3, pp. 308–9, 310–11; Harford, *Recollections*, p. 141.

for Wilberforce. 'Have you any votes in Manchester for Yorkshire, whom you could engage for Wilberforce?' he asked in a letter to John Wadkin. 'It is absolutely necessary that he should be in Parliament ... in Case any Attempt should be made to reverse the late Bill – It is necessary too that We should watch every Violation of the late Act – He desires only to be in Parliament, till he can see this great Measure out of danger.'[5]

A message addressed to the Society of Friends quoted Clarkson's *Portraiture of Quakerism* on the Society's disinclination to join in politics, adding that in this contest the consistent Friend must, when voting for Wilberforce, give another vote to Lord Milton as equally in favour of abolition and also a friend of 'just religious freedom'. 'The other Candidate, Mr. Lascelles, cannot be called either a Friend to the Abolition of the Slave Trade, or to Genuine Religious Liberty.' Other voices contended that Friends and Methodists should support Wilberforce and Lascelles and forgive the latter for his former stand on a 'favourite question'.[6]

To Lascelles's supporters, suggestions that the slave trade act would be repealed were a 'Jacobin electioneering trick'. They were annoyed that Milton had the effrontery to portray himself as virtually the equal of Wilberforce. But copies of Milton's modest Commons speech were printed by the thousands. The Rev. Thomas Dundas, requesting a bundle for canvassing, said that 'going to Yarm unprovided with them will be quite useless'. Countless broadsides proclaimed 'NO SLAVERY, NO PLUNDER ... MILTON FOR EVER'. A favourite song at Milton gatherings concluded

> Then choose one those rights to defend,
> Who n'er will permit you to lose 'em;
> The *West-Indian* to *Coventry* send,
> And young ROCKINGHAM clasp to your bosom.
>
> Let the first o'er his slaves still preside,
> The terror of dusky Barbadoes;
> Be the latter the Yorkshireman's pride,
> And the terror of white renegadoes![7]

---

[5] *York Courant*, 27 October 1806 and *York Herald*, 9 May 1807, for example; *Hull Packet*, 8 May 1807; StJC: GBR/0275/Clarkson/Folder 1–5/26, Clarkson to Wadkin, 1 May 1807.
[6] SCC:LAI: WWM, E221, handbill; *Leeds Mercury*, 31 May 1807; *Sheffield Iris*, 26 May 1807; *Yorkshire Election*, 22; YML: Y/H 8.421, Election Squibs, 1807, A Yorkshireman, 11 May 1807.
[7] *Leeds Intelligencer*, 11 May 1807; Smith, *Whig Principles*, p. 286; SCC:LAI: WWM, E167/11, Dundas to Milton committee, 19 May 1807; Election Squibs, 1807.

'Africanus', speaking for Wilberforce, thundered, 'All England will be astonished to hear that no Slave Trade is on the banners of a Man who has done his worst to ruin Mr. Wilberforce & turn him out of Parliament by forcing him into a contest'. Milton was a babe in his nurse's arms when Wilberforce began the arduous conflict and he came to public notice only months ago 'to share the Honours of an easy Victory'. Wilberforce and Lascelles made capital of the fact that Fitzwilliam had given William Windham, a right-wing Whig and avowed anti-abolitionist, the seat at Higham Ferrers when he lost Sudbury in Norfolk. Windham hoped to be able to return it when a suitable borough could be bought. Such were the wonders of pre-reform politics that he gave back Higham Ferrers at the end of May, having obtained Appleby.[8] The fathers were regularly abused for their contending sons. 'Lord H–re–d's Address to the Clothiers of Yorkshire', for example, contained such lines as

> What reason has a LORD to fear
> The Yorkshire Renegadoes
> With forty thousand pounds a year
> *All* coming from Barbadoes!!

which were answered by 'Lord F–z–m's Address' diverting the freeholders' thoughts to youth and popery:

> Room for a noble Peer to pass,
> Whose party strong and squirish
> Will govern all the County as
> He *govern'd* the *wild Irish* ...
>
> Stick to your *Lord*, desert your King
> And bring in BABY BUNTING,
> The *Maids and Nurses* all shall sing
> And Daddy go a hunting.[9]

If the Harewood family wished 'to float on the tide of popularity' it must become munificent in charity, liberal in civil and religious principles, and, above all, divest itself

> of that Milstone, *Barbadoes*, which counteracts every effort they may make to rise in public estimation. The *ancient* Baron ... and his sons

---

[8] KINCM:1982.895.409, Account of the Proceedings, fols 286–8; NRO: F(M), 72/1, Laurence to Fitzwilliam, 3 May 1807; 72/5, 7, 36, Windham to Fitzwilliam, 5, 8 and 26 May 1807.

[9] *Yorkshire Election*, pp. 3, 4, 70, 72.

may still support the Slave Trade if they choose, but let the public see that they give it their support, from *principle*, and not from *interest*

said one comment.

'To what does the Name of Lascelles owe its Consequence?' demanded the handbill entitled 'A Few *Plain* QUESTIONS *Answered*', and the answer was 'Ask BLEEDING AFRICA'. A West Riding proclamation read:

> WANTED
> A Hundred NEGRO DRIVERS
> to be employed in the
> ISLAND OF BARBADOES
> Apply at Har–w–d House
> No Yorkshire Clothier need apply, as they have
> been found too refractory to be insulted and trampled upon by
> THE SON OF THE PROPRIETOR
>
> N.B. Should the Slave Trade be revived in the
> next Session of Parliament, with a view to which the
> Proprietor is labouring to procure for his Son the
> Representation of the County of York, the Number
> of Negro Drivers wanted will not be limited, but
> may extend to Two Thousand at least.[10]

Lascelles had to endure much more of this sort of thing; for example, the squib

> THE PUNCH BOWL
> Which has long been manufacturing at the Leeds
> Pottery, for Lord H–w–d, is expected to be fin
> ished next week: and filled with Punch ... as
> will furnish one GALLON to each Freeholder ....
> The ingredients are the most exquisite ... par
> ticularly the RUM and SUGAR: the former is very old
> and ... the latter is from Barbadoes; and though
> it has been refined 500,000 times, it still retains
> a BLOODY tinge ....

---

[10] *Leeds Mercury*, 27 June 1807; SCC:LAI: WWM, E221, handbills; YML: Y/H 8.421, Election Squibs, 1807; *Yorkshire Election*, pp. 33, 34, 39, 40–1.

There were jolly japes as well:

MILTON'S FREEHOLDERS

Whilst poor Negro Wenches must shrink
Beneath the hard smack of the Whip,
The Lasses of Yorkshire all think
There's no smack like the smack of the LIP!

Whilst *Rogues* of *Barbadoes* apply
Their *Strokes* to the back and the shoulders,
I'll promise, my Girls, you'll enjoy
Better STROKES from Lord Milton's Freeholders.[11]

Lascelles's enraged friends were not idle in defending him against his traducers, as one declaration 'To the Middle and Lower Classes of Freeholders' showed: Friends of the 'INSOLENT ARISTOCRAT, LORD MILTON', it said, regarded them as a *'swinish Multitude'* who could be duped into thinking that Lascelles was actively engaged in the slave trade, a *'most impudent Falsehood'*:

> Of the ample Possessions derived by Lord Harewood from his Ancestors, is a small Estate in the West Indies, which has been in Possession of the Family since the original Occupation of that Country by the English, and which all the Parties employed, White or Black, have been at all Times treated with a Liberality, a Kindness, and Humanity, which have reflected the highest Honour on the Family throughout all the West Indian Islands. The Hon. Henry Lascelles is a Younger Brother, and has no more to do with this West Indian Property, than any One of you. He has also publicly pledged himself, if any Attempt should be made to repeal the Abolition, to give it his decided Opposition.

But his critics insisted that the 'recantation' looked suspiciously like it had been extracted from him at public meetings and London organs of the Whigs questioned whether his conversion was the result of a 'religious contact' with Wilberforce or a 'temporary lure to reclaim his own faded popularity'. To share the Wilberforce interest in Yorkshire was his main hope in the contest, contended 'A Man and A Brother!!!' in both *The Times* and *Morning Chronicle*.

'AN ABOLITIONIST' insisted that Lascelles from earliest youth had been taught to view the slave trade complacently 'and in 10 years in Parliament never opened his mouth or gave a single vote against' it. Lord Harewood was

---

[11] YML: Y/H 8.421, Election Squibs, 1807.

the largest slave owner in Yorkshire and the family 'as deeply interested in the revival of slavery as any family in England. And all Yorkshire knows that the *besetting Sin of that family is not a disregard to their own interest*'. 'Shall the Wealth of BARBADOES be the Price of your Independence?' the county was asked.

In a report on the contest, *The Times* concluded that abolition was a 'public cause of first-rate importance, which preserves a near equilibrium between ... Lord Milton and Mr. Lascelles, making up to the former the disadvantage he sustains from the reigning feelings of the day in regard to general politics, and from the influence of Government; while it rescues Mr. Wilberforce from the danger of being left behind for the want of ... party spirit which pushes forward his competitors.'[12]

Popery

Just as a Lascelles was helpless in untying the bond to slavery, so was a Fitzwilliam saddled with a record of favouring Catholic relief. This was often linked to slavery:

> Popery with a vengeance, Popery and Slavery, always have, and always will go hand in hand. ... The grand aristocrat, the father of Lord Milton ... is the avowed patron, protector and emancipator of Papists. He has returned for this most immaculate borough of Higham Ferrers, the right Hon. William Windham ... (a most strenuous advocate for the Slave Trade) ...
> NO POPERY! NO SLAVERY!
> *Wilberforce and Lascelles for Ever*[13]

How effective it was in deciding the Yorkshire outcome is arguable. Others may feel that the contest was determined chiefly by money – certainly there was a lot of it about. But in my view, the election was decided less by the length of purses than by the determination of large numbers of freeholders, aroused by both the political debate and the social change around them, to express themselves. If the issues were of little consequence and bribery all, why would each side have gone to such lengths to influence attitudes? People were less certain, more open to ideas in the early nineteenth century than they had

---

[12] *Yorkshire Election*, pp. 22–4, 47–8, 68–9; *Halifax Journal*, 16 and 23 May 1807; *The Times* and *Morning Chronicle*, 29 May 1807; KINCM:2006.3657, Wilberforce Election Papers, Box 1; *The Times*, 2 June 1807.

[13] *Yorkshire Election*, p. 95.

been in most of the previous one.[14] Circumstances and events quite beyond their control were rapidly and visibly altering their lives: the enclosure of common land; the opening of factories; the American and French revolutions which unleashed fresh thinking, and the gagging bills that restricted discussion of these dangerous ideas; the shortages and taxation imposed by decades of war; the evangelical movement in the Established Church; the stirrings of social consciousness; the rapid growth of Methodism – to name but the more obvious ones. These strands were the warp of the 'public opinion' of the day. Self-interest – the protection of one's livelihood or rank – would finally settle the choice for the individual voter, but each needed greater justification than that for his action and this was especially true for the West Riding clothiers, many of them influenced by the Methodists, basically Tory in outlook, who were for the second time turning to an untried Whig on what others decried as narrow grounds. It was to them and other Nonconformists that the 'No Popery' cry was chiefly directed in Yorkshire, and it was the established order, in the shape of the government of the day and the Anglican Church, which raised it. Could the hoary fear of Catholicism overcome concern for the remote slave trade and the immediate fears for their own livelihoods? Lascelles's success depended upon its doing so. This and his amicable relationship with the highly regarded Wilberforce were his strongest cards.

Wilberforce, still wrestling with the question of religious toleration, did not oppose the strategy so far as we know. For better and worse, most of his supporters were also Lascelles's friends and Lascelles, the 'tool of the Government party had "No Popery" displayed in Letters of Gold upon every banner; a Trick which must convince every man either of his wickedness, or weakness; either of his wish to deceive others, or of his incapacity in being deceived himself,' according to Robert Grimston. On nomination day, Lascelles's brother Edward had been seen to saunter around the Castle Yard and 'amongst the thickest of the Spectators lisp in his elegant way "No popery" "No popery"', and later the same message was bellowed by Lascelles orators from the windows of the George Inn.

One instance was found where Wilberforce and Lascelles jointly disclaimed such tactics, but for obvious reasons. A handbill with the words 'NO MILTON, NO DISSENTERS, NO POPERY' was publicly rejected by the Halifax committees of the two men who said they were 'highly grateful for the Support and Assistance they have received from Dissenters'.[15]

---

[14] E.R. Taylor, *Methodism and Politics, 1791–1851* (Cambridge University Press: Cambridge, 1935), discusses this transition period on pp. 88–90, 92–3; H. Donaldson, 'The Yorkshire election of 1807', unpublished MA thesis (University of York, 2006), pp. 14–31.

[15] Wrangham MSS, Robert Grimston's account; *York Herald*, 11 July 1807 and KINCM: 1982.895.409, Account of the Proceedings, fols 422–4; *Leeds Intelligencer*, 25 May 1807.

In 1807, Wilberforce had not yet reached the stage where he could tolerate Catholicism in the way that he could not only tolerate but happily work with (as in the abolition campaign or the Bible Society) Methodists, Unitarians or Quakers, unlike many Church of England communicants. He was often criticized for his broad-mindedness. According to 'Jay of Bath' (the Rev. William Jay), Wilberforce was neither 'censorious [n]or exclusive' and expressed a 'real and large liberality towards those who differed from him in some of the more external and subordinate parts of Christianity'. He attended Nonconformist chapels and on two occasions that Jay knew of had taken the sacrament in them. He expressed a 'oneness and sympathy with the cause of God at large'. His great concern was the numbers, rich and poor (and in slavery) who never heard God's message.[16]

Wilberforce's relative tolerance caused some confusion in Yorkshire over where he stood on the Catholic bill which had brought down the previous ministry. Most of his Yorkshire associates were strongly anti-toleration. One anonymous informant said Wilberforce was losing popularity because while professing to be an Anglican he built or encouraged the building of 'chapels and conventicles for Sectaries'. When the 1807 election was called, Jonathan Gray cautioned Wilberforce that some of his constituents wondered about his views on the 'r. Cathl.' issue. Wilberforce was surprised; in London it was well known that he was 'decidedly ag[ains]t the late Ministers in that quest[io]n [and] had told Ld. Grenville so'. To William Hey he explained his sorrow that he was not able to support the ministry which had passed the abolition. He had, he said, told Grenville that even after some concessions, the Irish Catholics would not be 'cordially attached' to a Protestant government and the church which was a part of it. Lord Holland was bitter over Wilberforce's behaviour, alleging that Wilberforce had privately approved the cabinet's 'conduct in their correspondence with the King' and had professed gratitude to the ministry for the abolition act. This had 'led the ex-Ministers to indulge hopes of receiving the sanction and support of him and of the powerful body [the Saints] with which he was connected', Holland wrote, but instead Wilberforce had 'condescended to take full advantage of the cry of "No Popery!"' in the Yorkshire election.[17]

Whatever he may have led others to believe (and wishing to please everyone had a lot to do with the criticisms levelled against him for insincerity), Wilberforce held many reservations about Catholicism which he was to shed later when, beginning in 1813, he supported Catholic emancipation for

---

[16] *Autobiography of Jay*, pp. 301, 302, 303; Furneaux, *Wilberforce*, p. 47.

[17] *Farington Diary*, vol. 4, p. 158; YA: Acc. 5, 6, 24, 235 Gray Family Papers, J13, Gray to Mrs Gray, 24 April 1807; Furneaux, *Wilberforce*, p. 319; Wilberforce, *Life*, vol. 3, p. 310; Holland, *Memoirs*, vol. 2, pp. 222–3.

his own reasons: 'No one could dislike popery more than he did; but he thought it reasonable that all its adherents should realize their civil rights and immunities; and that with regard to religious parties, all restraints and oppositions excited and strengthened their zeal the more, and resembled the dams in a river that caused the water to rise higher and spread wider.'

But in 1807 Wilberforce was adamantly opposed to Catholic relief. 'It is irreligion and immorality of which Ireland is sick. These popery has increased and fomented,' he wrote in his diary. The only long-term remedy was, he said, to 'enlighten, and, thereby, as I trust, to convert the Roman Catholics', which might take twenty or thirty years. The swift change of governments over the Catholic question might prove to be the 'means of arresting a very dangerous progress. ... But all this I say in strict confidence; for I should appear the most ungrateful man living, to those who do not or cannot discriminate between personal feelings and public duty.'[18]

Roman Catholics were not numerically strong in Yorkshire but the religion survived among landowners and gentry in the northern hills and dales. The West Riding was nearly bereft of them by the late eighteenth century. Among those outside the Anglican church, they were heavily outnumbered in the county by Presbyterians, Independents and Baptists, while the Methodists, still within the church, were the largest single group, thriving in the industrial areas neglected by the Anglican clergy and among the new bourgeoisie of the towns.[19]

Methodists in general were not politically minded, identifying for the most part with commerce, the state and the throne. Among them was an abiding fear and hatred of Catholicism although some of them conceded that English Catholics were not a threat, freed as they were from so many of the ancient superstitions and corruptions which had brought on the Reformation.[20] In 1807 a majority of Methodists became active allies of Wilberforce who endeared himself to them as the 'real Friend of Religion' and leading abolitionist. Ministers and principal laymen rallied voters and contributed to his election fund. But the schism which followed Wesley's death in 1791 had created a small breakaway Kilhamite or New Connexion faction, more radical in outlook, sometimes denounced as 'Tom Paine Methodists'. There were some 2,500 of the New Connexion in the West Riding.

---

[18] Pollock, *Wilberforce*, pp. 234–5; *Autobiography of Jay*, p. 317; Wilberforce, *Life*, vol. 3, pp. 310–11; Furneaux, *Wilberforce*, pp. 319–22.

[19] Bossy, *English Catholic Community*, pp. 8–9, 80, 86–7; Bogue and Bennett, *History of Dissenters*, pp. 327–8; Teale, 'Methodism in Halifax', pp. 26ff.

[20] Joseph Sutcliffe, *Review of Methodism, in a Discourse ... January 1, 1805* (Wilson & Spence: York, 1805), pp. 36–8, 42; Taylor, *Methodism*, pp. 112–13, 148–9. Methodist attitudes to Roman Catholicism are discussed in D. Hempton, *Methodism and Politics in British Society, 1750–1850* (Hutchinson: 1984), pp. 116–48.

Robert Oastler, a Thirsk grocer and Methodist lay preacher who moved to Leeds in the 1780s and became a prosperous cloth merchant, was one of them. (In later life he was steward of Thomas Thornhill's Fixby estate.) A conservative in early manhood, he became a Whig, took up abolition and parliamentary reform, read Paine, supported the *Leeds Mercury* and was one of the richest men to join the New Connexion. In the 1807 election he favoured Lord Milton. (His youngest son, Richard, then 18, got his first taste of election combat when at Wakefield he was hit by a brickbat meant for Wilberforce. He boasted of it for years.)[21]

The divided Methodists thus appeared in the election on both sides and, most unusually, in public. In their circular letter of 1806, the Leeds Methodists had urged Wilberforce's re-election but insisted, 'We are not engaging in any Political Contest, or making our Society the Tool of any Party', but nothing they did in that uncontested election compared with their hard-hitting approach in 1807. Fearful that the Catholic issue might produce Methodist votes for Lascelles, a contributor signing himself 'One of You' on 30 April addressed the 'Independent Freeholders of the Methodist Body' on Milton's behalf, declaring that those who shouted 'No Popery' now would be the first to cry 'No Methodism' if it suited their purpose. Milton (unnamed) was an 'old friend to Toleration' while the unnamed Lascelles was a 'known Advocate of Slavery and Intolerance'. Yorkshire readers would know that the last accusation fanned a smouldering resentment that Lord Harewood had refused to allow a Methodist chapel in his village. There had been Methodists there among the tenants, labourers and weavers since at least the 1770s, but they had to worship in a cottage. A letter to the *Mercury* entitled 'Protestant Popery' repeated an allegation that 'satan prevailed on the great man of the place' to give notice to tenants to give up Methodism or quit their farms. One of Lascelles's committees tried to rebut the charge by advertising that Lord Harewood now and for more than 20 years had employed as his steward a 'highly respectable Gentleman' who was a Methodist preacher. But 'One of You' returned to the attack to say that his lordship still would not permit a chapel and had required his steward to give up either his Methodism or his job.

The answer this time came from 'A Methodist' in Bradford who denounced 'One of You' as a Kilhamite; the majority of Methodists remained warm friends of Wilberforce and Lascelles, he said. But 'A Methodist of the Old Connection' responded that though Wilberforce was widely supported as a

---

[21] *Report of the Proceedings*, pp. 27–8; John Lyth, *Glimpses of Early Methodism in York and ... District* (William Sessions: York, 1885), pp. 206–8; *Minutes of Conversations between Preachers and Delegates in the Methodist New Connexion* (T. Allbut: Hanley [1806]), pp. 5–6; Driver, *Tory Radical*, pp. 5–6, 14, 19; Hargreaves and Haigh, *Slavery in Yorkshire*, pp. 79–89; SCC:LAI: WWM, G29/1, Oastler to Milton, 15 July 1807.

friend to humanity, 'dealers in blood' would never be approved by Methodists who believed that God had marked 'MEN-STEALERS with INFAMY!' The Lascelles' tainted past was contrasted with the Fitzwilliam history as guardians of civil and religious liberty. Lascelles was defended by 'A.B.' who deplored attempts to blacken him by those who delighted in 'Republicanism and confusion'. They joined the 'Papists whom they hate and the Methodists whom they despise' merely to defeat him.[22]

Many deprecated the indiscriminate use of 'No Popery'. Whigs tried to make the point that 'popery' existed only in heated imaginations; 'Catholics are not Papists any more than Englishmen are Turks.' Lord Grenville's criticism of the Society for Promoting Christian Knowledge (SPCK), to which he belonged, for its public statement that the Catholic bill was hostile to the church, was reprinted widely, as was the Bishop of Norwich's charge to the clergy in 1806 which said that modern Catholics no less than Protestants opposed compulsion in religious matters.[23]

Miltonians tried to match the 'No Popery' hucksters in, for example, 'revealing' that a Roman Catholic sat on Lascelles's Leeds committee, 'a Papist ... who is canvassing for your votes under the cry of No Popery!!' But 'A Catholic' replied that he and his fellow churchmen felt grateful to George III for his liberality towards them, within the constraints of his coronation oath, and so by implication were right to support Lascelles as the ministerial candidate.[24]

Lord Milton not only had to endure attacks on his father's abortive Irish rule (during which the earl allegedly 'exclusively courted and caressed the Papists') but accusations that he was himself a Catholic ('which throws a great Damp' on the Saddleworth canvass, a disconsolate supporter said) and kept a priest in his house. The Rev. Francis Wrangham told Milton, 'It is really ludicrous to hear myself called upon ... to depose gravely that "you are not a papist!" As I preached a Sermon about nine years ago at Scarborough against Popery, I assure you mine is fortunately ... no contemptible authority.' Milton was, however, expected in many quarters to garner the second votes of Wilberforce's Methodist and Quaker friends, chiefly on the slave trade grounds, and as soon as they thought Wilberforce was 'safe'.[25]

---

[22] *Report of the Proceedings*, p. 31; *Leeds Mercury*, 2, 16, 23 and 31 May 1807; Jones, *Harewood*, pp. 171–2; *Doncaster Gazette*, 29 May 1807; *Leeds Intelligencer*, 4, 11 and 25 May 1807; *Sheffield Iris*, 12 May 1807; *York Courant*, 4 May 1807.

[23] *York Herald*, 16, 23, 30 May 1807; *Leeds Mercury*, 6 June 1807; SCC:LAI: WWM, E221, Grenville handbill.

[24] YML: Y/H 8.421, Election Squibs, 1807, fol. 37; *Yorkshire Election*, pp. 20–1; *Leeds Mercury*, 9 May 1807.

[25] *Yorkshire Election*, pp. 51–2; SCC:LAI: WWM, E178/8, Whitehead to Lady Fitzwilliam,

The denials of government ministers – Perceval, Canning and Castlereagh were especially singled out as perpetrators of the charge that the Whigs were Papists – that they were encouraging bigotry were (and are) unconvincing. So often had ordinary people been told that the government alone upheld the church that constables escorting Lord Castlereagh from St James's Palace shouted to the throng to make way for '*Bishop* Castlereagh's carriage', fancying that all ministers must be 'Heads of the Church', one anecdote ran. A scare-mongering report was industriously circulated in London that the Pope had landed in Ireland.

'The Catholic question was little understood and less relished,' commented Lord Holland. 'The King, long the most popular man in his dominions, derived fresh favour ... from his age and infirmities. Our real vindication consisted in a charge of insincerity against him; but such a line of defence, at all times indecorous, would then have been odious, injudicious, and unsafe. ... Even the Dissenters, upon whom, in a contest with the Crown, the Whigs must always mainly rely, were alarmed at the report of our indulgence to Roman Catholicks, and ... joined in some places with the Cry of intolerance in favour of Court and High Church candidates against the friends of religious liberty.'[26]

'No Popery' had helped to decide the York city contest. 'That rascal Dr. Burgh is at the bottom of all this mischief,' Alderman Robert Rhodes, Dundas's committee chairman, told Fitzwilliam. The York Minster interest was clearly for Sykes then and Lascelles now. The aged archbishop remained discreetly uninvolved but directed those under his influence to vote for Lascelles. He was toasted at Lascelles's post-election dinner in London. Where, in Rockingham's heyday, the Whigs could count on the church interest, now with the issue of Catholic emancipation to the fore, the ministerial candidates were favoured. The wealthy clergy of York – and clergy throughout the county as well – had a tradition of meddling in elections which offended some strait-laced citizens. 'For persons of this description to be seen deeply engaged in party politics, canvassing their parishioners, encouraging mobs, and frequenting taverns, and ... to have their names bandied about, and their foibles exposed in electioneering squibs, cannot be esteemed very favourable to the cause of religion,' one such critic wrote. The noted Dr Burgh fitted this description in the 1807 election, if we take the word of a Milton champion who described

---

2 May 1807; E161/26, Benson to Milton committee, 18 May 1807; E173/17, Wrangham to Milton, 3 May 1807; F62/96, Danser to Fitzwilliam, 6 and 21 May 1807; E177, Scatcherd to Fitzwilliam, 4 May 1807; E173/65/1, Danser to Fitzwilliam, 10 May 1807; *Sheffield Iris*, 5 May 1807.

26 *Hull Chronicle*, 17 June 1807; *Morning Chronicle*, 16 May 1807; Holland, *Memoirs*, vol. 2, pp. 226–7.

the Wilberforce leader as an '*Irish Refugee*' seen nightly in public houses where Milton voters were lodged 'haranguing in the kitchen' to seduce them to give their second votes to Wilberforce or Lascelles. His activities inspired an epigram:

> No Freeman is BURGH; yet he bustles about,
> As if he was Lord of the Whole of York city!
> No Freeholder HE; yet he makes a great rout,
> Usurping the Chair of a County Committee!!
>
> But the Bull of all Bulls, which this Irishman, mark,
> And pray keep it steadily still in your view,
> 'Tis as clear as the day, though 'tis done in the dark,
> He serves the SLAVE's FRIEND and the SLAVE-DEALER too!![27]

Clergymen in the North Riding, busy on behalf of Wilberforce and Lascelles, resorted to 'Religious prejudices' which 'with some weak minds have had the desired effect', a Greta Bridge resident reported to the Milton committee. John Crosley of Bradford described the appearance of Wilberforce and Lascelles at the cloth hall there as ruined by a cleric from Bingley who had so castigated Milton that the crowd hissed and groaned. Lascelles 'was so much disgusted … that he turned his back' on the clergyman and chatted with some ladies. The clergyman in question pointedly complimented Wilberforce on his support of the church establishment.

One hapless clerical partisan, the Rev. Ware, was singled out by the enemy camp as a clergyman 'distinguished for his Piety and *Morality* in every brothel in York!!' The Rev. John Ware of Stockton appears in election records as a local Wilberforce committee member and canvasser in the Bulmer wapentake but his name vanishes at an early stage from the lists. He did pledge £100 to Wilberforce's subscription and he voted for Wilberforce and Lascelles.[28]

The religion furore seemed to have less impact on the Society of Friends than the question of slave trade abolition and its conceivable repeal, to prevent

---

[27] YML: Y/H 8.421, Election Squibs, 1807; SCC:LAI: WWM, E170/4, Rhodes to Fitzwilliam, 2 May 1807; Smith, *Whig Principles*, pp. 64–5, 306; SCC:LAI: WWM, E176, Markham to Fitzwilliam, 30 April 1807; E224, Haigh to Milton committee, 28 May 1807; E177/30, Elliot to Fitzwilliam, 8 May 1807; *York Chronicle*, 25 June 1807; *Poll for Members of Parliament [for] the City of York … 1818* (York, 1818); Wrangham MSS, Robert Grimston's account.

[28] SCC:LAI: WWM, E178/147, Lidderdale to Milton committee, 31 May 1807; WYAS(L): WYL250/6/3/10, Crosley to Hardy, 8 May 1807; Wrangham MSS, Robert Grimston's account; KINCM: 1982.895.409, Account of the Proceedings, fols 34, 44, 221.

which the return of Wilberforce was essential. Where they expressed a second choice it was often for Milton as a friend to 'liberty and toleration'. The Tuke family of York may have been typical of Quakers generally, although they favoured Lascelles over Milton. They were Pittites but William Tuke, a prosperous tea dealer, believed that voting, if done, should be quiet, without attempting to influence others. There were times, he conceded, when the Society had to be more open and help sympathetic MPs, and such a time was 1807. Wilberforce was universally esteemed for his abolition labours and also, in 1796, learning of Friends held in York Castle for non-payment of tithes, he had supported a bill to free them from these church taxes. In 1807, William and his son Henry were in London for the yearly meeting when the Wilberforce subscription opened at York and Henry's son Samuel, aged 22, enthusiastically pledged £50 for the family firm. 'Samuel's bold stroke gave his grandfather and me some surprise,' Henry wrote, 'whilst others are not a little entertained, and some pleased at it!' Back home the surprise changed to approval and the Tukes gave Wilberforce their unqualified help.[29]

A sample of the songs sung in the taverns, the handbills stuck on walls, and the drum-beat advertising carried in the press will show the use made of popery to stir lethargic Yorkshire electors into making the rough journey to York:

> Here's a bumper, my boys, to our Protestant King,
> Like children around him let Protestants cling;
> Let Jacobin Papists their venom disgorge;
> Old England for ever! and Protestant GEORGE! [30]

CLOTHIERS

The Merchants are going to conjure up another Bug-bear to frighten you: finding that you are grown rather too familiar with their 'NO POPERY' Scarecrow; ... this new one, they fancy, poor souls, will be . .. ten times more ugly, and more frightful than even poor old 'No Popery!' . .. Why they have Combined together to buy no more cloth of

---

[29] BI: Tuke 3, W. Tuke to H. Tuke, 3rd day noon [1807]; Charles Tylor, *Samuel Tuke; His Life, Work, and Thoughts* (Headley Brothers: 1900), pp. 31–3; John Stephenson Rowntree, 'Samuel Tuke', *Friends' Quarterly Examiner*, April 1895, pp. 3–6; W.K. and E.M. Sessions, *Tukes of York* (William Sessions: York [1971]), pp. 79–80; William Allen, *Life of William Allen*, 3 vols (Charles Gilpin: 1846), vol. 1, p. 179; Wilberforce, *Life*, vol. 2, p. 146. For Quakers and abolition, see Judith Jennings, *The Business of Abolishing the British Slave Trade, 1783–1807* (Cass: 1997).
[30] YML: Y/H 8.421, Election Squibs, 1807.

any one who votes for LORD MILTON! ... So if all the Clothiers vote for LORD MILTON, the Merchants will all shut up their counting houses, warehouses and shops, and give up business forsooth! – Very likely indeed – [31]

LOST

A DUN-COLOURED Spaniel, that answers to the name of FITZ. He will fetch and carry, and do every thing he is bid, excepting jumping over a stick for KING GEORGE, but will readily do it for the POPE.[32]

PROCLAMATION

Be it known ... that I ... Electioneering Vicar General for the East Riding of Yorkshire have full power and authority to grant compleat

ABSOLUTION

to all my dear children induced by my persuation to break their promises however solemnly given in favour of that Arch-Heretic MILTON ... [33]

And, from an Address to the Freeholders of Yorkshire and Freemen of York:

... At this moment the Pope is the organ of Bonaparte. In a Catechism lately imposed on the miserable slaves of the Corsican Usurper, sanctioned by a bull of the Pope that Monster is solemnly declared to be the IMAGE OF GOD upon EARTH!!! ... The Catholics have every religious privilege which you have. It is senseless to talk of their *Emancipation.* THEY WANT POWER ... Persecute not, but permit not Popery ...

> Our aid, then, like FREEMEN, we boldly will bring,
> Let him Bluster and threaten who likes.
> We'll Vote with our Conscience, we'll bear up our King
> With Wilberforce, Lascelles, and Sykes.[34]

---

[31] *Yorkshire Election*, pp. 25–9; *Leeds Mercury*, 16 May 1807.
[32] YML: Y/H 8.421, Election Squibs, 1807; *Yorkshire Election*, p. 93.
[33] Collection of political tracts and handbills, British Library catalogue no. 1850 d 26, 3 June 1807.
[34] *York Chronicle*, 7 May 1807; YML: Y/H 8.421, Election Squibs, 1807.

Coalition?

There never was a declared coalition of the Lascelles and Wilberforce interests. None was needed to guarantee that the names of the two old members would be coupled. They plainly preferred each other to the upstart Milton; their mutual friends set up joint local committees for them; speeches, letters and advertising (all concentrating their fire on Milton) constantly served them both; and agents who worked for one usually recommended the other. Milton and his father chose to regard such evidence as proof of a deliberate coalition, and they pressed this charge relentlessly. The tactic reaped for Milton the single votes or bullets he needed to prevail. Wilberforce suffered as the clothiers and abolitionists deserted him in doubt or disgust over the apparent juncture with Lascelles. By his own estimate, he was 'defrauded' of more than 8,000 votes, chiefly because of this persistent issue. Lascelles was not an entirely innocent bystander. Association with Wilberforce helped him greatly. He disclaimed the coalition, but not from the housetops.

The puzzle is why Wilberforce should have let himself fall into the trap. It showed a strange naïveté in an experienced politician that he could so soon forget the stigma Lascelles had acquired by 1806 throughout the West Riding. It sounds lame to say, as he did, that he had no *right* to interfere with the activities of those volunteer workers who were also Lascelles's friends. A clear signal from him might have altered their conduct, but of course it might also have cost him the votes of Lascelles's most active friends. It also seems odd, to put it no higher, that he never tried to influence any supporter in the casting of his second vote, or, indeed, ever asked for a plumper, as he solemnly affirmed.[35] One must wonder what he talked about as he travelled the county if he had discarded as unmentionable the perfectly proper gist of canvassing conversations. After 23 years in Parliament and the winning of renown, perhaps he was simply careless, confident that nine-tenths of the votes were in his pocket, believing that his unsupported word that – as the saying went – he stood 'on his own bottom' should have sufficed.

Coalition had been a dirty word at least since the 'unnatural' union of Fox and Lord North or the 'strange monster of county politics', that 'unaccountable' combination of Yorkshire reformers and Pittites which in 1784 broke Fitzwilliam's grasp on the county. It might have been logical to ambitious party or factional leaders to unite, on occasion, for mutually profitable ends or in times of national crisis, but the less worldly adherents of

---

[35] Wilberforce, *Life*, vol. 3, p. 332; Furneaux, *Wilberforce*, pp. 261–2, 266; *Yorkshire Election*, p. 84; William Wilberforce, *Letter to the Gentlemen, Clergy, and Freeholders of Yorkshire; Occasioned by the Late Election* (Luke Hansard: 1807).

one side or the other seldom saw things so dispassionately. 'All good people hate coalitions,' Lord Eldon, now again Lord Chancellor, had said.[36] A slight attempt was made in 1807 to give Milton a ride on Wilberforce's coat tails. 'An Abolitionist' warned that Wilberforce's re-election would be endangered by the efforts to join his name with Lascelles's but that it would be consistent to couple Wilberforce and Milton: 'the Veteran and the Young Abolitionist'.[37] But it soon became obvious to Milton's party that the appeal to many influential voters of the two old members – Wilberforce with his many virtues and Lascelles with ten years' experience in Parliament – might overwhelm Milton's advantage as the saviour of the clothiers. He had to concentrate, therefore, on plumpers and at the same time convince voters that in giving him a single vote they would not injure Wilberforce's chances. Wilberforce and Lascelles were regularly portrayed as the joint government candidates as in 'A New Song':

> There's **WILBERFORCE** tried, and **LASCELLES** beside,
> Who for years have been firm in your cause;
> Who have stuck to their King, and will do the same thing,
> Crown'd again with your votes and applause.

Support for them was always equated with support of the 'kind hearted good old King ... your Religion, your principles and your independency'. 'Be grateful and faithful to your long tried and upright Representatives,' asserted another scribbler, 'Friends of Humanity to Wilberforce you owe the Abolition of the Slave Trade. Friends of Commerce behold in Lascelles the asserter of her real interests, the true Friend of her manufactures, the genuine patriot – The steady protestant – the arduous Servant of his King and Country.'[38]

The view from Etridge's and Wentworth Woodhouse

The strength of the Milton assault on the 'coalition' was its underlying sincerity. 'There never was a doubt in the minds of the Gentlemen of Lord Milton's Committee that Mr. Wilberforce both during his canvass and thro'out the whole of the Election had joined his Interest with that of Mr. Lascelles,' Robert Grimston was to write. Although Wilberforce said he had vowed to remain neutral, after receiving the 'friendly wishes of Lord Fitzwilliam, the Duke of Norfolk, and others and the promised support of all the clothiers, and

---

[36] Martineau, *History*, p. 233.
[37] *Yorkshire Election*, pp. 32–3; *Leeds Mercury*, 9 May 1807.
[38] *Leeds Intelligencer*, 18 May and 1 June 1807; *Yorkshire Election*, pp. 12–13; *York Chronicle*, 21 May 1807; KINCM: 1982.895.409, Account of the Proceedings, fol. 335.

of nine-tenths or more of Lord Milton's supporters', Fitzwilliam never fully believed or trusted him. The earl left no document describing Wilberforce in such words as Windham used when Wilberforce allegedly prevented Pitt from giving Edmund Burke a state funeral: 'that little viper, creeping & full of insidious venom,' but he probably agreed with his wife's assessment of their opponent as a 'very artful man'. Wilberforce and his election aides publicly disavowed a connection with Lascelles but, said Lady Fitzwilliam, 'I do suspect that he will help Lascelles instead of Milton'.[39] And so said all of Milton's party.

The earl, observing that Wilberforce and Lascelles paid canvassing visits to various towns on the same days, warned Milton's committee chairman, 'so far ... they are separate, but still they chose the same day for the same place: consequently the Adherents of each are collected together, which produces the effect of each ... having ... the support of the Whole – This can hardly be the effect of accident, & therefore gives ground for suspecting a secret understanding ... we must push *for single* votes as much as possible.' Those who refused plumpers should be marked down as for Wilberforce, an ally concluded. 'I am perfectly aware of [his] guile ... and dread its effects.'[40] To Miltonians, their opponent's performance during the canvass was a breach of his pledge of neutrality.

There was abundant damaging evidence. Wilberforce and Lascelles not only canvassed Bradford together but dined together at the home of John Hardy. The handbills circulated ahead of their arrival requested friends of both to *'parade together, to canvass together* and to *feast together* with this inseparable pair'. In the East Riding Wilberforce's friends and agents likewise canvassed for Lascelles. And in York, 'The two parties paraded the streets with the same Music, the same Banners, and their adherents wore the Cards of each party in their hats. ... The Chairman of Mr. Wilberforce's comm[itt]ee [Dr Burgh] solicited second votes for Mr. Lascelles in their own Committee room.' In London, Lord Rendlesham, Lascelles's committee chairman, asked votes for both. Various committees published announcements in the same words, printed on the same paper. The Leeds committees of the pair sat together regularly until nomination day. Milton's headquarters received a stream of reports of joint canvassing. Some Milton agents were convinced that Wilberforce had not consented and the combined operations were carried out

---

[39] Wrangham MSS, Robert Grimston's account; Wilberforce, *Letter to the Gentlemen*; Wilberforce, *Life*, vol. 3, p. 328; SCC:LAI: WWM, F48/23 Laurence to Fitzwilliam, 6 June; NRO: F(M), 72/8, Lady Fitzwilliam to Wentworth, 9 May 1807.
[40] SCC:LAI: WWM, 173/61, Fitzwilliam to Wrightson [10 May 1807]; NRO: F(M), 72/10, Wentworth to Lady Fitzwilliam, n.d.

on local initiative. In the West Riding where the clothiers were single-minded in their defiance of Lascelles, this made no difference.[41]

Much of the anti-coalition fire was directed to Methodists, Friends and others to whom abolition and religious toleration were supreme issues. One ditty ran:

> How much it will shock
> The whole Methodist Flock,
> To learn that the Saint they take pride in,
> To gain a few Votes
> His time now devotes
> To the VICE of the wicked West-riding! [42]

and another in the same vein:

> What a base *Coalition* has lately ta'en place
> 'Twixt the *Driver of Slaves*, and the *Preacher of Grace*! ...
> Shall it ever be said that our County is sold,
> Or that Yorkshire is *purchas'd* with *African Gold*?
> While cant and low cunning with L–sc–lles unite,
> All the hopes of her Sons, and their wishes to blight;
> No! Cheer up, my Boys,
> For, in spite of their noise,
> The Flag of our MILTON in triumph shall wave!
> He's the Man we'll support
> 'Gainst the *bribes of the Court*,
> For *he'll crush Peculation*, and *rescue the Slave!*[43]

Milton signed a carefully worded address the day after the breakdown of negotiations over expenses for Wilberforce–Milton voters which spoke of 'strong reasons to suppose that a virtual, though not avowed junction of Interests will take place between many of the separate Friends of my Competitors'. He protested against such a union, quoting Wilberforce to the

---

[41] SCC:LAI: WWM, E175/8, a Freeholder, 28 May 1807; Wrangham MSS, Robert Grimston's account; *Yorkshire Election*, pp. 102–3, 82–4; *York Chronicle*, 4 June 1807; *Morning Chronicle*, 6 June 1807; SCC:LAI: WWM, E171/9, 10, Martin to Milton committee, 8 and 9 May 1807; E156/58, Rylah to same, 20 May 1807; E164/32, Hunter to same, 3 June 1807; WYAS(L): WYL250/6/3/11, Sawdon to Slingsby, 29 May 1807; SCC:LAI: WWM, E163/2, Tottie to Milton committee, 4 May 1807.

[42] Wrangham MSS, Robert Grimston's account; Y. Wilberforce, *Wilberforce*, pp. ii–iii.

[43] YML: Y/H 8.421, Election Squibs, 1807.

effect that a coalition would be 'unworthy of the dignity of a large County'. To this Wilberforce's committee replied that 'no coalition ... at present exists; nor is any such coalition in contemplation', not an explicit enough answer to stifle the opposition.[44]

A letter urging 'MILTON, and NO COALITION!' told freeholders that they were dupes of the 'most artful coalition ever formed'. The public considered Wilberforce more of a religious man than most in public life, and so accepted his assurance that he had not joined forces with Lascelles. But his agents 'directly contradicted' his word, and feeling he was safe, were collecting second votes for Lascelles.

More doubts were cast on Wilberforce's character by 'A Friend to the Methodists' who declared that his 'pretence' that his committee members acted without his approval 'is most assuredly a trimming kind of subterfuge too flimsy to impose upon an honest Yorkshireman'. Methodists, especially, must oppose all forms of slavery and tyranny by turning to Milton, 'wise above his Years, a Man of Business and an Orator; he is decidedly opposed to Slavery [and] a warm friend to Religious Toleration.'[45]

There were ungracious suggestions that Wilberforce should have retired to a borough and saved the county the fuss of a contest, as the withering barrage of attacks on Wilberforce for something he asserted steadfastly he had not done became increasingly raucous. An anonymous scribe in Halifax listed the reasons for voting against Wilberforce: his family had no claim to public notice; his fortune did not set him above the danger of undue influence by ministers; he was constrained to ask the pecuniary aid of freeholders to carry on his election; 'he keeps a fair outward shew towards all parties'; he had supported arbitrary principles for 23 years, and 'his proper interest ... is in the neighbourhood of Hull'.[46]

Versifiers rejoiced in their opportunities to castigate the 'Monstrous Coalition', reaching a climax in 'The Gentle Denial':

> 'Tickle me,' says pious Billy
> > Tickle me, good Lascelles, do
> If you but tickle pious Billy,
> > He, in return, will tickle you!
> To it, then, they fall a tickling,

---

[44] *York Chronicle*, 21 May 1807; *York Courant*, 18 May 1807; *York Herald*, 16 May 1807, among others.
[45] *Leeds Mercury*, 31 May 1807; YML: Y/H 8.421, Election Squibs, 1807; *Sheffield Iris*, 2 June 1807; *York Chronicle*, 4 June 1807.
[46] *York Chronicle*, 4 June 1807; KINCM: 1982.895.409, Account of the Proceedings, fols 301, 429; *Yorkshire Election*, pp. 86–7.

> Tickling pink, and tickling blue:
> 'Colleague Lascelles!' – 'Colleague Billy!'
> Runs the whole COMMITTEE through.
> Las. – 'Plainest of all pious creatures
> Quakers are not plain as you'.
> Wil. – 'Gentlest of WEST INDIA NATURES!
> I must give the Devil his due'.
> Las. – 'You of Holiness the beauty
> Stived in Methodistic stew!'
> Wil. – ''Mongst your Slaves you know your duty,
> Blue is black, and black is blue'.
> Las. – 'But DEAREST SAINT! our plans concealing,
> Tho' join'd, we must appear in Two:'
> Wil. – 'sweet Sugar Cane! at double dealing,
> You need not furnish me my cue'.
> To it then they fall a tickling,
> 'You don't know me', – 'I don't know you':
> Groaning, grunting, humming, squibbling
> Runs the whole Committee thro'.

Lord Milton 'breathes the funeral of Bigotry; the destruction of Slavery; the commencement of universal and perpetual Freedom', trumpeted his supporters. He deserved the votes of 'every true born Briton'. 'CONSCIENCE, PLUMPERS, and INDEPENDENCE.'[47]

The View from York Tavern

The depth of Wilberforce's pain at the unprecedented questioning of his integrity can be judged by the *Letter to the Gentlemen, Clergy, and Freeholders of Yorkshire* which he published that summer. Vilified, victimized, as he saw it, and with his bright reputation, however lightly, tarnished, he composed a self-justification of events which – from the scant attention paid to the pamphlet in the Yorkshire press – had almost faded from memory. According to his biographer sons, Wilberforce here 'absolutely annihilated the slander' of a secret coalition in 'an admirable specimen of perfect self-defence without recrimination'. An earlier explanation of his conduct had appeared in the Yorkshire press under the pseudonym of 'A Freeholder'. It was advised and possibly written by Henry Thornton who spent the final hectic days at the

---

[47] Y. Wilberforce, *Wilberforce*, p. ii; YML: Y/H 8.421, Election Squibs, 1807; *Morning Chronicle*, 2 June 1807; Wrangham MSS, Robert Grimston's account; Furneaux, *Wilberforce*, p. 267.

'seat of war' with his friend. He gave Wilberforce a plumper, from his freehold in Sutton in Holderness. Thornton did more than a little of the scribbling while in the city, having discovered the press 'sadly mismanaged', and when the polls closed he encouraged Wilberforce to prepare a vindication with a short version to be issued at once. 'Remember, that though Yorkshire knows what was done, the rest of England knows nothing about it,' Thornton told Wilberforce. The latter was not easy about defending his character against 'ye false charge' but 'Happily', he told Thomas Babington, 'my Conscience is quite clear & therefore I can commit my Cause unto God & be at peace'.[48]

These accounts together with the election record kept by David Russell[49] revealingly trace his attitudes from the advent of the election to the wreck of his hope of a nearly unanimous endorsement by his constituents. He finished well ahead of his rivals in the poll, but his victory did not alter the sadness with which he looked back on this episode. Far from avoiding recrimination, he turned harshly upon the Miltonians who had, he believed, cheated him of his due. He did not comprehend the reaction provoked by his considerate treatment of Lascelles, with all that Lascelles had come to represent. There is bitter realization of the tricks by which Milton, his father and friends manipulated this insensitivity.

Wilberforce implied that he had been gulled into giving his pledge of neutrality in return for the friendly good wishes of Fitzwilliam, Norfolk and the clothiers. Knowing that he could also count on Lascelles's Tory friends and his own strength in the East Riding, a pact would be of no use to him. It would bring no more votes than he already could count on, except for a few of Lascelles's high-born friends, and it could lose him Milton adherents. It would be more expensive than his return as an independent and it could never be kept a secret.

But the pledge of neutrality was 'quite wrong – I should have made a conditional engagement, and then the Miltonians would not have dared to act as they did'. The bargain was a 'gross political error'. Questioned later on the hustings, Wilberforce repeated that he stood alone for he had given his word that he did. In his camp, however, were those who argued plausibly that a coalition with Lascelles could not be 'odious' because the two men had 'long been generally agreed in their politics and long generally supported the illustrious Pitt'. In this particular election, they also agreed on the Catholic question and that the King had acted correctly in dismissing the

---

[48] Wilberforce, *Life*, vol. 3, pp. 336–7; Wilberforce's *Letter to the Gentlemen* was, so far as I could find, described with excerpts only in the *Hull Advertiser*, 15 and 22 August 1807 and *Sheffield Iris*, 18 August 1807; *York Chronicle*, 9 July 1807; WLCT: EHC18/M786, Thornton to Mrs Thornton, 10 June 1807; BOD: AWP, Wilberforce to Babington, 16 June 1807

[49] KINCM: 1982.895.409, Account of the Proceedings; Wilberforce, *Life*, vol. 3, pp. 328ff.

'Talents', although Wilberforce recognized the debt that abolition owed to that government. A coalition would have been 'natural and honourable', a union of 'loyalty and patriotism' and would have guaranteed the election of both men. The slave trade – the most important issue dividing them in the public mind – was never a *party* question, and Lascelles had promised that he would never support repeal of the Abolition Act. But Wilberforce stuck to his original commitment to remain 'neutral', and in his own eyes he was impartial, which only made worse the double injury he sustained in suffering the obloquy of a presumed coalition and failing to bring in his old parliamentary friend with him.

On the question of his supporters' active aid to Lascelles, Wilberforce contended that he had no right to intervene in their friendships. His 'really independent and volunteer supporters' could not be commanded like Milton's 'deluded vassals'. But if we accept, as we must, that Wilberforce did not know what all his friends were doing, we may also feel that he ought to have cared. One is inclined to sympathize at least with an antagonist who argued that Wilberforce's York committee was no less liable to discipline than those of the other candidates. A coalition 'in its essential particulars' existed which left Wilberforce 'indebted to the imprudence of his friends and the indecision of his own conduct, for the odium which attached to his character during the late Election'. Wilberforce men afterwards said that they spoke for him only when they acted as a committee. When they canvassed for him and Lascelles, they were acting as private individuals. This 'quibble' reminded Samuel Henry Copperthwaite of the late Bishop of Derry who was also Earl of Bristol. Reproved for 'Profane swearing', he good-humouredly apologized, 'I do not swear as the Bishop of Derry, but merely as the Earl of Bristol'.[50]

Wilberforce blamed coincidence for his appearances with Lascelles in various West Riding towns, but admitted that he had not been guarded enough: it was his first contested election and he felt he had nothing to hide. It surprised him that after his denials, the question of a coalition ever arose again. His stance of being above the battle encouraged his opponents to think Wilberforce was guileful. Not for the first time was the old campaigner derided for cant. But his own scribblers turned the charge to his advantage in a rollicking song which ended with the verse

> Let the foes of our Friend and his noble Designs,
> Repeat their worst charge that he *cants and he whines*;
> O we've heard of his Cants in Humanity's Cause
> While the Senate was hush'd and the land wept applause.

---

[50] Copperthwaite–Hey post-election debate in Leeds press, including *Leeds Intelligencer*, 13, 22 and 29 June 1807.

The Public Argument

> Then shew us the Man, that talk like him can,
> Our interest we find in Such canting and whining,
> He shall cant for the County again and again.[51]

In the last analysis, Wilberforce and his friends credited Milton's success to his money. In a widely printed letter signed by the ubiquitous 'Freeholder', Milton was accused of buying the election:

> Money gets agents. Agents can raise a cry of popery or no popery, of Coalition or no Coalition. Money makes a ride to York from the greatest distance ... extremely commodious and agreeable; it can turn water into strong beer, or beer into wine, and a glass of wine into a bottle or a couple of bottles. It not only produces abundance of yellow ribbons in the hats, but ... the yellow goes also into the pocket. Money can also produce squibs, puffs, hand bills of all sorts and sizes, and can secure the circulation of them: it can command the press; it can secure the exact organization of all Committee business, can supply multiplied lists of polled and un-polled votes, and ensure in every hamlet and village of the county, the most perfect canvass. It can glean what a poorer Candidate has left ungleaned, and at the close of the Poll, it can bring straggling votes from the North and from the South, from the East and from the West, from Scotland or from Cornwall; and if Parliament would but consent to give a little more time for polling, from the East Indies and from the West Indies; it moreover can purchase sense; it can provide six Counsel instead of two to contend against the two Counsel of the adversaries ... and it can provide double sets of Attornies in the towns of Yorkshire; the one to contend by day and the other by night, against the mere voluntary Agents of a Wilberforce.[52]

In reply, 'Another Freeholder' put such awkward questions as, if money were so critical a factor, why had the opposition candidates dismissed Milton's chances as trifling? Why could

> *poor* Mr. Lascelles provide only two counsel? [actually, three] Has the Abolition of the Slave Trade effected a revolution in the fortunes of the House of Harewood? There was a time when its Lord, in his wealth,

---

[51] Furneaux, *Wilberforce*, p. 265.
[52] Printed in *York Courant*, 15 June 1807; *Leeds Intelligencer*, 15 June 1807 and most of the county press.

found a sufficient reason for bringing his son forward as a Candidate for the County.[53]

The Times's election correspondent also attributed much of the result to the excellent state of Fitzwilliam's treasury at a time 'when a ten per cent tax upon all income, as well as a recent General Election, has drained the purse of almost every other political man, and has most essentially diminished the spirit of subscribing to Elections'. Milton had now begun political life by letting fly a 'cool sixty or eighty, or, as we perhaps should rather say, a cool hundred thousand, for the benefit of the Party'. But he conceded that Lascelles's purse 'and the influence of his House' were hardly inferior, and the battle in that respect had been fairly fought between the 'two Chieftains'.[54]

Even had their means been larger, Wilberforce and his intimates had no taste, as he put it, for 'parade and profusion'. Looking back, he was still glad that economy had been their watchword. 'Our triumph was of a different sort. We may perhaps have too much indulged our love of simplicity, but to our eyes and feelings, the entrance of a set of common freeholders on their own, and those often not the best horses, or riding in their carts and waggons, often equipped in a style of rustic plainness, was far more gratifying than the best arranged and most pompous cavalcade.'

---

[53] *York Herald*, 20 June 1807; *Leeds Mercury*, 27 June 1807; *Sheffield Iris*, 23 June 1807, among others.

[54] *The Times*, 5 June 1807.

PART III

THE POLL

CHAPTER TWELVE

The First Ten Days, 20–30 May

POLLING BEGAN at 1 o'clock on Wednesday 20 May, at the close of a set piece election rite very like the nomination ceremony the week before. The Castle Yard was packed with substantial numbers from the West Riding. 'It is impossible to keep back the clothiers,' Milton wrote to his father the night before. 'Multitudes' had not waited for a call under the calculated plan for 'feeding' the polling booths but had set out unprompted for York. Henry Ramsbotham at Bradford apologized for sending so many but feared that if the clothiers were thwarted they might take offence and fall prey to the 'other party' which was using every tactic 'even to treating' to win them away from Milton. They were safer at York than at home, he concluded.[1] A few days before, Fitzwilliam, who although fifty miles from York kept abreast of every move by express messengers travelling around the clock, had learned that Wilberforce and Lascelles might persuade the sheriff to postpone the opening of the booths until Thursday, and he had insisted that this trick be nipped in the bud. If the possibility were to become known, many voters would not go into York on Wednesday and Milton's show of hands would be thin – 'a most serious evil'. His letter to the York chairman continued: 'I hope we shall make a good figure that day, & a good figure in *single* votes ... to counteract the effect of W & L bringing votes, who will support them jointly: we must look forward to neither of them bringing a man, who will give a second vote to Milton. If by any means we could place M at the head of the Poll, it would produce a most advantageous effect: it would create a jealousy between the other two ... from that moment, each would take single votes, where he could, instead of throwing a second vote into the scale of the other.'[2]

The election opened on a sunny day. The candidates on horseback, clad in blue with cocked hats, swords and spurs, led their respective friends into

---

[1] NRO: F(M), 72/21, Milton to Fitzwilliam, 19 May 1807; SCC:LAI: WWM, E156/147, Ramsbotham to Milton committee, 20 May 1807.
[2] SCC:LAI: WWM, E173/88, Fitzwilliam to Wrightson [16 May 1807].

the Castle Yard, circling it before they dismounted and climbed upon the hustings to join the high sheriff and official party at this 'special county court'.[3] 'O Yes, O Yes, O Yes,' intoned the crier to silence the immense crowd, and the ritual began with the county clerk reading the election proclamation and the bribery act. Sheriff Wilson then called for nominations. Wilberforce was proposed once more by Sir Robert D'Arcy Hildyard with Bacon Frank as his seconder. Lascelles was nominated and seconded by John Bacon Sawrey Morritt and William Fenton Scott, while Sir Francis Lindley Wood and William Wrightson performed these services for Lord Milton. The candidates did most of the speechifying and along now familiar lines.

Wilberforce denied the irrepressible rumour that he had linked his fortunes with anyone else and boldly appealed for money – the first time such a plea had been heard on this hustings. He hoped that all freeholders would contribute according to their means and come to poll at their own expense. He staked his election on their patriotism and gratitude. 'I have been plain with you,' he told the Yorkshiremen, 'but on this occasion it is necessary for me to speak the truth. I trust that independent spirit which has so long characterized the inhabitants of this county, has not forsaken you.' In this way he asserted his own virtuous independence by praising that quality in the Yorkshiremen he was addressing.[4]

Lascelles, following him, was forced to disavow any coalition with Wilberforce and he sharply rejected an imputation from Wood that he was a 'courtier' although he would always support the King. ('Cries of no bugbear! No Pledges! No Melville!', according to the *Mercury*.)

It was Milton's turn to defend himself, this time against charges that he had disturbed the peace of the county. The freeholders' privilege could not be surrendered to a 'nondescript' nomination meeting, he said. He professed his great attachment to the Constitution, which he defined as embodying the King, the Lords and the Commons. When he boasted of the success of his canvass, loud laughter burst from Lascelles's friends on the platform who were hissed by some of the crowd.

The high sheriff then called each nominee's name in turn for the show of hands, but the size and density of the crowd made the result inconclusive. The names were quickly painted on three large boards which were held up in succession. This time the sheriff declared Lascelles and Milton had the majority. It became therefore Wilberforce's unpleasant task to demand

---

[3] 'Election day', *York Courant*, 25 May 1807; *York Chronicle*, 28 May 1807; *York Herald*, 23 May 1807; KINCM: 1982.895.409, Account of the Proceedings, fols 7–13; *Hull Advertiser*, 23 May 1807; *Leeds Intelligencer*, 25 May 1807; *Leeds Mercury*, 23 May 1807; Gray, *Account of Proceedings*, pp. 22–4.
[4] McCormack, *Independent Man*, pp. 44–52.

the poll. He was shocked and disconsolate at this first inkling that he was not, perhaps, a universal favourite. Even the barrister he had brought from London as counsel, William Reader, was traitorously pessimistic, saying 'Mr. Wilberforce has obviously no chance, the sooner he resigns the better'.[5]

The election formalities were followed by a brief adjournment to swear in deputy sheriffs and poll clerks before the booths were opened to the hordes. In five hours, 1,532 men voted, but Milton came third with 656 votes to Wilberforce's 751 and Lascelles's 774. 'We had certainly more people in the Castle Yard,' Milton informed his father, blaming a 'partial sheriff' and a disciplined enemy for carrying the day. The arrangement of the booths had proved highly inconvenient for his voters who clustered mainly at a few while Wilberforce and Lascelles voters were scattered among them all. A notice was rushed into print to say that Milton's foes had won a 'paltry majority' by unfair collusion, but that there were 20,000 voters and 14 days still to go.[6]

So began an uproarious battle 'of such strength and perseverance as has never, *at any period*, been equalled at any County Election in the Kingdom', an observer wrote. He continued,

> Nothing since the days of the Revolution has ever presented to the world, such a scene as has been for fifteen days and nights, passing within this great County. Repose or rest have been unknown in it, except it was seen in a messenger, totally worn out, asleep upon his post-horse or on his carriage. Every day the roads, in every direction, and to and from every remote corner ... have been covered with vehicles loaded with Voters, – and Barouches, Curricles, Gigs, Flying Waggons, Military Cars with eight horses to them, crowded sometimes with 40 Voters – have been scouring the Country – leaving not the smallest chance for the *quiet* traveller to urge his humble journey, or find a chair at an Inn to sit down upon ...
>
> It is reckoned that ... about eight horses a day were found dead upon the different roads. And every house, every room, every bed in York, by an incessant change of Voters, at the rate of about two thousand a day, – created a consumption of provisions, – that might have otherwise served this City the twelve months.

---

[5] Wilberforce, *Life*, vol. 3, p. 324.
[6] All voting figures are as cited in Introduction, *Poll for Knights of the Shire* (York, 1807). NRO: F(M), X515, Milton to Fitzwilliam, 21 May 1807; 72/22, Foljambe to Wentworth, 20 May 1807; SCC:LAI: WWM, E224, Cooke to Fitzwilliam, 21 May 1807; YML: Y/H 2..421, Election Squibs, 1807.

Needless to say, the inhabitants of York did not hesitate to profit by this influx of 2,000 strangers a day. Seven shillings was the charge for the 'most pitiful' accommodation and a guinea for a comfortable lodging.[7]

The shape of each day was the same: the castle gates opened at 8, the booths admitted voters at 9 and the polling continued without pause until 5. Each deputy sheriff then carried his booth's returns to the sheriff who was quartered in the court house. As soon as they were tallied, the sheriff read out the totals from the hustings and the candidate who headed the poll that day commented first. The other candidates and their friends said their pieces after which the Castle Yard emptied into the streets and inns of York where the electioneering continued at full voice over dinners and drinks.

Thousands of broadsheets carrying the day's results were issued at the print shops and bundles were carried nightly to all the towns where crowds gathered at the local committee rooms or coaching inns to hear the news. The state of the poll was reported weekly in newspapers all over Britain, for no contest save possibly the one at Westminster attracted so much attention that year. The candidates produced their own versions of the day's results, cheering on their unpolled battalions. The chief agents began to call in subscriptions and deposit funds in York banks for the voters' beds, meat and drink. Lascelles's agent, Edward Wolley, had estimated that it would cost £5,000 a day from the nomination to the close of the poll – a total of £120,000 – and he proved to be nearer the mark than Bowns, Milton's chief agent, who thought (perhaps hoped) the bills would be half as much. Wolley told Bowns that Lord Harewood had placed £100,000 for the West Riding and £40,000 for the North and East Ridings in banks at York and Leeds the week before election day.[8]

The first five days of polling saw Milton's hopes realized and then dashed. On the second day, 21 May, the orange flood carried him to the top of the poll when, in the first eight-hour day, 2,293 electors registered their choices thus: Milton 1,295, Wilberforce 923 and Lascelles 914 (with aggregates respectively of 1,951, 1,674 and 1,688). Miltonites gloated:

> Last night, how triumphant were Lascelles' host!
> How clamorous their joy! How grotesque their grimaces!
> 'Blue! Blue! was the cry; but the accent seems lost:
> The colour has fallen from their hats – to their faces.

---

[7] *Leeds Intelligencer*, 8 June 1807; *York Herald*, 6 June 1807, among others; *Hull Advertiser*, 13 June 1807.
[8] SCC:LAI: WWM, F48/7, Bowns to Fitzwilliam, 16 May 1807; F48/10, same to same, 18 May 1807.

And handbills gloated 'The Wentworth-House Infant Has attained his *constitutional*, as well as *legal* MAJORITY, And will continue it to the End of the Poll'.

On Friday, 22 May, Milton repeated his triumph, with 1,081 votes to 1,173 for Wilberforce and 1,010 for Lascelles. The Milton camp was jubilant. Lascelles 'seems obstinate, but I hope he will give up', the elated Milton said. The clothiers were rallying strongly and almost to a man giving plumpers. Where they split, their second votes went to Wilberforce. But Wilberforce had ruined his cause by his 'equivocal conduct & Mr. Burgh has by his finessing precipitated the fall of his friend', said the Rev. John Lowe, now at Milton's elbow in York. 'Joy, Joy to you, my dear fellow,' wrote Bryan Cooke from the Doncaster committee rooms, where a cavalcade of plumpers was being organized to descend on York on Monday.[9]

But the week ended on a less glorious note for Milton when on the fourth day he dropped to third place as 2,509 electors gave Wilberforce 1,422, Lascelles 1,196 and Milton 1,126. The first four days had brought out 8,600 voters and the candidates stood: Wilberforce 4,269; Milton 4,158 and Lascelles 3,894 as the Sunday hush descended. After Saturday's results, the Lascelles stable of scribblers came up with a parody of Milton's verse, a composition which became known as the 'dirty epigram', to celebrate

MILTON'S MINORITY!
Last Night, how triumphant were MILTON's rough Host;
But Support from Republican Clamour, a Farce is:
And their Colour will soon be their Shame, not their Boast,
For the Yellow will fall from their Heads to their A***s.

The Milton committee seized upon this and re-printed it as an illustration of the *'delicate refinement'* of the *'Gentlemen* at the GEORGE'.[10]

The sight of Wilberforce coming last on Thursday's poll electrified his supporters. The ever-available 'Freeholder' asked

WHAT are you doing? *Is* Wilberforce *last upon the Poll?* That friend of humanity – that enemy of the Slave Trade – that tried, that faithful, that upright Senator, *is he last upon the Poll?* Shame where is thy blush!

---

[9] *York Herald*, 23 May 1807; Wrangham MSS, Robert Grimston's account; YML: Y/H 2..421, Election Squibs, 1807; NRO: F(M), 72/28, Milton to Fitzwilliam, 22 May 1807; 72/24, Lowe to same, 21 May 1807; SCC:LAI: WWM, E178/96, Cooke to Milton, 22 May 1807.

[10] Wrangham MSS, Robert Grimston's account; YML: Y/H 2..421, Election Squibs, 1807.

... Exert yourselves without delay! Rouse from your apathy! Come forwards like men.

By Saturday Wilberforce was first again, but 'To relax is dangerous. Your Independence may STILL be lost, United we Conquer – Divided we fall.' With carriages taken up by others, Hull had sent its Wilberforce voters by boat, farm wagon, donkeys and on foot. On Friday Sir Robert Hildyard led a train of freeholders from the North Riding into the Castle Yard. They had expected to vote for Wilberforce and Lascelles but with the former in danger, they gave him plumpers. That night Wilberforce wrote to his wife, 'You would be gratified to see the affection which is borne me by many to whom I am scarcely or not at all known.'[11]

Lascelles billed the city with dire warnings that Milton was an avowed Foxite and enemy of the King, and Milton's friends, putting on a brave face, hailed the name-calling as proof of their opponents' 'imbecility'. 'They call us "desperate and dangerous" ... We are "dangerous" – to their schemes of political intrigue and corruption, but it is *they* who are "desperate".'

On the Friday night the *Herald* printer set up a 'CAUTION' to 'honest Freeholders' not to be deflected from giving their plumpers to Milton by emissaries of other candidates 'as it is by Plumpers only that they can ... defeat the UNNATURAL COALITION of their Enemies', and bill stickers were out early Saturday to paper the town. Lascelles released his own warning to his voters to ignore the clamour against him for so strenuously 'promoting the general prosperity of the Country'. 'The worthy Freeholders in my Interest,' he added meaningfully, 'may depend upon every indulgence and accommodation which the law will permit. My Opponents, whatever they may promise, dare to allow no more.'[12]

The first week of the election coincided with the spring race meeting, an inspiration to the industrious propagandists:

> To Start for the County Plate
> Earl F–W–M's chestnut colt Independence, *by* Rockingham:
>   rode by a Yorkshire Clothier in White and Gold.
> Lord H–W–D's black horse Barbadoes, by Slavery:
>   rode by a Leeds Merchant in *deep* Mourning.
> Mr. W–B–E's piebald gelding TRIM, by Cant:
>   rode by the Owner in a Cloak.
> 5 to 1 on the Chestnut Colt, on account of the Rider.

---

[11] *Yorkshire Election*, p. 61; *Leeds Intelligencer*, 25 May 1807; Wilberforce, *Life*, vol. 3, pp. 324–6.
[12] YML: Y/H 2..421, Election Squibs, 1807; *York Herald*, 23 May 1807; SCC:LAI: WWM, E178/184, Bartholoman to Milton committee, Friday, n.d.; *York Courant*, 25 May 1807.

and from the other side

> A List of the Horses to run for the Parliament Stakes
> His Majesty's Bay Horse, Loyalty, *by* Patriot, out of Constitution:
> Rider, *Honest Harry – Blue.*
> Mr. Africa's Horse, Perseverance, by Humanity, own
> Brother to Rectitude, Independence &c.:
> Rider, *Will Steady – Pink.*
> Lord F–W–M's Dun Poney, Paddy Whack,
> (train'd *by* the Whig-Club) by Discontent, out of Anarchy, own
> Sister to Sedition:
> Rider, *Old Jumper – Orange.*
>   10 to 1 on *Loyalty*, and 20 to 2 on *Perseverance*.[13]

By Saturday night even the young colt was 'amazingly fagged', and happy for the day of rest ahead, not much consoled by the fact that his father's horse Sir Paul won a sweepstakes with the betting 11 to 5 against. His committee, however, spent the Sabbath drawing up further instructions to agents, and even Wilberforce had to devote the evening to committee work after attending two services at York Minster. The spring weather was kind and the city was abloom with lilacs. On Sunday, with the thermometer at 77 degrees fahrenheit, the Minster was filled with freeholders, stripped of their cockades and behaving with utmost propriety. The sublime scene reminded Wilberforce of the 'great Jewish Passover in the Temple, in the reign of Josiah'.[14]

Miltonians hoped that Wilberforce would fall back on Monday since 'many of his voters among the saints will not travel on Sunday' and Milton had a thousand unpolled voters waiting in York. But Wilberforce never lost his top place again. Lascelles passed Milton by 1,402 to 1,037 on the Monday and by 101 in the aggregated total. 'We have had a terrible day,' Milton admitted. His strength especially among the clothiers could beat Lascelles 'if he was not carried on W's shoulders', but their split votes could crush him. 'I dread the combination between W & L which nobody now doubts.'[15]

The choked West Riding booths where Milton's voters waited impatiently, contrasted with the easily accessible polling stations for other wapentakes, caused Milton's workers to ask the election officials to open all the booths to the air and public gaze. They claimed that voters were suffocated in

---

[13] YML: Y/H 2..421, Election Squibs, 1807.
[14] NRO: F(M), 72/29, Milton to Fitzwilliam, 23 May 1807; *York Herald*, 30 May 1807; SCC:LAI: WWM, E221, Further instructions; Wilberforce, *Life*, vol. 3, pp. 326–7.
[15] SCC:LAI: WWM, E224, Dundas to Fitzwilliam, 25 May 1807; NRO: F(M), 72/34, 35, Milton to same, 25 May 1807.

their struggles to reach the admission bar in the unseasonal heat. The other candidates, however, allowed only minor adjustments to the entrances. But by common consent, the occupants were shifted so that a booth serving a heavily populated wapentake was next to one with fewer voters.

Some voters were reported to be reluctant to come to York, having heard of the pushing and shoving, or took one look and went home, unpolled, promising to come back if a casting vote became necessary. *The Times* carried a happily false report that two Halifax men were trampled to death. The *York Herald* published 'Election Consolation':

> *Two Voters*, by zeal for the Candidate led
> Press'd down by the mob at the Hustings lay dead.
> What a *loss* to their friends when their fate shall be told!
> 'Not at all', cried an agent: – *'They'd both of them poll'd'*.

It was officials in the Strafforth and Tickhill booth who invented the queue. At this booth, the 'waiting voters formed in rank and file in a line without side the booth, and gradually moved up to the door; those who chose were accommodated with benches to sit on; and no one was allowed to break into the line, but every new comer was sent to the rear.' Such a sensible plan, commented Jonathan Gray, would never have survived in the first excited days. The other booths did not copy this curious method. At best, Milton could not expect to poll more than 1,000 a day with a concentration of voters from three wapentakes and most of them giving single votes.[16]

Each day's experience tested the plans of each side for 'feeding' the booths. William Gray's notes for 1784 had urged that great attention be paid 'to fill the Pens of the Booth as early as possible on each day with freeholders in our interest' and to keep a secret reserve in the city ready to poll in case the flow from the countryside slackened.

Voters had to be summoned on days that did not conflict with their local markets and fairs. The Stokesley Trinity Saturday fair followed by races on Monday meant voters from the Cleveland area were unavailable for the first week, for example. Daily contact between York and local agents and committees was maintained by express messengers on horseback and the letters and lists sent with conductors of batches of voters or by a conveniently timed mail coach. The system did not work perfectly for any candidate: promises were forgotten, agents were guilty of duplicity, supplies of horses and carriages ran out unexpectedly, voters turned greedy or succumbed to the other side by one form of skullduggery or other. But it was remarkably

---

[16] SCC:LAI: WWM, E224, Dundas to Fitzwilliam, 25 May 1807; NRO: F(M), 72/34, 35, Milton to same, 25 May 1807.

effective, all the same. The York committees knew in a general way how many voters they could expect in the Castle Yard on a given day and when to direct a new canvass. From Castle Howard, for example, came the request to know what day would be best to bring voters from Lord Carlisle's vast estates, mostly Milton plumpers and none for Lascelles. It is curious to find in the poll book only three votes from the neighbourhood of the great house itself: the postboy, a joiner and the innkeeper.[17]

The fierce competition for vehicles and horses never ceased. Estates were stripped of farm carts and wagons. Gentlemen's barouches, coaches and carriages which would hold up to twenty were borrowed, chaises were engaged at posting inns, and seats on the mail coaches booked whether filled or not. River boats and canal barges were commandeered. Even a hearse was employed and Mrs Wroughton, wife of Milton's chairman at Doncaster, gave up her sociable.[18]

Milton's flying start owed much to the thorough way in which his agents had secured transport in advance. Besides the cavalcade from Leeds for the opening day, 500 plumpers were carried by barges from Wakefield and another 442 by road from Halifax. Lascelles's Hull committee offered a sloop for freeholders willing to go by water but had few takers. Most men preferred carriages to being crammed in the hold of a ship and working men often chose to walk the 38 miles from Hull at a profitable 1s. 6d. a mile for expenses.

'The Devil is in the freeholders for there is no hold[in]g them or getting things into order,' Lascelles's Hull agent, Edward Codd, protested. 'They run away for York without giv[in]g us time to Examine them or even to let us take down their names.'[19]

Around Boroughbridge Lascelles's agent found a handful of votes to send but more would go if expenses were guaranteed them. Forty had headed for York under Milton control because arrangements had not been agreed for the Lascelles and Wilberforce people there. 'There are Conveyances ready at *all points* for Lord Milton,' he stressed. When the Duke of Northumberland's steward asked how the tenants at Stanwix (about twenty and ready to vote for Milton and Lascelles) were to be carried to York, Milton's Richmond chairman stalled, insinuating 'as delicately as I could that their presence at

---

[17] YA: M90:52, Hints for a Contested Election; WYAS(L): WYL250/6/3/10, Clarke to Wolley, 17 May 1807; SCC:LAI: WWM, E178/143, Forth to Wilson, 16 May 1807.

[18] WYAS(L): WYL250/6/3/10, Fox to Lascelles committee, 24 May 1807; SCC:LAI: WWM, E177/98, Warde to Milton, 1 June 1807; E178/90, Newton to Milton committee, 21 May 1807; E161/85, Wroughton to same, 31 May 1807.

[19] SCC:LAI: WWM, E178/71, Higgins to Wroughton [19 May 1807]; E171/18a, Sandwith to Milton committee, 19 May 1807; WYAS(L): WYL250/6/3/10 and WYL250/6/3/11, Codd to Wolley, 21 May 1807.

York would not be immediately necessary'. The joint Wilberforce–Lascelles committee at Richmond was trying to hire carriages at the inns, but 'I have ventured to engage them all until Wednesday next, & beyond, if necessary. They are angry,' Chairman Readshaw added.

Lascelles's committees seemed to have plenty of wagons, though often at the wrong places, and many times the money for hire was slow to reach the local agents. 'The cause languishes at Whitby for lack of ways and means,' John Piper of Pickering reported on 24 May – a message echoed from many parts of the county. Freeholders often refused a seat in a wagon, yielding only if some gentleman volunteered to rattle along with them.[20]

Many electors in Dent would not stir an inch unless picked up at their doorsteps with post chaises, complained the Lascelles agents at Skipton. They insisted on vehicles on springs 'as neat as may be' and covered if possible. Milton's committees had similar troubles. Wakefield ran out of carriages and could not coax voters into wagons. An effort was underway to dispatch them on foot headed by a knot of faithful gentry. Huddersfield voters at one point refused any mode but carriages and the only inn which had any would not let them for Milton's use. His voters at Leeds refused wagons, too. Henry Ramsbotham at Bradford was confronted with 'Cargoes of Halifax Voters' who arrived at the committee room hourly without money or instructions, many insisting on chaises.[21]

All local committees appeared to be confused about how much voters might expect in compensation for travelling costs and in the last resort the voters set their price. Early talk of a sixpence a mile soon gave way to thrice as much but even that did not satisfy everyone and voters in addition expected to find 'open houses' along the way. All the candidates yielded to this demand. Sums mentioned for 'expenses' as having changed hands to win a voter from Lascelles or Milton or to cast a split vote instead of a plumper varied from one to five guineas.

William Ward, representing Lascelles in Richmond, told his York committee that Milton's agents 'make no Hesitation about giving their Voters 3 g[ui]n[ea]s a piece to go to York in whatever way they please without being accountable for any Balance that might remain in their Hands'. This had

---

[20] WYAS(L): WYL250/6/3/10, Sergeantson to Lascelles committee, 22 May 1807; SCC:LAI: WWM, E167/16, Readshaw to Milton committee, 22 May 1807; WYAS(L): WYL250/6/3/11, Ingham to Lascelles committee, 23 May 1807; 1/10, Donkin to Fawell, 22 May 1807 and Piper to Wolley, 24 May 1807.

[21] WYAS(L): WYL250/6/3/11, Alcock and Preston to Ingham, 29 May 1807; SCC:LAI: WWM, E156/97, Lee to Milton committee, 26 May 1807; E224, Heywood to Fitzwilliam, 26 May 1807; E163/28, Wailes to same, 28 May 1807; E156/147, Ramsbotham to same, 20 May 1807.

much embarrassed Ward 'with the lower Orders of freeholders' but it seemed contrary to his original instructions. Generous friends who, unlike agents, could not be prosecuted for treating were rarities and when they appeared they often were given publicity to stimulate imitators. Marmaduke Spencer of Addingham, enclosing a list of plumpers for Lascelles and hinting that numbers of Milton voters 'might turn', said the latter had inquired about expenses, 'for answer I told 'em, if they went with me I would make 'em a present of all reasonable expences'. Thomas Thornhill of Fixby sent thirteen Milton plumpers from among his tenantry by wagon and chaise and paid for all of them. Thomas Binks of Stonykeld 'headed a phalanx of 70 freeholders from Bowes and vicinity' to and from York at his expense. The liberality of Robert Bell, a Hull merchant willing to spend £200 on conveyances for Lascelles and Wilberforce electors, was duly reported in the press when he took 100 freeholders to York, and Lady Johnstone paid for a hundred voters from Scarborough.[22]

'Voters continually pour in and want more Money,' Joshua Crossland informed Milton's York committee from Huddersfield. 'Some walk to York and ride back again, & some walk back part of the way &c but their Demands generally exceed your Directions pray send me further instructions. I am also drained of my Money – if you should wish a further allowance to be made I think you had better appoint a *Friend* to make them presents.'

It was impossible to follow the committee instructions, declared William Tindal, Milton's agent for Skipton. He was obliged to pay voters before they set out and those from west of Skipton were being allowed five guineas each. A hundred Milton plumpers from Gilling West wapentake were held up because an agent had run out of money. He appealed to Richmond where two committeemen dug into their pockets for an advance of £100.[23]

The insatiable voters seemed to delight in travelling to York at one candidate's expense and then voting for another. The New Inn at Delph in the Saddleworth area even ran up a bill of more than £150 to Milton's account in drinks and rides for spurious voters, all of whom, luckily, were discovered by the time they reached Huddersfield and sent back home. John Wooler, a Mirfield clothier, spent eight days in York at Milton's expense and voted for Wilberforce and Lascelles. A Wilberforce plumper, who said his journey from south Yorkshire had cost him nothing, was asked how he had done it. 'Sure

---

[22] WYAS(L): WYL250/6/3/10, Ward to Wolley, 25 May 1807; 1/11, Spencer to Ingham, 13 May 1807; SCC:LAI: WWM, E156/18, Voters from Huddersfield; *York Herald* and *Leeds Mercury*, 4 July 1807; WYAS(L): WYL250/6/3/10, Codd and Garland to Wolley, 17 May 1807; *Hull Chronicle*, 2 May and 3 June 1807.

[23] SCC:LAI: WWM, E156/17, Crosland to Milton committee, 25 May 1807; E162/10, Tindal to same, 31 May 1807; E167/16, Readshaw to same, 22 May 1807.

enow I cam all' d-way ahint Lord Milton's carriage,' he was quoted as saying. John Read, a Yarm grocer, who was paid £5 for his costs and expected in return to give Lascelles a plumper (but 'Get him polled as soon as you can', the York committee was warned) voted instead for Wilberforce and Milton. Several voteless common labourers from the village of Carlton were taken to York by chaise, stayed some days, and back at home boasted they had cost Lascelles £7 or £8 each. A gentleman escorting his tenants to poll was asked by a friend where he was headed. *'Don't you see,'* he said, *'I am going with a* FEW BEASTS *to Poll for Wilberforce and Lascelles?'* 'Zounds!' cried his friend when the party reached the booths, 'they have polled for LORD MILTON!' 'Why, yes!' said one of the countrymen, *'We be* STURDY BEASTS, *and have got on our own side of the Poll.'* [24]

An indeterminate number of voters wended their way to York under duress. How many unwillingly voted in their landlord's, customer's or employer's interest cannot be said and at least some of the threats made seemed to boomerang. There was an anecdote told of a tenant of a peer who had been pressed to vote for Milton. His reply had been that he loved his landlord and would go to the devil for him but he would go even further for 'our Good old King' so this time would please himself. George Poole, the Pudsey agent for Lascelles, could name eleven men who promised to vote for Lascelles and Wilberforce but who at York chose Milton, and Poole believed they had been threatened 'to be deprived of their Connections and Business' if they did not do so. Ten appear in the poll book, including two butchers, a miller and seven clothiers.

At Scarborough where the Corporation favoured Lascelles, a great number of Milton's promised voters turned tail from 'threats & other undue means'. But nearly half the 347 voters from there gave Milton one vote (155, often split with Wilberforce). Proprietors of the Aire & Calder Navigation prevented employees from voting for Milton. Luke Green, a lock keeper at Woodlesford, wanted to plump for Milton but for fear of dismissal recorded votes for Wilberforce and Lascelles instead. The two iron companies at Bowling near Bradford allegedly used threats to hold the Milton plumpers down to three, but the poll book discloses seventeen, of whom six were in the cloth trade and none of the rest related to ironmaking. Among the seventeen who voted for Wilberforce and Lascelles were ironmaster John Green Payley and four others connected with that trade. Wilberforce received a plumper from a weaver there. At Horton (Great and Little) where Lamplugh Hird claimed 'the most

---

[24] SCC:LAI: WWM, E156/143, Ainley to Milton committee, 11 June 1809; E156/31, Ingham to same, 1 June 1807; Wilberforce, *Life*, vol. 3, p. 335; WYAS(L): WYL250/6/3/10, Clarke to Lascelles committee, 31 May 1807, and Barton to Upton, 2 June 1807; *Yorkshire Election*, p. 91.

unjustifiable threats' were uttered and many 'absolutely forbidden by their employers to give a vote at all for Ld. Milton', Milton tallied 42 plumpers (half from men in cloth making) and divided four votes with Wilberforce, while Wilberforce and Lascelles received the votes of 28 (13 from the cloth trade) and Wilberforce got four plumpers to Lascelles's one.[25]

According to Roger Martin of Bedale, the Duke of Leeds ordered his tenant freeholders to split their votes between Milton and Lascelles, although they had indicated a preference for Milton. The Sheffield area tenants of James Stuart Wortley, a close friend of Lord Melville, were instructed to oppose Milton.

Joshua Walker, the iron manufacturer, headed Milton's Rotherham committee but it was no secret that he desired Wilberforce's return as well and in the canvass pushed for divided votes. This brought a sharp rebuke from Fitzwilliam who sent an agent to work for plumpers. When Walker first offered to look after Milton's interest, the earl chided him, it was not understood that Milton would be sacrificed to Wilberforce. 'Time will no longer permit forbearance,' he added. The end result (Milton 73 plumpers and only 31 divided votes with Wilberforce) so exasperated Walker that he 'demanded his bill of various tradesmen to settle & discard them for ever'. Two freeholders were dragged out of a carriage belonging to innkeeper Thomas Carnelley and left behind when they said they were giving Milton plumpers. Lascelles got only three votes in the town, divided with Wilberforce.

On their way to Skipton for 'conduct money' from Milton's agent, Thomas Walker, a farmer from Airton, and James Walker, a weaver of Kirkby Malhamdale, were accosted by a Lascelles agent who invited them into the Black Horse Inn. 'What he did with them there I know not, but they were got out of town ... to vote against us,' Milton's headquarters was told. (Both voted, as feared, for Wilberforce and Lascelles.)[26]

The roads to York were full of such ambushes. The Leeds committee for Milton complained publicly about the 'outrageous violence' used against its freeholders there. Lascelles's friends felt 'in danger of our lives' at Otley and without protection could be 'lamed or worse'. It was suggested that they remove the blue tickets from their hatbands before entering Otley where the

---

[25] *Morning Post*, 30 May 1807; WYAS(L): WYL250/6/3/38, Account of George Poole, 15 June 1807; SCC:LAI: WWM, E166/7, 8, 9/1, Allen and Robson to Milton committee, 24 and 25 May 1807; E156/110, Carr to same, 31 May 1807; E156/151, Hird to same, 26 May 1807.

[26] SCC:LAI: WWM, E168/8, 9, 10, Martin to Milton committee, 24, 25 and 26 May 1807; E224, Vernon to Fitzwilliam [8 June 1807]; E226, Fitzwilliam to Walker, 28 May 1807; E224, Observer to Fitzwilliam [29 May 1807] and Cooke to same [29 May 1807]; E162/7, Tindal to Milton committee, 29 May 1807.

current slogan was 'Milton for ever Lascelles down River with a Knife in 'is Heart and a Fork in 'is Liver'. At the wool village of Stanningley where all ten of the freeholders cast Milton plumpers, Lascelles's travelling friends were pulled from a wagon and beaten up.

Tadcaster with its one long curving street and single bridge across the Wharfe was a principal waystop, incredibly jammed with election-goers, many of whom paused overnight, and some of whom were stalled there for long periods waiting for carriages. Most of the West Riding had to pass through this bottleneck and there was much haggling with innkeepers over who was to pay and when for refreshing the voters. Postboys took to extorting three and four shillings a head for bringing voters back from York and one demanded 15s. to carry three Sheffield voters from Tadcaster to Ferrybridge, a 12 mile stage. Postboys from York infuriated the agents when, instead of taking their horses and carriages onwards, they loitered the day away. The boys from Etridge's were said to be the worst.[27]

The normal tumult in the little town turned into an uproar on 26 May when a body of Milton voters on horseback, tenants of Sir Thomas Gascoigne, were met on the narrow stone bridge by a column of Lascelles supporters, led by Charles Duncombe, Wilberforce's county chairman, who had been parading with drums beating and flags flying. Some of the Gascoigne horses took fright at the music and their riders veered off to the river bank. The band stopped playing. The parties might then have passed in peace, but Duncombe rode back in a rage, commanded the band to resume and began chasing the Milton stragglers as if to drive them into the river, but they escaped into a field. John Crossland, acting for Milton there, burst out of the Angel Inn and while he was upbraiding Duncombe, an instant mob pulled Duncombe off his horse and gave him a head bruise and bloody nose. 'I'm very glad I had no concern therein,' Crossland said virtuously, 'only receiving among the Crowd some part of the dirt thrown.'[28]

Once they reached the walls of York, voters had to be bedded, nourished and above all protected from seduction by opponents until they had registered their votes. Agents and local committees sent word about arrivals who might be susceptible to blandishments or who required some flattering attention to clinch their loyalty. Charles Mitchell of Forcett was a high-spirited gentleman, rather capricious, who 'by a little more attention' would be of more use, William

---

[27] KINCM: 1982.895.409, Account of the Proceedings, fols 50–1; WYAS(L): WYL250/6/3/11, Spencer to Ingham, 22 May 1807; SCC:LAI: WWM, E156/149, Hird to Milton committee, 22 May 1807; E157/6, Hartley to Wrightson, 19 May 1807; E157/7, Crossland to Milton committee, 25 May 1807; E163/16, Lee to Leeds committee, 21 May 1807; E157/10, Candler to Milton committee, 30 May 1807.
[28] SCC:LAI: WWM, E157/8, 9, Crossland to Milton committee, 26 and 29 May 1807.

Ward of Richmond told the Lascelles committee, and while Dr Samuel Swire of Melsonby, escorting some parishioners, did not need attention, he was equally entitled to it 'being the most intimate friend of the Lord Chancellor [Eldon]'. Both voted for Lascelles and Wilberforce.

Lascelles was eager to get such Wilberforce activists as Humphrey Osbaldeston of Hunmanby, as devoted to Wilberforce as his relations at Hutton Buscel were to Milton, to share the votes they controlled. Osbaldeston had refused all Milton overtures and would be glad to see Lascelles trounce him. Lascelles was notified when Osbaldeston would arrive at the York Tavern with his 'little Regiment of Freeholders' so that not a moment would be lost in greeting him. Osbaldeston held to his own plumper for Wilberforce and 15 of his flock of 39 did the same. All the rest also voted for Wilberforce but Lascelles got 14 and, surprisingly, Milton 10.

Dispatching three freeholders from Beeforth, Thomas Harland explained the arrangement that would prevent their falling into the hands 'of the Philistines' at Beverley or York and all three – bricklayer, farmer and miller – survived to record their votes for Lascelles and Wilberforce. A party of 51 from Bridlington and Kilham in the close custody of Ralph Creyke of Marton, John Graeme of Beverley and Bryan Taylor of Bridlington were safely delivered in the Wilberforce–Lascelles interest.[29]

Milton's forces took similar precautions. Christopher Lightfoot, a farmer near Scarborough, had promised a plumper but must be ushered to the very door of the booth, as apparently he was, for the record shows the single vote. Tom Scatcherd, sending 100 'bullets' from Hull advised the Milton committee to put 'active young gentlemen' into every public house in York by 9 a.m. to get the voters out before they started wandering the streets. 'No good to be don after 1 o'c. this is why we were last on the 1st day,' he counselled. A well-wisher pointed out that coachloads of Milton voters were not properly met but allowed to disperse and fall into the hands of the enemy.[30]

Voters who became dissatisfied with their reception or accommodation might go home without polling. The landlord of the Robin Hood Inn in Castlegate was heard to say near the hustings that voters at his house were determined to leave because of neglect from Lord Milton. Others without proper escorts became confused in the teeming city or jostling hubbub of the Castle Yard and failed to find, or being illiterate could not read the inscriptions on, the booths they were seeking. The Milton agent at Leeming persuaded

---

[29] WYAS(L): WYL250/6/3/10, Ward to Lascelles committee, 25 May; Harland to Lascelles, 24 May; same to Wolley, 1 June; same to same, 24 May.

[30] SCC:LAI: WWM, E172/19, Holmes to Milton committee, 25 May 1807; E173/121 Dobson to same, n.d.; E173/135, Cooke to Wrightson, 30 May 1807; E178/70, Scatcherd to Milton committee, Thursday [21 May 1807]; E175/7, A Friend to same, 28 May 1807.

twenty Wilberforce plumpers whom he met on the road to give second votes for Milton, but they should be met outside York for they were country people and did not understand vote splitting. 'If you dont some of Lassel's party will & poison their minds.' A short handbill was soon put out to guide electors through the intricacies of voting.[31]

York was never able to match the electioneering frenzy of a Westminster or Middlesex. To sophisticated Sydney Smith, rector of Foston but not yet required to reside in the Yorkshire wastes, who saw only two drunks and one 'battle', the provincial city at the height of the drama was 'as riotous as London in the middle of the Night'. He voted for Milton ('one of the most ungainly looking young men I ever saw') and – because Africans could not speak for themselves – for Wilberforce. But county folk had never seen such a 'saturnalia'. They recalled the roads thronged night and day, horse-drawn vehicles packed with voters and draped with flags, and hardy walkers who thought nothing of thirty-mile treks to vote and thirty miles back. Arrivals at the outskirts of York were cheered by fevered onlookers perched in the trees. Small boys and idle men sat on the Ouse bridge parapet to watch coaches sweep past and make the sharp left turn into Spurriergate and Coney Street towards the principal inns. Walter Spencer Stanhope, unlike the Rev. Smith, found the city indescribably confused and the roads lined with tipsy men who molested travellers or slept in heaps on the verge.

The consensus, however, was that Yorkshire did not disgrace itself. A Hull editor, inured to the racket of the freemen there at election time, was pleased to see 'order and propriety of conduct ... opposed to the noise, riot, and disorder too commonly prevalent in borough elections' in the thousands of freeholders crowding York, each with a 'solid property to protect'.[32]

On Doghouse Farm at the edge of Wakefield, Matthew Tomlinson watched his 73-year-old father set out on 24 May 'to York and be polled'. Matthew, who was inordinately fond of solitude and dismayed by the discord of the general election, was amused by the spectacle of his 'aged sire' so 'diverted by trifles'. He seemed wonderfully pleased by the novelty of a journey which would take him from Wakefield by canal to Selby and up the Ouse past Cawood, where he was born, to York. Father returned on 30 May having given a plumper for

[31] SCC:LAI: WWM, E178/181, Hartley to Wrightson, n.d.; E163/21/1, Your Friend to Milton, 21 May 1807; E178/209, Nicoll to Bowns, Tuesday [19 May 1807]; E178/159, Simpson to Townend, Monday evening [1 June 1807]; E178/139, Smith to Milton committee, 29 May 1807; SCC:LAI: WWM, E151, copy of instructions.

[32] *Letters of Sydney Smith*, vol. 1, p. 122; *The Creevey Papers: a selection from the correspondence and diaries of the late Thomas Creevey, M.P.*, ed. Sir Herbert Maxwell, 2 vols (J. Murray: 1903), vol. 1, p. 167 (erroneously dated 1812); Peel, *Spen Valley*, pp. 304–5; Bradley, *Old Coaching Days*, p. 66; Stirling, *Letter-Bag*, vol. 1, p. 141; *Hull Chronicle*, 3 June 1807.

Milton (as had his squire at Lupset Hall). He was unwell and ready to agree with Matthew that 'Electioneering is dissatisfaction and vanity'. Four days later he was dead. 'Ah life!' Matthew brooded in his diary, 'uncertain vapour! dancing fancy! – aiery dream!!'[33] Martin Tomlinson was not the only casualty of the election. Three West Riding men died from injuries sustained when their carriages overturned. A Doncaster publican and a Halifax hosier died of natural causes in their York lodgings and the body of a Spofforth man was fished out of the Ouse; he had fallen from the bridge before he got to the polls. Jonas Jackson of High Town was so badly injured when his coach overturned that he could not work. Milton paid the surgeon's bill and compensation for time lost at work, although Jackson never got to the booths either.[34]

Thousands of tales probably were told of the election stir and a few were preserved. An 'honest farmer' who voted for Milton against the *'commands'* of his wife no sooner got home 'than she flew to the dresser, and seizing a *rolling-pin* ... so belaboured her *Lord and Master*, that during the whole of next day his recovery was much doubted'. Neighbouring women hoped that this castigation would serve 'useful warning to all *married voters* in future'.

Thomas Stuart, a yeoman from Hawes, was making his way home after casting a single vote for Milton when he encountered a special messenger riding for the opposition. 'I made him Intoxicated with Licker till he was not Capable to Dow any Bisuness for that time,' he reported to Milton. A 'sensible old man' on his donkey with Wilberforce and Lascelles cards in his hat and Milton's card on the donkey's brow was accosted by two Milton canvassers who asked him how he intended to vote. 'Why gentlemen! he replied, I shall vote for the two old members, but my ass is like all other asses, he'll vote for M–lt–n.' Milton at least had the sympathies of many a debtor confined at York Castle for Robert Dixon, an inmate, requested a supply of orange cards to wave from the windows overlooking the voting precinct.

A 'poor curate' sent by his vicar to vote for Wilberforce erroneously gave his vote for Milton. He had been told to 'think of the *Church*, and vote for the – *Lord*', and, as he explained, he had found only one lord at the election. A dashing young freeholder from a village near Halifax came back from York unadorned with badge or ribbon of any colour. 'Finding himself in the company of several young people, of *both sexes*' and being asked to 'intimate his partiality to *that* WHICH always had claimed his attention most, he cried out

---

[33] WLM, MS Journal of Matthew Tomlinson of Doghouse Farm, Lupset, 1806–12, vol. 5.
[34] *The Times*, 17 June 1807; *Halifax Journal*, 20 June 1807; *Doncaster Gazette*, 12 June 1807; *York Courant*, 15 June 1807; *Leeds Mercury*, 13 June 1807; SCC:LAI: WWM, E179/76/1, Crosland to Milton committee, 13 October 1807.

"LASSES for ever!'" and was knocked down by a carter who thought he had said 'Lascelles'. Hard luck, since he had, in fact, voted for Milton.[35]

At the polls by the fifth day, Monday 25 May, Milton had lost his early momentum and came in bottom of the list. Wilberforce steadily augmented his lead and for the next five voting days Lascelles kept ahead of Milton in the contention for second place by around 300 votes, but it never entered the minds of Milton or Fitzwilliam to concede. When Milton stood up to speak on Tuesday, Morritt shouted, 'This is the last dying speech and confession!' but Milton had observed that the booths where Lascelles usually polled best were quiet while his – for Agbrigg, Morley and Strafforth and Tickhill – were crowded as ever, which kept his spirits up. On Wednesday, his committee began to summon outvoters, and there were still resources at Sheffield, Huddersfield and Leeds. The knowledge that by Saturday, Lascelles 'did not consider himself at all secure' gave fresh hope after a dismal week which ended with Wilberforce 10,025 (and technically now 'safe'), Lascelles 9,047 and Milton 8,717. Nearly 18,000 freeholders had polled; no one was quite sure how many more there were to come.[36]

Milton wrote to his father on Sunday that his friends predicted 500 votes on Monday 1 June but he hardly credited it. 'I am now so resigned to be beaten, that I don't much care about it,' he confessed. 'We have fought a glorious battle, & that is sufficient, particularly when I think that we have ruined Wilberforce's popularity.'[37]

When Wilberforce reached the magic total of more than 10,000 votes on the tenth polling day he was absolved from further expense for voters who divided between him and Lascelles. But his count was not nearly so high as he had expected to chalk up by this time. In their search for single votes, the Miltonites had circulated a rumour at an early stage that Wilberforce already was 'safe' and those who would have voted for him could feel free to give Milton a plumper. This 'artful misrepresentation' was 'wonderfully successful', Wilberforce's side asserted. The accusation of a secret coalition continued to damage his standing, too. The shortage of agents or trustworthy friends meant that many voters went to York on their own, vulnerable to tampering from the other sides. The business of receiving voters, keeping them together,

---

[35] *Halifax Journal*, 20 June 1807; SCC:LAI: WWM, E178/155, Stuart to Milton, n.d.; *Leeds Intelligencer*, 6 July 1807; SCC:LAI: WWM, E178/195, Dixon to Milton committee, n.d.; *York Herald*, 13 June 1807; *Halifax Journal*, 6 June 1807.

[36] Wrangham MSS, Robert Grimston's account; NRO: F(M), 72/37, Milton to Fitzwilliam, 26 May 1807; 72/40, 41, same to same, and Shearwood to same, 27 May 1807; 72/44, Milton to same, 29 May 1807; 72/45, 46, same to same, 30 May 1807; *York Herald*, 30 May 1807.

[37] NRO: F(M), 72/47, Milton to Fitzwilliam, 31 May 1807.

supervising them at the inns, and recording them was all somewhat neglected, Wilberforce's agents admitted.³⁸

Wilberforce badly needed the advice and comfort of old friends beyond those in Yorkshire who, like Thomas Thompson of Hull, gave up all his other business to stay near him for eighteen days. He wrote to Thornton, 'I cannot ask you to come down to me, but O how I long for some kind and sympathizing friend, for my heart is sickened by the treachery and ingratitude that I have met with!' The letter reached Thornton on 23 May and he would have set out that night but had only just reached home himself, 'fagged and shabby', as Mrs Thornton related to Hannah More. At midnight, however, James Stephen and his son, Henry's brother Robert, and Charles and Robert Grant – a carriage load of Saints – drove out of London 'resolved not to stop till they reached ... poor dear Wilberforce [Monday] morning'. Thornton followed on Sunday (acutely uncomfortable to be seen travelling on that day) and as soon as he crossed the Yorkshire border he began to 'speechify' for Wilberforce. He arrived at Wilberforce's door at 8 o'clock Monday night. He reported to his wife that he had met her brothers, Daniel and Richard Sykes, in the Castle Yard, both Milton men. The electoral civil war divided many families and Mrs Thornton had remonstrated with her brothers. Daniel, the more moderate Miltonite of the pair, assured her he would do nothing to harm Wilberforce but like the rest of Milton's committee he was incensed by accusations of Wilberforce's friends that the Miltonians lied in speaking of a coalition which they knew did not exist. 'Mr. W is, as I knew he always was, secure of his Election, & Lord Milton will be defeated by the mutual assistance afforded by the friends of the other two. Though beaten,' Daniel wrote at Milton's nadir, 'we are not dismayed ... having shewn much greater strength than I expected.'³⁹ Daniel voted for Milton and Wilberforce but Richard gave a Milton plumper and Thornton and he had a 'fine row' about it in the Castle Yard. At first Thornton enjoyed the bustle: 'it is a grand contest, and fills one with grand ideas,' and, comfortably ensconced in a bedroom and sitting room at William Gray's, relaxed in morals so much that he was rising as late as 10.⁴⁰

Lascelles's camp was fortified by government emissaries as well as personal friends. The solicitor-general Sir Thomas Plumer canvassed the law courts in

---

³⁸ Wilberforce, *Letter to the Gentlemen*; *York Chronicle*, 9 July; KINCM: 1982.895.409, Account of the Proceedings, fol. 32.

³⁹ L.G. Johnson, *General T. Perronet Thompson, 1783–1869* (Allen & Unwin: 1957), p. 24; WLCT: EHC18/M786, Thornton letters, Mrs Thornton to H. More, 25 May 1807; CUL: GBR/0012/MS Add 7674/1/I, Thornton Papers, D. Sykes to Mrs Thornton, 31 May 1807; WLCT: EHC18/M786, Thornton to Mrs Thornton, 25 May 1807.

⁴⁰ WLCT: EHC18/M786, Thornton to Marianne, 28 May 1807; Thornton to H. More, 27 May 1807; Thornton to Mrs Thornton, n.d. [June 1807].

London and voted on his freehold at Thornton le Clay for Wilberforce and Lascelles, as did his brother Hall of Bilton in Ainsty, one of Lascelles's most caustic orators. Milton supporters insinuated that the government was making extraordinary and unfair efforts to bring Lascelles back into Parliament. Lascelles's use of the royal arms and King's name on his election cards and cockades had outraged his opponents, but he brushed off their criticisms saying this was commonplace among those greatly attached to the Crown. Each day that Lascelles was ahead of Milton, the state of the Yorkshire poll was merrily circulated in London by ministers, and the government's friends coursed the London streets for 'army agents, Shopkeepers, Contractors et hoc genus omne' who could vote or influence votes.[41]

An elated Lascelles brought his biggest single day's force of 1,402 to the booths on Monday 25 May. This was followed by another good showing of 1,160 on the Tuesday. It was a close fought race from then to the end of the week, however, although Lascelles steadily raised his lead over Milton in the aggregated total from 101 to 330 on the Saturday. Signs were developing that the wapentakes were nearly bereft of his supporters as agents swept the county for any unpolled friends. Both sides were scraping the barrel for stragglers now and Lascelles pointedly warned his supporters to take no notice of an inspired rumour that he had won his election and they need not bother to come to York.[42]

Open letters proliferated in the newspapers, usually attacking Milton on behalf of both old members. But one from 28 Yorkshire freeholders living in and around Manchester singled out Lascelles as the 'ZEALOUS FRIEND and PROTECTOR of our INDUSTRY, MANUFACTURERS, and TRADE'. The signatories included the eminent cotton spinner, Robert Peel of Accrington, one of the few who actually crossed the Pennines to vote for Wilberforce and Lascelles.[43] Lascelles was popular with the 225 Lancashire outvoters who divided 158 for him and Wilberforce, 25 for Lascelles alone, 5 single votes for Wilberforce, 65 plumpers for Milton, and 3 votes for Milton and Wilberforce.

Milton's enthusiastic young friends and relations contributed glamour to the contest and ultimate victory. His canvassing of Beverley, Holderness and Hull was led by 'high spirited young Men of fortune … who spare

---

[41] *York Herald*, 11 July and 23 June 1807; SCC:LAI: WWM, E224, Wentworth to Fitzwilliam, 2 June 1807; E174/19, same to same, 30 May 1807; E224,) same to same, 1 June 1807; *Morning Chronicle*, 25 May 1807; NRO: F(M), 72/71, Innes to Milton, 15 June 1807.

[42] WYAS(L): WYL250/6/3/10, Kitching to Morritt [25 May 1807]; *Sheffield Iris*, 26 May and 2 June 1807; SCC:LAI: WWM, E162/8, Tindal to Milton, committee 29 May 1807; WYAS(L): WYL250/6/3/11, Codd to Wolley [26 May 1807]; *Halifax Journal*, 30 May 1807.

[43] *York Chronicle*, 4 June 1807; *York Courant*, 1 June 1807.

neither trouble nor expense', a Lascelles agent complained. The Marquess of Hartington canvassed the Skipton area with the Earl of Thanet from Skipton Castle. William Haigh of the Doncaster wine merchants lent his *'full weight'* at York for a week, and, as he told Fitzwilliam, 'Zeal with seventeen stone upon its back, is of no small consequence, particularly when we meet our Opponents late in the Even[in]g endeavouring to seduce our Friends'. Convinced that each vote was the winning one, gilded youth took the reins of wagon- and coach-loads of voters and headed towards York. They ferreted out voters in the public houses and conducted them to the polls. They dashed off squibs and verses. The 25-year-old Viscount Althorp, heir to Earl Spencer, having successfully held on to his Northamptonshire seat, hurried to York to help Milton and gave sterling service. The *York Herald* gushed:

> Were the popular cry – the mere assemblage of all that was fashionable – the union of all the most distinguished talents for wit and pleasantry – the unceasing activity of many of the finest young men of the age – the zealous patronage of all the beautiful women – all the laugh of gaiety and good humour – and every possible display of gallant show: – were these only to characterize an Election, and give it popularity – then indeed that of Lord Milton would stand supereminent over every Election, the Kingdom had witnessed. Nothing ever equalled it. Never before, were whole streets taken up by carriages in line – from military cars, carrying 40 voters, barouches and four, down to waggons, ornamented with orange banners, with honourable and right honourable drivers, and preceded by incessant bands of music, the populace all the time rending the air with shouts of *Milton for Ever*! Never before could any Election show such displays; because the extent, the number of inhabitants, and the wealth of the County of York, are alone equal to it.[44]

The passions of two of Milton's friends rose to the pitch of a duel which became the talk of the country, a rustic version of the celebrated meeting between Sir Francis Burdett and James Paull at Westminster. Henry Francis Mellish of Hodsack Priory in Nottinghamshire, who had a vote from property at Austerfield, was rapidly adding to an already colourful reputation as a

---

[44] WYAS(L): WYL250/6/3/10, Codd to Wolley, 28[?] May 1807; SCC:LAI: WWM, E224, Haigh to Fitzwilliam, 28 May 1807; R.W. Smith, 'Political Organization', p. 1555; SCC:LAI: WWM, F48/20, Bowns to Fitzwilliam, 26 May 1807; Forrester, *Northamptonshire Elections*; Denis Le Marchant, *Memoir of John Charles Viscount Althorp Third Earl Spencer* (R. Bentley: 1876), p. 89; SCC:LAI: WWM, E224, Wentworth to Fitzwilliam, 19 May 1807; *York Herald*, 13 June 1807.

gambler and racing man by his flamboyant speeches from the hustings or Etridge's window ('Why don't you pay your debts?' hecklers would shout) when he and Martin Bladen Hawke, brother of Lord Hawke of Womersley and Scarthingwell, quarrelled on the night of Sunday 31 May at a Tadcaster public house over who was doing the most for their mutual friend. A fist fight followed and although Mellish was getting the better of Hawke, both soon were exhausted and agreed that this was no way for gentlemen to settle a dispute. Next morning they met with pistols and seconds.

'Take care of yourself, Hawke, for by G— I shall hit you,' shouted Mellish.

'I will, my lad! and let me recommend you to take care of your *own cannister!*' Hawke retorted.

On signal, they fired. Mellish missed but Hawke's bullet shattered Mellish's left forearm.

'Hawke, You have *winged* me! lend me your neckcloth to tie up the broken *pinion!*' the wounded man cried.

It was done. With the limb bound, Mellish and Hawke climbed into the same chaise and drove off 'as good friends as ever'.

No more picturesque character adorned Milton's electioneering than the 'celebrated Horse breaker', Old Jumper, whose stubby form could be found daily outside Etridge's. According to Francis Hawksworth, he was as well known in Yorkshire as the King. 'That he has had ever bone in his skin broken & that he has been in every Jail in England' was his boast. 'He is (I suppose) the greatest scoundrel *in every particular* that ever existed,' Hawksworth added when he sent a drawing of Orange Jumper to Gillray to etch.[45]

Calling upon outvoters was expensive, especially those from London, 200 miles and 25 hours away, and only to be considered as a last resort. By the second week of the struggle, Lascelles and Milton were sending for their London votes as was Wilberforce, to a lesser extent, for he would have the second votes of most of the Lascelles contingent.

Milton had been first with a London committee, little thanks to him or his father. There were possibly 500 Yorkshire votes in the London area. F.F. Foljambe, writing to Milton on 2 May, pointed out the folly of forgetting '*this little spot*' and reported that he and others had set up a committee to sit at Fitzwilliam house on Grosvenor Square and sponsored a public meeting at the Crown and Anchor on 5 May. Among their most useful recruits were two men who had served as counsel for the clothiers the previous year. The committee

---

[45] Smith, 'Yorkshire Elections', p. 82; NRO: F(M), 72/42, Milton to Fitzwilliam, 28 May 1807; Leeds City Libraries Reference Room, MS letter, W. Powell to Thomas Wilkinson, 1 June 1807; *Morning Chronicle*, 12 June 1807; *York Chronicle*, 18 June 1807; *Doncaster Gazette*, 5 June 1807; *The Times*, 5 June 1807; Gray, *Account*, p. 36; BL: Add Ms 27,337, fol. 112, Hawksworth to Gillray, 16 February 1809. See Plate 10: 'Orange Jumper'.

later established itself at St Alban's Tavern in Pall Mall. Members canvassed for votes, published Milton's news in the metropolitan press and, when the time came, fixed passages for voters to York. Walter Fawkes, Lord Howick, William Denison, Conyers Norton, the Duke of Norfolk, Lord St John, William Windham, William Elliot, Lord Downe, Lord Spencer and Lord Crewe were among the men who shared the work while C.M. Wentworth acted for Fitzwilliam, not least in trying to keep down the expenses. The London allies had the aid and inspiration of Lady Mary Milton who, from her letters to her mother-in-law, seemed to relish every moment of the contest. She canvassed her linen drapers and persuaded them to get their Yorkshire acquaintances to vote for Milton. Whatever the state of the poll, 'We grow more keen every day,' she said.[46]

Fitzwilliam on 26 May sent for whatever London votes could 'frank themselves down' but the committee, 'sitting on thorns', was uneasy at its news from York and hired extra carriages for Saturday 30 May, partly to keep them out of the hands of the Lascelles and Wilberforce committees. Wentworth reported 'strong reason to believe that Mr. Lascelles' Friends have given £30 a man as a gratuity for going to York'. When finally word came to send all available voters, carriages along the way were unobtainable but an outpost sub-committee was established at the Saracens Head, Snow Hill, to seize any space open in the stage coaches and mails heading north, usually at a guinea a head, leaving it to the York committee to make sure the passengers were not impeded on the road. It was expected that another hundred votes could be produced by Friday 5 June.[47]

As the descent of the London voters approached, the opposition scribblers poked fun at Milton's 'PLUMPER MANUFACTORY' and the immense machine it was constructing to carry 4,007 single votes from London (!) patterned on a French raft lately intended for the invasion of Britain.[48]

---

[46] WYAS(L): WYL250/6/3/10, Names of Freeholders, listing 414 names and their preferences; SCC:LAI: WWM, 6173/9, Foljambe to Milton, 2 May 1807; E177/11, same to Fitzwilliam, 2 May 1807; E177/13, same to same, 4 May 1807; E224, Williams to same, 14 May 1807; E174/1, Foljambe to Milton committee, 6 May 1807; E224, Wentworth to Milton, 22 May 1807; E174/8 same to Bowns, 13 May 1807; NRO: F(M), 72, Lady Milton to Lady Fitzwilliam, 11 May 1807.

[47] NRO: F(M), 72/38, Fitzwilliam to Wentworth, 26 May 1807; SCC:LAI: WWM, Bag, Wentworth to Fitzwilliam, 28 May 1807; E174/16, Wentworth to Milton committee, 30 May 1807; E224, Fawkes to Fitzwilliam, Saturday [30 May 1807]; E174/20, Wentworth to Milton committee, 1 June 1807; E174/10, 28, 25, Swale to Milton committee, 1 and 2 June 1807; E174/21, Wentworth to same, 2 June 1807.

[48] YML: Y/H 2..421, Election Squibs, 1807; *Yorkshire Election*, 72; KINCM:2006.3657,

Lascelles's committee in London, with a list of 414 Yorkshire freeholders, discovered by a quick and thorough canvass that Milton would beat Lascelles in plumpers and, as the Milton committee had also learned, most London electors could not be enticed to 'go into Yorkshire' at all. A committee was not properly set up until after a public meeting at the White Horse, Fetter Lane on 26 May. William John Bethell took the chair but the principals wanted someone of greater consequence to head the body and at a second meeting the following day at the British Coffee House, Cockspur Street, Lord Rendlesham was installed as chairman. 'We labo[u]r under the Greatest & most cruel inconvenience from our adversaries having had the start of us by many days,' Rendlesham pointed out on discovering that all places in the stage coaches had been reserved by Milton's men. No Lascelles votes could go before Tuesday. As in Yorkshire, the electors were choosy: no outside places for them. Rendlesham doubted that more than 200 of the potential voters would travel to York but Milton would clearly have most of the votes of those who did.[49]

Wilberforce's London committee, based at the Crown and Anchor, was founded to raise money but did a certain amount of canvassing for votes as well. Until the final week, no one was asked to travel to York. Then freeholders were asked to journey in Lascelles or Milton carriages depending upon their second choices. Finding that Milton's people were only interested in plumpers, Wilberforce's group sent one party of three for Wilberforce and Milton in a chaise. When the task force of Saints reached York, they had sent an insistent letter to say that although Wilberforce was the choice of the majority he could be defeated if Lascelles and Milton fought the full 15 days. 'I heartily wish that those Gentlemen who may have doubted the necessity of large pecuniary support ... could witness what I have already seen,' the writer (one of the Stephens?) said. 'The bulk of the Freeholders are men who cannot afford their travelling charges, and *these* are unavoidably very great. Mr. W's ... Election Funds, are in the hands of men conscientiously frugal in moderating the claims of the Voters to the strictest line of mere indemnity ... yet the multitude of Claimants ... is so great, that the aggregate ... is formidable.' This message launched a provisional subscription which would enable Wilberforce to carry on to the end.

Wilberforce Papers Box 1, biographical memoir of William Wilberforce, by T. Tindall Wildridge.
[49] WYAS(L): WYL250/6/3/10, Names of Freeholders; Eyre to Hardy, 25 May and 26 May 1807; Rendlesham to Slingsby, 30 May 1807; 1/11, Rendlesham to Lascelles, 2 June 1807.

So many gentlemen preferred not to make the tiresome journey to York that 'pairs' were arranged by the three committees. One jubilant Milton man thought he had kept away three plumpers for Lascelles by not going himself.[50]

London also was the fount of propaganda for the whole country. A subscription of £600 had been raised by the Whigs 'for the management of the press, and the distribution of hand-bills' on the day of dissolution, though Lord Holland considered a third of it had been frittered away before a committee was organized under Henry Brougham who, with Holland and John Allen, did most of the writing. Within days, their pamphlets were in all booksellers' shops, letters, paragraphs and verses were flowing to the press and handbills were being printed keyed to local contests.[51]

Even Lord Rendlesham's cautious prediction of the size of the London area vote in Yorkshire's election proved optimistic. The poll book records 160 voters from London and vicinity. Milton polled 77 plumpers and another 10 voters divided with Wilberforce. Lascelles won 16 single votes and 54 in conjunction with Wilberforce, who himself received only three plumpers: those of Henry and Robert Thornton and Joseph Jackson, tea dealer. During the election it became increasingly clear that, with due regard for the strength of other groups, the outcome would turn on the clothiers, for the margin between Lascelles and Milton remained slim. Their antipathy to Lascelles had seemed a sufficient stimulus to get them into the Castle Yard. 'Mount your Horses then with alacrity, appear without delay ... & give your votes for Milton, the heroic and virtuous Youth, who has boldly stood forth in the hour of difficulty,' as one exhortation put it.

The response reached its peak between the second and fifth days and after that initial wave, Milton fell behind. Milton's Leeds committee met with the trustees of the Mixed Cloth Hall on 26 May and a new canvass for plumpers was quietly set on foot. A public call to unpolled clothiers went out two days later: 'The ELECTION now depends on your Exertions; you may if you please have the MAN OF YOUR HEARTS, Your Opponent is nearly exhausted, and you have only to come in a Body and decide the Election. A strong Pull – a long Pull – and a Pull altogether.' Calls were sent as far afield as Manchester for coaches and chaises to travel towards York via Huddersfield, picking up voters along the route. 'It seems very much as if the clothing country had not been completely roused till they found Lascelles was

---

[50] Wilberforce, *Letter to the Gentlemen*, pp. 34–6; BL: Add Ms 35,129, fol. 428, Circular 28 May carrying York letter of 25 May 1807; *The Times*, 29 May 1807; SCC:LAI: WWM, E177/85, 93, Eyre to Milton, 30 May 1807; E174/31, WLD to Sykes, Saturday [30 May 1807].

[51] Holland, *Memoirs*, vol. 2, pp. 227–9; Arthur Aspinall, *Politics and the Press, c.1780–1850* (Home & Van Thal: 1949), pp. 284–9.

likely to be returned,' Milton commented. As Lascelles climbed in the poll, the alarmed clothiers' ardour for Milton mounted. Their ensign was a leather apron, which they shook in the face of any fellow worker taking an opposite side: 'What thee vote against t'apron!' The Wentworth home territory of Strafforth and Tickhill wapentake, where industry mingled with agriculture, was also combed and as the results streamed into York, Milton marvelled, 'they must come from under ground'.[52]

The realization that a body of working people could wield such political power inspired a public debate in the latter days of the election and for weeks afterwards. The clothiers were reprimanded for acting out of pique. Not so, they replied. Lascelles's rudeness to their representatives (and his incivility was never denied; his friends could only say it was not the sort of remark he would make, i e, to tell anyone to 'go & be d—d', but outbursts of a similar nature, as when he called one man a 'Damn'd Blackguard' in the Castle Yard, revealed Lascelles's sadly short temper) had been more important than his stand on their bill. The clothiers thought for themselves and demanded respect.

'Wealth we know does not give Independence, personal labour may. Whatever they may be these Men and others in similar Stations are the Men who if roused will always determine contested Elections for the County of York,' one spokesman predicted. 'Unless therefore Mr. L. can make Friends of his Neighbours he may spare himself the Expence of another Contest ... The community will experience no inconvenience if the House of C. should learn a lesson of humility' from his defeat.

Lascelles's spokesmen argued that it was natural for the clothiers to 'wish to increase the value of [their] labour, beyond what was convenient to the public good', but their prejudice against him personally was irrational. They repeatedly called on Milton to say what he would do when the bill which would open the floodgates to factory development reappeared in Parliament but he, discreetly, refused to be drawn, preferring to see in the clothiers' support an endorsement of his Whig principles. A Wilberforce supporter jeered that when Milton heard such words as gig mills and croppers he meditated on 'the number of his coaches, his chaises, and his gigs, and of the number of crops whom he has riding in them'.[53] But a clothiers' spokesman responded that Milton had not humbugged them; they had never asked

---

[52] *The Times*, 6 June 1807; KINCM: 1982.895.409, Account of the Proceedings, fols 266–7; SCC:LAI: WWM, E163/24, Lee to Milton, 26 May 1807; *Leeds Mercury*, 31 May 1807; NRO: F(M), 72/55, Milton to Fitzwilliam, 2 June 1807; E163/32, Copperthwaite to Wrightson, 30 May 1807; Wilberforce, *Life*, vol. 3, p. 330n.; NRO: F(M), 72/59, Milton to Fitzwilliam, 3 June 1807.

[53] *York Herald*, 11 July 1807; *Leeds Mercury*, 31 May 1807; *York Courant*, 15 June 1807; *York Herald*, 27 June 1807.

from him any pledge to support a particular bill, but they knew he would most certainly 'hunt out those vipers that crawl about the King's throne and feed upon the public property' and such concern for public economy would relieve every tradesman of unnecessary taxes. Lascelles had erred in counting too completely on the merchant class, and the election would show that the merchants had less influence and the clothiers more independence than had previously seemed possible.[54]

---

[54] *Leeds Intelligencer*, 13 July 1807; *Leeds Mercury*, 18 July 1807; *York Herald*, 1 August 1807.

CHAPTER THIRTEEN

The Final Stretch, 1–5 June

THE HUE AND CRY about a Wilberforce–Lascelles coalition rose to a crescendo in the closing days of the election with the explicit purpose of generating plumpers for Lord Milton. What was 'so artfully tho' not perfectly veiled from public observation' in the beginning appeared to Miltonians now as a force powerful enough to 'rob' Milton of election. On Monday 1 June, with four days left, Milton was still third: the figures, Wilberforce 10,511, Lascelles 9,550 and Milton 9,336. But more electors were recorded for Milton on that day (619) and on each of the other remaining days than for either of the other candidates.

The Milton forces did not hesitate to destroy Wilberforce's character if that was the price they had to pay because, as their private correspondence shows, his public denials were regarded as impudent in the face of overt evidence that his friends and agents were touting for Lascelles even more busily after his own return was certain. *'Let him be Judged'* by the conduct of his 'Bosom Friends', the voters were told. Quakers were said to be changing to Milton plumpers out of abhorrence at the deception and on 1 June Samuel Tuke felt compelled to issue a denial from Wilberforce's Committee of Friends that the Society had deserted him.[1]

To the 'pretended coalition' accusation, Wilberforce supporters replied 'Because an Elector happens to be a friend of Mr. Wilberforce, or a member of one of his Committees, is he to have no choice in giving his second vote, or is he thereby deprived of the liberty of expressing his opinions? Do the friends and agents of Lord Milton abstain from expressing their opinions … they do not. Some of them have offered to canvas for Milton and Wilberforce jointly

---

[1] SCC:LAI: WWM, E224, Wentworth to Fitzwilliam, 1 June 1807; Wroughton to same, 28 and 30 May 1807; Cooke to same, 30 May 1807; *Leeds Mercury*, 31 May 1807; Election Squibs, 1807, To the Society of Friends; Wrangham MSS, Robert Grimston's account; *Yorkshire Election*, p. 97 (as also in county press).

... Mr. Wilberforce has never swerved from his original declaration, that *he stood alone* ... His noble and independent mind is above all artifice.'²

Naturally Milton advocates were not appeased and continued to rant about the 'juggling Coalition' and Wilberforce's responsibility for the acts of his central committee, if not all the others. The *Mercury*, conceding Wilberforce was by now re-elected, thundered 'if the people had been as thoroughly aware of the artifice ... as they are at present, he would ... have been the falling Candidate', adding ominously, 'There may come another contested Election, and he will then see and feel the effect of this abandonment of public principle. Mr. Lascelles ... has in this particular acted the more *manly* part – he from the beginning sought a coalition. Mr. Wilberforce has long been accused of a trimming, accommodating, and wheedling disposition; we are sorry to say it, but the transactions of this election wring the declaration from us, that this charge seems not without foundation.'

A set of verses, 'The Culprit's Lamentation', contained a supposed dialogue between Wilberforce and Lascelles in which the latter pleaded in vain for Wilberforce to avow their union and the two fell out. The concluding 'Moral' came in broad Yorkshire from the turnkey at the Castle prison:

> Vell I remembers these here Fellers,
>> In one dark cell they lied together:
> 'Till one or t'other growing jellers,
>> Why then you zee, they blow'd foul Weather.
>
> And thin as zoon as Sintance came,
>> Why BILL, he took the sneveling part;
> But HARRY wint off didly Game,
>> And BILL psalm-singing in a Cart.³

To the *Leeds Intelligencer* the Orange Men were reduced to paltry shifts indeed if they had to attack Wilberforce in such a fashion. 'The fact is simply this – Lord Milton's friends confess that he has little chance; they must find some one to bear the *brunt* of their disappointed hopes.'⁴

Wilberforce considered the Milton strategy utterly shameful. The assault upon his integrity was almost unbearable and, in addition, from a practical standpoint, the charge did him great harm, for he did not gain the wholehearted assistance of the Lascelles organization and he lost the votes of the heated Miltonians. Wilberforce's committee was driven to denouncing both his

---

² *Leeds Intelligencer*, 1 June 1807.
³ *Leeds Mercury*, 31 [30] May 1807; YML: Y/H 2.421, Election Squibs, 1807.
⁴ *Leeds Intelligencer*, 1 June 1807.

The Final Stretch, 1–5 June

opponents: 'YOUR independence is at stake,' it warned the freeholders. 'If the representation of this great county be confirmed to the two houses of _____ ___ _____ [i.e. Fitzwilliam and Lascelles] then you will never be able to regain your liberty.'[5]

Barracking candidates was a hallowed election custom. During the first week of the poll, Milton was continually interrupted and his boisterous friend Mellish stopped cold. The London committee inquired whether, for the 'good management of the crowd', it might be useful to have a few men *'conversant in the mobs of London'*, and the Leeds agents forwarded 28 young hearties to serve as standard bearers 'or whatever wanted', while a colonel in the volunteers seconded three stout sergeants for duty in the Castle Yard. The 100 constables enlisted at the beginning of the poll regarded themselves so much as retainers of their respective candidates that Undersheriff Gray had to hire another twenty or so to keep order – or try to.[6]

Wilberforce claimed that the Milton men began a 'mob-directing system' using twenty 'bruisers' including John Gully, the celebrated prize-fighter. Gully's life is a Georgian success story. He began work as a publican in his father's footsteps but in 1804, at the age of 21, landed in the King's Bench prison for debt. There he was visited by Henry Pearce, the current boxing champion, and a match between them prompted fight lovers to pay Gully's debts and train him. In October 1805 he fought Pearce for 64 rounds but lost. A few months later Pearce died and Gully became his acknowledged successor. His fame inhibited challengers from coming forward for the next two years, however, in which interval he was at liberty to attend the York election. After a heroic but short career in the ring, Gully retired, and became successively a respected tavern keeper, racehorse owner, proprietor of extensive lands and mines and MP for Pontefract.

Wilberforce, who was repelled by the rough stuff at elections, might have cast his mind back to his first election for Hull when he had, reluctantly, canvassed the butcher Johnny Bell, having been told he was 'a fine fellow if you come to bruising'. The day after his chairing – during which a stone was thrown at the new MP – Bell had offered to find the culprit and 'kill him tonight'. Wilberforce had dissuaded him, cautioning, 'You must only frighten him'.[7]

---

[5] Wilberforce, *Life*, vol. 3, pp. 328, 329; *Yorkshire Election*, pp. 80–1.
[6] *Hull Chronicle*, 3 June 1807; *Hull Advertiser*, 30 May 1807; SCC:LAI: WWM, E224, Wentworth to Fitzwilliam, 19 May 1807; E163/19, Lee to Milton committee, 23 and 25 May 1807; Gray, *Account*, p. 14.
[7] Wilberforce, *Life*, vol. 3, p. 329; Furneaux, *Wilberforce*, p. 269 and note; G.C. Boase, 'Gully, John (1783–1863)', rev. Emma Eadie, *Oxford Dictionary of National Biography*; Wolffe, 'Wilberforce', *Oxford Dictionary of National Biography*; Wilberforce, *Life*, vol. 1, pp. 13–14.

The rowdiness at the Castle Yard now reached new and notorious heights. The crowd hooted at Lascelles but even more at Wilberforce, who had always before been able to quiet the most unruly audience. According to one story, he was astonished to find his constituents so changed, and said so. 'Ah! Sir, – cried a bye-stander – You see what it is to set the Slaves free.' The chant used to silence him was 'No Coalition'. 'Wilberforce was hard pressed by us,' Milton reported unrepentantly on 28 May. 'He was quite out of temper & did not know what to say, & the people were quite against him, he has lost much of his popularity; he is now accused by them of hypocrisy & duplicity ... it is delightful to see that people begin to find him out.'[8]

According to the *Leeds Intelligencer*, Milton was browbeating the freeholders with a 'Banditti of hired Pugilists' and word was carried to London of Milton's own coalition of 'men of strong fists and Stentorian throats'.

'There is no earthly thing talk'd or thought of but duels and the Yorkshire Election,' observed Lady Bessborough. 'An Express arriv'd in Town this Morning with an account of the Death of H. V. Tempest [false] and people only ask'd the man if he pass'd thro' York!!!'[9]

Wilberforce was not easily driven from the election stage and not before he had provided Henry Thornton with 'A Story for Mim', his daughter Marianne:

> While Wilberforce was speaking the other day, the mob of Milton interrupted him. W. was attempting to explain a point which Milton had misrepresented. W. endeavoured to be heard again and again, but the cry against him always revived. 'Print, print', cried a friend ... 'print what you have to say in a hand bill, and let them read it ... .' They read indeed!' cried Wilberforce, 'What! do you suppose that men who make such a noise as these fellows can read – They read!' holding up both his hands to his eyes ... 'They must hear me now, or they'll know nothing about the matter.' Immediately there was a fine Yorkshire grin over some thousand friendly faces.

After Monday 1 June, Wilberforce never again faced a Yorkshire audience. That day he was heard only after Milton had appealed to the crowd on his behalf. His reception was cool: 'he could not raise a Hat even from Mr. Lascelles's Friends'. 'That Voice which has so often and so eloquently pleaded for the poor and helpless ... which is listened to with so much respect in our Senate ... which has shaken every quarter of the Globe in the cause of

---

[8] *York Herald*, 20 June 1807; WLCT: EHC18/M786, Thornton to Mrs Thornton, 4 June 1807; NRO: F(M), 72/42/43, Milton to Fitzwilliam, 28 May 1807.

[9] *Leeds Intelligencer*, 22 June 1807; *The Times*, 5 June 1807; [Gower], *Private Correspondence*, vol. 2, pp. 251–2.

human liberty and suffering human nature ... that voice was drowned ... by the clamour of *Pugilists*, and *Blacklegs* and impertinent ... *Schoolboys*,' mourned his friends.[10]

Until that day, Wilberforce had goaded his frail person into almost ceaseless activity, breakfasting with his committee at the Tavern, taking a cold lunch before going to the hustings, and dining late with forty or fifty supporters. His agent David Russell found that the best time for a few words with him was when he returned from the Castle Yard to dress for dinner. Each day Russell found Wilberforce repeating, like a mantra, a verse of Cowper's:

> The calm retreat, the silent shade,
> > With prayer and praise agree,
> And seem by Thy sweet bounty made
> > For those that follow Thee.[11]

On 2 June Wilberforce suffered a violent gastric attack which put an end to his electioneering. It was his old 'constitutional complaint', but his political enemies could not let him endure it in peace. A York physician was said to have diagnosed his ailment as a 'severe attack of the *Coalition* Cholick'. The problem of designing a suitable stool for his chairing was taken up in another paper and even the Rev. John Lowe wrote seriously to Earl Fitzwilliam, 'Mr. Wilberforce has been politically ill – and has not ventured to shew himself at the Hustings. ... Were the Election to commence now ... he would go out. His conduct has been marked by strong duplicity, while Mr. Lascelles's has been manly, liberal & handsome. He made some strong allusions in his speech today [3 June] to Mr W– and expressed his hope that the result ... would justify both himself & his noble opponent from the charge of having disturbed the peace of the County, without having fair grounds of hope.'

Wilberforce himself had wondered whether his repeated denials of a coalition did not hurt his friend and former colleague. A man less generous than Lascelles, he said, would have been alienated by the constant repetition of this theme.[12]

---

[10] Wrangham MSS, Robert Grimston's account; WLCT: EHC18/M786, Thornton to Mrs Thornton, n.d. [June 1807]; Wilberforce, *Life*, vol. 3, p. 330; Furneaux, *Wilberforce*, p. 269; YML: Y/H 2..421, Election Squibs, 1807; SCC:LAI: WWM, E2243, Wrightson to Fitzwilliam, 1 June 1807; *York Chronicle*, 9 July 1807.
[11] Furneaux, *Wilberforce*, pp. 269–70; Wilberforce, *Life*, vol. 3, p. 331.
[12] Furneaux, *Wilberforce*, p. 270; Wilberforce, *Life*, vol. 3, p. 331; *Leeds Mercury*, 13 June 1807; *York Herald*, 27 June 1807; NRO: F(M), 72/60, Lowe to Fitzwilliam, 3 June 1807; Wilberforce, *Letter to the Gentlemen*, p. 24.

Disturbances erupted in several West Riding towns towards the end of the polling period, at Sheffield, Halifax, Huddersfield and Wakefield, all brought on by the election rivalries and all starring Milton's turbulent partisans. Of the lot, the Wakefield episode was the least troublesome and is mentioned only as another illustration of the tinderbox atmosphere. It occurred the night the election ended when a great crowd had assembled to meet a messenger from York with the result. It was a Milton crowd, hoping for joyful news, but peaceable and patient. A local justice of the peace (and Lascelles committee member), William Wood, ignoring the objections of Milton's committeemen and the local constable, summoned troops to disperse the people. The soldiers behaved impeccably and merely paraded the streets until the express arrived, after which the citizens went home.

At Sheffield on Saturday 30 May, a number of youths joined a Milton parade led by a band with banners emblazoned 'Milton for ever' and 'No Plunderers', and in passing the Paradise Square house of Charles Brookfield, Lascelles's agent, and the Angel Inn, where his committee met, shouted rude slogans, were yelled at in return, and retaliated by throwing stones, smashing windows at both places. The houses of some of Lascelles's leading supporters also were attacked.

At Halifax, mobs began making trouble on Monday 25 May and kept the place in turmoil most of that week. The first night Milton enthusiasts collected opposite the White Swan Inn where the separate Wilberforce and Lascelles committees met and contented themselves with verbal abuse. The next night, however, they were back in swollen numbers, strutting about with an effigy of Lascelles and vandalizing the homes of Wilberforce and Lascelles supporters. On Wednesday, with a youthful crowd still in the streets, 60 special constables were sworn in and an express was sent to Leeds for the Inniskilling Dragoons who arrived shortly after midnight. But the magistrates did not use them against what the irate *Halifax Journal* pictured as a 'riotous and disorderly Rabble'. All 'Parents and Masters of Families' were asked to keep children and servants indoors under a 9 o'clock curfew and the week of 'disgraceful outrages' finally ended without bloodshed.[13]

Huddersfield was not to be so lucky. There on Tuesday 2 June a throng collected in front of the George Inn, Lascelles's local headquarters, 'hustling and bawling' their devotion to Milton. They then paraded with an effigy of Lascelles to the deep annoyance of many of his substantial friends, including Joseph Radcliffe, a magistrate, who sent to Halifax for the idle dragoons,

---

[13] *Leeds Mercury*, 13 June 1807; *Sheffield Iris*, 2 June 1807; *Halifax Journal*, 30 May 1807; *Leeds Intelligencer*, 1 June 1807; *York Chronicle*, 4 June 1807 (same report in *The Times*, 4 June 1807 and *Doncaster Gazette*, 5 June 1807).

read the Riot Act and ordered the troops to disperse the mob. This time the military adopted the methods used to clear the streets in Leeds. Several men were wounded, including one whose cheek was cut away. But the crowd gathered again on Wednesday and was not routed until 26 had been arrested. Three innocent victims of the soldiers were Thomas Drake, Joseph Cocking and Joseph Hutchinson, neighbours at Honley, who had come to the cloth market. Hearing the uproar when they were ready to start home they waited in the Ramsden Arms until about 10 o'clock. As they entered the market place, the dragoons rode at and trampled them. All were injured but most seriously Drake, who was badly bruised and slashed by a sword which cut through his hat and into his head. Prodded by the soldiers' swords, the trio was locked in an upstairs room at the George without bandages, food or a bed until noon the following day when they were taken before Radcliffe and bound over to Bradford assizes to answer, as it later transpired, a charge of assaulting that self-same magistrate.

The 53 freeholders of Honley had voted with but six exceptions for Milton but the three injured men were not electors. Their neighbours testified to their honesty, sobriety and industry. The 'Orange party' believed they were being sacrificed to 'appease the anger and satisfy the revenge of the Blue Merchants'. The case came to Milton's attention after the election and he provided legal counsel for them. Months later, to save the cost of litigation, which would have to be transferred to London if they were to get a fair trial, a bargain was struck under which the three admitted improper behaviour (though generally believed to be innocent) and the indictment was quashed. Milton paid costs amounting to £193 4s. 6d.[14]

Extraordinary measures were taken during the last week to uncover every unpolled freeholder and bring him into the booths before the contest ended on 5 June. Wilberforce continued steadily to add to his commanding lead but it was touch and go between his opponents and Lascelles's reservoirs in particular were running low. The weather had turned rainy and voters were even more reluctant than usual to venture out.

Milton's committee was showered with advice, some sharply delivered by 'A Friend':

> Distinctions of rank and fortune should give place on such trying occasions to the services which every Gent[lema]n should render ... All gentlemen who may have influence ... should sally forth in

---

[14] *Halifax Journal* 6 June 1807; *Leeds Intelligencer*, 8 June 1807; *Leeds Mercury*, 13 June 1807; SCC:LAI: WWM, E156/42, Hirst to Fitzwilliam, 11 June 1807; E156/43/2, Examination of three men hurt by soldiers; E179/188/1, Maude to Bowns, 28 May 1808; E92, Election expences, Agbrigg.

different directions and scour the country of voters ... and ... forward them immediately in their own carriages accompanied by themselves stewards tennants or trusty servants ... So great a number of gentlemen remaining in York inactive lookers on ... are not doing their best to serve his Lordship. ... Bringing one freeholder to vote is doing more service ... than all the songs and satires.

Trickles of voters should join others on the road so as to enter York in procession, William Fenton suggested as he dispatched an agent from Rothwell (exhausted of voters) into the Barnsley–Dewsbury vicinity; and another, well-mounted, tireless and once a clothier himself, was sent into Saddleworth in a last minute flurry. The clothiers indeed seemed to be the only class of voters still pouring into York. As the final week began, 500 passed through Leeds in two days.[15]

A Lascelles friend called attention to a Beverley butcher, Francis Denton, confined in York Castle for debt, and urged that someone check on his vote. He had one but it went to Milton and Wilberforce. John Forster of Bedford, *en route* to Scotland was hauled off his coach in York to vote (on a freehold at Tong) for Milton. Milton himself informed his father about an old freeholder living at Wentworth who had so far resisted all pleadings to stir. 'You will perhaps be able to move him, we must absolutely have him,' he wrote, but the old man did not give in even to the great Fitzwilliam. William Denison, pursuing voters in London, heard of one on board a vessel in the Thames about to sail for Gibraltar. He took a boat to the ship, brought back the Yorkshire freeholder and shipped him to York in time to vote on 4 June.[16]

Probably never had those pitilessly designated as 'aged and infirm' felt so much solicitude as they experienced in making their halting way to the polling booths. As the candidates ran out of able-bodied voters, what remained were chiefly old, unwell and phlegmatic. 'The grand thing is to move them from their homes,' said Bryan Cooke, but they could be extremely stubborn; some had not left their firesides in years.[17]

At the Castle Yard special arrangements were made to allow all elderly or disabled voters, unable to battle the crowds at the doors of the busier polling stations, to appear before representatives of the three candidates in

---

[15] SCC:LAI: WWM, E224, Cooke to Milton committee, 3 June 1807; E178/151, A Friend to same, 31 May 1807; E178/156, Fenton to same, 1 June 1807; E163/35, Lee to same, 31 May 1807.

[16] WYAS(L): WYL250/6/3/10, Shepherd to Wolley, 3 June 1807; SCC:LAI: WWM, E174/20, Wentworth to Brent, 1 June 1807; NRO: F(M), 72/51, 52 Milton to Fitzwilliam, 1 June 1807; *Morning Chronicle*, 8 June 1807.

[17] SCC:LAI: WWM, E224, Cooke to Fitzwilliam, Tuesday [2 June 1807].

the court house and, if qualified and no objections arose, to be given passes to enter the booths by the back doors at midday. Hundreds applied and sometimes the crowd at the rear was as large as the one at the front of the booths. Most of the applicants had been dug out in Milton's second canvass. His York sub-committee watched over them at Swift's Coffee House and shepherded them to the Castle Yard. Among their charges were two plumpers from Whitby, William Swailes, old and shaky, and Amos Dennis who had lost his speech 'so that great care must be taken when he is carried to vote as he cannot articulate the word 'Milton'. Dennis Davy, a deaf mute farmer near Keighley, also was sent to poll for Milton. He could write his name and understand what was going on, the Keighley agent promised. Seven aged men were routed out of the hospital of St John the Baptist at Kirby Ravensworth on legal advice that their votes were good. Lascelles's scrutineers contested them, and from the poll book, successfully. The anti-Milton press claimed that with his 'total contempt of expence', Milton polled more than 200 pensioners who had never been regarded as freeholders but were now said to be qualified through pensions arising from freehold lands, but this is undoubtedly partisan exaggeration.[18]

Jonathan Gray resented the difficulties presented by the hordes of superannuated freeholders of the 'lowest class' who tried to get tickets and was frankly sceptical about their frailties. Back-door admissions sometimes seemed to be a perquisite of friends of the candidates or of election officials. 'The pressure at the iron-gate leading into court was such that the Most *robust* of the *soi disant* aged and infirm, rushed in, and bore down the really infirm; the court was crowded with a disorderly mob ... the agility with which *the aged and infirm* climbed over seats and tables to procure tickets, was astonishing; and in this hurry and uproar, very little discrimination was practised by the distributers. Several hundreds departed daily without tickets ... because being real objects, they were too infirm to make their way to the commissioners,' said Gray afterwards. Adding to the disorder were quarrels between factions 'anxious to facilitate the polling of poor cripples on crutches or sedans!'. The restless voters at the front of a booth, pent up in a mob while the handicapped were admitted to the rear at noon, caused such near rioting as to bring a shift in the special hour to 4 to 5 p.m.[19]

The expensive outvoters, brought up towards the end of the poll, besides those already mentioned, came from Buckinghamshire (1), Cambridgeshire (3), Cheshire (14), Cornwall (1), Cumberland (3), Derbyshire

---

[18] Gray, *Account*, p. 31; SCC:LAI: WWM, E164/26, Hunter to Milton committee, 31 May 1807; E147, 148, lists; E167/17, 21, 22, Readshaw to Milton committee, 23, 28 and 29 May 1807; WYAS(L): WYL250/6/3/10, Ward to Wolley, 29 May 1807; *Morning Post*, 9 June 1807.
[19] Gray, *Account*, pp. 31-4.

(62), Dorsetshire (1), Durham (195), Hertfordshire (1), Huntingdonshire (1), Ireland (County Fermanagh, 1), Kent (9), Leicestershire (2), Lincolnshire (59), Northamptonshire (2), Northumberland (18), Nottinghamshire (63), Oxfordshire (2), Pomerania (Dantzig, 1: Henry Etherington, a Baltic merchant who owned a freehold at Great Driffield), Scotland (Shire of Clydesdale, 1), Shropshire (1), Somersetshire (2), Staffordshire (13), Sussex (1), Warwickshire (5), Westmoreland (49) and Wiltshire (1).

Correspondence and election rhetoric gave an impression that Milton supporters were working harder, spending more and bringing larger numbers of nonresidents to York. But the figures tell a different story. A total of 825 men (3½ per cent of the electors) from beyond the Yorkshire borders cast 1,245 votes in their appropriate wapentakes. Thirty per cent of them came to vote for Wilberforce and Lascelles and with their single votes or votes divided with Milton, these two candidates carried 70.46 per cent of the outvotes. The totals were Lascelles, 449, Wilberforce 431 and Milton 365. Lascelles received 73 single votes and Wilberforce only 12 but Milton had 320 plumpers – 87.67 per cent of his non-county vote. A higher proportion of wealthier voters – gentlemen, Anglican clergy, farmers, merchants and yeomen – appears in the non-resident lists.[20]

Some of the lesser outvoters experienced trouble collecting their expenses, George Fowler, a Manchester carpenter, for example, who cast a Milton plumper. He lost a week's wage (£2 2s. 0d.) and his food, drink, postboys and turnpike tolls amounted to £3 12s. 0d. but at York the committee gave him only £1 1s. 6d. towards his outlay. Charles Stacey of Broadholme in Nottinghamshire also had reason to consider Milton's committee stingy when he got only half his expenses after riding 'one hundred and sixty or seventy Miles to serve Lord Milton'. An offer by another to come from Fakenham in Norfolk for the cost of the journey was rejected as 'too far'. And two gentlemen who promised Milton plumpers if he would pay their way before they left Lincoln were 'taken no notice of'. Against these examples, the Lascelles agent in Durham appears generous in giving George Saunders, a yeoman living in Northumberland, £5 towards his expenses between Durham and York plus the cost of his journey from Newcastle to Durham. An Oldham voter who managed to travel at Lascelles's expense both ways polled for Milton.[21] Milton received four plumpers from the Oldham party of 13, two gentlemen, a tinplateworker and a hatter, and we must look among them for the guilty

---

[20] Analysis of voters from my study of poll book, expanded in Chapter 14.
[21] SCC:LAI: WWM, E179/83, 93, Fowler to Bowns, 3 and 18 November 1807; E179/147, Stacy to Bowns, 17 March 1808; E178/129, Catton to Milton committee, 28 May 1807; E173/129, Elgie to same, 29 May 1807; WYAS(L): WYL250/6/3/10, Clarke to Wolley, 3 June 1807; *York Chronicle*, 2 July 1807.

man. The others voted for Wilberforce and Lascelles. These were difficult journeys as 70-year-old Thomas Harrison, 'gent.', of Kendal could attest. Francis Wrangham had summoned him and he set out in a chaise at 11 p.m. on the first leg of a four-day, 182-mile expedition, sharing vehicles for some stretches with other voters. After travelling all one night, he reached York at 9.30 a.m. on 5 June, drove directly to the Castle Yard, stood in a pressing crowd until after 2 p.m. when his vote (for Wilberforce and Milton) was recorded. He returned by chaise and fish cart until he was met at Settle by his own servant and gig.[22]

Milton's electors were severely tested in the booths and their chief obstacle to proving a right to vote lay in the out-of-date, often confused land tax assessment lists. Qualified voters were rejected in their hundreds because their properties had not, intentionally or otherwise, been correctly rated, or the current ownership properly described. A minority of those refused on their first appearance were willing or able to come back with acceptable additional proofs. Since 1781 the right to vote had depended on certified payment of the land tax and the system from the start was open to abuse. An attempt was made in 1788 to get a uniform published list of assessments for each parish but the act was soon repealed because of cost. From then until 1832, the land tax commissioners' fallible lists were the only record. Barristers acting for the candidates, together with the sheriff's assessors, had to adjudicate on the spot any disputes over title at elections.[23]

In all, 1,852 voters were turned away in 1807, 1,490 of them Milton supporters. Only 300 Lascelles votes were rejected. Milton's foes blamed his disproportionate loss on the gamble his side took in sending questionable voters; 'many of them are the scum of the country', Lascelles's agent at Yarm snorted. The majority of the rejected voters did not appear on the land tax lists, but this was not necessarily because they were unqualified. Lascelles's agents were much more vigorous than the others in challenging credentials. Milton had employed six legal counsel to the others' two and three, but his seeming advantage was dissipated by their poor attendance record. Sometimes all six were absent when the assessors were meeting late and had to be dragged from their dinners. 'Mr. Courthope, the leader for Mr. Lascelles, was indefatigable: he was continually on his legs, and battled every case pertinaciously,' Jonathan Gray recalled.[24]

---

[22] SCC:LAI: WWM, E179/2/2, Harrison to Wrangham, 9 June 1807.
[23] *York Herald*, 20 June 1807; *York Chronicle*, 28 June 1807; Porritt, *Unreformed House*, pp. 25–8; Gray, *Account*, pp. 25–7.
[24] *York Herald*, 20 June 1807; KINCM: 1982.895.409, Account of the Proceedings, fols 118–66; WYAS(L): WYL250/6/3/10, Fawell to Wolley, 26 May 1807; SCC:LAI: WWM, E173/106, Scatcherd to Wrightson, 26 May 1807; Gray, *Account*, p. 27.

Too many Milton voters were eliminated without any reference to the assessors and without a proper discussion of their qualifications. Votes dismissed as bad for Milton were accepted for Wilberforce and Lascelles, it was frequently alleged. At the three booths handling the bulk of Milton electors (Agbrigg, Morley, and Strafforth and Tickhill) the spokesmen for his opponents spent much time on every doubtful case, slowing down the proceedings and of course the total vote which could be amassed that day. Robert Oastler proposed that Milton's election aides should screen his voters first and put those with clear qualifications ahead of the others.

Sometimes, local agents could send voters back with fresh evidence of their claims to the franchise. The brothers George and Robert Atkinson of Adwicke went back twice and 'woud travel 20 times to York rather than be unjustly foiled', Milton's Doncaster chairman wrote. He was confident that their inherited property duly qualified them but a tenant's name had been inserted erroneously in the land tax list and they never polled.

Charges of favoritism or undue influence were hard to prove but Milton's friends firmly believed them to be true. Tom Scatcherd claimed that voters who turned up wearing an orange favour were thrown out and that gentlemen friends of Lascelles and Wilberforce walked in the rear doors '*for Money*'. Humbler freeholders at the Morley booth were so 'dismayed by the Brow beating of Mr. Lascelles' Poll Clerk, Mr. Thompson, that they return hither unpolled', reported the Halifax committee, blaming Milton's representatives for negligence. In the Agbrigg booth, the Lascelles and Wilberforce men insisted on the delaying tactic of administering the freeholder's oath to all comers. Distant friends heard that Milton had no hope because Lascelles had decided to put the 'long oath' to each Milton voter to keep their numbers down.[25]

'A sincere well-wisher' informed Milton's committee that a 'decided partiality' towards the other candidates ran through all those conducting the election, from highest to lowest. Milton's voters were kept out of the booths as long as possible and once admitted were 'teased with a long string of questions' and subjected to oaths while friends of Wilberforce and Lascelles 'slipt thro'', as another anonymous correspondent put it. Milton faced the 'most *unnatural*, unjustifiable, and unprecedented Coalition in election history', said this regular observer of events in the Castle Yard. Many Milton freeholders

---

[25] SCC:LAI: WWM, E163/30, Walker to Sykes, 28 May 1807; E156/32, Crosland to Milton committee, 2 June 1807; E178/178, Oastler to same, June, n.d.; E151, Memorandum for the Scrutineers; E161/88, Wroughton to Milton committee, 1 June 1807; E173/106, Scatcherd to Wrightson, 26 May 1807; E224, same to Fitzwilliam, 30 May 1807; E156/77, Stocks to Milton committee, 1 June 1807; NRO: F(M), 72/62, Bowns to Fitzwilliam, Thursday [4 June 1807]; *Farington Diary*, vol. 4, p. 140.

– and undeniably he drew out voters from classes seldom if ever involved in an election before – were completely baffled by the examinations they were forced to undergo and could not describe their freeholds correctly. Yet Milton's agents stood by without cross-examining. In this friend's opinion, bribery was afoot.[26]

Gray flatly denied any partiality on the part of assessors or deputy sheriffs, in proof of which assertion he noted that committee members of all three candidates had at one time or another complained about decisions. The deputy sheriffs all bore respectable characters, he added, and they had been furnished with written instructions well known to the agents sitting with them who, therefore, need not submit tamely to any irregularity. Nine of the deputies voted: William Iveson, Robert Scott and Anthony Thorpe for Wilberforce and Lascelles; Samuel Hall, Thomas Ewbank and James Iveson for Wilberforce and Milton; Thomas Paul and John Lockwood for Wilberforce alone, and William Powell for Milton alone.[27] If this were the whole of the story, Lascelles should have been the one to feel injured.

Because Milton attracted Roman Catholic support, religious tests were invoked against suspected or known Catholics who braved the poll. The Milton committee had advised agents to send propertied Catholics only if they would be willing to take the oath of supremacy. Lascelles's agents in the East Riding alerted his York committee that every Holderness Catholic would support Milton and that to foil them, all men from that wapentake should be asked whether they were Catholics; they would not all be spotted and many would not 'swallow' the oath taking.

William Sheldon, a London barrister, managed to give a Milton plumper without being asked to swear anything. He was 'happy to find the Catholics had polled in considerable numbers, and many were so provoked at having the oath of supremacy &c &c tendered to them that they *leap'd farther than I confess I cou'd do even in a cause to which I wish so well*, and they took it'.[28]

Dissenting ministers voted heavily, as a group, for Milton but some were challenged to take the freeholder's oath. If they could be 'removed at pleasure' they were not qualified. The Anglican clergy voted almost as solidly for Wilberforce and Lascelles, especially the latter. A man who proffered a Milton

---

[26] SCC:LAI: WWM, E175/11, Sincere Well Wisher to Milton committee, n.d.; E178/149, Freeholder and Friend to Milton, 31 May 1807.
[27] Gray, *Account*, pp. 34–6.
[28] SCC:LAI: WWM, E164/7, Hunter to Milton committee, 20 May 1807; E167/33, Readshaw to same, 3 June 1807; WYAS(L): WYL250/6/3/10, Codd to Wolley, 31 May 1807; Dickinson to Wolley, and Burnstall to Lascelles committee, 31 May 1807; SCC:LAI: WWM, E224, Sheldon to Fitzwilliam, 27 May 1807.

vote was bluntly told by Bacon Frank that 'no man of his cloth ought to vote for Lord Milton ... the established church ... was in danger'.[29]

There was no pause in the polling on Thursday 4 June to celebrate the King's 69th birthday but the bells of the Minster and parish churches rang, flags flew and a salute was fired. In the evening, a ball took place in the Assembly Rooms and the Theatre Royal performed a comedy, 'The Birth-day', followed by a three-act melodrama called 'Tekeli or the Siege of Montgatz'. The Mansion House was brilliantly illuminated and at Etridge's, the windows of the Great Room where Milton's committee met, blazed with candles.[30] Milton and his friends had cause to rejoice on the eve of what now seemed certain victory.

He had been told to expect 500 votes on Monday 1 June and achieved 619, after which his fortunes steadily rose and Lascelles's sagged. A total of 19,741 persons had voted by Monday evening, and the poll stood at Wilberforce 10,511, Lascelles 9,550 and Milton 9,336, but Milton had brought in 123 more than 'the Negro' as Tom Scatcherd persisted in calling Lascelles, which made it 'A most blest & glorious day'. Scatcherd predicted Milton would 'beat ye two Coalis'd Knaves To morrow'. (Seven votes were disputed and added to Milton's total only later in the week.) Milton's people were confident they had greater numbers on the road or in the city than either of the others but the contest had narrowed to him and Lascelles.

Milton's strength should have been registered earlier but for the fact that his opponents' voters were spaced over eight or nine polling booths (thus processed more speedily and sent home) while Milton's were concentrated in three 'crammed beyond their faculties of digestion'. Gray believed that Lascelles's friends foolishly relaxed after nine straight days of leading Milton and should have noticed the 'thin concourse of freeholders about the doors of their favourite booths' in contrast to the 'busy hum of the crowding swarms at ... the hives in Lord Milton's favour'. If Lascelles was over-confident, the friends who had told him that Milton could not win more than 1,300 votes in the West Riding (where Milton's total reached 7,625 by the end) were surely to blame. Milton's 'engaging manners endear him more every day to the Freeholders', his father was glad to hear. His throat was sore on Monday but some cold meat and a basin of broth had enabled him to make an 'excellent speech' before he left the Castle Yard.[31]

---

[29] Male, *Treatise*, pp. 272–3; SCC:LAI: WWM, E224, Cooke to Fitzwilliam, Thursday [28 May 1807].
[30] *York Courant*, 1 and 8 June 1807.
[31] SCC:LAI: WWM, E224, Scatcherd to Fitzwilliam, 1 June 1807; Wentworth to same, 1 June 1807; Gray, *Account*, p. 9; *Leeds Mercury*, 6 June 1807.

Tuesday added another 506 to Milton's total and only 363 to Lascelles's, who was now only 71 votes ahead: another 'victorie over ye Black Blue, & little Jackall ... Oh, for such another day.' Scatcherd's dream came true on Wednesday when Milton passed Lascelles by 130 votes on the day's poll and 59 on the aggregate. Lascelles was all but conceding defeat. His friends were 'said to have got the Blue devils, I fear it will be a fatal disorder', Milton reported gleefully.

In London Milton's supporters had been taunted daily by the 'Ministerialists' who triumphantly brandished the latest news from Yorkshire in the faces of their Whig opponents. When the 3 June results reached town, Sir William Cunnynghame called on Charles Innes to say, 'Come now Charles, let us walk out, and insult the Rogues in our turn', which they did. *The Times* reported that Milton was expected to carry the county with Wilberforce. From his sickbed, Wilberforce wrote to Matthew Montagu, 'This day fortnight, though I had the promise of at least 9 votes out of 10 throughout the whole County, I was scarcely more confident of my own success than of Mr. L's but I now fear he will loose it. If he does it will be chiefly owing to the various faults, to call them by the slightest name, of his agents. What think you of his principal agent [Wolley] voting ... for Lord M. as well as L. I have been treated by the Miltonians most shamefully; but it is very wholesome ... such usage teaches us to remember that we are here but strangers & Pilgrims where we must therefore expect our Characters to be often traduced & our best intended actions calumniated.'[32]

Lascelles faced the emerging facts stoically. Although he went through the motions of summoning every rejected voter in the vicinity of York to try again on Friday, he expected to fail. He spoke at length with Bryan Cooke, and during the conversation remarked, 'I should be the happiest man in the world if I had a son who at the age of Lord Milton was able to conduct himself with the discretion, judgement & ability he has done'. Cooke wasted no time in reporting these words to Earl Fitzwilliam along with the York gossip about Wilberforce's current unpopularity. Lascelles, so far as possible, had refrained from 'inflamation & objects of irritation', the Milton side was saying, now that Lascelles was no longer a threat.

As Wilberforce had observed, Lascelles was ill served by Wolley who climaxed his mediocre electioneering with the split vote for Milton. Rumour had it that several letters directing Lascelles's West Riding agents to send certain convoys of voters had been held up until too late. Much of the benefit

---

[32] SCC:LAI: WWM, E224, Scatcherd to Fitzwilliam, 2 June 1807; NRO: F(M), 72/59, Milton to same, 3 June 1807; 72/71, Innes to Milton, 15 June 1807; *The Times*, 6 June 1807; KINCM: Wilberforce letters, Wilberforce to Montagu, 3 June 1807.

he might have hoped to derive from the collaboration of his and Wilberforce's organizations had been dissipated by the coalition outcry. The clothiers' implacable opposition had cost him more than 2,000 votes.[33]

On Thursday 4 June, Milton polled 101 more votes than Lascelles and came 160 ahead on the total count. Mrs Osbaldeston swept into the Castle Yard with a fine force from the Pickering Lythe wapentake just before polling ended for the day. It was only the latest of her energetic contributions and Peregrine Wentworth had already declared that 'a Bust of that good creature Mrs. J. Osbaldeston is worthy of being placed in the best Apartment in Wentworth House.' Milton's friends rather hoped that this spirited show would encourage Lascelles to 'make his bow' to Milton on the hustings. Like many of Milton's aristocratic friends, however, Wentworth was unhappy with Lascelles's imminent defeat: 'Oh that we could have thrown that little *Importer* out' was his real ambition.[34]

The great Yorkshire election ended at 3 p.m. on Friday 5 June. From 1 o'clock onwards, disputed cases were settled in the booths by the deputy sheriffs without reference to the assessors. Freeholders still inside when the cannon signalled 3 were allowed to finish voting. Then the deputy sheriffs adjourned to the grand jury room to compute the figures. It was fully two hours before Sheriff Wilson mounted the hustings to proclaim the results. The heat of the day had been broken by a violent rain storm and much of the tense crowd was standing impatiently in puddles.

The state of the poll was Wilberforce 11,806, Milton 11,177 and Lascelles 10,989, with Walter Fawkes (at the insistence of two diehards) 2. Wilberforce and Milton were declared duly elected.[35]

Much was to be made of the narrowness of Milton's edge over Lascelles of a trifling 188 votes and of Wilberforce's margin over Milton of a healthy 629. But if contemporary accounts are correct, Milton still had 'some hundreds' (the *Mercury* said 600) unpolled voters on hand at 3. Had the booths where he was strongest been less swamped or had his voters been less relentlessly and successfully challenged, he could have beaten even Wilberforce himself. He and his friends did not argue the point: they were too busy celebrating. He had run up 9,049 plumpers, a record for any election.[36]

---

[33] SCC:LAI: WWM, E224, Vernon to Fitzwilliam, Wednesday [3 June 1807]; Cooke to same, 3 June 1807; *The Times*, 8 June 1807.
[34] SCC:LAI: WWM, E224, Wentworth to Fitzwilliam [4 June 1807] and 1 June 1807.
[35] See Appendix for Gray's 'General Summary of the Whole Poll'.
[36] Gray, *Account*, 37, 18; *Yorkshire Election*, pp. 105–8; *Leeds Mercury*, 13 June 1807; accounts of the end of the poll in the county press as *York Courant*, 8 June 1807; *York Herald*, 6 and 13 June 1807; *Hull Advertiser*, 13 June 1807. The two Fawkes votes were cast by Auctioneer William Bell of Hull and Mark Laybourn, turner, Great Driffield.

In profound relief, Fitzwilliam summed up the election for his aunt, Mrs Weddell:

> there was one whole week, very cloudy and threatening, not one glimpse of sunshine from the Monday to the Saturday. Happily, on the Monday following our prospects brighten'd, but our anxieties did not lessen ... But yesterday [5 June] has put an end to all our fears ...
>
> It has been a great struggle, against the greatest combination that ever got together – a strong party in the County, grown powerfull by long possession: popular cry of the day, aided by the innate spirit of Toryism, which together led even good men astray: Ministerial faction, & Court Faction – the Ministers & (I am sorry to think it, but there is no shutting out the glare of Evidence) the King himself – all these were to be contested against, having on their side the incalculable advantage of Wilberforce's duplicity & effrontery. But they are all beaten, & I believe, if the Law had not limited the time, Milton would have come out *first* on the Poll. Such a battle could not have been fought, but with zealous & hearty troops, with friends, who exerted all their powers to the utmost.[37]

Wilberforce, still ailing, was absent at the close and Sir Robert Hildyard spoke briefly for him but nobody listened. In his published thanks for his sixth election the next day, which was strongly if obliquely critical of his new parliamentary partner, Wilberforce called attention to the peculiar circumstances of a contest in which he had to 'struggle against the combined power of high rank, immense wealth, and extended family and political connections' as well as 'strong local and temporary prejudices, in which, though I was not their immediate object, means were diligently and very successfully found to involve me; and neither a very sparing nor a very scrupulous use made of what are understood to be Election Manoeuvres'. He indicated his future intention to answer at length the charge of coalition and, free now from the risk of being misconstrued, heartily applauded Lascelles's dignified conduct.

Henry Thornton walked over to the Castle Yard at 3 to take in the scene and carry the news back to Wilberforce. He pushed into the 'mob' at 5 to hear the speeches. Milton's, he thought, 'half reflected on W– but I doubt whether he meant to do so – It is the fashion with us to be quite sure that he did.' But Thornton regarded Milton as 'too much of a party man ever to be very respectable for the County of York'.[38]

---

[37] WYAS(K): WYL 109/2b/152, Fitzwilliam to Mrs Weddell [6 June 1807].
[38] WLCT: EHC18/M786, Thornton to Mrs Thornton, 10 June 1807.

Milton's speech did evoke the shades he venerated – Hampden and Sidney – and claimed his victory was a vindication of the previous administration's policies. He urged his friends to be magnanimous in their hour of triumph and he extended to the clothiers his hearty thanks for 'firm and efficient' support. 'When I forget them, may my right hand forget her cunning,' he said. He concluded with praise for Lascelles's honourable behaviour in the contest but made no reference at all (in published accounts) to Wilberforce.

Lascelles did not air his private view of Milton or return the compliment. The small majority convinced him that he still represented the 'sense of the county'. (Cries of 'No, no'.) True, the clothiers had supported his opponent but this was because of their misbegotten prejudice which Milton had cleverly turned to his advantage. He forgave them; their animosity would subside. Lascelles concluded, 'I do most solemnly declare before God and my country, I had rather be in my present situation than in that of the noble Lord, supported as the noble Lord has been'. The proud effect was ruined by shouts of 'Fox and Grapes!' An Irish joke circulated about a man who saw his horse lose a race: '"Jontilmen!" said he, "I am quite happy that I am after coming in last; for, do you see, had I been winning, I should have taken money out of *your* pocket, and now I only take it – *out of my own*."' Lascelles left the hustings and proceeded to the George with a crowd of friends, cheered by onlookers and some of the 'first families' from their windows, leaving Milton in possession of the Castle Yard. The victor fastened on the sword of the knight of the shire and clambered into his chair for the tumultuous victory parade.[39]

Such scenes are never enacted nowadays and other paraphernalia of eighteenth- and nineteenth-century elections such as bands, parades, election dinners and the general blaze of colour in posters, flags and personal adornments survive mainly in American elections. To a newly chosen member today, the loss of the chairing ceremony, at least, must seem a blessing. An actual chair – in Milton's case smothered in laurel leaves and orange silks and ribbons – was mounted on the platform of a coach to give the victor a precarious seat well above the heads of the crowd. It was usually drawn by six horses and on this occasion postillions, outriders and special constables were decked in orange. Much of Milton's immediate escort was made up of exultant clothiers from Pudsey where 98 out of 117 votes had been recorded for him, 94 of them plumpers. Milton, perched on his chair, and his retinue circled the Castle Yard three times before leaving by the postern followed by a thousand or more cheering partisans to traverse the city. From windows ladies waved orange handkerchiefs ('one of the most enchanting scenes the imagination can paint,' we are told) and the shouts of joy ricocheted from the buildings which

---

[39] *Sheffield Iris*, 9 June 1807, and press accounts as in note 36; *Leeds Mercury*, 27 June 1807.

lined the crooked streets. Opposite the George Inn a disgruntled onlooker threw a brick which barely missed Milton's head and several 'ruffians' rushed out of hiding to try to pull him off his chair. They failed to dislodge him but succeeded in stripping his throne of its wreaths and silks. In a moment they were being chased by angry supporters. Safe at Etridge's, Milton addressed the crowd from a window before going on to the Assembly Rooms for dinner with 200 distinguished guests who had in their several ways worked for his victory. 'Harmony and hilarity universally prevailed,' we can readily believe. Meanwhile, the Pudsey men set off for home with the chair, which became the centrepiece for a local celebration before it was given an honoured resting place in the trustees' room of the Mixed Cloth Hall at Leeds.[40]

Wilberforce's health ruled out a chairing and his presence at his election dinner at the York Tavern. There his health was drunk and rousing speeches made by James Stephen and Robert and Samuel Thornton. Henry Thornton slipped out to join Wilberforce at their retreat at William Gray's and review frankly, as only old friends could, the history of the election which had ended sourly for Wilberforce in spite of his massive poll, the highest vote thus far recorded by any candidate in a British election. The contest left him 'thin and old beyond his years', Thornton was to write to Hannah More. He had been pained to lose the support of friends from earlier times, wounded to discern suspicion where he had known confidence and regard. Writing to his constituents later, however, Wilberforce took justifiable pleasure in the fact that 'without high birth, great wealth, aristocratical connection, or family alliance' he had been chosen for the sixth time to represent the greatest county in the kingdom. The *Sheffield Iris* in an effusive tribute prayed 'Long may he live to advocate the cause of the oppressed. ... God grant that it may yet be in his power to ameliorate ... the condition of the poor reprobates of man, who must still be slaves, in the West Indies! We fearlessly acknowledge that we shall never be satisfied till all is done, that can safely be attempted, towards the gradual and eternal abolition of Negro-slavery.'[41]

Four years later, around the time of his 52nd birthday, Wilberforce decided to give up the county seat. He had no fear of being turned out at another election: he was sure the clothiers would return to his side but the county representation absorbed too much time. He believed that to do the job fairly he must attend every parliamentary session and open his house to any Yorkshire caller. His health was no better – he thought his memory was

---

[40] Camidge, *York*, pp. 31–3; *Yorkshire Election*, pp. 107–8; S. Rayner, 'Great Yorkshire Election Contests' in Smith (ed.), *Old Yorkshire*, 1 (Longmans: 1881), pp. 120–1.

[41] WLCT: EHC18/M786, Thornton to Mrs Thornton, 10 June 1807; and Thornton to H. More, 22 September 1807; Wilberforce, *Letter to the Gentlemen*, pp. 23, 25, 27; *York Chronicle*, 2 July 1807; *Sheffield Iris*, 9 June 1807.

failing – but, above all, he worried about the 'moral education' of his children which only a parent could provide. He would have many regrets at 'closing my account' with Parliament 'when one knows not what may be intended in favour of popery, or against morals' and Lord Calthorpe's offer of Bramber in Sussex gave him a comfortable half-way house. There he was returned in the 1812 election without having to stir from his holiday retreat at Sandgate. It was a matter for Christian satisfaction that, as an independent MP who had long shunned honours and offices, he retired from Yorkshire voluntarily, without a peerage and amid a hail of testimonials from his long-time constituents.[42]

---

[42] Wilberforce, *Life*, vol. 3, pp. 533–44, 551–2; vol. 4, pp. 44–7, 62–8.

CHAPTER FOURTEEN

Afterwards

So the 'Imbecile Infant of a factious Aristocracy' won his election and the defeated *Leeds Intelligencer* announced with 'inexpressible regret' the 'triumph of *Jacobinism* over the friends of the King and Constitution'. 'The Fifth of June will long be remembered as the most disgraceful æra in the history of Yorkshire – a day on which the independence, the honour and the loyalty of the county were sacrificed to the gratification of personal revenge.'[1]

But to Whigs it was the 'Glorious Fifth of June' and in an election often disastrous for supporters of the previous ministry, a beacon of hope. Twenty-three years after it was sent into the political wilderness by the Pittite–Reformer coalition, the Fitzwilliam interest had recovered its old importance. For the first time the family sat in both houses of Parliament. Nationally many of the Whig leaders were humiliated – scurrying from strongholds like Northumberland, where Lord Howick bowed out when menaced by an enormously expensive contest, to 'such close boroughs as their friends could provide', as Lord Holland admitted with commendable frankness. 'Lord Fitzwilliam, indeed, rescued us from the reproach of universal failure,' he wrote.[2]

An exuberant ballad, 'Lascelles and the Baby', reflected the joy:

> Our Joe's come from York
> > Where, he says, they'd strange Work
> > For that Mr. Lascelles
> > And *A Legion* of Yells
> Did furiously fight with – a Baby,
> > They *call'd him* a pitiful Baby,
> > A white-looking, red-headed Baby,
> > But he laugh'd at *their Rattle*,

---

[1] *Yorkshire Election*, p. 19; *Leeds Intelligencer*, 8 June 1807.
[2] Smith, *Whig Principles*, p. 56; Holland, *Memoirs*, vol. 2, pp. 229, 230.

> Then offer'd them Battle,
> And *manfully* fought, though – *a Baby!* ...
> For full *fifteen Days*
> (Our Joe further says,)
> The Giant was fought by the Baby!
> When *the Snake in the Grass*
> And each big-looking Ass
> Join'd their *Notes* – 'gainst the *conquering Baby*.
> The *Low-Great* and the *Knowing*, half crazy,
> Vow'd – that they never more should be *asy*!
> And did haughtily gabble,
> 'Bout *the insolent Rabble*,
> Who had triumph'd, in *choosing* – *the Baby*![3]

'We are quite mad with joy,' Lady Milton wrote when the news reached London on Sunday, 'and are covered with Orange ribbons, Milton for Ever &c – ... we intend to go into Hyde Park on purpose to Shew ourselves, with the Servants & Horses bedecked with furious Orange Cockades.' 'The defeat of Lascelles appears to have produced a stronger impression in London than the fall of Dantzig,' said Lord Sidmouth, 'orange ribbons are to be seen in every street decking men, women, children, servants and horses.' The equipages of all the Whig families who were in town paraded through the West End that Sunday to hail Milton's return[4] and great men rained congratulatory notes upon Fitzwilliam and his son. Thomas Grenville declared, 'as a party triumph it is also in every respect compleat, & you must have heard enough of the earnestness & anxiety with which the new ministers pursued this contest, to leave no doubt as to the degree of mortification that they will have suffered ... their base & wicked hypocrisy has been justly punished.' 'If my poor uncle [Fox] could have fixed on the person and family in which distinguished talents and true Whig principles should appear he would have named Lord Milton,' Lord Holland wrote.

William Elliot saw Milton's victory as a 'complete triumph over the wicked and hypocritical clamour of "no popery"'. Lord Howick, brushing aside his own troubles, thought the glorious victory in Yorkshire of incalculable value and 'I had almost said it is worth all the money it has cost. For no price almost would be too dear to place Milton in a situation in which at the commencement of his political career he has shown so much energy of character, & so much

---

[3] *Yorkshire Election*, pp. 98–9.
[4] SCC:LAI: WWM, E225, Fawkes to Fitzwilliam, Monday [8 June 1807]; SCC:LAI: WWM, 116, Lady Milton to Mrs Sanderson, 7 June 1807; Smith, 'Yorkshire Elections', p. 85, n. 93; *The Times*, 8 June 1807; *Leeds Mercury*, 13 June 1807.

real ability.' William Adam called the Yorkshire result 'the most splendid & the most usefull contest in the country'. Congratulations also arrived from the Duke of Gloucester, and the Prince of Wales, once thought to be somewhat opposed to Milton, 'quite exulted in Milton's triumph, and did not ... spare the present Ministers', a mutual friend reported.

The Earl of Carlisle found in it the 'first important step that had been taken calculated to turn the current of Ministerial deception, & does most essentially tend to open the eyes of the public: & restoring to the people anything like the powers of vision, this ministry is at an end.' His single regret was that 'I am not yet in condition to get drunk to day with Milton & yourself'.

The loyal Rev. Richard Sykes recalled, 'We who fought under his banner had to contend with Partiality, Prejudice, the Weight of Government, & a Phalanx of well disciplined Mercenaries.' He humbly begged a lock of Fitzwilliam's hair to set in a souvenir ring and when Fitzwilliam insisted upon providing the entire ring, joyfully sent his finger size.[5]

As the Fitzwilliams, Milton, Lord Harewood, Lascelles and Wilberforce all departed for London, celebrations for Milton were occurring all over the county while Lascelles's resentful supporters collected signatures for addresses of thanks to their champion and searched for evidence to justify a petition to void Milton's election. The Milton festivities so riled 'A Freeholder' and Wilberforce supporter at Halifax that he demanded

> Why all this racket? *Where* the honours won
> By this fam'd Stripling, great Fitzwilliam's Son;
> While unregarded by the public eye
> By far the greater Champion passes by?[6]

But Wilberforce gave no encouragement to such acclaim and most of the compliments paid him were buried in the adulation heaped on Lascelles.

At Calverley on Saturday 6 June a society of bell ringers rang 5,040 changes in 3 hours and 14 minutes in Milton's honour. Among the smart parties were those given by Lady Strickland at the Hotel at Bridlington Quay, Frances Fawkes at Barmborough Grange, St Andrew Warde at Hooton Pagnell and Frederick Lumley at Tickhill Castle. The Earl of Thanet opened

---

[5] SCC:LAI: WWM, E225, Grenville to Fitzwilliam, 7 June 1807; Holland to same, 7 June 1807; Elliot to same, 8 June 1807; Howick to same, 8 June 1807; F32/57, Adam to same, 13 June 1807; E225, Gloucester to same, 6 June 1807; [Gower], *Private Correspondence*, vol. 2, p. 249; SCC:LAI: WWM, E225, Dorchester to Fitzwilliam, 7 June; NRO: F(M), 72/70, Carlisle to same, 9 June 1807; SCC:LAI: WWM, F42/59, Sykes to Fitzwilliam, 11 June 1807; E225, same to same, 19 June 1807.

[6] *Halifax Journal*, 27 June 1807.

the inns of Skipton to free public refreshment and from a window of his castle his wife tossed orange cockades and handkerchiefs to the happy populace. Communities made up their own parties, as at Billingley where 100 neighbours dined and danced or Rawmarsh where the local squire contributed a fat sheep, five guineas to drink his health and a wagon load of coal for the poor.

Throughout the county, and especially in the West Riding, bells rang, folk marched, bonfires roared and sheep were roasted during the week following the last day of the election. Numerous villages and towns staged chairings. At Halifax a crowd followed a band with a proxy Milton in one chair and his lady in another. (Their 'dresses' cost a guinea, charged to Milton's committee.) In Wakefield they chaired an old woman who lived on Clayton Hill and she was known ever after as Lady Milton and her street was called Milton Street.[7]

One of the most significant celebrations was at Leeds, where the trustees of the Mixed Cloth Hall hung two giant banners over the entrance on market day, one printed with Milton's pledge, 'When I forget the Clothiers, may my right hand forget her cunning' and the other, 'King and Constitution: The Glorious Fifth of June 1807: Trade and Independence'. Leeds gentlemen dined at the Music Hall with Richard Lee, the wool merchant, in the chair, speeches by the Rev. John Lowe and H.F. Mellish calling the election a triumph of independence over ministerial influence and intolerance, and among the guests an 'animated, but well regulated, feeling of exultation and hilarity'.[8]

Sheffield magistrates felt constrained to warn the jubilant inhabitants not to stage any public demonstration except the authorized parade which had been demanded by the Miltonians. It was held on 6 June replete with band, banners and thousands of marchers – 'triumphant yet orderly'. But private festivals abounded in Sheffield, as throughout the Strafforth and Tickhill wapentake which had overwhelmingly favoured Milton. There were flags in every street, eleven sheep roasted at as many steam grinding mills and a dinner attended by 170 was held at the Tontine Inn.

At a dinner at Doncaster Mansion House guests feasted on venison around a centrepiece composed of a freshly cut vine bearing large bunches of grapes fashioned by the daughters of Michael Humble of Shooter's Hill, who joined the Queen, Lady Milton, Mrs Osbaldeston and Lady Strickland in the roster of toasts. No dinner was complete without bumpers to the clothiers 'to whom Europe is indebted for her Cloathing, and Yorkshire for her Independence'; to the 11,177 freeholders who voted for Milton and to his 9,000 plumpers. Daniel Sykes, chief speaker at Hull, reminded his audience that the election

---

[7] *Leeds Mercury*, 13 and 27 June 1807; *Doncaster Gazette*, 19 June 1807; *Sheffield Iris*, 16 June 1807; *Halifax Journal*, 13 June 1807; Clarkson, *Memories*, p. 185; SCC:LAI: WWM, E92, expenses, Morley.

[8] *Leeds Mercury*, 13 and 27 June 1807.

had proved that the county could be polled and need never again be fobbed off with a 'sham election at the Nomination Meeting'.[9]

The Liverpool celebration dinner, attended by 300, was unusual for being held in a strongly Tory town which had just dumped its reformist abolitionist MP William Roscoe to return both old members, Generals Tarleton and Gascoyne, proven friends of the slave trade. Roscoe's election in 1806 had resulted from a split among the Whig supporters of Tarleton and his votes in Parliament for both abolition and Catholic emancipation sealed Roscoe's fate with the Liverpool ruling class. A 'No Popery' mob of seamen greeted him on his return from London and Gascoyne and Tarleton, promising to restore the slave trade, were elected.[10]

But it was the glittering London dinner for Milton that constituted the Whigs' 'declaration of war' against the ministry, at least in the opinion of William Cobbett, who was pleased that Milton had won, 'first because it was a triumph over no-popery; and secondly, because it *put political hypocrisy personified* into bodily fear'. The London gathering of 500 notables at the Crown and Anchor on 13 June was presided over by Walter Fawkes, who stoutly claimed the Yorkshire decision was a fundamentally political one and a true test of popular opinion. It was made, he said, between two equally matched opponents, both young, active, powerful and with spotless reputations, but differing widely in politics 'and on these grounds ... alone, I conceive Yorkshire was called upon to make her election between them'. Milton endorsed these views, defended the previous ministry and called the clothiers as 'independent a set of men as ever lived'. They had taught the King's ministers that it was not wise to raise a senseless cry or circulate abominable falsehoods against any man. '(Incessant applause).'[11]

Milton inspired some odd tributes. An elegant clothes brush, guaranteed to last twenty years, was named after him. Children were baptized Milton, booksellers enjoyed a run on [John] Milton's *Paradise Regained*, and 'on account of this increasing *rage* for everything that is MILTON', the price of Milton

---

[9] KINCM: 1982.895.409, Account of the Proceedings, fol. 396; *Sheffield Iris*, 9 June, 14 and 28 July, 18 August 1807; *Doncaster Gazette*, 27 June 1807; *Hull Advertiser*, 27 June 1807; *Hull Packet*, 30 June 1807.

[10] *Leeds Mercury*, 13 June 1807; F.E. Sanderson, 'Liverpool Abolitionists', in *Liverpool, the African Slave Trade and Abolition* (eds), Roger Anstey and P.E.H. Hair (Historic Society of Lancashire and Cheshire: Liverpool, 1976), pp. 221–6; Henry Roscoe, *Life of William Roscoe*, 2 vols (T. Cadell: 1833), vol. 1, pp. 355–99; *The Times*, 8 May 1807; *Hull Advertiser*, 1 August 1807; *Sheffield Iris*, 14 July 1807.

[11] Cobbett's *Weekly Political Register*, 27 June 1807, pp. 1113–21; *York Courant*, 22 June 1807; *York Herald*, 20 June 1807; *Sheffield Iris*, 23 June 1807; *The Times*, 15 June 1807; *Morning Chronicle*, 15 June 1807; *Morning Post*, 15 June 1807; *Leeds Intelligencer*, 22 June 1807.

oysters, a delicacy pickled in London, rocketed by a shilling per hundred. Nine thousand orange and yellow decorated earthenware jugs, bearing the fateful words 'Milton Plumper' were distributed to this happy band. J.R. Smith painted Milton's portrait, at the request of his political friends, and engravings of it were available in August at one to three guineas.[12]

To crown his joy, Milton's first child, Charlotte, was born on 10 July and the two highlights of his year were celebrated by a splendid ball and fête for 400 guests at Milton.[13]

Lascelles's defeat evoked the same rash of addresses as his withdrawal in 1806 had done. Once more Yorkshire was reminded of his virtues, and dark hints were thrown out that Milton's election was fraudulent. At every gathering a petition against Milton on grounds of treating was bruited. A popular final toast was to 'Those Freeholders whose hearts were with us, but whose votes were against us'. On the whole, the unpleasant work was left to committeemen, for the Harewood and Wentworth families consorted amicably at the York races in August where there was the usual competition for best display of equipage as well as best performance on the track. Fitzwilliam, who never allowed himself to be outshone in status symbols, arrived with his party in a coach with 10 outriders, a landaulette and a chariot; Lord Harewood and his two sons in two coaches with eight outriders. Lord Milton made a separate entrance in a coach drawn by a pair of bays, a landaulette and eight outriders. After their sport, the two great families left the city's prisoners richer by 10 guineas from each of them. Lord Harewood also gave money for 150 poor people and Fitzwilliam dispensed his annual donation to 400 needy recommended by their parish priests. York was back to normal, having enjoyed since the election bustle the trial and hanging of John Robinson for the hatchet murder of a pregnant maid servant; a panorama of the Battle of Trafalgar and death of Lord Nelson which was exhibited for a month to much acclaim; and six nights at the Theatre Royal of Mrs Siddons's farewell tour, with the star appearing in a different and exacting role each night.[14]

Lascelles had been returned to Parliament for Westbury in Wiltshire. His brother had been conveniently elected for both family boroughs and chose Northallerton after Henry lost in Yorkshire.

The Lascelles entertainments and addresses occupied the government's friends for most of the summer. One of the first and largest turnouts was in York where Sir Thomas Slingsby presided over a meeting at the Black Swan

---

[12] *Leeds Mercury*, 6 June 1807; *Halifax Journal*, 13 June 1807; KINCM: 1971.17, Election Souvenirs, Milton plumper jug (see Plate 11); *York Herald*, 22 August 1807.

[13] *York Chronicle*, 13 August 1807; *Leeds Mercury*, 15 August 1807.

[14] *York Herald*, 25 July and 29 August 1807; *York Chronicle*, 3 September, 9 April, 16 and 23 July 1807; *York Courant*, 13 June 1807.

in Coney Street. Four hundred and thirty-eight men approved resolutions and signed an address expressing their deep disappointment at the wound inflicted on the honour and independence of the county. The York meeting regretted that Milton and his powerful friends had 'courted and encouraged a description of persons ... whose general principles they must condemn', including in this confederacy 'certain religionists' and numerous 'deluded persons' mistakenly persuaded that they would be supported in future against the county's commercial interests. In contrast, the conduct of Lascelles and his friends was uniformly independent and dignified. Not one had been heard to utter 'No Popery'.

The meetings and addresses at Beverley, Halifax, Hull, Leeds, Northallerton, Richmond, Ripon, Sheffield, Wakefield and one representing the Staincliffe and Ewecross wapentakes in the north-west of the county, which was held at Lord Ribblesdale's seat, Gisburne Park, all conveyed similar sentiments and often in identical language. The Staincliffe and Ewecross address was signed by 827 men from 24 communities in the Craven area, well over half the 1,533 voters from a district which had recorded 1,025 votes for Lascelles, 923 for Wilberforce and only 501 for Milton. Their address proclaimed their 'exultation' at the manner of Lascelles's failure which had resulted not from Milton's lavish spending or crafty agents but because of 'local prejudices'. 'The Triumph is ours,' it concluded, 'for notwithstanding the great Majority your Opponent obtained in the Four populous Wapentakes [booths] into which this mistaken Prejudice ... had extended ... in the Nine other Wapentakes [meaning booths again] where it did not exist, and where every Man of common Discernment must see the Sense of the County was spoken, you had a Majority of Two Thousand Five Hundred and Seventy.' (Milton actually carried five wapentakes in the West Riding and one in the North, Lascelles six in the West and seven in the North and Wilberforce four in the North Riding and all six in the East.)

The 'accidental antipathy' of small clothiers was a popular theme in the addresses. Lascelles, said the Halifax signatories, was not the actual but the 'virtual and legitimate representative' of the 'intelligent part of the Community, and of the supporters of the establishments of the Country'.

There were no surprises in the list of 406 names appended to the Leeds address; there stood the whole of the professional and mercantile establishment, 'Convinced that a large Majority of dispassionate and unbiassed suffrages have actually been given' to Lascelles. At a Sheffield dinner, Chairman James Stuart Wortley took issue with Milton's position that his election was an endorsement of political principles and he condemned the interference at Sheffield of the patron, the Duke of Norfolk. 'I hope,' said Wortley in what from other lips than those of a very wealthy landed proprietor might seem subversive, 'that the overbearing authority which the Duke of Norfolk, or rather his agent, assumes will rapidly decrease ... for it is really grating to my feelings, that in a great town of such acknowledged commercial importance, so many men ... are commanded by a nod from his Grace's Steward.'

At Richmond as at York, an indignant meeting agreed to set up a committee to correspond with counterparts in other towns and 'look into the causes' of the election outcome.

In his polite acknowledgements, Lascelles likewise blamed his defeat on cleverly revived prejudices and held that on the constitutional questions behind the election, he not Milton represented the sense of the county. His personal unpopularity alone had cost him election; political principles had nothing to do with it. His major statement came at the testimonial dinner of a 'select company' on 17 June at the British Coffee House in London where Lascelles accused the clothiers of trying to restrain the use of capital so much as to ruin the British woollen trade and workmen generally of trying to keep out all machinery.

Lascelles gave private encouragement to the efforts in Yorkshire to void Milton's election even though he conceded in his London speech that it was impractical to challenge the result: no contest for that vast county could be carried on without making each candidate liable to charges of treating. Allegations of bad votes were a 'miserable artifice employed by the treasury writers to cover a mortifying and humiliating defeat', declared the Whig *Morning Chronicle* after this speech.[15]

But as Lascelles's network of agents scouted for proofs, Charles Bowns directed Milton's men to send in whatever they knew of their opponent's wrongdoing. Both sides had tales to tell of apparent bribery, broken promises, rough justice, duplicity and treating, which was a major reason why so few petitions ever reached Parliament even after the most stormy elections.

'If we have been guilty of violating these Acts there cannot be a doubt of our Opponents being equally so,' Bowns wrote when he invited evidence that Wilberforce or Lascelles, their committees, friends or agents had exceeded the treating and bribery acts. All through the election agents had collected information on irregularities.[16] The archival evidence is not complete enough

---

[15] WYAS(L): WYL250/6/3/30, York address, 22 June 1807 with other addresses, lists of signers and Lascelles's replies; *York Herald*, 27 June and 4 July 1807; *Leeds Intelligencer*, 27 July, 17, 24 and 31 August, 7 September 1807; *Leeds Mercury*, 11 July and 12 September 1807; *York Chronicle*, 25 June and 20 August 1807; *Sheffield Iris*, 21 July 1807; *York Courant*, 15 and 22 June 1807; *Doncaster Gazette*, 29 June 1807; SCC:LAI: WWM, G83/3, Lowe to Milton, 27 June 1807; G83/2, Mellish to same, 16 June 1807; *Morning Chronicle*, 18 and 19 June 1807.

[16] SCC:LAI: WWM, E151, Bowns circular letter, 27 June 1807; E163/21, Blakelock to Milton committee, 23 May 1807; E178/148, Wharton to Wrightson, 31 May 1807; E168/16, Martin to Bowns, 9 July 1807; WYAS(L): WYL250/6/3/10, Ward to Wolley, 29 May 1807;

to venture a judgment on which party stretched the law the most but a few examples will show that few active participants were innocent and agents were often swindled by venal voters.

Thomas England, a Tadcaster shoemaker, promised a Lascelles plumper but after reaching York and being told by the committee that they could give him no promise as to what he might expect for this favour (all electioneering officials avoided that trap), he was about to walk home again without voting when he met several men who told him that if he voted for Milton he would have a guinea. He did and received the guinea, which was laid down to travelling expenses and loss of a day's work.

According to Robert Overend, Lascelles's agent of Clayton near Barnsley, Matthew Firth, a farm worker, voted for Milton and Wilberforce after promising to vote for Lascelles. He had asked Overend what he would give him and was told expenses only: 7s. for his walk to Wakefield from where he would be taken to York. A Milton agent offered him two guineas and 'he had the villainy' to take it. He stayed overnight in York, charged to Lascelles's account, and at the inn told companions, 'You are dam–d fools, here's plenty of Money stirring. You ought to make the most of your Votes. I have.' John Parrott, a miller from Skipsea, refused to vote for Lascelles and Wilberforce for expenses only, announced he would vote for the 'best Bidder' and gave a Milton plumper for 6s. a day and expenses, reportedly promised him by Sir George Strickland's clerk.[17]

On the other side, Cuthbert Metcalf, Milton's Keighley agent, said that Lascelles's agents had treated freeholders who promised votes during the canvass to a dinner and liquor. This so irritated voters pledged to Milton that they rebelled; if they were not to have so much as a drink they would 'turn their votes', so Metcalfe capitulated and spent two guineas as a gift from himself. John Carr at Skipton told of a bill against Lascelles at the Black Horse Inn 'for treating the Electors amounting to upwards of 1,400 Guineas, which I understand he has engaged to discharge'. A Bedale man was allegedly given £14 by Lascelles's committee to travel to York from London and another £4 to continue on to Bedale. Charles Carr of Gomersal claimed to have complete evidence of several cases of bribery – including one of a voter paid £20 – by Lascelles's committee 'but none on the part of the c—ting Hypocrite'.[18] Even his worst enemies seemed unable to pin any misdeeds on Wilberforce.

While the threat of a petition hung in the air, Milton's agents would not

---

1/11, Sawdon to Slingsby, 29 May 1807; Jackson to Atkinson, 8 June 1807; Wilkinson to [?], 16 June 1807; Statement of Joshua Whiting; Statement of William Eggleston.

[17] WYAS(L): WYL250/6/3/11, Upton to Pullan, 18 June; Overend to Atkinson, 25 June 1807; William Eggleston statement.

[18] SCC:LAI: WWM, E162/29, Metcalf to Milton committee, 7 July 1807; E162/13, Carr

pay a farthing on the accumulated election bills. An attempt to invalidate his election would result in a further delay to the settling-up and make Lascelles extremely unpopular, another reason Milton's friends were confident that no challenge would be made, and Lascelles's friends were divided on the wisdom of a petition. Milton was urged to prepare a counter-petition against Wilberforce (as well as Lascelles), a step 'which if it did not put a stop to the proceedings of Mr. Lascelles' party, would sow a division in the Enemy's Camp', said the Rev. John Lowe. (Apparently such a petition was got up and its existence was said to have induced Wilberforce to persuade his government friends to see that the anti-Milton petition was dropped.)

The merchants of Wakefield were so furious at Lascelles's defeat that they started a subscription to defray the cost of prosecuting Milton, though 'there certainly was no difference in the conduct of the Candidates in this respect', barrister Francis Maude believed. Thomas Lee, Milton's Wakefield agent, confirmed the report: 'the blues are very sore, they won't speak to one, but that I don't mind – This Party talk of a Scrutiny & say that the Merchants are to be at the Expence, but I think that they are to [sic] fine calculators for such an undertaking and will be cautious in putting their Hands to Paper after being called upon for their full Subscriptions to Mr. Wilberforce.'[19]

Edward Baines wrote philosophically in the *Mercury*, 'At the close of a contested Election, much conversation always takes place in the discomfited ranks of the vanquished party, about setting aside the election by scrutiny, petition, and all the other engines of nullification. These bubbles serve to break a fall, and to revive expiring hopes, but ... we do not believe that there ever was a contested election conducted by all parties with less departure from the strict letter of the law. ... one can easily imagine that a minute investigation might develop circumstances not strictly accordant with the Acts ... but these circumstances would apply with equal force to each of the Candidates.' Furthermore, should a petition go forward and the people lose the 'man of their choice' by a 'collection of quibbles ... the consequence may be to unseat both the Members' and force another election.[20]

The 10 July deadline for filing petitions passed with no move from Lascelles. Three petitions, one from each Riding, had been drawn up by Richard Pullan of Leeds but when he submitted them to a London committee of Lascelles's friends, they were rejected on legal advice. For allowing London to have a

---

to same, 7 [July 1807]; E168/16, Martin to same, 9 July 1807; E156/64, Carr to same, 5 August 1807.

[19] SCC:LAI: WWM, G83/3, Lowe to Milton, 27 June 1807; G83/1, Maude to Milton, 15 June 1807; *Journal of Lady Holland*, vol. 2, p. 228; SCC:LAI: WWM, El56/127, Lee to Milton committee, 19 June 1807.

[20] *Leeds Mercury*, 4 July 1807.

veto, Pullan was censured by the irate mercantile supporters of Lascelles in Sheffield for his 'most palpable and unjustifiable breach of confidence' but it was too late to do more than grumble.[21]

There were other scores to settle, however, the most notorious case being Malton, and a petition against the election of Lord Headley was presented on Fitzwilliam's behalf. An intensely proud proprietor, Fitzwilliam was obsessively concerned with his responsibilities for his vast estates. One of his duties was to propose for the electors of Malton 'the most honorable Objects of Parliamentary suffrage', selected by him for their public distinction or from among intimate friends or the bosom of his family.[22] As we know, this year two candidates had presented themselves (Lord Headley and Isaac Leatham) against Fitzwilliam's choices of his nephew Robert Dundas and his friend Bryan Cooke, the sitting MP. Headley and Dundas were elected after Leatham left the field.

Although Fitzwilliam with the county to fight made no move until after Milton's election, some at least of his Malton rebels were contrite enough to bestow on Mrs Osbaldeston and her entourage, returning from York to Hutton Buscel, 'those marks of approbation they had no opportunity to show Lord Milton', she wrote to the earl after her rapturous welcome there.

'The *misled lower* orders of People were ... most forward to show their zeal – the *higher Leaders* exhibited Blue – Might I *presume* to *offer* an Opinion ... that not ONE of your Confidential Agents at Malton shoud be listened to *without* caution; as I fear more are to blame than have been named and the Evil has arisen from too much being kept from your Lordship's observation.'

Her conclusion, that certain voters went astray because it was the only way open to them to protest at their high-handed treatment by William Hastings, the earl's steward, was substantiated by others, but Fitzwilliam, to restore his authority, had to move against the people rather than appear to yield to their revolt by turning out his employee. He directed Hastings to collect evidence of bribery and treating and served notice on all tenants who had given one or both votes against his interest to quit his premises. His heretofore modest tolls for coal and corn carried on the Derwent Navigation were raised for opposition barge owners and Fitzwilliam and the Earl of Carlisle, whose seat was only five miles away, withdrew their patronage from Malton shops. Carlisle thoroughly approved:

I am convinced you must act with firmness, and all will be recovered. I have done so at Morpeth, & taking my full rents have precisely the

---

[21] *Leeds Intelligencer*, 13 and 20 July 1807; *Leeds Mercury*, 18 July 1807.

[22] Smith, *Whig Principles*, p. 33; SCC:LAI: WWM, Gov/88, Memoir of Circumstances Relative to Malton Election, C.W.F. [probably Lord Milton], April 1808.

same influence I had when I was such a dupe as to make very injurious sacrifices desired of me ... my rascal of an Apothecary ... shall Blister & Clyster no more of my family or tenants I promise him.[23]

A flurry of comment broke out in the county press with the *Mercury* editor one of the few participants who was not critical, pointing out that this was exactly the line Lord Harewood would follow if Westbury or Northallerton staged an uprising. Until the corrupt system of representation was reformed, 'It is merely skimming the surface to declaim against the exercise of Borough influence'.[24]

John Walker, banker and 'upstart gentleman' who was identified as the chief fomenter of the voters' rebellion, explained to Fitzwilliam that he had intended to vote for Milton and Cooke, but when Milton stood for the county instead, Walker 'was released in part'. He went on to rebuke his landlord: 'If at a period and on an occasion when every Man who can read a Newspaper thinks himself qualified and entitled to give a Political opinion, it sh[oul]d be deemed, my Lord, a crime in me to have formed an opinion on Measures which have lately engaged Public attention and animadversion, I certainly must plead Guilty. I voted both at Malton and at York [for Lascelles and Wilberforce] from a sense of Duty.'

The difficulty of proving bribery or treating, in spite of loose talk of money thrown about, was no less at Malton than elsewhere, but Hastings in any case could not win confidences and it was Mrs Osbaldeston who finally established the evidence on which a parliamentary committee found Headley's election void. She talked with Edward Leefe, who had been Leatham's local agent, and from him learned that Leatham had resigned in Headley's favour in return for all his election expenses and £500. She took Leefe to London for the hearings, lodged him at her house, and the moment the decision came on 16 March 1808 sent word to her steward to canvass Malton for Bryan Cooke at the coming by-election.[25]

On 24 March, the Malton electors atoned. Bryan Cooke was opposed by Robert Bower of Welham, a local landowner, and in a brief poll, Cooke won

---

[23] SCC:LAI: WWM, E225, J. Osbaldeston to Fitzwilliam, 8 June 1807; G29/2, Oastler to Milton, 18 July 1807; F76/118, Bartindale to Fitzwilliam, 26 October 1807; F72/17, Cooke to same, Tuesday [12 May 1807]; Smith 'Earl Fitzwilliam and Malton', pp. 61, 62, 66; *York Chronicle*, 25 June 1807; *York Herald*, 4 July 1807; *Leeds Intelligencer*, 13 July 1807; B.F. Duckham, 'The Fitzwilliams and the Navigation of the Yorkshire Derwent', *Northern History*, 2 (1967), 45–61; SCC:LAI: WWM, F72/24, Carlisle to Fitzwilliam, 9 August 1807.
[24] *Leeds Mercury*, 11 July 1807.
[25] SCC:LAI: WWM, F72/21, Fenton to Fitzwilliam, 27 June 1807; F75/44, Walker to same, 21 June 1807; F78b/32, 34, 35, 36, J. Osbaldeston to same, 12, 19, 23 and 24 February 1808.

by 319 votes to 82. Bower was an unenthusiastic champion recruited by Lord Headley with promises of money from himself, Sir Mark Sykes and the Rev. Christopher Sykes to pay the cost. Bower was to put up £3,000 of his own. The effort cost him £2,800 and only £500 (of the £6,000 promised) was paid by his sponsors. Again an appeal was taken to the House of Commons but Bower failed. He had fought his corner noisily, attacking Fitzwilliam for 'popery' and 'tyranny' in Malton, and what was worse, charging that the earl had been involved in a scheme to sell one of his Malton seats. Borough jobbing was still legal, but repugnant to Fitzwilliam, who accused Bower of slander. Bower carried the vendetta into the newspapers and Fitzwilliam then publicly demanded reparation for the stain on his character. A duel was fixed for the Doncaster race course on 12 April at 4.30 a.m. Fitzwilliam made known his last wishes to Lord Milton and proceeded to the rendezvous with Cooke. There Bower's second told Cooke that Bower would recant if one of his sources changed his story. The two seconds rode into Doncaster to interview the man and returned with a written statement which satisfied Fitzwilliam's honour and caused Bower to agree to publish a formal retraction. 'Than Lord Fitzwilliam we believe a purer character does not exist; and we have no doubt that the necessity he felt of exposing his life to vindicate his character, having been thus removed, will be the cause of heartfelt pleasure to every good man,' declared the new Hull paper, the *Rockingham*. The two Malton elections and petition cost Fitzwilliam £1,532 0s. 2½d. The usual election gifts to the voters and £200 for church repairs – all forfeited in 1807 – were distributed. The eviction notices against electors who had come back into the fold were withdrawn but their rents were raised by about 25 per cent. Canal tolls were restored to their previous level. But forty persons on a list headed by John Walker (who had voted correctly this time but refused to pay the higher rent) were to be turned out of their houses, shops and yards on Lady Day.[26]

Psephologists of the time devoted countless hours to the great Yorkshire election. In sum, they tended to agree that Milton had won the 'rabble' (known to Whigs, according to one scornful Tory, as 'the People') while Lascelles and Wilberforce carried the 'respectable' and 'independent' landed and commercial classes. 'Lascelles's electors are *angels*, Milton's merely mortals, and yet these human beings have had the insolence to vie and vanquish this *seraphic host*,' a Miltonite contributor to the argument observed sarcastically. It followed in the minds of Lascelles's friends that because Milton's strength

---

[26] *Hull Packet*, 28 March, 12 and 19 April 1808; Ward, *East Yorkshire Estates*, pp. 40–1; *Rockingham*, 26 March and 16 April 1808; Smith, 'Earl Fitzwilliam and Malton', pp. 63, 64, 65 n. 2; *Memoir of Circumstances Relative to Malton Election*; SCC:LAI: WWM, F72/19 Names of persons to be turned out in Malton.

arose from the working class, political issues could have nothing to do with the outcome; only selfish motives and prejudices could explain the phenomenon.

'It was not a political contest,' insisted the *Morning Post*. 'Lord Milton ... has succeeded by the assistance of the Clothiers ... They supported him, not as the friend of the present Opposition, but as the friend of the ancient exploded mercantile system. They loved him not as the enemy of the present Ministry, but as the enemy of the present system of commercial improvement.'

Prejudices, however, came in many forms and by the reckoning of one analyst in the *Leeds Mercury*, Lascelles benefited by prejudices far more than Milton. He estimated the prejudices of the wool merchants and iron masters, eager to embark in factory production, furnished Lascelles with 700 votes; Leeds Corporation interest 100, the 'covert coalition' with Wilberforce 3,000; the effect of personal favours granted during his 10 years in the Commons 200, his early canvass 1,000; the prejudice roused by Milton's age 500 and the 'whole weight of Administration, including Government Contractors, and the Freeholders in the public offices in London' 300 for a total of 5,800 prejudiced votes.

Against this, Milton gained only 2,400 votes from prejudice: 1,500 if the cloth district vote was considered as arising solely from prejudice; 500 from family connections, 200 from his anti-slave-trade stance, and 200 from people's disgust at the violence of Lascelles propaganda and the intervention of troops on several occasions. This theorist pointed out that he was taking no account of the loyalty of tenantry, for one side offset the other in this respect, nor of the prejudice raised by the 'No Popery' cry – highly effective in the North and East Ridings.[27]

But Milton's enemies would not have it so. There were easier explanations.

> As Milton now is all the Go,
>   Attend ye Britons hearty;
> I'll sing a song, 'twill let you know,
>   Who are of *Milton's* Party

one bellicose song ran, with successive verses listing as members of 'sedition's num'rous clan' 'fierce sec'trists', ruffians, wretches 'from justice 'scaped', even prostitutes (voteless though they were):

> Ask'each ragg'd Cyprian that you meet,
>   Which part espouses she;
> Quoth she, 'I live in *Milton-street*,
>   *Milton's* the lad for me.

---

[27] *York Chronicle*, 23 July 1807; *York Herald*, 11 July 1807; *Morning Post*, 9 June 1807; *Leeds Mercury*, 27 June 1807.

and pointing sternly to the guilty men of the woollen districts, it continued:

> And Clothiers! ye, whom we have seen,
>   For Church and King so hearty;
> Blush, and lament that ye have been
>   The tools of this vile party.
>
> The great, the loyal and the good,
>   Of Yorkshire's Sons the pride,
> And Yeomen of true English blood,
>   These are on LASCELLES' side.[28]

The abuse heaped on Milton voters spoke volumes on the significance of an election in which the 'lower orders' had snatched from the previously determinant elite the power to control the outcome. It was a startling result, a beginning of the decline of 'country house politics', brought about largely by the single-mindedness of the clothiers but with the assistance of others of their social and economic station in alliance with Whig aristocrats. It would discourage any early attempt to widen the franchise. The unity of the clothiers had its later counterpart in the political rôle played by coal miners throughout much of the twentieth century, for the clothiers likewise lived in tightly knit single industry communities. They mingled with those from other such places at the cloth markets. They controlled their production and managed their cloth halls in addition, and with their smallholdings they maintained an independence lost by wage earners in later years. In this sunset of the domestic system, they had triumphed over the landed proprietors, merchants and factory owners. Writing a few years afterwards, Samuel Nicoll, president of the York Whig Club, reflected that the years since the French Revolution had changed the English people more than had many a century before. 'Something of learning has become universal amongst them', he said, 'and that learning is chiefly political.'[29]

A study of the 1807 poll book, which lists the electors' occupations (with negligible exceptions) as well as their preferences, proves the class alignments in the voting. The poll was published at the request of Milton people because of the aspersions cast upon their side.[30] The pursuits of the 1807 electorate –

---

[28] *Leeds Intelligencer*, 22 June 1807.
[29] Linton, *Sheffield*, p. 145; S.W. Nicoll, *Second Letter to Members of the York Whig Club* (Hargrove, Gawthorpe & Cobb: York [1819?]), p. 8.
[30] *Sheffield Iris*, 9 June 1807. The analysis of voters by occupation is from my study of the poll book (see Plate 12). It covers voters resident in Yorkshire and includes Hullshire and York although both were administratively separate from the county. Voters from

about 350 different occupations are mentioned – make a colourful list, and I cannot forebear to point out that a single comedian appears at Beverley and plumped for Lascelles. Among the 'respectable' voters who, in the opinion of Lascelles and Wilberforce, represented the 'sense of the county', Milton collected only about 27 per cent of the votes while Wilberforce received 37 per cent and Lascelles just over 36. This was the established order, composed of men of title, landed gentry, professional men, military officers and high public officials, the Anglican clergy, large merchants or factory owners (sometimes retired to country seats), farmers (chiefly tenants) and yeomen, the owners of small estates which they cultivated (and were invariably denoted as honest or sturdy in the literature of the times). These men gave 16,281 votes in 1807, nearly 48 per cent of the total.

Agriculture, the nation's most important industry, was represented in the poll (in addition to the farmers and yeomen above) by such persons as husbandmen, surveyors, castrators, cow doctors, gamekeepers, mole-catchers, shepherds, bailiffs and land agents. Together they cast 11,757 votes, 35 per cent of the poll and showed as a group the same preference as the 'respectables' of which most of them were a part: both Wilberforce (36 per cent) and Lascelles (just under 36 per cent) did marginally worse and Milton (28 per cent) did marginally better.

In the broad commercial area of retail and wholesale trade, taking in among others linen drapers, silk mercers, beast jobbers, fishmongers, clerks, bookkeepers, grocers and shopkeepers, who cast 1,489 votes (just over 4 per cent of the total) the proportions vary, with Wilberforce winning almost 41 per cent, Lascelles 31 and Milton nearly 28.

Turning to those performing services, from carters to chimney sweepers, hairdressers, seamen and soldiers and the less exalted professions such as dissenting ministers, musicians and schoolmasters, who gave 1,687 votes (almost 5 per cent of the total), Milton surges ahead with 38 per cent, followed by Wilberforce with 32 and Lascelles 29.

Among producers – manufacturers, skilled craftsmen and artisans including such elites as apothecaries, architects, sculptors and portrait painters, but not including the textile or metal trades which will be examined later – there were 6,652 votes (19.5 per cent of the total) of which Milton again took the most, almost 37 per cent; Wilberforce 33 and Lascelles just under 30.

Because of their significance in the Yorkshire result, the metal trades,

---

London, Manchester etc. are not included in these figures but have been discussed in the previous chapter. The voters resident within the Yorkshire boundaries – 96.5 per cent of the electorate – were taken for study together on the grounds that they were subject to influence by the same county events, interests, newspapers and electioneering and, of course, represent the great majority of the electorate.

county-wide but centred on Sheffield, and the West Riding's wool trade need to be looked at separately. The metal trades included skilled workers from anchorsmiths to wire drawers who turned out silver, brass, tin, iron and steel products. They cast 1,194 votes at the election, 3.5 per cent of the poll, and Milton was a clear favourite taking 46 per cent of the vote compared with 30 per cent for Wilberforce and less than 24 for Lascelles.

This leaves only the cloth trade, the focus of so much electioneering attention. Wool preoccupied the West Riding but there was a small cotton industry, too, and every market town in the North and East Ridings had a few weavers, usually producing heavy linens. The latter tended to vote along the same lines as others in their rural communities. Taking all workers in cloth and its associated trades (such as scribbling millers or shuttle-makers) into account, Milton achieved 50.7 per cent of the vote compared with 25.8 per cent for Wilberforce and 23.5 per cent for Lascelles. When the militants in the wool trade are looked at separately, Milton's margin grows: 55.7 per cent to 23.5 for Wilberforce and only 20.6 per cent for Lascelles – although this latter figure, a fifth, may seem a great deal considering the maledictions poured on Lascelles. As a whole the cloth trade accounted for 3,518 votes, more than 10 per cent of the poll, of which more than 8 per cent came from workers in wool. Electors who identified themselves as clothiers numbered 1,416.

Clothworkers were not alone in helping Milton pull ahead of Lascelles. Milton outscored both Lascelles and Wilberforce among such relatively large groups as carpenters, cordwainers and butchers throughout the county. For their own reasons, other artisans, craftsmen and unskilled workers contributed to Milton's victory, their first opportunity for genuine political choice since the war began, or indeed in their lifetimes. To complain that Lascelles was defeated solely by the 'pique' of the clothiers, the only reason he publicly admitted, is to ignore the long-standing 'prejudices' of other groups – for example, the usually decisive partiality of the merchants of whom, in 1807, 81.24 per cent were for Lascelles and Wilberforce. Similarly, of the clergy, 80.95 per cent were for the two old members. And, not least, 73.43 per cent of the gentry voted for the pair. That the customary ruling class viewpoint did not prevail between Lascelles and Milton, representing poles in the political spectrum, suggests more than the perversity of a single group, even if one concedes that a clannish community concentrated in two or three wapentakes might have an impact beyond its actual numbers. But Lascelles's apologists in their post-election comments made a surprising assumption that Strafforth and Tickhill was a clothing district similar to Agbrigg, Morley or Skirack, when they tried to belittle Milton's achievement. Strafforth and Tickhill in 1807 offers a prophetic glimpse of elections to come, but well after reform. Here it can be shown that despite the protests of Lascelles and his friends, there was a political dimension to the result, whether or not it was exactly the one claimed by the elated Whigs. Both Lascelles and Wilberforce had been scrupulous in their attentions to the interests of the metal trades, and the Cutlers Company had supported them heartily – though Fitzwilliam had known its limited influence, yet Milton won 115 out of the 209 votes cast by cutlers.

Strafforth and Tickhill, the southernmost and largest wapentake in Yorkshire, containing besides Sheffield the market towns of Bawtry, Doncaster, Rotherham and Tickhill, sent voters representing 172 occupations to York. The list included butchers, bakers, and, yes, a candlestick maker. In all, 2,398 persons voted from this wapentake, second only to Morley, the heart of the woollen area, which sent 2,487 electors to the polling stations. Even Milton, whose home wapentake it was, had marvelled that 'they must be coming out of the ground'. Milton's vote in Strafforth and Tickhill was an astonishing 1,898 against 483 for Lascelles and 691 for Wilberforce – 61.78 per cent of the votes cast, the highest ratio won in any wapentake by any candidate. Here, against the trend of the county as a whole, Milton won three out of the four most eminent bodies of voters:

	Wilberforce	Lascelles	Milton
Clergymen	15	13	33
Farmers	117	92	484
Gentry	76	52	159
Merchants	49	39	40

as well as carrying the artisans and mechanics with him.

This landslide cannot be explained by personal prejudice against Lascelles on the wool issue for here the wool, cotton and linen trade combined mustered an insignificant 29 votes, 23 of them for Milton. There were only two voting clothiers and three woolcombers in the wapentake. It would seem that the North and East Ridings where industry and commerce counted for less, still deferentially followed the lead of the squirearchy in support of the Church, the King and his government of the day. In the perverse West Riding, two factors produced a 'protest vote' in 1807. First, of course, the revolt of the clothiers, the 'Billymen' who had rallied to Pitt in 1795 and who now had changed sides over the searching issue of the future of their domestic system of manufacture. They attracted the support of others in their neighbourhoods and beyond, not least from the small manufacturers of the Sheffield area whose workshops also were threatened by the advent of a factory system.

But the second factor was the underlying radicalism of the Sheffield region, widely expressed in the 1790s, which always opposed Pitt's repressive laws, resented wartime taxation and supported civil liberties and parliamentary reform. Wilberforce and Lascelles were against them in all these matters. The personal influence of such great landlords as the Duke of Norfolk and the

Earl Fitzwilliam must have had its effect, perhaps an important one with the clergy (for the 'church in danger' slogan seemed to cut little ice here), and with their fellow landed proprietors, tenantry and some tradesmen. But landlord pressures were exerted everywhere and even Fitzwilliam's acknowledged electioneering skill and a lingering affection for the Rockingham tradition could not have brought about such a conclusive result. Lascelles could well argue that he still had won the 'sense of the county' as it always had been known. His friends went through various mathematical exercises to show that without the 'prejudice' of the 'industrial' areas, he would have led Milton by 4,000 votes. But the industrial areas could not be dismissed in this way. For their part, Milton's friends pointed out that if the law had permitted only one vote per man, that is, a total of 23,007 in this election, Milton's 9,049 plumpers would have left fewer than 14,000 votes to be shared between the other contenders.[31]

A letter to the *Leeds Intelligencer* of 15 June 1807 and another in the *Sheffield Iris* of 23 June sum up contemporary reactions. The Leeds letter attributed Lascelles's defeat to Milton's dextrous exploitation of local and temporary antipathies and his jacobinical talent for inflaming the 'lower orders' against the government. His single most powerful weapon had been the opposition of the clothiers to new machinery. Both Wilberforce and Lascelles had recognized that it was common sense to repeal obsolete restrictions, but the clothiers were bitter towards Lascelles because of an intemperate expression he was said to have voiced. Without this bias, the clothiers would as soon have voted for the Pope as for Milton.

In the *Iris*, a Strafforth and Tickhill observer chose a broader perspective. He argued that no private fortune could compete with the public funds available to Lascelles and that he 'would much rather see my native country return, as in feudal times, to the control of its native chieftains, than be under the influence of Treasury Clerks and their supporters. The former would have some degree of common feeling with myself, while the latter live only by fleecing me'. He noted that the London press had misrepresented Strafforth and Tickhill as a clothing district; he guessed not five clothiers lived there and Lascelles should have had the substantial support of the iron manufacturers if self-interest alone had dictated their votes. 'But really the people seem ... to have risen superior to private considerations, and to have given their support to him whom they thought the real friend to the general welfare of the nation.'

The writer discounted Fitzwilliam's influence for in this district large numbers of freeholders pursued independent trades and pressures were not

---

[31] *York Herald*, 27 June 1807.

strong upon them. The role Wilberforce had played in the 'stab given to the constitution by the treason and sedition bills' was in the writer's mind. He had witnessed Wilberforce's dramatic arrival at York Guildhall to speak in support of those bills. This history had not been forgotten. The Yorkshire voter had lost his liberties and gained the burdens of war. 'The different shackles and fetters which he now wears, and the imposts he now pays ... will convince the most stupid and uninformed' that if there were no possibility of change, the country was in a deplorable state. Perhaps he, like others, believed Lascelles had gained much by the support of Wilberforce's friends: 8,880 had voted for the two of them. But Wilberforce had been of little help to Lascelles in Strafforth and Tickhill for he had never supported the 'cause of the people' and, in preferring Lascelles to Milton, he might even have opened the way to letting Lascelles give a casting vote should repeal of the abolition act arise – not a question to be trifled with. The letter writer had given both time and money to bring in Wilberforce for the county in 1784, but both he and Lascelles had been tried and found wanting.

Before leaving the poll figures, a note of interest: 544 men who described themselves as labourers had and used the franchise. They divided their votes fairly equally, giving 289 to Milton, 255 to Wilberforce and 225 to Lascelles.

The advance in political power made by the Yorkshire electors in the 1807 election was not to be a springboard. The old system of election by negotiation returned in the other elections that preceded the 1832 Reform Act. In 1812, Wilberforce vacated his seat; James Stuart Wortley, a moderate Tory, was bluffed out of a contest by Lascelles, and Milton and Lascelles were returned together. Six years later, Lascelles withdrew to Northallerton because of ill health and Milton was returned with Wortley by acquiescence. No opposition faced them in 1820 (by now Lascelles had succeeded his father in the House of Lords) but the 1826 election was notable as the first in which Yorkshire chose four MPs. Two more seats had been acquired by the disenfranchisement of Grampound in Cornwall for gross corruption. Wortley had been ennobled and Milton, his popularity now enlarged by his support of parliamentary reform, was returned with John ('Unitarian') Marshall, a self-made flax spinner and manufacturer who embraced reform and religious toleration, while William Duncombe and Richard Fountayne Wilson represented the 'Protestant Cause' of 'No Popery' and no reform. Because religious passions threatened to bring on a contest, Milton and Marshall were forced to spend more than £27,000 each. By 1830, with Earl Fitzwilliam failing, Milton left his Yorkshire seat for a short tenure at Peterborough and Northamptonshire before succeeding to the peerage in 1833. Marshall retired, too, and the Whigs brought in Lord Morpeth and Henry Brougham. Richard Bethell and Duncombe were now the Tory choices. A fifth candidate, Martin Stapylton of Myton Hall, withdrew after one day of polling. A year later, with the reform issue paramount, in the last election for the undivided county constituency, Yorkshire returned unopposed four men who favoured reform.

By the Reform Act, Aldborough, Boroughbridge and Hedon lost their parliamentary representation entirely; Northallerton and Thirsk were reduced to one member each and Bradford, Halifax, Huddersfield, Leeds, Sheffield, Wakefield and Whitby were enfranchised at last.[32]

On the critical issue of the wool trade's future, Lord Milton, contrary to prediction, remained in spirit on the clothiers' side, but their cause was hopeless against the new technology. It was not until June 1809 that the hard-fought bill was passed. It maintained the clothiers' system of apprenticeship but held it was not a necessary qualification for setting up in the wool trade. Most of the old restraints were repealed. The law against combinations of workmen was strengthened. For workers displaced by the introduction of machinery a sop was offered in a provision that they would be free to take up any other trade or business without the curbs imposed by local custom or by-laws. Suffering in addition from a wartime slump in trade and soaring food prices, the clothiers lashed out at the tangible symbols of their plight – the shearing frames and gig mills – and by 1812 Luddite riots and machine-breaking had spread over the West Riding. In January 1813, seventeen men were hanged at York's Castle Yard for their parts in the disturbances.[33]

After the vote counting was over came the financial reckoning which each side postponed just as long as possible. Some unhappy creditors were not paid until 1808 or 1809. When William Sheardown of Doncaster submitted to Lascelles his printing bill of £9 16s. 9d. he attached the unpaid bills of £3 8s. 5d. for 1802 and £13 5s. 8d. for 1806, and the account was settled – in March of 1808. It was not until April 1808 that Milton's freeholders in and around Hull were notified that they could apply for their 'reasonable expences'

---

[32] R.W. Smith, 'Political Organization', pp. 1556–7; Gooder, *Parliamentary Representation*, pp. 114, 154–5; Gash, 'Brougham', pp. 78–9; Spring, 'Earl Fitzwilliam and the Corn Laws', p. 301.

[33] *Leeds Intelligencer*, 27 July 1807; *York Herald*, 1 August 1807; *Leeds Mercury*, 1 August 1807; *Journals of the House of Commons*, vols 63 and 64 (1808–09); A Bill to repeal and amend Acts respecting Woollen Manufacture, *House of Commons Sessional Papers* (145), 1809, vol. 1, pp. 231–5; *The Statutes of the UK*, vol. 3, pp. 899–902, 15 June 1809 [49 Geo. III, c.109]; Crump and Ghorbal, *Huddersfield Woollen Industry*, p. 95; Frank Darvall, *Popular Disturbances and Public Order in Regency England* (Oxford University Press: 1934), pp. 106–8, 130; Peel, *Risings*, pp. 269–70; Thompson, *Making of the Working Class*, pp. 608–18, 624–6; R. Reid, *Land of Lost Content. The Luddite Revolt, 1812* (Heinemann: 1986); A. Brooke and L. Kipling, *Liberty or Death. Radicals, Republicans and Luddites* (Huddersfield Local History Society: new edn, Huddersfield, 2012), pp. 27–67.

at the Cross Keys Inn on three days in May. Milton at least gained some credit for having paid all his bills by the time of the 1812 election.[34]

The enormous cost of the Yorkshire election fascinated observers of the county's convulsion and estimates at the time spoke of half a million, £400,000, £336,000 and £250,000 as the sum spent on this 'Austerlitz of Electioneering'. No figures precise enough survive to verify any of these suppositions but this has generally been acknowledged to be the most costly election in British annals, with money gushing out in 'frightful profusion'.[35] The figure of £250,000 has come to be accepted as the round total, with more than £100,000 each probably dispensed by Earl Fitzwilliam and Lord Harewood. Wilberforce's frugal team are said to have spent only £28,600 and it may well be true considering his numbers of unpaid volunteers, the joint electioneering appeals put out by Lascelles's friends, and the fact that three-quarters of his voters came to York to vote for the two of them. Wilberforce's agreement to pay half their expenses lasted only until about the tenth polling day when he had enough votes to assure his return, and he polled only 1,173 plumpers for whom he would be wholly responsible. A partial list of Wilberforce's expenditure, amounting to £7,713 16s. 1d., shows that his committee paid Lascelles's committee £4,500 under their mileage agreement. There were 1,753 split votes with Milton for whom the expenses were also divided. At his York Tavern headquarters, Wilberforce's bill came to £953 19s. 1d.[36]

Lascelles's surviving accounts are much bulkier but still fall short of a conclusive statement. One informative record is a 128-page leather-bound ledger, 'Robe Cattle's Statement of Expences &c Incurred at the General Election for ... 1807'. Beginning on 26 May, Cattle itemized expenditures of £28,054 18s. 6½d. for York alone and Edward Wolley's disbursements as chief agent for the North and East Ridings came to another £35,405 4s. 1½d., as nearly as Cattle could make out, for Wolley, indifferent to the end, apparently did not keep careful track. But there would be in addition the heavy costs incurred in the West Riding, some of which are indicated in other jumbled records in the Harewood archive which have been estimated to show total

---

[34] WYAS(L): WYL250/6/3/13, William Sheardown's bill; SCC:LAI: WWM, E151, Bowns notice, 8 April 1808; SCC:LAI: WWM, E221, handbill 'six Reasons'.

[35] T.H.B. Oldfield, *Representative History of Great Britain and Ireland*, 6 vols (Baldwin, Cradock & Joy: 1816), vol. 5, pp. 267–8; Brock, *Great Reform Act*, p. 29; *Halifax Journal*, 6 and 13 June 1807; YML: Y/H 2.421, Election Squibs, 1806–37, handbill, 3 June 1807; *Morning Post*, 8 June 1807; Grego, *History of Elections*, pp. 325; Baines, *Life*, p. 63.

[36] Smith, 'Yorkshire Elections', pp. 86–9; Furneaux, *Wilberforce*, p. 271; Wilberforce, *Life*, vol. 3, p. 335; KINCM: 1982.895.409, Account of the Proceedings, fols 444–5.

spending of more than £93,600. To this might be added the £491 13s. 0d. it cost to return Lascelles for Westbury.[37]

Amid details redolent of the event are 10s. 6d. for hauling a coach out of the Ouse river, 12s. for watering a dusty street, and £8 17s. 4d. for hairdressing. Lascelles's printing bill in York alone was £949 7s. 6d. after Cattle had corrected the bills submitted for a cash discount and overcharges. Thomas Deighton of the Shambles, who printed the 'dirty epigram' and most of the other creations of that ilk, earned the highest sum, £353 11s. 6d. for 53,200 handbills and 53,800 blue cards and 150 circular letters. George Peacock of the dispassionate *Courant* received £170 17s. 0d. and William Blanchard of the sympathetic *Chronicle* £163. Alexander Bartholoman of the Whiggish *Herald* was paid a meagre £33 14s. 0d. for advertising.

Griffith Wright of the *Leeds Intelligencer* was paid another £461 14s. 8d. for handbills, circular letters, addresses, squibs and advertising paragraphs, and from Doncaster J. Sparrow sent a bill for £96 6s. 4d. for the songs, handbills, and printed ribbons he had produced and circulated. He had had to pay three men overtime (2s. 6d. each) for Sunday and night work. Similar bills must have been run up in other major towns. There were additional expenses for copying land tax assessments, 'alphabeting' the polling records, sending express messengers far and wide and the services of agents (including their attendance at polling booths when called). The account sent by William Dawson of Wakefield included a figure of £3 13s. 6d. for the indictment and conviction of William Batty, a waterman, for sheep stealing (he had voted a Milton plumper).

The account from Travers and Woodhall of Scarborough in the Pickering Lythe wapentake, where Lascelles came in second, suggests the scale of the agents' expenditures even in a lightly populated area. The firm was paid £822 14s. 5d. for canvassing, service in the voting booth, and the hire of chaises, gigs and horses to dispatch voters to York. The expenses of 160 Lascelles–Wilberforce voters came to £275 0s. 8d. exclusive of their chaises and horses; eight who gave Lascelles plumpers received £26 12s. 0d., and one person who divided for Milton was given half his expense or 6s. 3d. But the greatest part of the money flowed into the pubs and inns. Cattle's record showed payments, after careful pruning by a sub-committee, of £15,891 18s. 10d. to 38 York inns, public houses or lodgings. In total, Lascelles seems to have engaged at least fifty inns or houses in York. The largest debt, of course, was run up at the George Inn headquarters in Coney Street where £1,763 15s. 3½d. was paid, including six guineas for broken furniture and £3 8s. 3d. for smashed window

---

[37] WYL250/6/3/17, Robert Cattle's statement; 6/92, Lord Harewood's Accounts, 1807; Smith, 'Yorkshire Elections', p. 86.

panes. A typical account, for Francis Elgin's Old George Inn, Pavement, where many voters were housed and fed, shows the landlord's daily record of breakfasts, dinners, suppers, teas, liquors, beds and horses supplied. Elgin provided the Hang West booth with sandwiches, wine and porter, too. His final account was settled for £1,060.[38]

The bill presented by Mr J. Fletcher's wayside inn at Skip Bridge near Kirkhammerton, only eight miles west of York, where voters wearing Milton cards could scarcely get a drink while Lascelles's friends 'could have anything they chose', caused a stir even at the time. It totalled £3,393 1s. 8¼d. and was settled for £1,383 6s. 8d., less than the amount originally charged for wine alone after Fletcher was made to produce his wine invoices. He had also claimed more than £200 for spirits, £195 for ale and porter, £55 for beef, mutton and veal, £88 for hams, £59 for bread, £18 for tea and coffee, the same for tobacco and pipes, £199 for horses, hay and corn; £55 for sugar, lemons, candles and cheese; nearly £3 for mustard, pepper, salt and vegetables; £23 for butter and more than £12 for broken glasses and pot measures.[39]

In the account of innkeeper John Fairgray, forwarded by the Ripon committee for the joint attention of Lascelles and Wilberforce, was an item of £31 10s. 0d. for a 'Capital Grey Horse died at Skipbridge' and £26 5s. 0d. for a 'Capital black Mare died out of the Coach', both of which, as the committee explained, were on the road every day in their behalf and had died of fatigue, but Lascelles's scrutineers – who claimed they saved him in all more than £4,200 by their review – disallowed both deceased horses along with a charge of £20 for 'Broken Glasses, Tables, Chairs &c' by what seems to have been a rather disorderly committee.[40]

On 13 July 1807, Charles Bowns sent out a circular letter announcing that 'No Petition having been presented against LORD MILTON' he was now ready to receive the agents' bills. When they had been reviewed he would fix a date to visit each wapentake and pay them.

Even the abundant Fitzwilliam archives (where mention is made of 16s. spent on a packing box and two guineas for a trunk to move the election papers from York) do not satisfy us that we have the whole story when we find a 'final' figure of £98,614 14s. 0d., adjusted downwards later by some £2,000. But the sums are impressive enough and the details highly entertaining.

The general expenses for the West Riding came to £36,869 8s. 3d. plus

---

[38] WYAS(L): WYL250/6/3/11, sundry bills; WYL250/6/3/13, election accounts; WYL250/6/3/17, Cattle's statement; WYL250/6/3/12, innkeepers' accounts.

[39] WYAS(L): WYL250/6/3/17, Cattle's statement; SCC:LAI: WWM, 178/88, Cox to Cox, 21 May; *Sheffield Iris*, 4 August 1807; E. Fearnside, 'The Great Election Struggle', in *Old Yorkshire*, ed. W. Smith, vol. 1 (Longmans: 1881), p. 122..

[40] WYAS(L): WYL250/6/3/13, Ripon committee debt to Fairgray.

£6,925 'payments to voters' (totalling £43,795 5s. 1d.); for the North Riding £9,019 0s. 9d. with £1,223 9s. 9d. to voters (totalling £10,242 10s. 6d.), and for the East Riding £5,504 9s. 7d. and voter payments of £685 9s. 0d. (totalling £6,190 6s. 7d.), for a grand total of £60,228 2s. 2d. for the three Ridings. Except for £1,807 3s. 5d. spent in London, the rest was paid out in York. Milton used 110 inns and houses in York and they cost him £26,782 6s. 2d. Carriages and horses hired at York to take voters home or carry messengers cost a further £915 16s. 5d. The friendly *York Herald* topped the list of recipients for printing, stationery, ribbons and calico flags with its payment of £750 12s. 11d. Among other items at York were postage (over £53), candles and torches, bill stickers, copyists and writers (one a woman, Ann Locke), messengers and runners, Milton's victory chair (£32 17s. 0d.), ferry fees across the Ouse, 'superintendents' stationed in the public houses and inns or at the city gates, medical attention for infirm voters (£14 19s. 0d.) and 15s. to two men who lost their hats in the tumult of the chairing. The music came from Richard Brown's twenty-piece band and fifteen drummers and fifers who together earned £697 4s. 0d. during the contest. Payment was so tardy, however, that they had had to live on credit and might end up in jail, their families in the poor house, if Mr. 'Bounce' did not meet the bill, one frantic musician complained. As with Lascelles, the Milton accounts were audited by a sub-committee which met in York in late summer and the two groups agreed, after an acrimonious dispute, on how to divide the handful (314) of Milton–Lascelles voters' expenses.[41]

Robert Rhodes suggested that it would be prudent to settle the York publicans' bills before the August race meeting and most of them were paid in instalments, while the auditors looked into some of the more extravagant portions of them. Milton's bill at Etridge's came to £1,884 16s. 6d., so it was no wonder that the account for £2,649 4s. 9d. sent in by Mary Driffield of the Bird in Hand at Bootham Bar raised questions. A Sheffield silversmith, William Law, had taken the trouble on his way home from polling to warn Milton's committee that at this inn, wine was 'thrown away at every hower of the day'. Mrs Driffield pursued her claim stubbornly, finally appealing in April 1808 to Lord Milton. She had engaged her house solely for his friends, she said, and because of its convenient location at an entrance to the city she had served great numbers for twenty days. She had buried her husband only a fortnight before the election began and now, a poor widow, might lose her

---

[41] SCC:LAI: WWM, E151, Bowns circular letter, 13 July 1807; Smith, 'Yorkshire Elections', p. 86; SCC:LAI: WWM, E92, account of Charles Bowns; E175/19, ZY to Milton; E149, Minutes of auditing committee; WYAS(L): WYL250/6/3/17, Cattle's statement; SCC:LAI: WWM, E179/230, 232, Nicoll to Bowns, 8 September and 3 November 1808.

whole property. But she got no more than £1,268 10s. 8d. Unmoved, Milton told Bowns, 'I have had a long letter of grievances from Mrs. Driffield of the Bird in hand to whom I have given a very short answer; – you seem to have pinioned the said bird, but I fancy not more than she deserved.'[42]

Sarah Godfrey of Market Weighton, who had agreed to supply horses for Milton voters at two guineas a day per pair (and could have got, she said, £2 12s. 6d. from his opponents) insisted that she had suffered greatly because she had not been authorized to give refreshments to the passing electors. They had refused to pay for themselves because her competitors on the road to York kept open houses. She fervently prayed there never would be another election. She gave up her struggle in August 1808 and accepted £263 12s. 4d. for her £309 11s. 8d. bill. She, too, won no sympathy from Milton: 'I suspect she is a great cheat,' he told Bowns. Mrs Godfrey declared that Bowns was no gentleman.[43]

The incidental hazards of such a contest are reflected in the Milton ledgers, usually under the catch-all 'Promiscuous Expences'. He was charged 10s. 6d. for ruining the grass at the Piece Hall in Halifax and 7s. to repair the 'great Drum' of the Skipton band. Several ardent West Riding supporters were injured in their enthusiasm and Milton paid out compensation. Thomas Chadwick, run over by Milton's carriage as it swept into Halifax, was ill for 32 weeks and was given 10 guineas. Benjamin Atkinson, also run over but not badly hurt, received five guineas. A Sheffield grinder, William Hall, who was bruised in the course of giving his plumper at York, was awarded two guineas and Jonathan Eastwood, a carpenter from Wooldale in the Agbrigg wapentake, received £4 for his loss to a pickpocket in York. Thomas Wood went insane from his election wounds and was given £3 13s. 6d. Milton paid the funeral expenses of £13 4s. 6d. for William Blakeman, the Doncaster publican who died at York 'and was well when he left Doncaster'.[44]

The eleven meticulously kept books listing payments to voters do not even hint at bribery but it is hardly to be expected that they would. Perhaps the records came closest to such an admission with an item of £52 to reimburse J.P. Heywood for the extra money he had to give voters 'to make up the sum promised by the Wakefield Committee which was over and above the settled Allowance'. The 639 voters from in and around Leeds, for example, were

---

[42] SCC:LAI: WWM, E170/22, Rhodes to Bowns, 29 July 1807; E158/6, Law to Milton committee 22 May 1807; E112, Bird in Hand bill; E179/161 Mrs Driffield to Milton, 4 April 1808; E179/164, Milton to Bowns, 7 April 1808.
[43] SCC:LAI: WWM, E92, Harthill and Hullshire accounts; E178/101, Mrs Godfrey to Milton committee, 23 May 1807; E179/24, Clayton to Bowns, 17 August 1807; E179/191, Mrs Godfrey to Bowns, 27 June 1808; E179/221, same to same, 3 August 1808; E179/225 same to same, 9 August 1808.
[44] SCC:LAI: WWM, E92, Bowns's account.

paid on average less than £1 each. Gentlemen and squires rarely accepted anything and many shopkeepers, yeomen and artisans, including clothiers, also refused expense money. But Thomas Gibbon, a cropper, was not the only one who was disappointed when he went to the Bull and Mouth at Leeds at the advertised time in December 1807 to collect the £1 15s. 0d. due him only to receive a mere 14s., a guinea short. He was sure that Milton, in whose father's regiment Gibbon had served for six years, meant everyone to be paid a reasonable amount for his costs and 'a guinea is an object to a working man'. Since Gibbon had remarked that some chagrined voters might air the disagreement in the *Leeds Intelligencer*, Thomas Tottie, 'with a view to Lord Milton's permanent Interest', advised that claims of this sort not be 'wholly disregarded'.[45]

Raising the ready cash for the election was a problem shared by Lord Harewood and Earl Fitzwilliam and thousands were borrowed from bankers and friends to deposit at York and other points where needed. Fitzwilliam (and probably Harewood, too) sold shares, in the former's case £10,000-worth of government 4 per cents which yielded £8,000. In addition, his wife and sisters sold stocks worth more than £10,000 and Milton contributed £5,000. A small list in Fitzwilliam's hand gives in round figures where he expected to find £101,200 without borrowing upon mortgages, which he would not do. Outside the family, he obtained £8,371 from French Laurence, £20,000 from W.J. Denison, £10,000 from the Archdeacon of Northampton, £1,000 from Bryan Cooke, £2,300 from the Duke of Devonshire whose late duchess had owed Fitzwilliam that sum, £3,000 from Robert Rhodes, £13,000 from his Wicklow estate ('the largest remittance ever made at one time') and the rest from banks at London, York and Doncaster.[46]

What all these figures mean in modern and inflationary parlance is hazardous to guess. As a rough guide, £1 in 2005 has been estimated as having 43 times that value in 1810. If this is the case, then the sums expended on the 1807 election by each of the two great Yorkshire families could in present-day terms be worth the equivalent of around £4 million, with the total election costing as much as £9.47 million.[47]

---

[45] SCC:LAI: WWM, E98–108, payments to voters; SCC:LAI: WWM, E179/109, Gibbon to Milton committee, 29 December 1807.

[46] NRO: F(M), X515, Fitzwilliam to Baldwin, 1 May 1807 and Baldwin to Fitzwilliam, 15 May 1807; Smith, 'Yorkshire Elections', p. 86; SCC:LAI: WWM, F48/13, Snow to Fitzwilliam, 18 May 1807; NR0 767/84, Bank account book; SCC:LAI: WWM, F48/29, Fitzwilliam's list; F48/18, Laurence to Fitzwilliam, 22 May 1807; F48/17, Heaton to same, 22 May 1807; F89/355, Wainwright to same, 23 May 1807.

[47] Estimate taken from http://www.nationalarchives.gov.uk/currency/results2.asp#mid (values to 2005) and http://www.thisismoney.co.uk/money/bills/article-1633409/Historic-

At the close of the heated 1807 Westminster election, which had lasted from 7 to 23 May, a mob tore apart the hustings. Yorkshiremen were ever more canny. The hustings and booths at York were carefully dismantled and the timber sold at auction for £93 14s. 6d., which was divided among the three contenders who agreed to give most of it to the keeper of York Castle for his 'extra trouble and risque'. In the large oval of the Castle Yard, where deer had pastured in April but where election crowds had since shouted and shuffled, not a blade of grass was to be seen.[48]

---

inflation-calculator-value-money-changed-1900.html [consulted 14 August 2013]. Earl Fitzwilliam, *First, Second, and Third Addresses on the Corn Laws* (Ridgway: 1839 edn), p. 10, said the highest wage in south Yorkshire around this time was 15s. a week; the national minimum weekly wage in 2013 was around £236 for much shorter hours.

[48] *Morning Chronicle*, 25 May 1807; Election Squibs, 1807, auction notice, 17 June 1807; WYAS(L): WYL250/6/3/17, Cattle's statement; KINCM: 1982.895.409, Account of the Proceedings, fol. 440; *York Herald*, 13 June 1807.

APPENDIX

General Summary of the Whole Poll

	1807	State of the poll for each day				Daily aggregate			
	Days	No. of persons polled	Wilber.	Lasc.	Milton	No. of persons polled	Wilber.	Lasc.	Milton
1	20 May	1,532	751	774	656	1,532	751	774	656
2	21 May	2,292	923	914	1,295	3,825	1,674	1,688	1,951
3	22 May	2,266	1,173	1,010	1,081	6,091	2,347	2,698	3,032
4	23 May	2,509	1,422	1,196	1,126	8,600	4,269	3,894	4,158
5	25 May	2,594	1,641	1,402	1,037	11,194	5,910	5,296	5,195
6	26 May	2,194	1,354	1,160	948	13,388	7,264	6,456	6,143
7	27 May	1,753	936	845	871	15,141	8,200	7,301	7,014
8	28 May	1,394	766	689	698	16,535	8,966	7,990	7,712
9	29 May	1,165	600	592	561	17,700	9,566	8,582	8,273
10	30 May	913	459	465	444	18,613	10,025	9,047	8,717
11	1 June	1,128	486	503	619	19,741	10,511	9,550	9,336
12	2 June	870	373	363	506	20,611	10,884	9,913	9,842
13	3 June	797	291	341	471	21,408	11,175	10,254	10,313
14	4 June	902	381	401	502	22,310	11,556	10,655	10,815
15	5 June	697	250	334	362	23,007	11,806	10,989	11,177

York, December 7, 1807   JONA. GRAY, Under Sheriff

Source: Jonathan Gray, *An Account of the Manner of Proceeding at the Contested Election for Yorkshire, in 1807* (York, 1818), p. xxiii.

Bibliography

Manuscript sources

Bodleian Libraries, University of Oxford [BOD]
Additional Wilberforce papers (formerly belonging to Mr C.E. Wrangham) [AWP]
c.44–45, Correspondence
d.56, Letterbook

Borthwick Institute, University of York [BI]
Hickleton Papers, Halifax A4/12/1–26, Election Squibs, c. April – June 1807
Lascelles Barbados Papers, Printed Election Material, 1807 [uncatalogued]
Tuke Papers, Tuke 3, correspondence of William Tuke; and Tuke 108–10, Elections

British Library [BL]
Add MS 27,337, correspondence and papers of James Gillray
Add MS 28,060, correspondence of Francis Godolphin Osborne, Marquess of Caermarthen, and 5th Duke of Leeds
Add MS 35,129, letters addressed to Arthur Young
Add MS 45,130A, miscellaneous letters and papers, 1539–1894

Brotherton Library, University of Leeds [BRO]
MS 193: Benjamin Gott Business Papers

Cambridge University Library, Department of Manuscripts and University Archives [CUL]
GBR/0012/MS Add.7674, Thornton Family, Letters and Papers

City of York Archives [YA]
Accessions 5, 6, 24, 235, Gray Family Papers
M.22, Robert H. Skaife's Manuscript Catalogue of Lord Mayors & other Civic Officials of York (1895)
M.25, Yorkshire Association Letters, 1779–1786
M.32, Yorkshire Association Papers
M.90, Election Papers, 1784, 1787

Dr Williams's Library, London [DWL]
HCR Diary 17, Henry Crabb Robinson MS diary, 22 August 1837–26 October 1839

Doncaster Archives [DD]
DD/BW/P/63–66, William Wrightson: Chairman of Lord Milton's Election Committee for the County of York, 1807

East Riding Archives and Local Studies, Beverley [ERALS]
DDGR 42/29, Various letters relating to John Grimston, 1779
DDGR 43/27, Various letters relating to Thomas Grimston, 1807

Hull Museums, Kingston upon Hull [KINCM]
KINCM: 1982.895.409, Bound MS volume, An Account of the Proceedings Relative to the Election for Yorkshire [1807, compiled by David Russell]
KINCM: 2006.3657, Wilberforce Papers Box 1, biographical memoir of William Wilberforce, by T. Tindall Wildridge
KINCM: 1971.17 Election Souvenirs, Milton plumper jug
KINCM: Wilberforce House Museum, Wilberforce Letters

John Goodchild Collection, Local History Study Centre, Drury Lane, Wakefield [JGW]
POLITICAL: Yorkshire Election, 1807, Canvas returns on behalf of William Wilberforce's Committee

Leeds City Libraries Reference Room
SRP 324.42 Y82, MS letter, W. Powell to Thomas Wilkinson, 1 June 1807

Northamptonshire Record Office, Northampton [NRO]
F(M), Fitzwilliam Papers (Milton)

North Yorkshire County Record Office, Northallerton [NYCRO]
ZFW, Wyvill of Constable Burton archive, Wyvill Papers

St John's College Library, Cambridge [StJC]
GBR/0275/Wilberforce, Papers of William Wilberforce
GBR/0275/Clarkson, Papers of Thomas Clarkson

Sheffield City Council, Libraries, Archives and Information [SCC:LAI]
WWM, Wentworth Woodhouse Muniments, Rockingham, Fitzwilliam and Milton papers

Shropshire Records and Research Centre, Shrewsbury [SRRC]
Corbett of Longnor Papers
Katherine Plymley MS diaries

Society of Friends, London [SoF]
MS vol. 337/15: Gibson MSS

The National Archives, Kew [TNA]
Home Office 43/16, Domestic Letter Book, July 1806–June 1808

Wakefield Library and Museum [WLM]
MS diary: Vol. 5, Journal of Matthew Tomlinson of Doghouse Farm, Lupset. From 30 November 1806 to 25 October 1812

West Yorkshire Archives Service, Kirklees [WYAS(K)]
WYL109 vols 2a–2c, Ramsden Records (Rockingham Letters), Collection of Isabella Ramsden

West Yorkshire Archives Service, Leeds [WYAS(L)]
Earls of Harewood (Lascelles family), family and estate archive: WYL250 6/3/8–40 and Accn 3292/58 [77/4/10, 77/5/13]: Yorkshire Politics and Elections; 6/92: Lord Harewood's Accounts

Wigan Archives Service [WLCT]
EHC18/M786, Edward Hall Collection, Henry and Marianne Thornton, letters and diary, 1760–1815

Wrangham MSS (formerly belonging to Mr C. E. Wrangham (1907–1982) of Catterick, North Yorkshire) [current location not known]
Robert Grimston's unpublished account of the Yorkshire election, 1807

Official publications

Cobbett's Parliamentary History (1780–1803)
House of Commons Sessional Papers (145), (1809), vol. 1, pp. 231–5
Journals of the House of Commons, vols 61, 63, 64 (1806. 1808, 1809)
Parliamentary Debates, House of Commons, vols 6–9 (1806–07)
Parliamentary Debates, House of Lords, vols 7–9 (1806–07)
Report and Minutes of Evidence, on the State of the Woollen Manufacture of England, *Parliamentary Papers*, Reports from Committees (268, 268a), 1806, vol. 3, pp. 567, 595
The Statutes of the United Kingdom, vol. 3 (1809), pp. 899–902 [49 Geo. III c.109]

Journals, newspapers and periodicals

Annual Register (1780–1807)
Cobbett's *Weekly Political Register*, 27 June 1807
Courier, April–June 1807
Doncaster Gazette, October 1806–June 1807
Edinburgh Review, vol. 67, issue 135 (April 1838)
Gentleman's Magazine, vol. 17 (1842)
Halifax Journal, October 1806–June 1807
Hull Advertiser, October 1806–August 1807
Hull Chronicle, June 1807
Hull Packet, May 1807–April 1808
Leeds Intelligencer, September 1767, January 1779, October 1806–August 1807
Leeds Mercury, May 1780, September 1806–August 1807
Morning Chronicle, April–June 1807
Morning Post, May–June 1807

Northampton Mercury, May 1807
Quarterly Review, vols 61 and 62 (1838)
Rockingham, January–April 1808
Sheffield Iris, April–August 1807
The Times, May–June 1807
Wakefield Star, October 1806; May 1807
York Chronicle, March–April 1784; October 1806–September 1807
York Courant, October 1806–July 1807
York Herald, February 1806–August 1807

Other printed material published before 1850
(place of publication is London unless otherwise stated)

Allen, Thomas, *New and Complete History of the County of York*, 6 vols (J.T. Hinton: 1828–1831)
Allen, William, *Life of William Allen*, 3 vols (Charles Gilpin: 1846)
An Exhibition. A Lion broke loose (W. Rawson: Hull [1807])
Appeal to the Nation by the Union for Parliamentary Reform (J. Willan: Halifax, 1812)
Belsham, W., *History of Great Britain from the Revolution to the Commencement of the Year 1799* (R. Marchbank: Dublin, 2nd edn, 1825)
Bigland, John, *Beauties of England and Wales, XVI, Yorkshire* (Vernor & Hood: 1812)
Bogue, David and James Bennett, *History of Dissenters, from ... 1688, to ... 1808*, 4 vols (Williams & Smith: 1808–12)
Brougham, Henry, Lord, *Historical Sketches of Statesmen Who Flourished in the Time of George III*, second edn, 6 vols (C. Knight: 1845)
County of York. The Poll, for Knights of the Shire, Begun on Wednesday, May 20th, and finally closed on Friday, June 5th, 1807 ... (T. Wilson & R. Spence: York, 1807)
Election addresses, notices and other leaflets relating to the Parliamentary election for the County of York, 1807 (York, 1807) [in a collection of political tracts and handbills, British Library catalogue no. 1850 d 26(22)]
Election Squibs [1807] [York Minster Library, SC Folio, Y/H 8.421 ELE]
Election Squibs [1806–1837] [York Minster Library, SC Folio, Y/H 8.421 WIL]
Fawkes, Walter, *Speech ... on the Subject of Parliamentary Reform, Delivered at the Anniversary Celebration of the Election of Sir Francis Burdett* (Ridgway: 1813)
Fitzwilliam, 5th Earl, *First, Second, and Third Addresses on the Corn Laws* (Ridgway: 1839 edition)
[Gray, Jonathan], *An Account of the Manner of Proceeding at the Contested Election for Yorkshire, in 1807* (J. Wolstenholme: York, 1818)
Hazlitt, William, *Spirit of the Age* (Oxford University Press: 1825)
Hebblethwaite, B., 'To the Memory of the Spinning Wheel' [copy in Piece Hall Museum, Halifax]
Hutton, W., *A Tour to Scarborough in 1803; including a Survey of the City of York*, (Nichols, Son & Bentley: 1804; 2nd edn, 1817)
Jewell, John, *Tourist's Companion, or the History and Antiquities of Harewood* (Leeds, 1819)
Leatham, Isaac, *General View of the Agriculture of the East Riding of Yorkshire* (W. Bulmer & Co.: 1794)
Male, Arthur, *Treatise on the Law and Practice of Elections*, (J. Butterworth: 1818; 2nd edn, 1820)
Marshall [William], *Rural Economy of Yorkshire*, 2 vols (T. Cadell: 1788)

Minutes of Conversations between Preachers and Delegates in the Methodist New Connexion (T. Allbut: Hanley [1806])

Nicoll, S.W., *Second Letter to Members of the York Whig Club* (Hargrove, Gawthorpe & Cobb: York [1819?])

Oldfield, T.H.B., *Complete History, Political and Personal, of the Boroughs of Great Britain*, 3 vols (B. Crosby & Co.: 1792; new edn, 1805)

Oldfield, T.H.B., *Representative History of Great Britain and Ireland*, 6 vols (Baldwin, Cradock & Joy: 1816)

Parsons, Edward, *Civil, Ecclesiastical, Literary, Commercial and Miscellaneous History of Leeds, Bradford, Wakefield, Dewsbury, Otley, and the District Within Ten Miles of Leeds*, 2 vols (F. Hobson: Leeds, 1834)

Pearson, John, *Life of William Hey* (Hurst, Robinson: 1822)

Public Characters of 1799–1800 (R. Phillips, 1799)

Pick's Edition of the State of the Poll for Members of Parliament, to Represent the City of York (W. Pick: York, 1807)

Poll for Members of Parliament [for] the City of York ... 1818 (York, 1818)

Proceedings of the General Meeting of the Freeholders of the County of York ... March 25, 1784 (A. Ward: [1784])

Proceedings of the County Meeting ... 28 July 1803 (A. Bartholoman: York, 1803)

Report of the Proceedings Relative to the Election for Yorkshire, November 13, 1806, ed. A. Bartholoman (York [1806])

Roscoe, Henry, *Life of William Roscoe*, 2 vols (T. Cadell: 1833)

[Ryley, John], *Leeds Guide* (J. Ryley: Leeds, 1806)

[Silliman, Benjamin], *Journal of Travels in England* (T.B. Wait & Co.: Boston, 1812)

[Simond, Louis], *Journal of a Tour and Residence in Great Britain, During ... 1810 and 1811, By a French Traveller*, 2 vols (Constable: Edinburgh, 1815)

Stephen, James, *Essays in Ecclesiastical Biography*, 2 vols (Longmans: 1849)

Sutcliffe, Joseph, *Review of Methodism, in a Discourse ... January 1, 1805* (Wilson & Spence: York, 1805)

Tuke [John], *General View of the Agriculture of the North Riding of Yorkshire* (W. Bulmer & Co.: 1794)

Walker [George], *Costume of Yorkshire* (Longman: 1814)

Wilberforce, Robert Isaac and Samuel, *Life of William Wilberforce*, 5 vols (J. Murray: 1838; 2nd edn, 1839)

Wilberforce, William, *Substance of the Speech ... at the County Meeting ... on the First of December, 1795* (Thomas Wright: Leeds [1795])

Wilberforce, William, *Letter to the Gentlemen, Clergy, and Freeholders of Yorkshire; Occasioned by the Late Election* (Luke Hansard: 1807)

Wilson, Joshua, *Biographical Index to the Present House of Commons* (Thomas Goddard: [1808])

Wordsworth, C.F.F., *Digest of All the Election Reports, from the Earliest to the Present Time* (A. Maxwell: 1834)

Wyvill, Christopher, *Political Papers, chiefly respecting the attempt of the County of York and other ... districts commenced in 1779 ... to effect a reformation of the Parliament of Great Britain*, 6 vols (W. Blanchard: York, 1794–1802)

Yorkshire Election. A Collection of the Speeches, Addresses, and Squibs, Produced ... During the Late Contested Election ... (Edward Baines: Leeds, 1807)

BIBLIOGRAPHY

Editions of correspondence, memoirs etc.
(place of publication is London unless otherwise stated)

Bessborough, Earl of, and A. Aspinall (eds), *Lady Bessborough and Her Family Circle* (J. Murray: 1940)
Bessborough, Earl of (ed.), *Georgiana, Extracts from the Correspondence of Georgiana Duchess of Devonshire* (J. Murray: 1955)
Colchester, Charles, Lord (ed.), *Diary and Correspondence of Charles Abbot, Lord Colchester*, 3 vols (1861)
Copeland, T.W. *et al.* (eds), *Correspondence of Edmund Burke*, 10 vols (Cambridge University Press: Cambridge, 1958–78)
Davies, R., A. Petford and J. Senior (eds), *The Diaries of Cornelius Ashworth, 1782–1816* (Hebden Bridge Local History Society: Hebden Bridge, 2011)
de Selincourt, E. (ed.), *Journals of Dorothy Wordsworth*, 2 vols (Macmillan: 1959)
Fitzpatrick, W. (ed.), *Report on the [Grenville] manuscripts of J.B. Fortescue, Esq., preserved at Dropmore*, Historical Manuscripts Commission, vol. 8 (HMSO: 1912)
Fortescue, John W. (ed.), *Correspondence of King George the Third from 1760 to December 1783*, 6 vols (Macmillan: 1927–28)
Ginter, D.E. (ed.), *Whig Organization in the General Election of 1790: Selections from the Blair Adam Papers* (University of California Press: Berkeley, 1967)
Granville, Castalia (ed.) *[Lord Granville Leveson Gower], Private Correspondence 1781 to 1821*, 2 vols (J. Murray: 1916)
Grieg, James (ed.), *Farington Diary*, 8 vols (Hutchinson: 1922–28)
Harcourt, Edward William (ed.), *Harcourt Papers*, 14 vols (Oxford University Press for private circulation: 1880–1905)
Holland, Lord Henry Edward (ed.), *Memoirs of the Whig Party During My Time*, 2 vols (Longmans: 1852, 1854)
Ilchester, Earl of (ed.), *Journal of Elizabeth Lady Holland, 1791–1811*, 2 vols (Longmans: 1908)
Redford, George and John Angell James (eds), *Autobiography of the Rev. William Jay* (Hamilton Adams: 1854)
Kirk, R.E.G. (ed.), *Royal Commission on Historical Manuscripts [C.8551], Fifteenth Report, Appendix Part VI, Calendar of the Manuscripts of the Earl of Carlisle, preserved at Castle Howard* (Eyre & Spottiswoode: 1897)
Le Marchant, Denis, *Memoir of John Charles Viscount Althorp Third Earl Spencer* (R. Bentley: 1876)
Malmesbury, 3rd Earl of (ed.), *Diaries and Correspondence of James Harris, First Earl of Malmesbury*, 4 vols (R. Bentley: 1844)
Maxwell, Herbert (ed.), *The Creevey Papers: a selection from the correspondence and diaries of the late Thomas Creevey, MP*, 2 vols (J. Murray: 1903)
Smith, Nowell C. (ed.), *Letters of Sydney Smith*, 2 vols (Clarendon Press: Oxford, 1953)
Stirling, A.M.W. (ed.), *Letter-Bag of Lady Elizabeth Spencer-Stanhope*, 2 vols (J. Lane: 1913)
Wilberforce, Robert Isaac and Samuel Wilberforce (eds), *Correspondence of William Wilberforce*, 2 vols (J. Murray: 1840)

Reference works
(place of publication is London unless otherwise stated)

C[ockayne], G.E., *Complete Peerage of England, Scotland, Ireland, Great Britainn and the United Kingdom*, 8 vols (1887–98) revised edn, ed. V. Gibbs *et al.*, 14 vols (St Catherine Press: 1910–59)

Doyle, J.W.E., *The Official Baronage of England*, 3 vols (Longmans: 1886)

Matthew, H.C.G. (to 1999), Brian Harrison (2000–04) and Lawrence Goldman (2004–14) (eds), *Oxford Dictionary of National Biography*, 60 vols (Oxford University Press: Oxford, 2004); online edition at http://www.oxforddnb.com/ [current version May 2013]

Secondary sources
(place of publication is London unless otherwise stated)

Ahier, Philip, *Legends and Traditions of Huddersfield and Its District*, 2 vols (Advertiser Press: Huddersfield, 1940–45)

Aspinall, Arthur, *Politics and the Press, c.1780–1850* (Home & Van Thal: 1949)

Asquith, Ivon, 'James Perry and the *Morning Chronicle*', unpublished Ph.D. thesis (University of London, 1973)

Ashton, John, *Dawn of the XIXth Century in England* (T. Fisher Unwin: 1886)

Baer, M., *The Rise and Fall of Radical Westminster, 1780–1890* (Palgrave Macmillan: Basingstoke, 2012)

Baines's Account of the Woollen Manufacture of England, ed. K.G. Ponting (David & Charles: Newton Abbot, 1970)

Baines, Edward, *Life of Edward Baines, Late M.P. for the Borough of Leeds* (Longmans: 1851)

Barker, H., *Newspapers, Politics and Public Opinion in Late Eighteenth-century England* (Clarendon Press: Oxford, 1998)

Barrell, J., *Imagining the King's Death. Figurative Treason, Fantasies of Regicide, 1793–1796* (Oxford University Press: Oxford, 2000)

Bean, W.W., *Parliamentary Representation of the Six Northern Counties of England, 1603–1886* (C.H. Barnwell for the author: Hull, 1890)

Black, E.C., *The Association: British Extra-parliamentary Political Organization, 1769–1793* (Harvard University Press: Cambridge, Mass., 1963)

Bonsall, B., *Sir James Lowther and Cumberland and Westmorland Elections, 1754–1775* (Manchester University Press: Manchester, 1960)

Borenius, Tancred, *Catalogue of the Pictures and Drawings at Harewood House* (privately published by Oxford University Press: 1936)

Bossy, John, *English Catholic Community, 1570–1850* (Darton, Longman & Todd: 1975)

Bradley, Tom, *Old Coaching Days in Yorkshire* (Yorkshire Conservative Newspaper Co.: Leeds, 1889)

Brewer, John, *Party Ideology and Popular Politics at the Accession of George III* (Cambridge University Press: Cambridge, 1976)

Briggs, Asa, *Age of Improvement, 1783–1867* (Longman: 1959)

Brock, Michael, *Great Reform Act* (Hutchinson: 1973)

Brooke, A., and L. Kipling, *Liberty or Death. Radicals, Republicans and Luddites, 1793–1823* (Huddersfield Local History Society: new edn, Huddersfield, 2012)

Brooke, John, *King George III* (Constable: 1974)

Brown, Ford K., *Fathers of the Victorians, the Age of Wilberforce* (Cambridge University Press: Cambridge, 1961)
Buckle, Richard, *Harewood* (English Life Publications: Derby, 1950; paperback edn [1959])
Butler, J.R.M, *Passing of the Great Reform Bill* (Longmans: 1914)
Butlin, R.A. (ed.), *Historical Atlas of North Yorkshire* (Westbury Publishing: Otley, 2003)
Butterfield, Herbert, 'Yorkshire Association and the Crisis of 1779–80', *Transactions of the Royal Historical Society*, 4th series, 29 (1947), 69–91
Butterfield, Herbert, *George III, Lord North and the People* (Bell: 1949)
Cameron, W.S., 'A Famous Election Contest', in *Old Yorkshire*, ed. W. Smith, vol. 1 (Longmans: 1881), pp. 117–20
Camidge, William, *York: Parliamentary Old Time Elections* (York, 1907)
Cannon, J., *The Fox–North Coalition. The Crisis of the Constitution, 1782–84* (Cambridge University Press: Cambridge, 1969)
Carr, Mary, *Thomas Wilkinson: A Friend of Wordsworth* (Headley Bros: 1905)
Christie, I.R., *The End of North's Ministry, 1780–1782* (Macmillan: 1958)
Christie, I.R., *Wilkes, Wyvill and Reform. The Parliamentary Reform Movement in British politics, 1760–1785* (Macmillan: 1962)
Christie, I.R., *Myth and Reality in Late Eighteenth-century British Politics* (Macmillan: 1970)
Clark, A., 'Class, Gender and British Elections, 1794–1818', in M.T. Davis and P.A. Pickering (eds), *Unrespectable Radicals? Popular Politics in the Age of Reform* (Ashgate: Aldershot, 2008), pp. 107–24
Clarkson, Henry, *Memories of Merry Wakefield* (Wakefield, 1887)
Colley, L., 'The Apotheosis of George III: loyalty, royalty and the British nation, 1760–1820', *Past & Present*, 102 (February, 1984), 94–129
Collyer, C., 'Yorkshire Election of 1734', *Leeds Philosophical and Literary Society Proceedings*, 7:1 (1952), 53–83
Collyer, C., 'Yorkshire Election of 1741', *Leeds Philosophical and Literary Society Proceedings*, 7:2 (1953), 137–52
Collyer, C., 'The Rockinghams and Yorkshire Politics, 1742–1761', *Thoresby Miscellany*, 12 (Thoresby Society: Leeds, 1954), 352–82
Collyer, C., 'The Rockingham Connection and Country Opinion in the Early Years of George III', *Leeds Philosophical and Literary Society Proceedings*, 7:4 (1955), 251–75
Collyer, C., 'Politics in 18th-century York', York Georgian Society, *Annual Report* (York, 1955–56), 13–18
Coupland, Reginald, *Wilberforce* (Oxford University Press: 1923)
Craven, M.T., *New and Complete History of the Borough of Hedon* (Ridings Publications: Driffield, 1972)
Crump, W.B. (ed.), *Leeds Woollen Industry 1780–1820* (Thoresby Society: Leeds, 1931)
Crump, W.B. and G. Ghorbal, *History of the Huddersfield Woollen Industry* (Tolson Memorial Museum: Huddersfield, 1935)
Cuming, E.D., *Squire Osbaldeston: His Autobiography* (John Lane: 1927)
Curtis, L.P., *Chichester Towers* (Yale University Press: New Haven, 1966)
Darvall, Frank, *Popular Disturbances and Public Order in Regency England* (Oxford University Press: 1934)
Derry, J.W., *Charles James Fox* (Batsford: 1972)
Dinwiddy, J.R., *Christopher Wyvill and Reform, 1790–1820* Borthwick Papers, 39 (St Anthony's Press: York, 1971)
Donaldson, H., 'The Yorkshire election of 1807', unpublished MA Thesis (University of York, 2006)

Driver, Cecil, *Tory Radical: The Life of Richard Oastler* (Oxford University Press: New York, 1946)

Duckham, B.F., 'The Fitzwilliams and the Navigation of the Yorkshire Derwent', *Northern History*, 2 (1967), 45–61

Eastwood, D., 'Contesting the Politics of Deference: the rural electorate, 1820–60', in J. Lawrence and M. Taylor (eds), *Party, State and Society. Electoral Behaviour in Britain since 1820* (Scolar Press: Aldershot, 1997), pp. 27–49

Ehrman, John, *The Younger Pitt: The Years of Acclaim* (Constable: 1969)

Emsley, C., 'An aspect of Pitt's "Terror": prosecutions for sedition during the 1790s', *Social History* 6:2 (May 1981), 155–84

English, B.A., 'Harewood MSS', *Bulletin of the National Register of Archives*, 12 (1963) 9–14

Fairfax–Blakeborough, J., *Sykes of Sledmere* (Allan: 1929)

Farrell, S., M. Unwin and J. Walvin (eds), *The British Slave Trade; Abolition, Parliament and the People* (Edinburgh University Press for The Parliamentary History Yearbook Trust: Edinburgh, 2007)

Fearnside, E, 'The Great Election Struggle', in *Old Yorkshire*, ed. W. Smith, vol. 1 (Longmans: 1881), p. 122

Foord, A.S., *His Majesty's Opposition, 1714–1830* (Clarendon Press: Oxford, 1964)

Forrester, E.G., *Northamptonshire County Elections and Electioneering, 1695–1832* (Oxford University Press: 1941)

Forster, E.M., *Marianne Thornton, 1797–1887* (Arnold: 1956)

Fraser, D. (ed.), *A History of Modern Leeds* (Manchester University Press: Manchester, 1980)

Furneaux, R., *William Wilberforce* (Hamilton: 1974)

Gash, N., 'Brougham and the Yorkshire Election of 1830' in *Pillars of Government and other essays on State and Society, c.1770–c.1880* (Arnold: 1986), pp. 77–92

George, M.D., *Catalogue of Political and Personal Satires ... in the British Museum*, vols 5–11 (British Museum: 1935–54)

Gibb, M.A. and F. Beckwith, *Yorkshire Post: Two Centuries* (Yorkshire Conservative Newspaper Co.: Leeds, 1954)

Girouard, Mark, *Life in the English Country House* (Yale University Press: New Haven, 1978)

Gooder, A. (ed.), *Parliamentary Representation of the County of York, 1258–1832*, Yorkshire Archaeological Society Record Series, vol. 91 (1935) and vol. 96 (1938)

Grego, Joseph, *History of Parliamentary Elections and Electioneering from the Stuarts to Queen Victoria* (Chatto & Windus: 1892)

Hague, W., *William Wilberforce. The Life of the Great Anti-Slave Trade Campaigner* (Harper Perennial: 2008)

Haigh, E.A.H. (ed.), *Huddersfield. A Most Handsome Town* (Kirklees Cultural Services: Huddersfield, 1992)

Halévy, Elie, *History of the English People in 1815* (1912; reprinted, Penguin Books: 1937)

Hall, R. and S. Richardson, *The Anglican Clergy and Yorkshire Politics in the Eighteenth Century*, Borthwick Papers no. 94 (Borthwick Institute: York, 1998)

Hallett, M. and J. Rendall (eds), *Eighteenth-century York: Culture, Space and Society* (Borthwick Institute: York, 2003)

Hammond, J.L. and B. Hammond, *Skilled Labourer, 1760–1832* (1919; second edn, Longmans: 1920)

Hanson, T., 'Diary of a Grandfather: Cornelius Ashworth, of Waltroyd, Wheatley', *Halifax Antiquarian Society Papers* (1916), 233–48

Harford, J.S., *Recollections of William Wilberforce* (1864)

BIBLIOGRAPHY

Hargreaves, J.A., *Halifax* (Edinburgh University Press and Carnegie Publishing: Lancaster, 1999)

Hargreaves, J.A. and E.A.H. Haigh (eds), *Slavery in Yorkshire. Richard Oastler and the Campaign Against Child Labour in the Industrial Revolution* (University of Huddersfield Press: Huddersfield, 2012)

Harris, A., *The Rural Landscape of the East Riding of Yorkshire, 1700–1850* (Oxford University Press: 1961)

Harvey, A.D., *Britain in the Early Nineteenth Century* (Batsford: 1978)

Hawkin, R.Y., *History of the Freemen of the City of York* (City of York Guild of Freemen: York, 1955)

Heaton, Herbert, 'Leeds White Cloth Hall', *Thoresby Society Miscellanea*, 22 (Thoresby Society: Leeds, 1915), 131–71

Heaton, Herbert, *Yorkshire Woollen and Worsted Industries* (Clarendon Press: Oxford, 1920; 2nd edn, 1965)

Hempton, D., *Methodism and Politics in British Society, 1750–1850* (Hutchinson: 1984)

Hey, D., *Yorkshire from AD 1000* (Longman: Harlow, 1986)

Hill, B. W., *British Parliamentary Parties, 1742–1832* (Allen & Unwin: 1985)

Hinton, M., 'The General Elections of 1806 and 1807', unpublished Ph.D. thesis (University of Reading, 1959)

Hirst, J.F., 'William Wilberforce, A Commemorative Sketch', *Yorkshire Notes and Queries*, 2:5 (August 1905), 142–9

Hobhouse, Christopher, *Fox* (Constable: 1947)

Huddleston, M.A., *History of Malton and Norton* (G.A. Pindar & Son: Scarborough, 1962)

Hussey, Christopher, *English Country Houses: Early Georgian, 1715–1760* (Country Life: 1955)

Hussey, Christopher, 'Milton, Northamptonshire', *Country Life*, 129:3350–3352 (18 and 25 May, 1 June 1961), 1148–51, 1210–13, 1270–4

Ingledew, C.J. Davison, *History and Antiquities of North Allerton* (Bell & Daldy: 1858)

Jackson, Gordon, *Hull in the Eighteenth Century* (Oxford University Press: 1972)

James, David, *Bradford* (Ryburn: Halifax, 1990)

Jennings, Judith, *The Business of Abolishing the British Slave Trade, 1783–1807* (Cass: 1997)

Jephson, Henry, *The Platform: Its Rise and Progress*, 2 vols (Macmillan: 1892)

Johnson, L.G., *General T. Perronet Thompson, 1783–1869* (Allen & Unwin: 1957)

Jones, G.P., 'Political Reform Movement in Sheffield', *Hunter Archaeological Society Transactions*, 4 (1937), 57–68

Jones, John, *History and Antiquities of Harewood* (Simpson, Marshall & Co.: 1859)

Judd, G.P., *Members of Parliament, 1734–1832* (Yale University Press: New Haven, 1955)

Jupp, Peter, *British and Irish Elections, 1784–1831* (David & Charles: Newton Abbot, 1973)

Keir, D.L., 'Economical Reform, 1779–1787', *Law Quarterly Review*, 50 (1934), pp. 368–85

Lascelles, George, 7th Earl of Harewood, 'Harewood House', York Georgian Society Annual Report (1970), pp. 39–43

Lean, Garth, *God's Politician* (Darton, Longman & Todd: 1980)

Leys, M.R., *Catholics in England, 1559–1829: A Social History* (Longmans: 1961)

Linton, D.L. (ed.), *Sheffield and Its Region: A Scientific and Historical Survey* (British Association: Sheffield, 1956)

Loch, A., 'The Electoral Management of the Yorkshire Election of 1784', *Northern History*, 47:2 (2010), 271–96

Lyth, J., *Glimpses of Early Methodism in York and … District* (William Sessions: York, 1885)

Maccoby, S., *English Radicalism, 1786–1832* (Allen & Unwin: 1955)

McCormack, M., *The Independent Man: Citizenship and Gender Politics in Georgian England* (Manchester University Press: Manchester, 2005)
McKenzie, K., '"My voice is sold, & I must be a Slave": Abolition Rhetoric, British Liberty and the Yorkshire Elections of 1806 and 1807', *History Workshop Journal* 64:1 (2007), 48–73
Markham, John, *The 1820 Parliamentary Election at Hedon: A Study of Electioneering in a Yorkshire Borough before the Passing of the Reform Act* (J. Markham: Beverley, 1971)
Mathieson, W.L., *England in Transition, 1789–1832: A Study of Movements* (Longmans: 1920)
Mauchline, Mary, *Harewood House* (David & Charles: Newton Abbot, 1974)
Mee, Graham, *Aristocratic Enterprise: The Fitzwilliam Industrial Undertakings, 1795–1857* (Blackie: Glasgow, 1975)
Milnes, R.M., 'Wentworth Woodhouse and Its Owners', *Yorkshire Archaeological and Topographical Journal*, 6 (1881), 343–84
Mingay, G.E., *English Landed Society in the Eighteenth Century* (Routledge & Kegan Paul: 1963)
Morrell, J.B., *Biography of the Common Man of the City of York As Recorded in His Epitaph* (Batsford: 1947)
Namier, L. and J. Brooke, *History of Parliament. The House of Commons, 1754–1790*, 3 vols (Oxford University Press: 1964)
Navickas, K., '"That sash will hang you": Political Clothing and Adornment in England, 1780–1840', *Journal of British Studies*, 49:3 (July 2010), 540–65
O'Gorman, F., *Whig Party and the French Revolution* (Macmillan: 1967)
O'Gorman, F., *The Emergence of the British Two-Party System, 1760–1832* (Arnold: 1982)
O'Gorman, F., *Voters, Patrons and Parties. The Unreformed Electorate of Hanoverian England, 1734–1832* (Clarendon Press: Oxford, 1989)
O'Gorman, F., 'Campaign Rituals and Ceremonies: the social meaning of elections in England, 1780–1860', *Past & Present*, 135 (May 1992), 79–115
O'Gorman, F., *The Long Eighteenth Century. British Political and Social History, 1688–1832* (Arnold: 1997)
Ormrod, W.M. (ed.), *The Lord Lieutenants and High Sheriffs of Yorkshire, 1066–2000* (Wharncliffe Books: Barnsley, 2000)
Pakenham, Thomas, *Year of Liberty: The Story of the Great Irish Rebellion of 1798* (Hodder & Stoughton: 1969)
Pares, Richard, *Historian's Business and Other Essays* (Clarendon Press: Oxford, 1961)
Paterson, Alexander, 'Yorkshire Journalism in the Eighteenth Century', in *Old Yorkshire*, ed. William Smith, new series 2 (Longmans: 1890), pp. 182–95
Patterson, M.W., *Sir Francis Burdett and His Times (1770–1844)*, 2 vols (Macmillan: 1931)
Peel, Frank, *Risings of the Luddites, Chartists and Plug-Drawers* (Senior & Co.: Heckmondwike, 1888, 4th edn, Cass: 1968)
Peel, Frank, *Spen Valley: Past and Present* (Senior & Co.: Heckmondwike, 1893)
Penson, L.M., 'London West India Interest in the Eighteenth Century', *English Historical Review*, 36 (1921), 373–92
Pevsner, Nikolaus, *Buildings of England: Northamptonshire* (Penguin Books: Harmondsworth, 1961)
Phillips, J.A., *Electoral Behaviour in Unreformed England. Plumpers, Splitters, and Straights* (Princeton University Press: Princeton, 1982)
Phillips, J.A., *The Great Reform Bill in the Boroughs. English Electoral Behaviour, 1818–1841* (Clarendon Press: Oxford, 1992)
Phillips, N.C., *Yorkshire and English National Politics, 1783–1784* (University of Canterbury Publications: Christchurch, 1961)
Plumb, J.H., *First Four Georges* (Batsford: 1956)

Pollock, J., *Wilberforce* (Constable: 1977)
Porritt, Edward, *Unreformed House of Commons: Parliamentary Representation Before 1832*, 2 vols (Cambridge University Press: Cambridge, 1903, reprinted Kelley: New York, 1963)
Quinn, J.F., 'Yorkshiremen Go to the Polls: County contests in the early eighteenth century', with a computer analysis of election results, 1734 and 1742 by P. Adman, W.A. Speck and B. White, *Northern History*, 21 (1985), 137–74
Ragatz, L.J., *Fall of the Planter Class in the British Caribbean* (Century: New York, 1928)
Ragatz, L., *Old Plantation System in the British West Indies* (Educational Research Bureau: Washington, D.C., 1953)
Rallings, C. and M. Thrasher (eds), *British Electoral Facts, 1832–2006* (Ashgate: Aldershot, 2007)
Rayner, S., 'Great Yorkshire Election Contests', in *Old Yorkshire*, ed. W. Smith, vol. 1 (Longmans: 1881), pp. 120–1
Read, Donald, 'North of England Newspapers (c.1700–c.1900) and their Value to Historians', *Leeds Philosophical and Literary Society Proceedings*, vol. 8:3 (1957), 200–15
Read, Donald, *Press and People, 1790–1850: Opinion in Three English Cities* (Arnold: 1961)
Read, Donald, *English Provinces c.1760–1960: A Study in Influence* (Arnold: 1964)
Reid, Robert, *Land of Lost Content. The Luddite Revolt, 1812* (Heinemann: 1986)
Rimmer, W.G., 'Leeds and Its Industrial Growth: 2. Historical Survey', *Leeds Journal*, 24:11 (1953), 391–4
Rimmer, W.G., *Marshalls of Leeds, Flax-Spinners, 1788–1886* (Cambridge University Press: Cambridge, 1960)
Robson, R.J., *Oxfordshire Election of 1754* (Oxford University Press: 1949)
Rowntree, John Stephenson, 'Samuel Tuke', *Friends' Quarterly Examiner* (April 1895), pp. 3–6
Royal Commission on Historical Monuments (England), *Inventory of the Historical Monuments in the City of York*, 5 vols (HMSO: 1962–81)
Rutherford, R., 'A Distinguished West Indian House', *West India Committee Circular*, 21:172 (5 January 1906), 10–11
Sanderson, F.E., 'Liverpool Abolitionists', in *Liverpool, the African Slave Trade and Abolition*, eds Roger Anstey and P.E.H. Hair (Historic Society of Lancashire and Cheshire: Liverpool, 1976)
Sessions, W.K. and E.M. Sessions, *Tukes of York* (William Sessions: York [1971])
Sigsworth, E.M., 'Leeds and Its Industrial Growth: 8. The Leeds Cloth Halls', *Leeds Journal*, 25:11 (1954), 415–18
Singleton, Fred, *Industrial Revolution in Yorkshire* (Dalesman: Clapham, 1970)
Smith, E.A., 'Earl Fitzwilliam and Malton: a Proprietory Borough in the Early Nineteenth Century', *English Historical Review*, 80 (1965), 51–69
Smith, E.A., 'Yorkshire Elections of 1806 and 1807: a study in electoral management', *Northern History*, 2 (1967), pp. 262–90
Smith, E.A., *Whig Principles and Party Politics: Earl Fitzwilliam and the Whig Party, 1748–1831* (Manchester University Press: Manchester, 1975)
Smith, H.S., *Parliamentary Representation of Yorkshire* (J.R. Smith: 1854)
Smith, Juliet, *Shell Guide to Northamptonshire and the Soke of Peterborough* (Faber: 1956)
Smith, R.W., 'Political Organization and Canvassing: Yorkshire Elections Before the Reform Bill', *American Historical Review*, 74 (1969), pp. 1538–60
Smith, S.D., *Slavery, Family and Gentry Capitalism in the British Atlantic. The World of the Lascelles, 1648–1834* (Cambridge University Press: Cambridge, 2006)
Smith, William (ed.), *Old Yorkshire*, first series, vols 1–5 (Longmans: 1881–84); new series, 3 vols (Longmans: 1889–91)

Spring, David, 'Earl Fitzwilliam and the Corn Laws', *American Historical Review*, 59:2 (1954), 287–304

Stapylton, H.E. Chetwynd, *Stapletons of Yorkshire* (Longmans: 1897)

Stirling, A.M.W., *Annals of a Yorkshire House from the Papers of a Macaroni and His Kindred* (J. Lane: 1911)

Sykes, Christopher, *Four Studies in Loyalty* (Collins: 1946)

Tait, Hugh, 'Sèvres Porcelain in the Collection of the Earl of Harewood', *Apollo*, 83:52 (June 1966), 437–43

Taylor, E.R., *Methodism and Politics, 1791–1851* (Cambridge University Press: Cambridge, 1935)

Taylor, R.V., *Yorkshire Anecdotes* (Whittaker: 1887)

Teale, A.M, 'Methodism in Halifax and District, 1780 to 1850' unpublished M.Sc. thesis (University of Bradford, 1976)

Thomas, P., *John Wilkes. A Friend to Liberty* (Clarendon Press: Oxford, 1996)

Thomis, M.I. and P. Holt, *Threats of Revolution in Britain, 1789–1848* (Macmillan: 1977)

Thompson, E.P., *Making of the English Working Class*, (Gollancz: 1963; 2nd edn, Pelican Books: Harmondsworth, 1968)

Thompson, F.M.L., *English Landed Society in the Nineteenth Century* (Routledge & Kegan Paul: 1963)

Thorne, R.G. (ed.), *History of Parliament. The House of Commons, 1790–1820*, 5 vols (Secker & Warburg: 1986)

Thornton, D., *Mr Mercury. The Life of Edward Baines, 1774–1848* (Merton Priory Press: Chesterfield, 2009)

Tomkins, S., *William Wilberforce: A Biography* (Lion: Oxford, 2007)

Trevelyan, G.M., *History of England* (Longmans: 1926; 3rd edn, repr. 1948)

Turberville, A.S. and F. Beckwith, 'Leeds and Parliamentary Reform, 1820–1832', *Thoresby Society Miscellany*, vol. 12 (Thoresby Society: Leeds, 1954)

Turner in Yorkshire, ed. D. Hill *et al.* (York City Art Gallery: York, 1980)

Tylor, Charles, *Samuel Tuke; His Life, Work, and Thoughts* (Headley Brothers: 1900)

Veitch, G.S., *Genesis of Parliamentary Reform* (Constable: 1913, reprinted 1965)

Victoria History of the County of York, ed. W. Page, 3 vols (Constable: 1913)

Ward, Bernard, *Eve of Catholic Emancipation*, 3 vols (Longmans: 1911–12)

Ward, J.T, 'The Earls Fitzwilliam and the Wentworth Woodhouse Estate in the Nineteenth Century', *Yorkshire Bulletin of Economic and Social Research*, 12 (1960), 19–27

Ward, J.T., *East Yorkshire Landed Estates in the Nineteenth Century* (East Yorkshire Local History Society: York, 1967)

Webb, R.K., *Modern England from the Eighteenth Century to the Present* (Allen & Unwin: 1971)

Whellan & Co., *History and Topography of the City of York; and the North Riding of Yorkshire*, 2 vols (Beverley, 1857)

White, R.J., *Age of George III* (Heinemann: 1968)

Wilberforce, Yvette, *William Wilberforce, An Essay* (C.E. Wrangham: 1967)

Williams, Eric, *Capitalism and Slavery* (University of North Carolina Press: Chapel Hill, 1944)

Wilson, R.G., *Gentlemen Merchants: The Merchant Community in Leeds, 1700–1830* (Manchester University Press: Manchester, 1971)

Yorkshire Notes and Queries (Bingley, 1888; Bradford, 1905)

Index

A

Abbot, Charles, 1st Baron Colchester 105
abolition of slavery 102, 105, 112, 153, 157, 257
abolition of the slave trade 3, 50, 51, 53, 55, 56, 59, 62, 65, 71–3, 78, 90, 92, 109, 111, 112, 114, 126, 128, 135, 137, 140, 148, 150, 157–9, 175, 176, 178, 179, 185–91, 193, 198, 199, 202, 204, 208, 209, 263, 278
Accrington 231
Acklam Hall 134
Act of Union (1800) 90
Adam, William 49, 261
Addingham 222
Addington, Henry, 1st Viscount Sidmouth 62, 91, 260
advertisements, advertising 49, 71, 81, 141, 156, 180, 181, 195, 199, 201, 281
Adwicke 148, 250
Africa, Africans 71, 123, 125, 157, 158, 175, 178, 185, 189, 204, 218, 227
agriculture 21, 22, 24, 30–2, 74, 105, 107, 237, 274
Airton 224
Aislabie, William James 120; Aislabie family 16
Aldborough 14, 15, 17, 279
Alexander, Lewis 147, 152, 172
Allanson, Charles Winn, 2nd Baron Headley 163, 269, 270, 271
Allanson, Elizabeth 18

Allen, John 236
Allerton Mauleverer 143
Alverley Grange 148
America 4, 39, 41, 186, 256; War of Independence 17, 33–7, 89, 103, 122, 192
Amherst, Dowager Lady Elizabeth 134
anti-Catholicism 54, 86, 89, 90, 95, 96, 150, 164, 176, 191, 192, 194. *See also* anti-popery; popery
anti-slave trade 102, 125, 272, 188, 196, 216
anti-slavery 4, 6, 39, 92, 113, 116, 185, 186, 190, 191, 193, 195, 204–6
Appleby 17, 188
apprentices, apprenticeship 1, 14, 23, 25, 27, 141, 151, 279
aristocracy, aristocrats 6, 20, 22, 35, 37, 53, 65, 77, 86, 100, 110, 111, 148, 190, 191, 259, 273
Armley 26, 183
Armytage, Sir George 58, 77
artisans 4, 16, 23, 24, 37, 274, 275, 276, 285
Ashworth, Cornelius 25
Assembly Rooms, York 35, 156, 252, 257
Association for the Preservation of Liberty and Property Against Republicans 55
Athorpe, Robert 45, 55
Atkinson, Benjamin 284

301

Atkinson, George 250
Atkinson, Robert 250
Atkinson, Thomas, 127

attorneys 47, 121, 133, 143, 147, 148, 166.
  See also lawyers, solicitors
Austerfield 232

B

Babington, Thomas 178, 207
Bailey, Rev. James 148
bailiffs 274
Baillie, Charles, Archdeacon of Cleveland
  126, 134
Baines, Edward 109, 126, 131, 138, 139,
  143, 150, 268
bakers 276
ballads 110, 141, 259. *See also* songs
Baltic 13, 32, 113, 248
Baptists 89, 95, 194, 247
Barbados 37, 99, 102-4, 139, 187-91, 217
Barnsley 60, 142, 143, 148, 246, 267
Bartholoman, Alexander 181, 281
Bawtry 276
Bayley, Sir John 167
beast jobbers 274
Beauclerk, Aubrey, Earl of Burford 51
Beaumont, Richard Henry 128
Beckett, John 27
Bedale 45, 224, 267
Beeforth 226
Belasyse, Henry, 1st Earl of Fauconberg
  41, 42, 44
Belasyse [Thomas Edward Wynn] 120
Bell, Johnny 119, 241
Bell, Robert 222
bells 34, 57, 67, 111, 145, 153, 252, 261,
  262
Benson, John 174
Bernard, George 69
Bessborough, Lady Henrietta Frances
  Ponsonby 242
Bethell, Richard 135, 278
Bethell, William 235
Beverley 15, 32, 51, 60, 82, 83, 119, 135,
  155, 168, 178, 226, 231, 246, 265, 274;
  elections 82
Bible Society 110, 113, 176, 193
Billingley 262
Billymen 56, 136, 276

Bilton in Ainsty 231
Bingley 198
Binks, Thomas 222
Birmingham 179
Birstall 149
Blakeman, William 284
Blanchard, William 181, 281
Bonaparte, Napoleon 25, 54, 95, 200
bookkeepers 274
Boroughbridge 15, 17, 220, 279
Bower, Robert 270, 271
Bowes 222
Bowns, Charles 49, 74, 142, 147, 166, 215,
  266, 282, 284
Bradford 1, 14, 29, 34, 50, 60, 66, 68, 70,
  77, 128, 131, 139, 149, 150, 168, 195,
  198, 203, 212, 221, 223, 245, 279
Bramber 258
Bramham Park 136
Bramley 183
Bramley, John 128
Bramley, Richard Ramsden 70, 130, 151,
  183, 184
bribery 82, 121, 135, 169, 170, 191, 213,
  251, 266, 267, 269, 270, 284
bricklayers 226
Bridlington/Burlington 31, 95, 127, 133,
  143, 145, 177, 226, 261
Brighthelmstone 179
Brisco, Edward Dyne 143
Broadley, Robert C. 127; Broadley family
  30
broadsheets, broadsides 7, 94, 123, 135,
  180, 187, 215
Brompton 142
Brook, John 166
Brookfield, Charles 244
Brougham, Henry 236, 278
Bubwith 144
Buckinghamshire 247
Burdett, Sir Francis 17, 232

Burgh, Dr William 49, 66, 124, 174, 197, 198, 203, 216
Burke, Edmund 18, 22, 39, 40, 41, 49, 53, 63, 163, 203

Burton Constable 135
Burton, Lt General N.C. 82
butchers 119, 162, 223, 241, 246, 275, 276

C

Calverley 261
Cambridgeshire 247
Canning, George 93, 158, 197
canvassing 6, 13, 18, 30, 38, 43, 46, 50, 61, 65, 66, 68–70, 73–5, 77–80, 81, 83, 84, 97, 98, 100, 111, 119–22, 124–8, 133–7, 142–6, 153, 160, 162, 163, 169, 175, 187, 196–8, 202, 203, 208, 209, 213, 220, 224, 228, 230–2, 234–6, 241, 247, 267, 270, 272, 281
capitalism 2, 26, 62, 71, 137, 159, 266
Carey, Henry Thomas, 7th Viscount Falkland 142
Carleton, Guy, 1st Baron Dorchester 109, 152
Carlisle, Earls of. *See under* Howard
Carlton 223
Carnelley, Thomas 224
carpenters 248, 275, 284
Carr, Charles 267
Carr, John 42, 103, 155
Carr, William 79, 142
Castle Howard 119, 220
Castle Yard 13, 42, 46, 56, 58, 60, 75, 78, 122, 134, 147, 155, 156, 158, 159, 161, 167, 171, 182, 184, 192, 212–15, 217, 220, 226, 230, 236, 237, 241–3, 246, 247, 249, 250, 252, 254–6, 279, 286
Castlereagh, Lord. *See* Stewart, Robert
castrators 274
Catholic relief 52, 53, 58, 62, 86, 88–93, 95, 98, 105, 110, 157–9, 162, 185, 186, 191, 193, 194, 195, 196, 197, 207, 263
Catholics, Catholicism 18, 52, 53, 85, 89, 90, 91, 93, 95, 134, 135, 141, 144, 150, 160, 166, 169, 184, 193–7, 200, 251
Cattle, Robert 181, 280
Cautley, Rev. William 181
Cavendish, Lord John 42, 44, 47, 82

Cavendish, William, 5th Duke of Devonshire 16, 58, 143, 285
Cavendish, William George Spencer, Marquess of Hartington 143, 232
Cavendish-Bentinck, William, 3rd Duke of Portland 41, 49, 53, 54, 88, 91, 93, 97, 132, 158
Cayley, Sir George 142, 146
Chadwick, Thomas 284
chairing ceremony 7, 46, 47, 58, 67, 241, 243, 256, 257, 262, 283
Chaloner, William 134
Cheshire 247
chimney sweepers 274
Cholmley, Henry 72
Church and King 86, 97, 273
Church of England 18, 20, 57, 85, 86, 89, 94, 100, 110, 112, 126, 128, 129, 131, 132, 136, 148, 150, 153, 154, 160, 169, 176, 192–4, 196, 197, 228, 248, 251, 274, 276
Clapham Sect 115
Clarence, Prince William, Duke of [later William IV] 23, 49
Clarke, Robert 135
Clarkson, John 178
Clarkson, Thomas 51, 56, 102, 178, 186, 187
Clayton 262, 267
Cleckheaton 136
clergymen 18, 21, 30, 35–7, 65, 67, 68, 84, 86, 91, 95, 98, 106, 108, 111, 114, 116, 120, 128, 130, 133, 134, 144, 148, 150, 152, 153, 161, 173, 175, 178, 179, 181, 186, 187, 196–8, 216, 227, 228, 230, 243, 248, 249, 251, 261, 262, 268, 271, 274–7, 285
clerks 274
Cleveland 135, 172, 219

Cloth Hall trustees (Leeds) 1, 66, 70, 77, 129, 138, 139, 149, 236, 257, 262
cloth halls 1, 25, 26, 28, 62, 273; Bradford, Piece Hall 29, 198; Halifax, Piece Hall 13, 25, 29, 50, 59, 67, 77, 128, 136, 143, 152, 153, 284; Huddersfield 29, 77, 153, 245; Leeds 60, 65, 66, 70, 77, 129, 137, 139, 151; Leeds, Mixed Cloth Hall 28, 77, 137, 183, 236, 257, 262; Leeds, White Cloth Hall 1, 27, 28, 137, 138, 149, 150, 160; Wakefield, Tammy Hall 30; Plate 7
cloth industry 223, 224, 275. *See also* woollen industry; worsted industry
cloth workers 1, 2, 7, 58, 149, 275. *See also* croppers; weavers
clothiers 1–4, 6, 21, 22, 24–6, 46, 56, 62, 65, 66, 69–71, 76–8, 100, 106, 125, 136–43, 149, 151, 157, 164, 172, 176, 183, 188, 192, 199, 200, 201, 202, 204, 207, 212, 216, 218, 222, 223, 233, 236, 237, 246, 254, 256, 257, 262, 263, 265, 266, 272, 273, 275–7, 279, 285; Plate 2
clothing districts 20, 56, 58, 75, 78, 136, 143, 272
coalitions: Fox-North 41, 42, 44, 201; Lascelles-Wilberforce 65, 99, 129, 173, 174, 176, 185, 201–9, 213, 217, 218, 229, 230, 239, 240, 242, 243, 250, 254, 255, 272; Pittite-Yorkshire Association 43, 45, 46, 98, 113, 201, 259. *See also* Ministry of All the Talents
Cobbett, William 169, 263
Cocking, Joseph 245
Codd, Edward 133, 135, 220
coffee houses 33, 34, 151, 180, 235, 266; Swift's Coffee House (York) 182, 247
Combination Acts 27, 279
combinations of workmen 27, 51, 62, 71
Coniston 43
Constable Burton 34
Constable family 30, 135

Constitution 22, 51, 56, 64, 78, 92, 93, 100, 118, 123, 129, 130, 138, 150, 153, 159, 162, 213, 218, 259, 262, 278
constitutionalism 108, 266
contested elections 4, 177
Conyngham, Elizabeth, Dowager Countess 179
Cooke, Bryan 79, 148, 163, 164, 216, 246, 253, 269–71, 285
Cookson, Robert 1, 65, 66, 138, 151
Cookson, William 56, 62, 70, 76, 128, 130
Copperthwaite, Samuel Henry 208
Corbett, Joseph, Archdeacon of Shrewsbury 178
Corbett, Rev. Stuart 130
cordwainers 275
Cornwall 209, 247, 278
Cornwallis, Charles, 1st Marquess 158
Cornwallis, Admiral Sir William 179
corruption 35, 51, 82, 94, 217, 278
Cottingham 32
cotton industry 1, 25, 231, 275, 276
Coulthurst, Rev. Dr William 67, 68, 128, 130
county meeting 35, 41–3, 56, 74, 94
Courthope, George 167
cow doctors 274
craftsmen 4, 82, 136, 156, 274, 275
Craven 265
Crewe, John, 1st Baron 234
Creyke, Ralph 56, 127, 140, 177, 226
Croft, Stephen 38, 47
croppers 3, 26–8, 151, 152, 237, 285
Crosland, Joshua 133
Crosley, John 198
Crossland, John 225
Crossland, Joshua 222
Crown 16, 20, 33, 34, 37, 39, 85, 91, 92, 94, 98, 131, 144, 197, 231
Cumberland 247
Cunnynghame, Sir William 253
Cusworth Hall 148
cutlers 276, Plate 1; Cutlers Company 66, 128, 130, 276

INDEX

D

Davy, Dennis 247
Dawes, William 178
Dawney, Henry Pleydell, 3rd Viscount Downe 22
Dawney, John, 5th Viscount Downe 234
Dawson, George 144
Dawson, William 281
deaths 40, 41, 61, 64, 82, 90, 101, 103, 104, 109, 113, 114, 144, 146, 214, 219, 228, 241, 242, 282, 284
Deighton, Thomas 281
Delaface, Thomas 147
Delph 222
Denby Grange 136
Denison, William Joseph 83, 84, 164, 165, 234, 246, 285; Denison family 30
Dennis, Amos 247
Dent 168, 221
Denton, Francis 246
Derbyshire 12, 247
Derwent Navigation 269
Devonshire, Duke of. *See* Cavendish, William
Dewsbury 29, 66, 133, 149, 168, 246
Dickens, Henry John 167
Dickinson, Stephen 133, 135
dinners 49, 50, 55, 58–60, 66, 78, 84, 145, 164, 197, 215, 243, 256, 257, 262, 263, 265, 266
Dissenters 37, 47, 52, 69, 71, 85, 150, 154, 192, 197. *See also* Nonconformists
dissenting ministers 18, 117, 251, 274
disturbances 1, 17, 27, 54–6, 82, 95, 180, 183, 184, 225, 227, 233, 241, 242, 244, 245, 247, 263, 269, 286. *See also* Gordon Riots

disturbing the peace of the county 75, 81, 129, 135, 213, 243
Dixon, Rev. James 148
Dixon, Robert 228
domestic industry 1, 2, 3, 25, 29, 62, 71, 77, 159, 185, 273, 276
Doncaster 47, 60, 108, 124, 136, 142, 148, 167, 168, 172, 175, 178, 216, 220, 228, 232, 250, 262, 271, 276, 279, 281, 284, 285; *Doncaster Gazette* 175
Dorsetshire 248
Drake, Thomas 245
Driffield 66, 248
Driffield, Mary 283, 284
drink 82, 84, 111, 147, 169, 170, 180, 183, 209, 215, 227, 248, 262, 267, 282–4. *See also* treating
duels 232, 242, 271
Duncombe Park 38, 127
Duncombe, Charles 40, 57, 58, 127, 177, 225
Duncombe, Henry 38, 44, 45, 46, 47, 50, 51, 56, 57, 60
Duncombe, Thomas 38
Duncombe, William 225, 278
Dundas, Charles 170
Dundas, Henry 164
Dundas, Henry, 1st Viscount Melville 45, 64, 150, 160, 213, 224
Dundas, Lawrence 72, 79, 92, 162, 197
Dundas, Rev. Thomas 187
Dundas, Robert Lawrence 163, 269
Dundas, Sir Thomas, 1st Baron Dundas 16, 53, 63, 72, 109, 134, 152, 163, 170, 172, 173, 175
Durham 12, 248
Dykes, Rev. T. 95, 175

E

Easingwold 133, 172, 173
East India Company 15, 41, 44, 103
East Retford 145
East Riding xv, 13, 20, 30, 31, 46, 65, 66, 72, 74, 76, 78, 126, 127, 129, 133, 135, 140, 142–4, 147, 162, 168, 200, 203, 207, 215, 251, 265, 272, 275, 276, 280, 283

305

Eastwood, Jonathan 284
Economical Reform 36, 39
Edwards, John 67, 68, 128, 130
Egerton, John William, 7th Earl of Bridgewater 135
elderly and disabled voters 172, 246, 247, 283
Eldon, Lord. *See* Scott, John
election agents 18, 36, 46, 49, 51, 66, 69, 70, 72, 74, 75, 85, 99, 100, 106, 117, 119–22, 124–7, 133–7, 142–4, 146–8, 152, 165, 166–9, 171–4, 182, 201, 203, 205, 209, 215, 218–26, 229, 231, 232, 239, 241, 243, 244, 246–51, 253, 265–70, 280–2
election analysis 265, 271–8
election colours: blue 40, 112, 122, 123, 162, 206, 212, 215, 218, 224, 245, 253, 268, 269, 281; orange 3, 86, 122, 123, 145, 183, 215, 218, 228, 232, 240, 245, 250, 256, 260, 262, 264; yellow 164, 209, 216, 264
election literature 6, 78, 149, 208, 216, 243. *See also* broadsheets; handbills; placards; posters; squibs

election petitions 169, 170, 261, 264, 266–8, 271
election propaganda 4, 123, 217, 236, 272. *See also* scribblers
election rituals 6–8, 67, 78, 213. *See also* street theatre
election symbols 3, 6, 27, 59, 81, 84, 122, 123, 131, 134, 145, 180, 183, 203, 209, 218, 224, 228, 231, 247, 256, 260, 262, 281–3
elections 6, 7, 8, 13, 16, 17, 18, 256, 275. *See also* under individual constituencies
Elizabethan statutes 1, 2, 27, 71, 277, 279
Elliot, William 63, 234, 260
England, Thomas 267
Etridge, Thomas 148
Evangelicals 50, 70, 110, 112, 116, 176, 192
Ewbank, Thomas 251
expenditure 4, 15, 38, 45–7, 65, 72, 73, 76, 78, 82, 84, 97, 99, 111, 114, 133, 135, 136, 146, 147, 161, 167, 170, 171, 173–5, 180, 204, 215, 220–3, 234, 248, 267, 270, 271, 279–85
Eyre, Vincent 148

F

factories 1, 25–8, 62, 63, 151, 192, 237, 272, 276
factory owners 3, 273, 274
Fairgray, John 282
farm workers 267
farmers 28, 31, 120, 136, 144, 224, 226, 228, 247, 248, 274, 276
Farnley Hall 57, 69, 97
Farsley 183
Fawkes, Frances 261
Fawkes, Walter 57, 58, 65, 67–79, 83, 86, 92, 97–100, 119, 129, 131, 138, 140, 142, 145–50, 152, 158, 159, 161, 165, 185, 234, 254, 263
Fenton, William 213, 246
Ferrand, Benjamin 128
Ferrybridge 172, 225
Filey 31
Firth, Matthew 267

fishmongers 274
Fitzwilliam, Charles William Wentworth, Viscount Milton 3, 7, 8, 13, 18, 59, 63–5, 78–80, 86, 92, 98, 99, 105, 106–11, 119–27, 131, 133–53, 156–8, 160, 161, 163, 166–8, 170–6, 179–84, 185–8, 190–2, 195–210, 212–37, 239–42, 244–57, 260–85; Plate 5
Fitzwilliam, William, 1st & 3rd Earl 21
Fitzwilliam, William Wentworth, 2nd & 4th Earl 3, 5, 14, 18, 21, 27, 40–7, 49–56, 58, 59, 62–4, 68, 69, 72, 74–80, 83, 84, 91, 92, 97–9, 101, 104, 106–10, 113, 119, 120, 130, 137, 140–2, 145, 149, 161–4, 172, 175, 179, 185, 188, 191, 196, 197, 201–3, 207, 210, 212, 217, 218, 224, 229, 232, 234, 243, 246, 253, 255, 259–61, 264, 269–71, 276–8, 280, 282, 285

Fitzwilliam, Countess Charlotte 106, 119, 145, 203
Fitzwilliam, George 40
Fixby 195, 222
flags 123, 145, 188, 225, 227, 232, 244, 256, 262, 283
Foljambe, Francis Ferrand 41, 45, 46, 47, 55, 233
Forster, John 246
Fowler, George 248
Fox, Charles James 13, 18, 41, 42, 44–7, 49, 51–5, 61, 62, 64, 65, 72, 74, 78, 84–6, 90, 109, 132, 160, 185, 201, 260
Fox, James Lane 136
France 30, 33, 56, 90, 93; French Revolution 48, 51, 52, 53, 55, 89, 108, 112, 192, 273
Frank, Bacon 127, 157, 213, 252
Frankland, Sir Thomas 15, 120
freeholders 4, 7, 13, 16, 20, 21, 31, 35, 39, 42, 44, 58, 65, 71, 74, 75, 77, 78, 84, 90, 98, 110, 117, 121, 122, 128, 131, 134, 136, 142, 144, 149, 168, 170, 172, 173, 175, 177, 180–2, 185, 188–91, 195, 198, 200, 205, 206, 209, 210, 213, 216–22, 224, 226, 227, 229, 231, 235, 241, 242, 245, 247, 250, 252, 254, 261, 262, 264, 267, 272, 277, 279
freemen 14, 15, 18, 21, 22, 39, 82, 162, 164, 200, 227
Friends. *See* Quakers

G

galloway horse 24
Galway, Lord. *See* Monckton-Arundel, Robert
Gambier, Admiral James, 1st Baron 179
gamekeepers 274
Gascoigne, Sir Thomas 46, 56, 225
Gascoyne, General Isaac 263
Gawthorpe estate 103
general elections 42, 45, 50, 57, 58, 61, 64, 81, 93, 96, 186. *See also* elections
gentlemen 21, 183, 226, 248
gentry 21, 22, 31, 34, 37, 65, 69, 100, 111, 136, 148, 156, 194, 221, 274–6
George I 86
George II 35, 86
George III 16, 22, 34, 36, 37, 39, 41, 42, 45–9, 55–9, 61, 65, 75, 78, 85, 86, 88, 90–5, 97, 100, 103, 122, 123, 125, 130, 132, 136–8, 152, 153, 157–9, 162, 169, 184, 186, 188, 193, 196, 197, 199, 200, 202, 207, 213, 217, 223, 231, 238, 252, 255, 259, 262, 263, 276
George, Prince of Wales 42, 49, 51, 83, 104, 108, 261
gig mills 1, 26, 28, 151, 237, 279
Gilbert, Nathaniel 178
Gillray, James 88, 233
Gisborne, Rev. Thomas 178
Gisburne Park 265
Glorious Revolution (1688) 22, 51, 52, 85, 86, 89, 122, 137, 150, 153, 214
Gloucester, Prince William Frederick, Duke of 261
Gloucestershire 1
Godfrey, Sarah 284
Gomersal 267
Gordon Riots 39, 89, 110, 122
Gott, Benjamin 26, 28, 151
Graeme, John 127, 226
Grampound 278
Grant family 178, 230
Grant, John 1, 138
Grantham, Lord. *See* Weddell, Thomas Philip
Grattan, Henry 79, 163
Gray, Jonathan 122, 166, 193, 219, 241, 247, 249, 251, 252
Gray, William 36, 38, 46, 48, 51, 60, 66, 122, 124, 219, 230, 247, 257
Greaves, George Bustard 130
Green, Luke 223
Green, Samuel 167
Greenup, William 130
Grenville, Lord. *See* Wyndham, William
Greta Bridge 133, 157, 198

Grey, Charles, Viscount Howick 64, 90, 91, 92, 109, 234, 259, 260
Grimston family 30, 127
Grimston, Robert 192, 202

grocers 274
Guisborough 101, 134, 173
Gully, John 241

H

habeas corpus 51, 105
Hailstone, Samuel 70
hairdressers 274
Halfpenny, William 167
Halifax 1, 13, 14, 25, 29, 59, 67, 68, 71, 77, 95, 128, 130, 136, 137, 147, 152, 160, 168, 172, 192, 205, 219–21, 228, 244, 250, 261, 262, 265, 279; *Halifax Journal* 67, 130, 137, 181, 244
Hall, Samuel 119, 251
Hall, William 284
handbills 65, 72, 78, 81, 88, 121, 123, 125, 131, 134, 135, 137, 138, 152, 180, 189, 192, 199, 203, 216, 217, 227, 236, 242, 281, 283
Hanover 41, 86, 169
Hardcastle, Joseph 178
Hardy, John 157, 167, 203
Harewood estate 103
Harewood family. *See* Lascelles
Harewood House 21, 37, 57, 58, 59, 60, 68, 69, 73, 99, 103, 104, 131
Harewood village 133
Harland, Thomas 226
Harrison, Thomas 249
Hartley, David 38, 46
Hastings, William 147, 163, 269, 270
hatters 248
Hawes 228
Hawke, Edward, 3rd Baron 143, 233
Hawke, Martin Bladen 233
Hawksworth, Francis 45, 77, 148, 233
Haworth 184
Headlam, Rev. John 133
Headley, Lord. *See* Allanson, Charles Winn
heckling 6, 7, 95, 158, 183, 233, 241
Heckmondwike 66, 136
Hedon 15, 51, 81, 147, 279; election 8
Hertfordshire 101, 248

Heslington xiii, 127
Hewitt, W.N.W. 159
Hey, William 51, 56, 59, 66, 130, 178, 193
Heywood, John 149, 167, 284
Heywood, Samuel 167
Hick, John 160
High Town 228
Higham Ferrers 63, 111, 188, 191
Hildyard, Sir Robert D'Arcy 35, 45, 157, 213, 217, 255; Hildyard family 30
Hill, Sir Richard 115, 179
Hilyard, Rev. Henry 134
Hoare family 178
Holderness 15, 31, 43, 135, 147, 231, 251
Holland, Lord. *See* Vassall-Fox, Henry Richard
Holmes, Charles 72
Honiton 169
Honley 245
Hooton Pagnell 261
Horbury 142
Horne, Rev. Melvill 178
horse racing 7, 22, 34, 49, 51, 63, 81, 82, 108, 117, 146, 156, 217–19, 233, 241, 256, 264, 271, 283
Horton, Bradford 223
Horton, Col. Thomas 130, 143, 160
Hotham, William 182
Howard, Charles, 11th Duke of Norfolk 44, 55, 58, 81, 148, 202, 207, 234, 265, 276
Howard, Henry, 4th Earl of Carlisle 20
Howard, Frederick, 5th Earl of Carlisle 43, 44, 119, 220, 261, 269
Howard, George, Viscount Morpeth 278
Howard, Richard, 4th Earl of Effingham 37, 55, 143
Huddersfield 1, 29, 60, 66, 70, 77, 127, 128, 130, 133, 137, 153, 166, 168, 172, 221, 222, 229, 236, 244, 279

INDEX

Huddleston, Rev. Wilfred 148
Hull 15, 22, 30, 31, 35, 38, 42, 43, 46, 51, 60, 82, 83, 95, 110, 112, 113, 117, 125, 127, 129, 133, 135, 140, 148, 155, 161, 164, 167, 168, 170, 172, 174, 181, 186, 205, 217, 220, 222, 226, 227, 230, 231, 262, 265, 271, 279; elections: (1780) 15, 83, 114, 129, 241; (1784) 83, 114; (1802) 83; (1806) 83, 84; (1807) 15, 164, 165; *Hull Advertiser* 94, 158, 165, 181; *Hull and Lincolnshire Chronicle* 181; *Hull Packet* 181
Hunmanby 91, 127, 148, 226
hunting 66, 68, 71, 101, 108, 145, 188
Huntingdonshire 120, 248
husbandmen 274
hustings 6, 17, 46, 50, 59, 73, 78, 84, 109, 119, 128, 138, 149, 157, 158, 160, 167, 180, 207, 213, 215, 219, 226, 233, 243, 254, 256, 286; Plate 9
Hustler, Thomas 134
Hutchinson, Joseph 245
Hutton Buscel 18, 145, 146, 226, 269

I

independence (concept) 6, 7, 13, 20, 21, 25, 30, 31, 34, 38, 47, 51, 59, 66, 68, 73, 76, 84–6, 92, 112, 118, 121, 125, 128–32, 139, 142, 144, 147, 150, 153, 154, 158, 160, 163, 164, 176–8, 191, 195, 202, 206–8, 213, 217, 218, 237, 238, 240, 241, 258, 259, 262, 263, 265, 273, 277
Independents 194
industrial areas 14, 37, 52, 71, 103, 128, 149, 153, 157, 194, 277
industrial revolution 3, 22
industrialists 37
Ingram, Frances, Viscountess Irwin 136, 177
Innes, Charles 253
innkeepers 8, 146, 160, 170, 171, 173, 220, 224–6, 241, 282
inns and taverns 33, 45, 66, 67, 126, 127, 134, 155, 172, 180, 197, 199, 214, 215, 220, 221, 227, 230, 262, 267, 281–3; (Delph) New Inn 222; (Doncaster) Red Lyon Inn 172; (Halifax) Talbot Inn 59, 77, 153; White Swan Inn 67, 244; (Huddersfield) George Inn 153, 244, 245; Ramsden Arms 245; (Hull) Cross Keys Inn 280; Neptune Inn 140; (Leeds) Bull and Mouth Inn 184, 285; (London) Crown and Anchor 235, 263; London Tavern 178; St Alban's Tavern, Pall Mall 234; (Malton) Head Inn 145; (Sheffield) Angel Inn 67, 244; Tontine Inn 153, 262; (Skipton) Black Horse Inn 224, 267; (Tadcaster) Angel Inn 225; (York) Bird in Hand 283; Black Swan 181, 264; Bluitt's Tavern 45, 46, 148; Etridge's Hotel 78, 123, 148, 156, 202, 225, 233, 252, 257, 283; George Inn 21, 72, 133, 181, 192, 216, 256, 257, 281; Old George Inn 282; Robin Hood Inn 226; York Tavern 35, 36, 45, 47, 60, 72, 78, 126, 226, 243, 257, 280
intimidation 120, 195, 223–5, 241, 242, 269, 271, 277
Ion, Rev. George 144
Ireland 40, 53, 54, 58, 63, 79, 90–2, 107, 141, 158, 164, 184, 188, 193, 194, 196–8, 248, 256, 285
iron industry 21, 23, 24, 26, 29, 66, 105, 137, 178, 223, 224, 247, 272, 275, 277. *See also* metal industries
ironmasters 128, 148, 223
Iveson, James 251
Iveson, William, 15, 147, 251

309

J

Jackson, Jonas 228
Jackson, Joseph 236
Jackson, William Ward 134
Jacobins 27, 54, 57, 152, 164, 187, 199, 259, 277

Jamaica 102, 103, 105
Jarratt, William 127
Jay, Rev. William 117, 193
Johnson, Sir Richard 177
Johnstone, Lady Margaret 222

K

Kaye, John Lister 68, 136
Keighley 147, 168, 247, 267
Kendal 249
Kent 248
Kilham 226
Kilham, Alexander 57
Kilvington, Rev. Edward 128

Kirby Ravensworth 247
Kirk Ella 32
Kirkby Malhamdale 224
Kirkhammerton 282
Kirkleatham 134
Knaggs, Thomas 133, 134
Knaresborough 16, 38

L

labourers 30, 195, 278
Lancashire 1, 12, 25, 231
land agents 120, 274
land tax 16, 46, 126, 143, 144, 168, 182, 249, 250, 281
landed classes 13, 20–2, 30, 31, 65, 68, 76, 95, 100, 113, 120, 137, 151, 271, 273, 274, 277
landed interest 17
landlords 22, 31, 37, 84, 120, 127, 223, 270, 276, 277
landowners 30, 31, 46, 134, 157, 194
Lascelles family 21, 37, 70, 101, 102, 103, 134, 188, 191
Lascelles, Daniel 38
Lascelles, Edward, 1st Earl of Harewood 2, 4, 57, 58, 99, 101, 102, 104, 105, 129, 131, 132, 160, 190, 195, 209, 215, 217, 261, 264, 270, 280, 285
Lascelles, Edward ('Beau') 57, 101, 104, 105, 129, 137, 186, 192, 264
Lascelles, Edwin 22, 37, 38, 57, 103, 104
Lascelles, Henry (b. 1713) 37
Lascelles, Henry 1–4, 7, 15, 24, 26, 27,
57–60, 61–79, 83, 86, 96, 97–106, 110, 111, 119, 120, 122, 125–40, 141–4, 147–51, 156–61, 164, 166, 167, 171–4, 179–92, 195–210, 212–18, 220–6, 228–31, 233–8, 239, 240, 242–56, 259–61, 264–83; Plate 4
Laurence, Dr French 63, 98, 108, 109, 285
Law, William 283
Lawson, Sir John 89
lawyers 49, 120, 131, 170, 179, 214, 249, 251, 268. *See also* attorneys, solicitors
Leatham, Isaac 163, 164, 269, 270
Lee, Richard 143, 149, 262
Lee, Thomas 268
Leeds 1, 14, 20, 22, 26–9, 33, 34, 36, 37, 47, 51, 54, 56, 57, 59, 65, 66, 70, 77, 95, 100, 103, 104, 106, 109, 128–30, 133, 141–3, 147, 149, 157, 160, 167, 168, 171, 172, 178, 183, 189, 195, 203, 220, 221, 224, 229, 241, 244, 245, 257, 262, 265, 268, 279, 284; *Leeds Intelligencer* 33, 38, 71, 73, 88, 92, 95, 126, 138, 141, 150, 152, 158, 161,

181, 183, 240, 242, 259, 277, 281, 285; *Leeds Mercury* 16, 33, 36, 47, 64, 71, 75, 126, 128, 131, 138, 139, 143, 150, 152, 161, 181, 183, 184, 195, 213, 240, 254, 268, 270, 272. *See also under* cloth halls
Leefe, Edward 270
Leeming 226
Legard, Digby 127
Leicestershire 248
Levitt, Qarton 95
Lightfoot, Christopher 226
Lincoln, Lincolnshire 84, 248
linen drapers 234, 274
linen industry 31, 275, 276
Lister, Thomas, 1st Baron Ribblesdale 265
Liverpool 175, 185, 263; elections 263
Liversedge 136

local election committees 121, 127, 130, 173, 201, 215, 221, 225
Lockwood, John 251
Lockwood, William 133
Lofthouse 173
London 12, 17, 30, 33, 37, 39, 49, 55, 73, 84, 122, 149, 167, 175, 177–9, 197, 203, 214, 227, 230, 231, 233–6, 241, 246, 251, 253, 263, 266, 268, 277, 283, 285; *London Courier* 93
London Corresponding Society 55
Lowe, Rev. John 111, 148, 153, 216, 243, 262, 268
Lowther, William, 1st Earl of Lonsdale 120
loyalism 42, 43, 45, 55, 57, 74, 79, 89, 93, 94, 130, 131, 138, 153, 208, 218, 259, 273
Luddites, machine-breaking 1, 279
Lumley, Frederick 153, 261

M

Macaulay, Zachary 178
machinery 266, 277, 279
magistrates 30, 55, 70, 73, 89, 244, 245
Maister, Henry 35, 127
Malton 14, 18, 46, 63, 79, 111, 145, 147, 148, 162–4, 178, 185, 269, 270; elections 21, 163, 271
Manchester 172, 187, 231, 236, 248
Manners, John Henry, 5th Duke of Rutland 16
manufacturers 28, 62, 130, 139, 151, 274, 277, 278
Market Weighton 284
Markham, George, Dean of York 70
Markham, Robert, Archdeacon of York 70, 73
Markham, William 69
Markham, William, Archbishop of York 69, 70, 197
Markington 43
Marshall, John 278
Marske 173
Martin, Roger 224
Martin, Samuel 95, 125

Marton 127, 134, 226
Marton Lodge 134
Mason, William 35, 38, 42
Maude, Francis 142, 167, 268
mechanics 276
Mellish, Henry Francis 232, 233, 241, 262
Melsonby 226
merchants 1, 2, 21, 22, 25–8, 30, 32, 34, 37, 39, 43, 45, 50, 62, 66, 68, 69, 77, 83, 95, 100, 104, 105, 107, 113, 114, 126, 127, 130, 136, 138, 139, 141, 143, 149, 150, 151, 156, 157, 183, 185, 195, 199, 200, 222, 232, 238, 245, 248, 265, 268, 269, 272–6
Melville, Lord. *See* Dundas, Henry
metal industries 22, 274–6. *See also* iron industry
Metcalf, Cuthbert 147, 267
Methley Park 143
Methodism, Methodists 18, 29, 50, 57, 60, 69, 71, 113, 125, 130, 144, 162, 176, 178, 187, 192, 193, 194–6, 204–6; New Connexion 57, 194, 195
Middlesex 5, 13, 34, 227

311

military officers 30, 89, 90, 121, 179, 274
millers 223, 226, 267
Milner, Rev. Isaac 114
Milner, Sir William 47, 49, 51, 72, 79, 92, 162
Milnes, Richard Slater 45, 47, 51, 58, 162
Milton House 63, 110, 111, 264
Milton, Lady Mary 63, 109, 161, 234, 260, 262
Milton, Northamptonshire 49, 107
Milton, Viscount. *See* Fitzwilliam, Charles William Wentworth
Ministry of All the Talents 62, 83, 88, 90–2, 186, 193, 208; Plate 3
Mirfield 222
Mitchell, Charles 225
mole-catchers 274
Monckton-Arundel, Robert, 4th Viscount Galway 14, 40, 47, 51
Montagu, Matthew 253
More, Hannah 179, 230, 257
Morning Chronicle 93, 94, 131, 190, 266
Morning Post 272
Morritt, John Bacon Sawrey 157, 160, 213, 229
Moxon, R.W. 95
Munkhouse, Rev. Dr Richard 130
Murray, Lindley 71
music, musicians 67, 78, 81, 111, 124, 145, 153, 155, 180, 203, 225, 232, 244, 256, 262, 264, 274, 283, 284
Myton Hall 278

N

Naylor, Jeremiah 130
Naylor, John 128, 130
Naylor, Joseph 128
Newby Hall 46, 136
Newcastle, Duke of. *See* Pelham-Holles, Thomas
Newcastle upon Tyne 248
Newman, William 147
newspapers 33, 34, 42, 48, 49, 65, 66, 71, 78, 92, 98, 121, 126, 127, 131, 133, 149, 158, 159, 179–81, 186, 199, 206, 207, 209, 215, 222, 231, 234, 236, 247, 270, 271, 277. *See also* individual titles
Nicholson, Lucas 66, 106, 133, 135, 151, 184
Nicoll, Samuel W. 142, 167, 273
No Popery 39, 77, 86, 88, 93, 96, 98, 149, 162, 163, 184, 185, 191–200, 209, 260, 263, 265, 272, 278. *See also* anti-Catholicism
nobility. *See* aristocracy
nomination day 6, 46, 58, 59, 67, 72, 78, 83, 84, 124, 126, 129, 134, 135, 139, 141, 146, 153, 155–65, 166, 169, 171, 175, 192, 203, 212, 213, 215, 263
Nonconformists 89, 91, 116, 192. *See also* Dissenters
Norfolk 188, 248
Norfolk, Duke of. *See* Howard, Charles
Normanby 134
North Cave 60
North Riding xiv, 13, 20, 30, 31, 34, 46, 66, 72, 74, 78, 126, 127, 133, 134, 142–4, 147, 152, 157, 168, 172, 181, 198, 215, 217, 265, 272, 275, 276, 280, 283
Northallerton 15, 38, 101, 103, 104, 148, 264, 265, 270, 278, 279
Northamptonshire 40, 49, 63, 97, 107, 110, 232, 248, 278
Northumberland 248, 259
Northumberland, Duke of. *See* Percy, Hugh
Norton, Conyers 143, 234
Nottinghamshire 12, 232, 248

O

Oastler, Richard 7, 195
Oastler, Robert 195, 250
oaths 18, 91, 144, 166–9, 250, 251
Oldham 248
Orange Jumper 218, 233; Plate 10
Osbaldeston, George 44, 145–7
Osbaldeston, Humphrey 127, 226
Osbaldeston, Mrs Jane 18, 145, 146, 254, 262, 269, 270

Osborne, George William Frederick, 6th Duke of Leeds 45, 224
Osborne, Robert 167
Otley 74, 148, 224
outvoters 120, 168, 229, 231, 233, 234, 236, 247, 248
Overend, Robert 267
Owen, Rev. John 179
Oxford 179
Oxfordshire 248

P

Paine, Thomas 24, 52, 54, 56, 57, 194, 195
Papists 88, 92, 93, 144, 153, 162, 191, 196, 197, 199. *See also* Catholics, Catholicism
Parker, Hugh 148, 153
Parliament 2, 34, 37, 41, 42, 45, 53, 55, 59, 62, 69, 89, 91–4, 109, 150, 159, 189, 259, 292, 293, 297; House of Commons 1, 2, 4, 6, 12–14, 16, 18, 22–4, 35–7, 39, 41–3, 48, 50–2, 55, 57, 59, 61, 62, 70, 74, 77, 78, 82, 83, 85, 86, 90, 92, 93, 97, 99, 102–6, 109, 110, 112, 113, 115–17, 122, 126, 130, 137–9, 141, 142, 146, 150–2, 158, 169, 170, 175, 178, 185–90, 201, 202, 209, 210, 213, 231, 237, 258, 263, 264, 266, 271, 272; House of Lords 22, 41, 48, 91, 92, 94, 106, 109, 110, 150, 164, 185, 213, 278
parliamentary reform 3, 23, 33, 35–7, 40, 48, 52, 54, 62, 64, 73, 98, 110, 165, 169, 195, 276, 278
Parrott, John 267
Patrick, Richard 175
patriotism 46, 47, 74, 79, 88, 93, 145, 147, 177, 202, 208, 213, 218
patronage 16, 37, 82, 85, 92, 93, 103, 232
Paul, Thomas 251
Paull, James 232
Payley [Paley], John Green 223

peace 52, 54, 56, 65, 105, 125, 135
Peacock, George 181, 281
Peel, Robert 231
Pelham-Holles, Thomas, 1st Duke of Newcastle 14, 15, 17
Perceval, Spencer 90, 91, 124, 159, 160, 178, 197
Percy, Hugh, 2nd Duke of Northumberland 220
Peterborough 63, 107, 278
Petre, Lady Juliana 120
Petty, William, 2nd Earl of Shelburne 39, 41
Phipps, Henry, 1st Earl of Mulgrave 16, 106
Pickering 31, 133, 221
Pierse, Henry 45
pig iron tax 24, 66, 105, 137
Piper, John 133, 221
Pitt, William (the younger) 17, 18, 24, 27, 40–8, 50, 51, 53–8, 61–4, 66, 74, 78, 85, 86, 90, 94, 99, 103, 105, 106, 113, 117, 125, 129, 132, 136, 142, 158, 159, 203, 207, 276
Pittites 43, 45, 46, 55, 69, 78, 83, 91, 95, 100, 119, 199, 201, 259
placards 157
Plumer, Sir Thomas 230
Plummer, Thomas 47
plumpers 15, 18, 65, 121, 125, 128, 134, 142, 144, 147, 173, 174, 176, 183,

201–3, 206, 207, 212, 216, 217, 220–31, 234–6, 239, 247, 248, 251, 254, 256, 262, 264, 267, 277, 280, 281, 284; Plate 11
political parties 20, 22, 41, 43, 52, 77, 85, 86, 112, 131, 150, 153, 180, 188, 248, 260, 273. *See also* Tories; Whigs
poll books 4, 19, 167, 168, 220, 223, 236, 247, 273, 278; Plate 12
poll clerks 166–8, 214, 250
Pollard, William 131
polling booths 46, 134, 166–8, 182, 184, 212, 214, 215, 218, 219, 223, 226, 228, 229, 231, 245–7, 249, 250, 252, 254, 265, 281, 282, 286; Plate 9
Pomerania 248
Pontefract 14, 60, 95, 120, 143, 168, 178, 241
Poole, George 223
popery 93, 95, 122, 138, 158, 185, 188, 191, 194, 195, 196, 199, 200, 209, 258, 271. *See also* anti-Catholicism; No Popery

population 12, 15, 23, 31, 155
Portland, Duke of. *See* Cavendish-Bentinck, William
posters 78, 81, 123, 125, 134, 138, 152, 153, 180, 256
Powell, William 251
Presbyterians 65, 85, 89, 141, 194
Price, Rev. W. 179
Priestman, Thomas 71
printers, printing 3, 8, 33, 34, 126, 142, 180, 181, 217, 279, 281, 283
prisons, prisoners 34, 50, 155, 183, 240, 241, 264, 286
professional men 17, 36, 121, 127, 136, 265, 274
public houses 49, 62, 198, 226, 232, 233, 281, 283. *See also* inns and taverns
public opinion 178, 192
publicans 146, 170, 228, 241, 283, 284. *See also* innkeepers
Pudsey 149, 183, 223, 256
Pullan, Richard 268

Q

Quakers 71, 72, 78, 89, 125, 150, 167, 176, 177, 178, 187, 193, 196, 198, 199, 204, 206, 239

R

Radcliffe, Joseph 70, 77, 127, 244, 245
radicals, radicalism 55–7, 169, 276.
 See also parliamentary reform
Ramsbotham, Henry 212, 221
Rawmarsh 262
Rawson, William 128
Read, John 223
Reader, William 167, 214
Reading 179
Readshaw 221
Redcar 173
Reform Act (1832) 81, 278, 279
regency crisis 49

repression in 1790s 52, 55, 58, 105, 116, 276
retail and wholesale trades 274
Rhodes, Robert 197, 283, 285
Richmond 16, 134, 220–2, 226, 265, 266
Rimington & Wake (Sheffield solicitors) 133
Riot Act 184, 245
Ripon 16, 18, 95, 127, 143, 163, 168, 177, 265, 282
Rise 135
Robson, Robert Smith 146
Rockingham 22, 271

Rockingham Club 21, 40, 44, 47, 49
Rockingham, 1st Marquess.
    See Watson-Wentworth, Thomas
Rockingham, 2nd Marquess.
    See Watson-Wentworth, Charles
Rockinghamites 22, 38
Rogers & Shearwood (Sheffield solicitors) 147
Romilly, Samuel 186
Roscoe, William 263
Rose, George 105
Rotherham 21, 23, 37, 55, 60, 65, 107, 143, 168, 224, 276
Rothwell 246
Rothwell, William 128
rotten boroughs 12, 16, 17, 48, 98
Royston, W. 147
Rudd, Bartholomew 134
Russell, David 117, 127, 174, 207, 243
Rylah, Thomas 133

S

Saddleworth 70, 77, 172, 196, 222, 246
St John, St Andrew, 14th Baron St John 234
St Quintin family 30
'Saints' 83, 92, 112, 116, 170, 193, 204, 206, 230, 235
Saltmarshe family 30
Sandwith, Robert 174, 175
Saunders, George 248
Savile, Sir George 21, 36, 37, 38, 41, 83, 89, 153, 158, 160
Savile, John, 2nd Earl of Mexborough 143
Savile, John, Lord Pollington 143
Sawdon, Thomas 133, 134
Scarborough 16, 20, 31, 44, 95, 103, 105, 126, 133, 146, 155, 172, 196, 222, 223, 226, 281
Scarthingwell 233
Scatcherd, Tom 68, 83, 84, 96, 226, 250, 252, 253
Schofield, John 142
schools, schoolmasters 31, 83, 110, 177, 274
Scotland 209, 246, 248
Scott, John, 1st Earl of Eldon 202, 226
Scott, William Fenton 213, 251
scribblers, scribbling committees 142, 152, 180, 207, 216, 234
Sculcoates 133
seamen 263, 274
Selby 103, 120, 136, 227
Settle 249
Sharp, Joseph 147
Sheardown, William 279
shearing frames 26, 28, 279
Sheffield 14, 22–4, 55, 60, 65, 66, 81, 95, 127, 128, 130, 133, 137, 147, 148, 153, 154, 168, 175, 178, 224, 225, 229, 244, 262, 265, 269, 275, 276, 279, 283, 284; *Sheffield Iris*, 93, 129, 154, 159, 181, 257, 277
Sheffield Constitutional Society 23
Shelburne, Lord. *See* Petty, William
Sheldon, William 251
shepherds 274
Sheridan, Richard Brinsley 84, 98
sheriff 35, 45, 46, 56, 102, 122, 157, 160, 166, 167, 212–15, 249, 254; deputy sheriff 167, 168, 214, 215, 251, 254; undersheriff 122, 166, 167, 241
shoemakers 267
shopkeepers 136, 144, 231, 274, 285
Shore, John, 1st Baron Teignmouth 178
Shore, Samuel 148
Shropshire 178, 248
Sidmouth, Lord. *See* Addington, Henry
Sierra Leone Company 178
silk mercers 274
Sinclair, Robert 58, 72, 76, 100, 142, 167
Skelton 173
Skelton Castle 134
Skipsea 267
Skipton 221, 222, 224, 232, 262, 267, 284
slave trade 65, 78, 102, 135, 137, 157, 186, 189–92, 208, 263
slaves, slavery 3, 7, 37, 59, 71, 79, 102,

125, 137, 138, 157, 160, 185, 187, 191, 193, 195, 196, 198, 200, 205, 217, 257
Slingsby, Sir Thomas (4th Bt) 38
Slingsby, Sir Thomas Turner (8th Bt) 133
Slingsby, Sir Thomas (9th Bt) 264
smallholders 16, 21, 25, 273
Smith, J.R. 264
Smith, Rev. Sydney 106, 108, 116, 227
Smith, Samuel 177
Society for Constitutional Information 23
Society for the Suppression of Vice 110, 113
solicitors, 127, 133, 146, 147.
   See also attorneys, lawyers
Somersetshire 1, 248
songs 164, 180, 187, 199, 202, 208, 246, 272, 281. *See also* ballads
Sorby, John 128
Sparrow, J. 281
Spencer, George John, 2nd Earl 234
Spencer, John Charles, Viscount Althorp 110, 232
Spencer, Marmaduke 222
splitters, split votes 125, 134, 148, 173–5, 216, 218, 221, 223, 224, 227, 253, 280
Spofforth 228
squibs 68, 121, 134, 180, 181, 189, 197, 209, 232, 281
squires 36, 50, 126, 127, 228, 262, 276, 285
Stacey, Charles 248
Staffordshire 248
Stanhope, John Spencer 97
Stanhope, Marianne 79, 97
Stanhope, Philip Henry, Viscount Mahon 165
Stanhope, Walter Spencer 19, 42, 44, 46, 48, 51, 56, 75, 128, 141, 227
Staniforth, John 83, 84, 95, 165
Stanningley 183, 225
Stanwix 220

Stapylton, Martin 278
Stapylton, Sir Myles 20
state of the poll 214–18, 229, 231, 236, 237, 239, 252–4
Steele, Thomas 94, 150
Stephen, James 178, 230, 257
Stewart, Robert, Viscount Castlereagh 158, 197
Stockton-on-Tees 134, 161, 198
Stokesley 134, 173, 219
Stourton, Charles Philip, 17th Baron 143
Stowe, William 149
street theatre 6, 156
Strickland, Lady Elizabeth Laetitia 145, 261, 262
Strickland, Sir George 267
Strickland, Sir William 20
Strong, William, Archdeacon of Northampton 285
Stuart, Thomas 228
Studley Royal 120
subscriptions 37, 38, 46, 73, 78, 108, 175–9, 198, 199, 213, 215, 235, 236, 268
Sudbury 188
sugar 37, 102–5, 123, 282
surveyors 274
Sussex 146, 248, 258
Sutton in Holderness 207
Sutton, Rev. Thomas 130
Swailes, William 247
Swire, Dr Samuel 226
Sykes family 30, 83, 127
Sykes, Daniel 83, 84, 165, 167, 230, 262
Sykes, Rev. Christopher 271
Sykes, Rev. Richard 84, 95, 148, 161, 230, 261
Sykes, Sir Christopher 44
Sykes, Sir Mark Masterman 66, 162, 163, 197, 200, 271
Sykes, Sir Tatton 30

T

Tadcaster 147, 172, 183, 225, 233, 267
Tarleton, General Banastre 263
Taylor, David 133

Temple Newsam 136
tenants 30, 31, 37, 110, 111, 120, 135, 147,

161, 163, 172, 195, 220, 223–5, 246, 269, 270, 274
Test and Corporation Acts 51, 60, 89
Tewkesbury 179
The Times 124, 190, 191, 210, 219, 253
theatres 51, 82, 117; Theatre Royal, York 156, 252, 264 *See also* street theatre
Thellusson, Peter Isaac, 1st Baron Rendlesham 203, 235, 236
Thirsk 15, 102, 172, 195, 279
Thompson, Beilby 81
Thompson, Thomas 129, 161, 230
Thorne 174
Thornhill, Thomas 195, 222
Thornton le Clay 231
Thornton, Henry 114, 115, 170, 178, 179, 206, 207, 230, 236, 242, 255, 257
Thornton, John 165
Thornton, Marianne 116
Thornton, Robert 230, 236, 257
Thornton, Samuel 46, 83, 84, 257
Thorpe, Anthony 251
Tickhill 276; Tickhill Castle 153, 261
Tindal, William 222
tinplate workers 248
Tobago 105
toleration 85, 86, 90, 93, 153, 154, 160, 192, 193, 195, 199, 204, 205, 278; Toleration Act (1689) 89
Tomlinson, Martin 228
Tomlinson, Matthew 227
Tong 246
Tooker, Samuel 55

Tories 20, 22, 28, 47, 62, 83, 85, 86, 92, 114, 122, 123, 132, 162, 176, 192, 207, 255, 263, 271, 278
Tottie, Thomas William 142, 143, 147, 171, 182, 183, 285
tradesmen 16, 31, 37, 49, 82, 89, 104, 224, 277
transport, transportation 3, 8, 32, 33, 46, 103, 119, 126, 127, 134, 145, 149, 152, 153, 167, 170–4, 177, 182–4, 210, 214, 217, 219–25, 227, 228, 232, 234–7, 246, 249, 281–4
Travers & Woodhall (Scarborough solicitors) 133, 281
treason 52, 151, 169; Treason and Sedition Acts 55, 56, 117, 192, 278
treating 135, 169, 170, 212, 222, 264, 266, 267, 269, 270
troops 89, 90, 105, 184, 244, 245, 272, 274; militia 30, 74, 101, 172; Volunteers 54, 74, 82, 153, 172, 183, 241; yeomanry 54, 63. *See also* military officers
Tufton, Sackville, 9th Earl of Thanet 143, 232, 261
Tuke family 199
Tuke, Henry 199
Tuke, Samuel 199, 239
Tuke, William, 71, 177, 199
Turner, J.M.W. 20, 73, 104
Turner, Sir Charles 40, 82, 134
Turner, Cholmondeley 20

U

unharnessing of horses 40, 49, 62, 66, 67, 77, 124, 145, 149, 152, 153
Unitarians 126, 278
United States. *See* America

unpolled voters 13, 47, 54, 192, 215, 218, 219, 226, 231, 236, 245, 248–51, 253, 254
unskilled workers 275

V

Valentine, George 179

Vane, William Harry, 3rd Earl of Darlington 143

Vansittart, George 179
Vansittart, Nicolas 179
Vassall-Fox, Henry Richard, 3rd Baron Holland 18, 64, 74, 193, 197, 236, 259, 260
Vavasour family 30
Vernon, Henry 143
violence 183, 184, 195, 197, 241, 272
Vyse, Lt General Richard 82

W

Waddilove, Robert Darley, Dean of Ripon 120, 127
Wadkin, John 187
Wakefield 1, 3, 20, 29, 34, 45, 60, 66, 70, 77, 95, 128, 130, 131, 136, 137, 143, 149, 167, 168, 172, 195, 220, 221, 227, 244, 262, 265, 267, 268, 279, 281, 284; *Wakefield Star* 77, 128, 179, 181
Walker, James 224
Walker, John 270, 271
Walker, Joshua 224
Walker, Samuel 128
Walker, Thomas 224
Walker, William 36, 137
wapentakes xiv, xv, 36, 121, 127, 134, 166, 167, 168, 173, 218, 219, 231, 248, 275, 282: Agbrigg 168, 229, 250, 275, 284; Ainsty 13, 135, 168; Allertonshire 168; Barkston Ash 168; Birdforth 168; Buckrose 168; Bulmer 168, 198; Claro 168; Dickering 168; Ewecross 168, 265; Gilling East 168; Gilling West 168, 222; Halikeld 168; Hang East 168; Hang West 168, 282; Harthill 168; Holderness 168; Howdenshire 168; Langbargh 168, 173; Morley 168, 229, 250, 275, 276; Osgoldcross 168; Ouse and Derwent 168; Pickering Lythe 46, 146, 168, 254, 281; Ryedale 168; Skirack 168, 275; Staincliffe 168, 265; Staincross 168; Strafforth and Tickhill 168, 219, 229, 237, 250, 262, 275, 276, 277, 278; Whitby Strand 168
war 33, 34, 51, 53, 54, 62, 93, 105, 112, 125, 137, 192, 275, 278
Ward, William 134, 221, 226
Warde, St Andrew 261
Ware, Rev. John 198
Warwickshire 248
Waterhouse, John 130
Watson, Percival 167
Watson, Shepley 148
Watson-Wentworth, Thomas, 1st Marquess of Rockingham 21, 107
Watson-Wentworth, Charles, 2nd Marquess of Rockingham 14, 18, 21, 22, 34, 35, 37–41, 44, 46, 49, 78, 83, 89, 107, 111, 146, 158, 160, 217, 277
weavers 24, 25, 56, 58, 195, 223, 224, 275
Weddall, Edward 144
Weddell, Elizabeth 255
Weddell (previously Robinson), Thomas Philip, 3rd Baron Grantham 136
Weddell, William 46, 47
Wentworth 148, 246
Wentworth Castle 143
Wentworth Woodhouse 21, 49, 50, 73, 83, 98, 107, 108, 110, 111, 141, 142, 149, 152, 202, 216, 237, 254
Wentworth, Charles Mary 179, 234
Wentworth, Peregrine 254
Wesley, John 57, 194
West Ayton 144
West Ella 32
West Indies 3, 7, 37, 102, 104, 158, 179, 186, 190, 206, 209, 257
West of England 2
West Riding xv, 7, 12, 20–2, 25, 26, 29, 30, 40, 42, 46, 50, 55–8, 63, 66, 70, 74, 77–9, 101, 103, 105, 106, 126, 127, 130, 133, 136, 140, 142, 143, 147, 149, 152, 156–8, 160, 168, 172, 186, 189, 194, 201, 204, 208, 212, 215, 218, 225, 228, 244, 252, 253, 262, 265, 275, 276, 279, 280, 282, 284
Westbury 105, 264, 270, 281
Westminster 215, 227, 232, 286

Westmoreland 248
Wetherby 18, 147
Wharton, John 82, 134
Whigs 20–2, 33, 34, 37, 39, 40, 43, 45–53, 57, 61, 62, 68, 72, 77–9, 84–6, 89, 90, 92, 96, 103, 107, 109, 122, 125, 131, 136, 140, 149, 153, 176, 181, 186, 188, 190, 192, 195–7, 218, 236, 237, 253, 259, 260, 263, 266, 271, 273, 276, 278
Whitby 31, 125, 133, 134, 172, 221, 247, 279
Wilberforce, William 2–7, 15, 24, 32, 39, 40, 42–8, 50, 51, 55–60, 61, 62, 64–79, 83, 86, 90, 92, 96, 97, 99, 100, 102, 105, 110, 111–19, 120, 122, 124–31, 133, 134–7, 139–44, 147, 150, 157–63, 166, 167, 172–7, 179–82, 185–8, 190–6, 198–210, 212–18, 220–31, 233–7, 239–46, 248–57, 261, 265–8, 270, 271, 274–8, 280–2; Plate 6
Wilkes, John 5, 34, 35, 40
Wilson, Richard Fountayne 122, 157, 254, 278
Wilson, Thomas 49
Wiltshire 1, 26, 27, 105, 248, 264
Windham, William 188, 191, 203, 234
Wolley, Edward 69, 72, 133–5, 166, 182–4, 215, 253, 280
women 6, 18, 19, 28, 80, 97, 119, 120, 123, 145, 156, 161, 163, 164, 177–9, 220, 222, 228, 230, 232, 234, 256, 260, 262, 283, 285

Womersley 143, 233
Wood, Catherine 175
Wood, Sir Francis Lindley 158, 213
Wood, Thomas 284
Wood, William 244
Woodlesford 223
Wool Committee 65, 137, 140; Report 2, 4, 18, 27, 62, 70, 140, 185
woolcombers 276
Wooldale 284
Wooler, John 222
woollen industry 1, 2, 7, 22, 24, 25, 29, 33, 62, 76, 105, 137, 140, 151, 185, 266, 273, 276, 279; legislation 50, 105, 159, 279. *See also* Elizabethan statutes
worsted industry 7, 29
Wortley 183
Wortley, James Stuart 130, 224, 265, 278
Wrangham, Rev. Francis 91, 148, 150, 152, 161, 186, 196, 249
Wright, Griffith 126, 150, 181, 281
Wright, Peter 127
Wrightson, William 148, 161, 174, 213
Wroughton, George 148, 172
Wyndham, George O'Brien, 3rd Earl of Egremont 136, 144
Wyndham, William, 1st Baron Grenville 62, 64, 65, 67, 74–6, 83, 88, 90–2, 94, 186, 193, 196, 260
Wyvill, Rev. Christopher 34, 35, 41–3, 48, 50, 54, 56, 98, 148

Y

Yarburgh, Henry 127
Yarm 134, 173, 187, 223, 249
yeomen 31, 121, 144, 147, 228, 248, 273, 274, 285
York 13, 14, 18, 22, 28, 33–5, 39, 40, 42, 46, 47, 49, 51, 56, 60, 63, 71, 72, 74, 78, 79, 82, 92, 99, 103, 105, 108, 138, 142, 145, 147, 148, 153, 155, 156, 162–4, 168, 172, 175, 177, 179, 181, 182, 184, 197, 198, 203, 206, 214, 215, 220, 224, 225, 227, 237, 246, 264, 267, 270, 276, 280, 281, 283; elections, 162; *York Chronicle* 33, 36, 49, 79, 130, 181, 281; *York Courant* 33, 49, 181, 281; *York Herald* 49, 125, 145, 181, 217, 219, 232, 281, 283
York Castle 50, 199, 228, 246, 286; Plate 8
York Minster 21, 35, 64, 156, 197, 218, 252
Yorkshire xiv, 2, 4, 6–8, 12, 14–16, 20, 22, 27, 31, 34–6, 40, 42, 45, 49, 54,

56, 63, 73, 74, 79, 81, 84, 88, 95, 100, 109, 112, 113, 121, 132, 140, 147, 148, 155, 160, 164, 168, 175, 176, 188–91, 194, 201, 204, 222, 227, 230, 231, 242, 248, 266, 271, 273, 278, 285

Yorkshire Association 23, 36–41, 46–8, 54, 57, 98, 101, 122, 148, 176

Yorkshire elections (1734) 20, 81; (1742) 81, 121; (1758) 21; (1780) 37, 38; (1783) 37; (1784) 5, 37, 42, 45, 47, 48, 278; (1790) 50; (1796) 57; (1802) 59; (1806) 1, 4, 23, 73, 74, 80, 81, 92, 99, 105, 109, 117, 119, 120, 124, 127, 136, 139, 143, 146, 157, 159, 195, 264, 279; (1807) 1, 3–6, 8, 24, 47, 81, 96, 104, 105, 117, 121, 122, 145, 171, 185, 186, 191, 193, 197, 236, 253, 254, 261, 274, 278, 280, 287; (1812) 278; (1818) 278; (1820) 278; (1826) 278; (1830) 81, 278; (1831) 278

Yorkshire Slavery 7

Young, Admiral Sir George 179

Young, Arthur 179